TERTULLIAN'S TREATISE ON THE RESURRECTION

BY THE SAME AUTHOR

Tertullian's Treatise against Praxeas
Tertullian's Tract on The Prayer
St Augustine's Enchiridion
Tertullian's Treatise on the Incarnation

Q. SEPTIMII FLORENTIS TERTULLIANI
DE RESURRECTIONE CARNIS LIBER

TERTULLIAN'S TREATISE ON THE RESURRECTION

*The text edited with an
Introduction, Translation and
Commentary
by*

ERNEST EVANS

*D.D. Oxford, Hon. D.D. Glasgow
Vicar of Hellifield, and
Canon of Bradford*

WIPF & STOCK · Eugene, Oregon

Wipf and Stock Publishers
199 W 8th Ave, Suite 3
Eugene, OR 97401

Tertullian's Treatise on the Resurrection
The Text Edited with an Introduction, Translation and Commentary
By Evans, Ernest
Copyright©1960 SPCK
ISBN 13: 978-1-4982-9500-0
Publication date 5/15/2016
Previously published by SPCK, 1960

CONTENTS

PREFACE	*page* vii
INTRODUCTION	
Tertullian's Theological Treatises	ix
Tertullian's Doctrine of the Resurrection	xi
The Argument of this Work	xvi
The Apologists and St Irenaeus	xxiv
The Textual Tradition	xxxv
LATIN TEXT AND ENGLISH VERSION	4
NOTES AND COMMENTARY	188
INDEX OF SCRIPTURAL REFERENCES	341
INDEX VERBORUM LATINORUM	346
INDEX NOMINUM PROPRIORUM	355
INDEX LOCORUM	356

PREFACE

With this volume I bring to an end work begun in 1917. When, some five years ago, it began to take its final shape, my inclination was to follow exactly the text constituted by Dr Borleffs. I have in fact differed from him in a few places: but my work still stands in great obligation to his, both in the text and in the *apparatus criticus*. I have not thought it necessary to follow accurately the spelling (for which Tertullian may or may not have been responsible) affected by the medieval copyists: supported by the powerful authority of Dr Cyril Bailey in his edition of Lucretius (the 1898 preface), *legenti commodius fore arbitrātus sum et re vera minus ineptum si orthographiam cum se ipsa constantiorem reddiderim et usitatae Latinitatis normae similiorem*. I have also made the text easier to read by removing a certain number of commas, especially from before relative pronouns: a relative pronoun is a connecting word, and not (as German printers seem to think) a disjunctive.

As it is probable that I shall not have time to produce any more books of this nature, I take a last opportunity of thanking the publishers for the generous interest they have taken in my work, and the readers of the Cambridge University Press, who with their keen eyesight and accomplished scholarship have rectified many errors and materially lightened the labour of proof-reading, as well as the keyboard operators and compositors, who, even in Latin and Greek, have read my handwriting with an almost entire absence of mistakes.

Those who read this book will do so with the intention of finding out what Tertullian and his contemporaries thought on this subject and with what arguments they supported their conviction. It was not necessary for me to indicate to what extent I find myself in agreement with him, though I believe I have done so. Far less was it necessary that I should attempt such a restatement of the doctrine of the resurrection and of the final judgement as would make it more acceptable to what is called the modern mind—which indeed is as old as Christianity, or even older. The 'hope of the flesh' (the expression is Tertullian's) does not stand or fall with his or any other's defence of it: but it will do no man any harm, and many men a great deal of good, to have first-hand acquaintance with the thoughts and words of a man who knew quite well what he had to say, and had no hesitation in saying it and no reserves in the expression of it.

E.E.

HELLIFIELD
July 1960

INTRODUCTION

TERTULLIAN'S THEOLOGICAL TREATISES

Tertullian's series of theological tractates appears to have been systematically planned, with the intention of discussing disputed points of Christian doctrine in their natural order. *Adversus Praxean* and *De Anima* are later additions, the former called for by a new form of heresy, the latter the expression of a new development, not so much of Tertullian's thought, as of the importance he attached to this particular aspect of it. The series begins with *De Praescriptione Haereticorum*, which makes the general claim against all heresies that they stand condemned by the fact of their recent emergence, since the truth must of necessity be that which is taught by the apostolic churches and those in agreement with them—a discreetly veiled and competently argued begging of the question, which has proved to be of much controversial value in both ancient and modern times. Although in his judgement this argument is of itself sufficient to silence all opposition, Tertullian proceeds to take the more influential heresies one by one, confuting them on the stronger ground of their failure to conform with Scripture and with natural reason. The five books *Adversus Marcionem* are a reply to the dangerous theory (which reappeared in a slightly different form, and acquired great popularity, in the third and fourth decades of the present century) that the God of the Old Testament, the Creator of the world, is in moral character as in substantive reality different from the Father of our Lord Jesus Christ. There appears to be no direct evidence of the immediate effect of this highly competent work: but as there are some indications that in the third century and afterwards Marcionism, though still troublesome, had lost most of its expansive power, it may well be that Tertullian's refutation was not without effect in checking the growth of that heresy.

Marcion had tried to solve the problem of the evil that is in the world by the postulate of a malevolent or incompetent creator. The treatise *Adversus Hermogenem* is a reply to a different attempt to answer this question, this time on the supposition that the Creator had to use a pre-existent matter which was too intractable for him to bring to perfection. This theory, of vaguely Platonic origin, though not it seems derived directly from Plato, reappears in various disguises, and evidently became in some quarters an acceptable solution of what is, after all, a real difficulty. It at least has the honesty of not denying that the problem exists, though the trouble with all these theorists is that they forget that evil is not primarily a matter of chemistry or physics but of morals: they shelve the real problem, while pretending to solve it by the introduction of the dangerous and offensive suggestion that material things (including the human body) are of necessity either totally evil or so contaminated with evil as to be beneath God's interest and beyond his saving power.

The gnostic sects attacked the same problem, with a similar result. Their theories are complicated and abstruse, there being almost as many doctrines as teachers, and it appears that the more involved an explanation was, and the more it was wrapped up in great swelling words, the more likely it was to find acceptance. But the sects had this in common, that they treated the creation of the world as a conscious or unconscious act of rebellion against the unknown and unknowable god, and, regarding all created things as evil, envisaged redemption not as the destruction of evil but as the disengagement from it of any sparks of good which may by accident have got entangled in it: they also made individual salvation dependent on knowledge of the secret passwords for the many stages of the upward ascent. The treatise *Adversus Valentinianos* is an account, translated from St Irenaeus, of some of these theories: the church writers thought that the mere setting forth of such pretentious nonsense would be the best refutation of it.

Concerning the two treatises *De Carne Christi* and *De Resurrectione Carnis* Tertullian several times observes that the former is designed to serve as *praestructio* or scaffolding for the latter. The former indeed has an importance of its own, since it is on the truth of Christ's human nature that the divine scheme for man's salvation depends, and any further aspect of Christian doctrine must be subsidiary to this. But in practice the lesser doctrine was turned back upon the greater. Doubts about the feasibility or necessity or desirability of the resurrection of the flesh of all mankind were easy enough to suggest: there are manifest difficulties, which it is easier to admit than to resolve. Once it was accepted that the so-called resurrection is of the soul alone, and that the body is to have no share in it, it seemed to follow that there was no need for the resurrection of Christ's body, and indeed that there was no need for him to have had a real body at all, but only such a phantasm of a body as should make him for a time visible to those he met. Also, since it now seemed to be proved by default that human flesh has no part in the life to come, being unworthy of God's interest and attention, it was thought to follow that the whole material creation must be the work either of a second god or of a rebellious or misguided angel. Thus the simple and unlearned (who are always, Tertullian remarks, the larger proportion of Christians), being ignorant of the Scriptures and of the power of God, were by virtue of a defective eschatology easily led on to deny the objective truth of the Incarnation, and beyond that to a doctrine of God which is no more than a thinly disguised polytheism.

TERTULLIAN'S DOCTRINE OF THE RESURRECTION

Throughout this series of works, on which he had been engaged for more than a decade, Tertullian had put first things first, the doctrine of God before the doctrine of man, the doctrine of creation before the doctrine of the last things: and now, the doctrine of the Incarnation having been clearly set forth against four heresies, he was in a position to maintain, as regards man's own destiny, that neither is any part of human nature unworthy or incapable of redemption, nor does God lack the power or the skill to redeem it. He might not have understood our terms, but he would have been at one with us and with the Scriptures in representing Christianity in its authentic form as a thoroughly (though not exclusively) materialistic religion, and in affirming that this present life is not a mere period of soul-making but is a preparation for the conservation and sublimation of the whole of manhood, body, soul, and spirit, in the life to come.

Along with other aspects of Christian teaching, this doctrine had been set forth in clear terms, though in summary form, in one of the earliest works, the *Apologeticus*, from which it appears that even in non-Christian circles it was well known that this is an essential article of Christian belief. And not only so, but it is clear from the works of previous apologists that however original are some of Tertullian's expressions and however characteristic his vigorous speech, the essentials of this doctrine and the main lines of its defence were not invented by him but were an inheritance from his predecessors in the faith: as likewise the cavils raised against the doctrine were no new thing, but had been canvassed here and there for at least half a century.

Some twelve or more years, then, before writing this monograph *On the Resurrection of the Flesh*, Tertullian had expressed himself as follows:[1]

If some philosopher states (Laberius suggests that Pythagoras thought so) that a mule is changed into a human being or a woman turns into a snake, and into support of that view distorts all manner of arguments by persuasive eloquence, he will certainly move some to assent and will establish this as a dogma. Thus some person will be convinced that he ought to abstain from flesh-meat, for fear of feasting on his great-grandfather when he thinks he is eating beef. Yet if a Christian puts it on record that a man will return to life as a man, John Doe as John Doe, he will be hounded, or even stoned, out of the company.

If there is some principle which demands that the souls of men must be brought back again into bodies, why should they not return into their own identity? For restoration means precisely this, that that which used to be, again is. Otherwise they will not be the same souls as they were: for in becoming what they were not they have to cease to be what they were. It would require many examples, and abundance of

[1] *Apologeticus* 48: on which there are valuable notes by J. E. B. Mayor. The translation here given is from Becker's text, which is substantially the same as that of Hoppe. The meaning of Tertullian's Latin is for the most part perfectly clear: but there probably does not exist another piece of Latin which it is so difficult to turn into satisfactory English.

leisure, if we were disposed to spread ourselves on the question which man would seem to be converted into which animal. But it has a closer bearing on our position when we postulate that it is much more dignified to suppose that human person will return to life as human person—anyone as anyone, provided he is human—so that the soul may regain its true nature by being restored to the same characteristics, even if not the same face and figure. And yet, seeing that the reason for this restoration is the judgement which God has appointed, it follows of necessity that the very same person who was before, will have to be brought into court to receive from God judgement upon his merits or demerits. For that reason men's bodies also will be restored again, because soul alone without that solid matter, the flesh, is not capable of sensation,[1] and because whatsoever the souls have to suffer by the judgement of God, they have deserved it in association with the flesh: for they were enclosed within the flesh when they did all that they have done.

But how, you ask, can matter which has been dispersed be brought together again for judgement? Look at yourself: in your own person you will find the evidence of it. Consider what you were before you were. Nothing. For if you had been anything you would remember it. As you were nothing before you were something, why, when you have become nothing by ceasing to be anything, should you not be able again to come into being out of nothing, by the will of that same Creator who has already out of nothing brought you into being? Nothing new will happen to you. You did not exist, yet were brought into existence. Describe, if you can, how you have come to exist: then you may ask how you will again come to exist. Moreover, it will be easier for you to be made once more what you have already been, in that equally without difficulty have you already been made what once you never were.

Doubts will be entertained, perhaps, of the power of God. Yet by him this great mass which is the world has been constituted out of that which was not, as it were out of the death of vacuity and nonentity, and has been animated with that spirit which gives life to all souls: it is itself a signed portrait of the resurrection of mankind, for a testimony to you. Daily the light is slain, and shines anew: darkness by the same sequence departs and returns: constellations which have died come to life again: seasons end and begin: fruits ripen and return: certainly grain rises in greater fertility only after it has decayed away and dispersed: all things

[1] Tertullian was still of this opinion when he wrote *De Testimonio Animae* 4: at *De Resurrectione Carnis* 17 he is seen to have changed his mind.

are preserved by being destroyed, all are brought into shape again out of perdition. If you have learned, at least from the Delphic inscription, to understand yourself, you know how noble is the name of man: and are you, the lord of all things that die and that rise again, to die only so as to perish? Whatever you are dissolved into, whichever of the four elements brings you to destruction, sucks you in, wipes you out, reduces you to nothing, that will give you back again: nothingness itself is subject to you to whom everything is subject.

In that case, you object, we shall for ever have to be dying and rising again. If the Lord of all things had so decreed, you would have obeyed the law of your being whether you would or not. But in fact he has decreed no otherwise than he has declared. That divine Reason which composed the universe out of things diverse, to the intent that out of opposing entities all things should stand together in unity—out of emptiness and fullness, animate and inanimate, comprehensible and incomprehensible, light and darkness, and even life and death—that same Reason has compacted time itself in such determinate and ordered sequence, that this first part of it, in which we have been living since the beginning of creation, should by limitation of time flow down to an end, but that that other part, which we stand in expectation of, should pass forward into endless eternity. So when it has reached that boundary, that gulf which gapes between, the fashion of this world, no less limited in time, which now is spread out like a curtain to cover that other eternal order, will itself suffer change: and thereupon will ensue a restoration of the whole human race, for the reckoning up of what of good or evil it has merited in this present age, and thereafter the paying up of what is owed, right on into the unmeasurable timelessness of eternity.

And so there will be no more death, nor any resurrection often repeated. We shall be the same persons as we now are, nor ever again shall we be other: the worshippers of God always in his presence, clothed upon with substance proper to eternity: but the profane, and such as are not perfect towards God, in the penalty of no less perpetual fire, receiving from the very nature of that fire, which is from God, a supplement of indestructibility. Even philosophers know the difference between mystic and natural fire. Far different is that which serves men's use from that which serves the judgement of God, whether it is hurled as lightning from heaven or belches forth from the earth at the mountain-tops: for this does not consume what it burns up, but restores while it destroys. Consequently the mountains remain, for ever burning: and

INTRODUCTION xv

one struck by lightning is safe for ever from again being burnt to ashes by fire. This then may stand for a token of the everlasting fire, an example of perennial judgement feeding its own penalty. Mountains burn up and yet endure: why not evil-doers and the enemies of God?

Here we have in summary form the doctrine, and the arguments in support of it, which Tertullian was to develop at greater length some ten or twelve years later. It is a doctrine of the continued life of the soul after death, and of the final reconstitution of the body, with the restoration of the complete personality of body and soul at the end of the world, at Christ's appearing. Neither in this summary nor in the larger treatise does Tertullian complicate matters by insistence on the millennial reign of Christ: though he was acquainted with the Apocalypse of John, and cannot, when writing the treatise, have been ignorant of Montanist expectations.

Of themes afterwards developed at greater length, we have here a reference to those of the philosophers who postulate the soul's survival and even, in some cases, its reincarnation. We have the claim that for purposes of divine judgement personal identity is required, and that this can only be ensured if each soul is returned to its own body. In reply to suggested or presumed difficulties in the reconstitution of bodies buried and decayed, we have the argument that God, who has once already brought things into existence out of nothing, evidently has power, and must find it easier, to reconstitute those same things out of dissolution. Examples, not entirely persuasive, but evidently a commonplace in such discussions, are given of phenomena akin to or suggesting resurrection in the natural order of the world: and, along with them, we find here a fair enough argument (which is not reproduced in the longer treatise) that as the world was made for man's sake it would be a strange thing if the world itself rises again while man who is its lord does not: for *eius est nihilum ipsum cuius et totum*. Unencumbered, as already remarked, by the millenary interval which others take over from the Apocalypse, we have the distinction between this age and the age to come, the present age falling like a curtain over that other eternal order—*quae illi dispositioni aeternitatis aulaei vice oppansa est*—so that the resurrection once accomplished becomes a permanent fact, not an event to be often repeated. It follows that there is no more death: and as neither Tertullian nor his contemporaries, nor the New Testament itself, is afraid of hard facts and hard sayings, there is a reference here, not repeated in this precise form in the treatise, to that penal fire which makes indestructible that which it even destroys.

THE ARGUMENT OF THIS WORK

Tertullian's original intention appears to have been to cast *De Carne Christi* and *De Resurrectione Carnis* into the form of *controversiae*, as if they had been the *actio prima* and *actio secunda* of a case argued in court. The earlier work has all the marks of the actual speech which it certainly never was. It fits into the conventional framework of *principium*, followed by *narratio* and *reprehensio*, with *amplificatio* and *conclusio*: it abounds in such asides as might have been supposed to embarrass an adversary, while moving the court to sympathetic amusement: and it answers, as it were in passing, pretended interjections by the opponent party. The later work retains very few traces of this. Certainly there is ordered arrangement of subject-matter: but it is that of a treatise rather than a speech. There are no asides, no hint of an adversary present in court, and no suggestion of an audience. In fact, the work is addressed to readers rather than listeners, or at least to such listeners as at a private reading can ask for abstruse and closely argued passages to be repeated once and again.

The argument is worked out in five stages. The first (§§ 1–4), which almost serves the usual purpose of an *exordium*, relates the heretical half-beliefs with which Tertullian is in conflict, to the opinions of philosophers and to the prejudices of the general non-Christian public. In part two (§§ 5–17) are set out the general principles which are to govern the interpretation of the relevant passages of Scripture: namely, the dignity of the flesh, the power of God, and the necessary requirements of divine judgement. Parts three (§§ 18–39) and four (§§ 40–56) take up the testimony of the Scriptures, first expounding their positive teaching, and then rescuing from perverse misunderstanding or misinterpretation a number of apostolic texts of which the adversaries have claimed the support. Part five (§§ 57–62) is a reply to a further set of difficulties and objections. The concluding chapter (§ 63) may be regarded as a sort of peroration: it summarizes the argument, and claims the support and enlightenment of the new prophecy.

Within this framework the details are worked out as follows:

(i) *Preliminary observations: the pagan origin of doubts about the faith*

The general public, which dishonours its dead by cremating them, and honours them by sacrificing to them, is inconsistent with itself. Philosophers also are not in agreement, some saying that death is the end of all things, while others allege that the soul survives, and even enters again into other bodies either animal or human (§ 1). Such heretics as deny the resurrection of the flesh are forced to deny both the verity of the flesh of Christ and the unity of God. On these matters we have already answered them: our present task is to maintain the completeness of man's salvation. Among such as profess to be Christians there seems to be no overt denial of the survival of the soul (§ 2). It is not always safe to base theological argument on popular opinions: this ought only to be done for affirmation, not for denial: and in any case divine truth does not always consist of what is obvious (§ 3): so it is without good warrant that heretics have borrowed from the heathen the whole fabric of the attack they make on the flesh (§ 4).

(ii) *General principles concerning the dignity of the flesh: the power of God: the rationale of divine judgement*

(a) The dignity of the flesh derives from the fact that it is God's handiwork, and that the clay shaped by God's hand was called 'man' even before God gave it a soul (§ 5). While the clay was taking shape under God's hand, his thought was of the manhood which Christ was to assume: for it says that man was made in the image of God, and 'God' here means Christ who was to take manhood upon him. In such a way as this can a thing become more honourable than what it is made of (§ 6). The suggestion that the coats of skins with which God clothed fallen man signify flesh (and thus that man's flesh is a consequence of his sin) cannot stand:

Adam already possessed flesh when Eve was formed out of him. Also if flesh is the servant of the soul, it is even more honourable on that account, since soul is the breeze of the breath of God, which yet without the flesh can bring nothing to effect (§ 7). The soul cannot obtain salvation unless while in the flesh it has become a believer, through the flesh as intermediary has received the divine mysteries, and by the flesh as agent has suffered for Christ's sake: and as soul and flesh are so closely united in act, it is inconceivable that they should be divided in reward (§ 8). These being the dignities of the flesh, it is not possible that God should abandon it to destruction (§ 9). Such reproaches against the flesh as are to be found in Scripture are really directed against the soul which has misused the flesh for lower purposes: and as there are other places where the flesh is spoken well of, we must think it more consistent with God's goodness to save that which he sometimes praises than to condemn it because he has at times expressed disapproval of it (§ 10).

(*b*) If there is any question whether God is competent to restore to existence flesh which has decayed, we answer that as it is easier to remake than to make, God is certainly able to recover what has been dispersed (§ 11). Nature itself, with its perpetual dying and coming to life again, is a standing example of God's power to bring life out of death (§ 12): and so is that strange bird the phoenix (§ 13).

(*c*) As the purpose of the resurrection is that mankind should appear before God's judgement-seat, evidently that judgement cannot be complete unless every man is presented entire (§ 14). The soul has never acted without the flesh: even its thoughts are mediated either by brain or by heart, and these are part of the flesh: also since God as judge is neither unjust nor negligent he has to treat the flesh as the soul's associate whether in penalty or in reward (§ 15). The quibble that the flesh, as a mere instrument of the soul, has no moral responsibility, is of no value: for if it is innocent it ought to be rewarded: and in practice even instruments are not exempt from praise or blame. Moreover the flesh is not an instrument of the soul, but its associate, as the apostle indicates when he enjoins us to glorify God in our bodies (§ 16).

Simple people suppose that the flesh will have to rise again because soul without flesh has no sensation, and thus can neither be punished nor rewarded. But in fact the soul, having a certain substantiality of its own, is not devoid of sensation. So it can before the resurrection be paying the penalty of its own misdeeds; but it needs also the resurrection of the flesh, so that it may pay its debts in full by the agency of the same flesh which has been the agent of its activities (§ 17).

(iii) *The evidence of Scripture:* (1) *its positive content*

(a) Since the Christian hope is of the resurrection of the dead, it follows that that which is to rise again must be that which has died, namely the flesh: for the soul does not die at death any more than it dies in sleep (§ 18). Consequently we cannot agree with such as desire to interpret the resurrection in an allegorical sense, alleging that those are already risen again who have put on Christ in baptism (§ 19). For, in the first place, it is not true that the prophets did all their preaching by allegory (§ 20): quite often they spoke in plain terms: and, as that is so, we must assume that so fundamental an article of faith as this would not just be darkly hinted at (§ 21). Secondly, the evidence of Scripture itself is that the resurrection has not yet taken place, its times being fixed at the second coming of Christ, the signs of which are not yet in evidence (§ 22). Again, it is true that the apostle, in saying that we have been buried with Christ and have been raised up again in him, refers to a spiritual resurrection: but he does so without any appearance of denying a physical one (§ 23): and the times of our Lord's coming and the signs of its approach are clearly set forth to the Thessalonians (§ 24) and in the Apocalypse of John (§ 25).

(b) Figurative speech, when it does occur, is rather in our favour. For example, since it was said, Earth thou art, anything of divine wrath or divine grace which the Scriptures threaten or promise to the earth, may be interpreted as referring to man's flesh (§ 26): so also references to clothing that did not wear out, and certain similar texts, can be allegories of the hope of the flesh (§ 27). We may also apply to the flesh anything the Scriptures say about blood (§ 28).

(c) If allegorical speech is in our favour, how much more is this true of prophecies which describe in set terms the resurrection of the flesh, as does Ezekiel's vision of the valley of the dry bones (§ 29). Attempts are made to convert this into an allegory of the restoration of the Jewish state after its dispersion: but we answer that nothing could be an allegory of anything unless it first represented a literal fact (§30): so that this parable, like a number of other prophecies, does not refer to the present state of Jewry but to the future hope of all mankind (§ 31). When it is written that the fishes of the sea and the beasts of the earth will give back the bodies they have devoured, this too must be taken literally: for it is remarkable that heretics never attempt to allegorize away any references to the soul, whereas whatever is written with reference to the flesh, or any part of it, they interpret as meaning anything or everything but what it says (§ 32).

(d) It is not true to say that our Lord spoke all things in parables: he spoke some things plainly, and must be taken to have meant what he said (§ 33). For example, he came to save that which was lost: and this means the whole man. When he says that of all that the Father has given him he will lose nothing, by 'all' he means complete manhood, combined of flesh and soul (§ 34). When he speaks of the possibility of soul and body being destroyed in hell, he cannot be referring to any but the natural body (§ 35). In his answer to the Sadducees he evidently affirms the resurrection in the sense in which they denied it, namely of both soul and body (§ 36). When he says that the flesh profiteth nothing he does not mean that it is incapable of receiving profit: it can receive profit from the Spirit which giveth life, that is, from the Word who was made flesh. And when he says that all who are in the tombs will hear the voice of the Son of God, and will live, he must be referring to the flesh: for souls are not buried in tombs (§ 37). His deeds also are in agreement with his words: when he raises the dead, he raises them entire (§ 38).

(e) The apostle, both before the Sanhedrin and in the presence of Festus, professed the same manner of resurrection as the prophets had spoken of: and the men of Athens understood him to the same effect (§ 39).

(iv) *The evidence of Scripture*: (2) *correction of misunderstandings*

(*a*) *The outer and the inner man* (2 Cor. 4. 16–5. 10). By the inner man the apostle means not (as some allege) the soul itself, but mind and spirit, which are functions of soul: and when he says that the outer man is being dissolved he means not that the flesh suffers destruction after death but that even now it is being worn down by toils and torments (§ 40). In the same sense, and in the same context, he refers to the earthly house of our tabernacle being dissolved, and to the building which we have from God, eternal in the heavens (§ 41): and when he says here that we desire not to be unclothed but to be clothed upon, he means the same as when he says elsewhere that the flesh when it has risen again will be changed by the addition of an angelic quality (§ 42). When he says that while we are at home in the body we are absent from the Lord, by absence from the Lord he means not the fact of being in the flesh, but that meanwhile we have to walk by faith and not by sight: and as he says (in the same connection) that we must all stand before the judgement-seat of Christ, evidently by 'all' he means the whole of each of us (§ 43). He has previously spoken of our having treasure in earthen vessels, not meaning that the vessels will be destroyed because of their earthly origin, but that they will be preserved because they contain divine treasure: for he adds that the life of Christ will be manifested in our body: and this can only be when we rise again, as Christ has already risen (§ 44).

(*b*) *The old man and the new man* (Eph. 4. 22; Rom. 8. 8, 6. 6; 1 Thess. 5. 23). We maintain that this distinction indicates a difference not of substance but of moral character (§ 45): for we frequently find the apostle condemning the works of the flesh in such terms as appear to involve a condemnation of the flesh itself, yet by the context of each of these expressions guarding against this misunderstanding: as, for example, when he says that those who are in the flesh cannot please God, and immediately adds, Ye are not in the flesh but in the Spirit, though physically they were still in the flesh (§ 46). So also the old man, crucified together with Christ, is shown by the context to indicate a worldly and sinful life: for it is not in fact true that in a physical sense we have been crucified with Christ. When writing to the Thessalonians, the apostle prays that their spirit, soul, and body may be made perfect: and that is to take place at the coming of our Lord, which will open the door for the resurrection (§ 47).

(c) *'Flesh and blood cannot inherit the kingdom of God'* (1 Cor. 15. 50). The answer to the doubt suggested by this sentence is to be found in the argument of the whole chapter. The apostle begins by insisting on the fact of Christ's resurrection, and argues that if there is no resurrection of the dead, then Christ cannot have risen and the whole Christian faith falls to the ground (§ 48). When he distinguishes between the first man, from the earth, earthy, and the second Man who is from heaven, he indicates a difference of character, and consequently of dignity, though not of substance: for both alike have the name and attributes of man (§ 49). It is true that flesh and blood by their own power are incapable of inheriting the kingdom, or of anything else: but the Spirit both quickens them and makes them capable of inheriting (§ 50). It is inconceivable that the apostle should have so peremptorily excluded flesh and blood from heaven, when Jesus is already there in the flesh and blood in which he ascended and in which he will come again (§ 51). The parable of the seed which is buried in the ground, and decays and comes to life again, indicates that the same flesh will rise which is buried, but in greater fullness: so also the reference to different kinds of flesh, and of bodies celestial and terrestrial, envisages different degrees of glory, but the same substance (§ 52). By 'natural' (or soul-informed) body the apostle does not mean the soul: for soul is not soul-informed but soul-informing: so that 'natural body' means soul-informed flesh. Also soul is not buried but flesh is: and it is that which is buried which is to rise again. The flesh is at present natural or soul-informed, and not yet spiritual or spirit-informed: for it has as yet received its full equipment of soul but only the earnest of the Spirit (§ 53). When the mortal thing is swallowed up of life it will not thereby perish. It is death which will perish, for death is not capable of immortality: the mortal thing, by the destruction of death, is so capable (§ 54). The apostle says, We shall be changed. Change is by no means the same thing as abolition: various examples prove that a thing or person can be changed, and yet remain the same (§ 55). Finally, it would be inconsistent with God's righteousness that one thing should do the works, and another thing substituted for it should receive the reward: so that any suggestion of a 'resurrection body', specially created for the purpose, is bound to fail (§ 56).

(v) *Answers to further cavils*

(a) The unbelieving ask whether the blind, the lame, and the diseased are to rise again to a renewal of their disabilities. These are wilfully ignorant that God is able, by the change the apostle speaks of, to confer both immortality and incorruption: and this implies the restoration of both health and integrity (§ 57). After the resurrection there is to be everlasting joy, with neither sorrow nor sighing: and how could this be, unless the causes of sorrow were removed (§ 58)? The apostle says that all things are ours, both things present and things to come. Thus the world to come is for man's sake, and there is no room for doubt that our earthly substance is capable of being brought into possession of things eternal (§ 59).

(b) The question is also asked, what need there is for the restoration of those members of the body for which in the life to come there will be no use. Our answer is, first, that even if their functions cease, they must at least be retained for judgement: also, their functions could not have ceased unless they themselves were still existent: and thirdly, that in God's sight none of our members will be without its function (§ 60): for when terrestrial functions cease, celestial functions take their place (§ 61). Angels are known to have assumed human substance while retaining their own: what is to prevent men from retaining their own substance while assuming the attributes of angels (§ 62)?

(vi) *Conclusion*

The flesh will rise again, the whole of it, in its own identity and in its full perfection. Any doubts there can have been on this matter, suggested by obscure places of Scripture, are now set at rest by the removal of all obscurities through the revelations of the new prophecy (§ 63).

THE APOLOGISTS AND ST IRENAEUS

The doctrine in its main lines is proved by Tertullian to be based on New Testament and other scriptural authority. The extracts which follow will show that both it and the forms of its defence are the subject of a continuous Christian tradition. The apologists indicate that even unbelievers were aware that this was a fundamental Christian doctrine, foolish enough in appearance to merit no less scorn than that other strange doctrine that there is one only God. Their remarks on this subject make it clear that they are aware of at least some of the arguments which Irenaeus and Tertullian were to set out in systematic form. Irenaeus, in controversy with heretics and not with pagans, can make more abundant use of scriptural evidence: there can be no doubt that Tertullian here as elsewhere knew and used his work.

At the same time it appears that in addition to heretics who have found dogmatic reasons for denying the resurrection, there are recurrent objections on what may be called practical grounds, which repeatedly call for an answer. It would hardly be true to say that there is evidence of a concurrent negative, or semi-negative, tradition: rather is it that, in the second century as in the twentieth, there are some who, influenced by the *communis sensus* (as Tertullian remarks) of their non-Christian neighbours, are moved by manifest difficulties of a physiological nature to a denial of this part of the Christian hope. The difficulties, we have to admit, are real ones: to second-century minds influenced by the bastard Platonism of the gnostics, as to twentieth-century minds fed on the bastard hinduism of theosophy and popular journalism, they seem insuperable, and it is possible that the solutions of them offered by orthodox apologists both then and now are calculated to persuade only such as are already disposed to be persuaded. Probably the most effective argument, and the one least often used, is the moral one that *nemo tam carnaliter vivit quam qui negant carnis resurrectionem: negantes enim et poenam despiciunt et disciplinam*:[1] a fact of which the present age provides evidence enough. In any case the strength of the Christian conviction that the body is to

[1] Tertullian, *De Res. Carn.* 11.

rise again is shown by the fact that Origen, who stands almost outside all tradition, the founder of a tradition of his own, is, unless Rufinus seriously misrepresents him, both aware of the difficulties, and insistent that the doctrine is what it is and that the Scriptures mean what they say.

Justin Martyr

At *Apology* 1. 8 Justin observes that Christians could, if they would, deny the faith and escape persecution: but they are in haste to be in God's presence, and have in mind the judgement of Christ. It appears from this that Justin was of the same mind as Tertullian, that only the martyrs pass on at death straight to Paradise.[1] Justin says that Plato speaks of judgement by Rhadamanthys and Minos, that they will punish the unjust who are brought before them: he continues 'We also affirm that this will be done, but by Christ, while men with their souls return into the same bodies to be chastised with eternal chastisement, not merely a period of a thousand years, which was all that Plato spoke of.'[2] By this last observation Justin should not be thought to dissociate himself from Christian millenarism: he had in fact learned that doctrine from the Apocalypse of John.[3] He adds that if we are in error in this we hurt no one but ourselves, and are not deserving of punishment: a sentiment echoed by Athenagoras.

At *Apology* 1. 18 and 19 Justin says that the survival of souls is proved by well-attested records of possession, haunting, and so forth, and is vouched for by philosophers and poets. 'You would do well', he suggests, 'to give us no less acceptance than you give them, seeing we trust God not less than they, but more, since we expect to receive back again even our bodies which have died and

---

[1] Tertullian however, *De Anima* 55, gives the impression that this was a new doctrine recently revealed to Perpetua near the day of her martyrdom.

[2] *Apol.* 1. 8: ἡμεῖς δὲ τὸ αὐτὸ πρᾶγμά φαμεν γενήσεσθαι, ἀλλ' ὑπὸ τοῦ Χριστοῦ, κἂν τοῖς αὐτοῖς σώμασι μετὰ τῶν ψυχῶν γινομένων καὶ αἰωνίαν κόλασιν κολασθησομένων, ἀλλ' οὐχὶ χιλιονταετῆ περίοδον ὡς ἐκεῖνος ἔφη μόνον. The Greek syntax is at fault, but its sense is clear.

[3] So *Dial.* 80, 81, quoted below.

been laid in the earth: for we say that nothing is impossible to God.' Resurrection, he adds, is no more inconceivable than, if we had never existed, would be the statement that it is possible that out of a small drop of moisture, human seed, bones and sinews and flesh should be built up, as we see they are.[1] He then quotes Luke 18. 27, Things impossible with men are possible with God: as do Athenagoras and Theophilus in connection with the same idea.

At *Apology* I. 52 and 53 he observes that the prophets have spoken of two comings of Christ, the one as a dishonoured and passible man, and the other when, coming with great glory, he will raise up the bodies of all men that have been: the bodies of those who are worthy he will clothe with incorruption, while those of the unrighteous he will in eternal sentiency send with the evil demons into the eternal fire. Justin quotes here Ezek. 37. 7, 'Joint to joint and bone to bone'. It would be possible, he proceeds, to produce other prophecies to the same effect: on such our faith is built: 'For by what reasoning should we have believed a crucified Man, that he is the first-begotten of the unbegotten God, and himself will conduct the judgement of the whole human race, unless before he came, and became Man, we had found testimonies published concerning him, and now saw them fulfilled?'[2]

At *Apology* II. 9, addressing the Senate, Justin argues that if there is no judgement, either there is no god, or else, if there is a god, he cares not for man, and there is no such thing as morality.

Dialogue 69. Here Justin says that our Lord's miracles were a challenge to the men of that day to acknowledge him: instead of which they called him a magician and a deceiver. 'Also he did these things to persuade those who should in the future believe on him that even though a man have some defect of body, but is a keeper of the doctrines delivered by him, he will at his second coming raise him up again and will also make him entire and

---

[1] *Apol.* I. 18, ἐκ μικρᾶς τινος ῥανίδος τῆς τοῦ ἀνθρωπείου σπέρματος δυνατὸν ὀστέα τε καὶ νεῦρα καὶ σάρκας εἰκονοποιηθέντα οἷα ὁρῶμεν γενέσθαι.

[2] *Apol.* I. 53. The last clause runs εὕρομεν καὶ οὕτως γενόμενα ὁρῶμεν. Perhaps read ὁρῶμεν: 'we had found...and now saw'.

INTRODUCTION xxvii

immortal and incorruptible and incapable of grief.'[1] With this we may compare what Tertullian writes, §§ 57, 58.

At *Dialogue* 80, 81 Justin warns Trypho that he may meet with some so-called Christians who deny the God of Abraham, of Isaac, and of Jacob, and allege that there is no resurrection of the dead, claiming that immediately they die their souls are taken up into heaven.[2] These, says Justin, are not to be reckoned as Christians, any more than you Jews would acknowledge as Jews people such as the Sadducees and a number of other sects. I, he continues, and all who are thoroughly orthodox Christians,[3] are assured that there will be a resurrection of the flesh, followed by a thousand years in Jerusalem, rebuilt, adorned, and enlarged: with a quotation of Isa. 65. 17–25, and, 'There was among us a man named John, who in a revelation which came to him prophesied that those who believed in our Christ would be in Jerusalem for a thousand years, and after that would come the catholic and (to speak briefly) eternal general resurrection of all men, and also the judgement: as our Lord also said, They will neither marry nor be given in marriage but will be equal to angels, being children of God and of the resurrection'. Here Justin professes the millenarism which at *Apology* I. 8 he has passed over. The expression 'catholic resurrection' is repeated by Theophilus.[4]

---

[1] The last sentence is, ὁλόκληρον αὐτὸν ἐν τῇ δευτέρᾳ αὐτοῦ παρουσίᾳ μετὰ τοῦ καὶ ἀθάνατον καὶ ἄφθαρτον καὶ ἀλύπητον ποιῆσαι ἀναστήσει.

[2] These could be Marcionites, and this would be one of the earliest references to them. The final claim has among modern non-practising professing Christians been expanded into the belief that all men go to heaven when they die: it would be undemocratic of God to make any distinction.

[3] ὀρθογνώμονες κατὰ πάντα Χριστιανοί.

[4] Concerning the authenticity of the fragments of a treatise *On the Resurrection*, attributed by John of Damascus to St Justin, philosopher and martyr (Otto, vol. II, pp. 208–45), there seems to be some doubt. Bardenhewer is non-committal, though inclined towards acceptance. In fact these are rather more than fragments, being a well argued and well arranged discussion of the entire question. They contain practically nothing which is not met with elsewhere, and probably no ideas which could not have occurred to Justin. What is unlikely is that he could have reduced his usual discursive style to such precise and logical order, or that he could to this extent, in arguing against Christians, have abstained

Athenagoras

Supplicatio 36. At the conclusion of his disproof of the accusation of ritual cannibalism Athenagoras claims that persons who believe there will be a resurrection could by no means be given to such a practice. It is ridiculous, he says, to suppose that while the earth will give up its dead, men would not give up the dead they had swallowed. It is more likely that persons who think they will have no account to give, will abstain from no sort of atrocity: whereas such as are persuaded that no act will be left unexamined before God, and that the body which has ministered to the irrational impulses of the soul will share in its punishment, will avoid even the slightest sin. If this seems like nonsense, it is at least not wicked: for by the arguments with which we delude ourselves, we injure nobody. Some of the philosophers think as we do: but the present is not the place for philosophical arguments, or for us to claim the support of Pythagoras and Plato.

The treatise *On the Resurrection of the Dead*, which in the manuscripts follows the *Supplicatio* and is commonly attributed to Athenagoras, is of doubtful authenticity.[1] It is much more discursive than either Irenaeus or Tertullian, its argument being for the most part based on natural reason. There are very few scriptural quotations—about three altogether, which is far fewer than Justin introduces in his addresses to the Emperors and the Senate. There is a freshness about this work similar to that of the treatise on this subject ascribed to Justin, a freshness which suggests that it is hardly beholden to anyone in particular, though it is true that many of the points of its argument appear also in other writers and seem to have become Christian commonplace. Such are the suggestion (§ 2) that it would only be possible for the adversaries

---

from scriptural quotations. Another extract from the same work by Methodius of Olympus (Otto, p. 250) may be either the original or a reflection of Irenaeus' and Tertullian's remarks on 1 Cor. 15. 50: κληρονομεῖσθαι μὲν τὸ ἀποθνῆσκον, κληρονομεῖν δὲ τὸ ζῶν λέγει, καὶ ἀποθνήσκειν μὲν σάρκα, ζῆν δὲ τὴν βασιλείαν τῶν οὐρανῶν.

[1] For a critical discussion of the ascription to Athenagoras see R. M. Grant in *Harvard Theological Review* (January 1954).

to disprove the resurrection if they could show that God would either find it impossible or think it undesirable to unify and collect into their previous human identities such bodies as had died and been entirely dissolved:[1] and with this its corollary that if God should think it undesirable this must be either because injustice would be involved in his doing of it, or because it would be beneath his dignity to do it:[2] with a further argument based upon this. In § 3 we have a reference to the undue respect of the wise for the doubts of the vulgar. In § 12 a description of the changes which the human body experiences during the present life concludes with the remark that the resurrection, as well as the change for the better in the condition of those still alive at that time, is itself a sort of metabolism, the last and final one.[3] In several places the author insists on the joint activity and the inseparable responsibility of soul and body, as in the eloquent passage (§ 15) which begins with the postulate that 'all human nature in general is composed of immortal soul and the body which at birth was compacted with it', and reaches the conclusion that 'he who has had conferred upon him mind and reason is not soul by itself, but man: so that it is man, who is composed of both soul and body, who must abide for ever'.[4] So again (§ 20) he repeats that the actor in all matters which come under divine judgement has been the man, not his soul alone: and (§ 21) that the body will suffer injustice if, having joined with the soul in the righteous acts, it does not share in the reward.

Although addressed to Christians this work is strangely sparing of scriptural quotations: and these, about three in number, are introduced not as the basis of a proof, but in illustration of a point already made. Such are the combined reference[5] to 1 Cor. 15. 53

[1] Athenagoras, De Res. Mort. 2, ἐὰν δείξαι δυνηθῶσιν ἢ ἀδύνατον ὂν τῷ θεῷ ἢ ἀβούλητον τὰ νεκρωθέντα τῶν σωμάτων ἢ καὶ πάντη διαλυθέντα ἑνῶσαι καὶ συναγαγεῖν πρὸς τὴν τῶν αὐτῶν ἀνθρώπων σύστασιν.
[2] Ibid.: τὸ γὰρ ἀβούλητον ἢ ὡς ἄδικον αὐτῷ ἐστιν ἀβούλητον ἢ ὡς ἀνάξιον.
[3] Ibid. 12: εἶδός τι μεταβολῆς καὶ πάντων ὕστατον.
[4] So also ibid. 23: οὐ γὰρ ψυχαὶ ψυχὰς γεννῶσαι τὴν τοῦ πατρὸς ἢ τῆς μητέρος οἰκειοῦνται προσηγορίαν, ἀλλ' ἀνθρώπους ἄνθρωποι.
[5] Ibid. 18.

and 2 Cor. 5. 10: 'It is clear to all that according to the apostle this corruptible must put on incorruption, so that...each one may justly receive the things which he has done by his body, whether good things or evil': which answers in advance Tertullian's question[1] about hyperbaton. In the following chapter we have a reference to 'Let us eat and drink for tomorrow we die', as a common dogma and single law highly in favour with the lecherous and gluttonous: which also is commented on by Tertullian.[2]

There are two themes which in this work are treated more fully than elsewhere at that early date. In sections 4 to 8 we have a curious argument addressed to those who wonder what will happen at the resurrection to those parts of one man's body which have become parts of another man's either by cannibalism or by their being consumed by animals and thus transferred to other men. The author replies that for each animal God has provided its proper food, from which alone it receives true nourishment: whatever does not satisfy these conditions is either rejected and ejected, or else is used for the building up of those corporal elements (such as the four humours) which will not be required at the resurrection. Thus the question, At the resurrection, to which body will this or that portion of matter belong? could only arise if it were first proved that the natural food of human beings is human flesh: which is impossible. The other side of this problem has already been touched upon in the *Supplicatio*, where the claim is made that persons who believe in the resurrection could not possibly be given to the cannibalistic practices of which Christians are accused. The suggestion that the blood and the other humours will not be required at the resurrection would not have met with Tertullian's approval.[3]

Much more significant is the emphasis laid on the teleological argument, which runs like a thread through the whole. So we have (§ 12): 'To those who bear in themselves the very image of their Creator, who are possessed of a mind and are endowed with rational judgement, their Creator has allotted continuity without

---

[1] *De Res. Carn.* 43.   [2] Ibid. 49.
[3] *De Res. Carn.* 28.

end, so that they might come to know their own Creator, his power and wisdom, and while following law and justice might without labour spend the life to come in the company of these virtues with which they had fortified their previous life, although they were then in corruptible and earthly bodies.'[1] This argument, Aristotelian in principle and method, but reaching a far from Aristotelian conclusion, shows the author of this work to have been a not unworthy student of the master of those who know.

Theophilus

Since Theophilus addresses his work to a single person, a friend or acquaintance, he is in a position to use the more personal argument of an appeal to the faith which can make unnecessary the more objective kind of argument. So he says,[2] 'Faith is a precondition of all acts and facts', and asks why his acquaintance cannot entrust himself to God who has given such manifest tokens of himself by having formed man out of almost negligibly small material:[3] 'Why not then believe that God, who has already made you, is able also to make you again?'[4] There is also[5] the standard argument about the decline and return of seasons, of days and nights, of seed and fruit, etc., with quotation of John 12. 24 and 1 Cor. 15. 36, 37: to which is added a further instance of a tree which grew on a mountain from a seed dropped in a bird's excrement. All these, Theophilus remarks, are works of God's wisdom, designed to show that God is able also to accomplish the catholic resurrection of all mankind. Again he observes[6] that the works of the third day of Creation, the replenishment of the seas, and so forth,

---

[1] Athenagoras, *De Res. Mort.* 12: τοῖς δὲ αὐτὸν ἐν ἑαυτοῖς ἀγαλματοφοροῦσι τὸν ποιητήν, νοῦν τε συμπεριφερομένοις καὶ λογικῆς κρίσεως μεμοιραμένοις, τὴν εἰς ἀεὶ διαμονὴν ἀπεκλήρωσεν ὁ ποιητής, ἵνα γινώσκοντες τὸν ἑαυτῶν ποιητὴν καὶ τὴν τούτου δύναμίν τε καὶ σοφίαν, νόμῳ τε συνεπόμενοι καὶ δίκῃ, τούτοις συνδιαιωνίζωσιν ἀπόνως οἷς τὴν προλαβοῦσαν ἐκράτυναν ζωήν, καίπερ ἐν φθαρτοῖς καὶ γηΐνοις ὄντες σώμασιν.

[2] Theophilus, *Ad Autol.* I. 8, ἁπάντων πραγμάτων ἡ πίστις προηγεῖται.

[3] Ibid. ἐξ ὑγρᾶς οὐσίας μικρᾶς καὶ ἐλαχίστης ῥανίδος ἥτις οὐδὲ αὐτὴ ἦν ποτε.

[4] This seems to be the meaning of the strange expression μεταξὺ ποιῆσαι.

[5] Ibid. I. 13.   [6] Ibid. II. 14.

illustrate the resurrection. But his first mention of the matter most clearly states his position:[1] 'Before all things let there prevail in your heart faith and the fear of God, and so you will understand these things. When you put off mortality and put on incorruption you will see God as you ought: for he will raise up your flesh immortal along with your soul, and then, having been made immortal, you will see the Immortal, if you now believe him: and so you will know that you have unjustly spoken against him.' This, it is to be observed, is not part of a formal defence of the resurrection, but of a general appeal to faith. Theophilus seems to have been acquainted with the work of Justin: but he had, none the less, a mind of his own.

St Irenaeus

The foregoing excerpts are evidence of a continuous tradition in expectation of a corporal resurrection, as well as of repeated need to defend it against heathen incredulity, heretical denial, and simple-minded doubt. There is no sufficient evidence that Tertullian was indebted to the apologists to the extent of copying their words or their arguments: the most that can be said is that he was not unacquainted with Justin and Theophilus, and that some of the themes and expressions used by the apologists had become common Christian property. With Irenaeus and Tertullian the case is different: the African was well acquainted with the work of the bishop of Lyons: and it seems likely that if he had not a copy of it before him as he wrote, he had committed its general argument and some of its expressions to a very retentive memory.

Besides casual references elsewhere, Irenaeus treats systematically of this subject in the first fifteen chapters of his fifth book *Against the Heresies*. With him, as with Tertullian, this question, or rather the defence of this doctrine, is intimately bound up with the truth of the Incarnation, and both these with the doctrine of creation and the unity of God. To recount here in detail Tertullian's borrowings from St Irenaeus would be tedious and would serve little purpose: in what follows only the most remarkable parallels will be noted.

[1] Theophilus, *Ad Autol.* I. 7.

INTRODUCTION xxxiii

Most of Tertullian's references to Scripture had already been made by Irenaeus. It is of some significance that the longest continuous quotations by both authors are of Ezek. 37. 1–14 (Irenaeus v. 15. 1, Tertullian 29) and 1 Cor. 15. 12–18 (Irenaeus v. 13. 4, Tertullian 48). But no less significant are the differences. In Ezekiel Irenaeus quotes the Septuagint with only three slight variants: Tertullian seems to have made, or procured, an independent translation from a faulty Hebrew text. Both agree that the last verb in verse 14 is future, as in LXX καὶ ποιήσω, where the Latin vulgate and the English versions (wrongly, as it appears) have the perfect. In 1 Corinthians again Irenaeus gives, as far as the Latin version shows, an accurate transcript of the Greek: while Tertullian to some extent abbreviates, evidently quoting from memory. Both writers pay particular attention to 1 Cor. 15, examining the whole chapter, with intent to place in its proper perspective the apostolic admission that flesh and blood cannot inherit the kingdom of God. They agree in the suggestion that flesh and blood, while incapable of inheriting anything, are not incapable of being inherited, and that the operation of the Spirit can even make them competent to inherit: and here Tertullian, while reducing to logical order the somewhat discursive argument of Irenaeus, deprives it of its impressive emphasis on the effect of sacramental grace. The conjunction at 'For this I say', which is not in the Greek, but on which Tertullian bases a small argument, is also found without special comment in Irenaeus. Galatians 5. 19ff., quoted in full by Irenaeus (v. 11. 1) in illustration of his interpretation of 1 Cor. 15. 50, is barely referred to by Tertullian (§ 45) in connection with something else.

Irenaeus (v. 5. 1, 2) cites Enoch and Elijah as evidence that natural human flesh is capable of being taken into heaven: and in answer to a doubt whether it can be supposed to have continued so long undecayed, he instances Jonah whose flesh remained undigested, and the three children whose flesh was unhurt by Babylonian fire. Tertullian (§ 58) reduces this to one sentence, placing Jonah and the three children first. Lazarus, and the daughter of Jairus, with the young man at Nain, are discussed at some length by Irenaeus (v. 13. 1): Tertullian mentions Lazarus at

§ 53, and refers to all three without naming them in one sentence of § 38.

The apostolic prayer, 1 Thess. v. 23, is cited as conclusive by both authors, but with a significant difference of emphasis: Tertullian treats it as clinching an argument already completed (§ 47), whereas Irenaeus makes it the basis of further and greater expectations and of an appeal to faith and righteousness.

The following details are worth recording. Irenaeus (v. 3. 2), in a description of the parts of the body, says that the blood is *copulatio animae et corporis*, a remark which Tertullian does not repeat. Irenaeus (v. 4. 1) makes the point, repeated by Tertullian, that if there is no resurrection the reason is either that God could not or that he would not do it: and that in the former case God is subservient to material things, or in the latter case is less beneficent than we have been taught to expect. At v. 6. 1 Irenaeus openly says that the Son and the Holy Spirit are *manus patris*, a proposition on which Tertullian will only use the indefinite *quaecumque sunt* (§ 6). At v. 7. 1 Irenaeus remarks that spirit cannot rightly be called *mortale corpus*: which perhaps suggested Tertullian's insistence that soul cannot be *corpus animale* or *corpus animatum*, but must be *corpus animans*. At v. 8. 1 Irenaeus, quoting Eph. 1. 13, explains *pignus* as *pars eius honoris qui a deo nobis promissus est*, with much more of great pastoral interest: Tertullian (§ 53), keeping the Greek word *arrabo*, drops most of the comment. At § 51 he uses the same word in a noble statement of the consequence of Christ's ascension for all humanity. Irenaeus (v. 10. 3), no less than Tertullian, insists that 'Those who are in the flesh cannot please God' has a moral, not a physical, implication; *etenim ipse in carne cum esset scribebat eis*. Both writers several times quote the LXX mistranslation of Isa. 25. 8, κατέπιεν ὁ θάνατος ἰσχύσας, usually in a context where its omission would involve no great loss to the argument. Finally, one may ask whether Tertullian's question (§ 56) *Quomodo canam illi novum canticum, nesciens me esse qui gratiam debeam?* was suggested by Irenaeus v. 13. 3, *Absorbetur autem mortale a vita quando et caro iam non mortua sed viva et incorrupta perseveraverit, hymnum dicens deo qui in hoc ipsum perficit nos.*

THE TEXTUAL TRADITION

[The information here given is for the most part adapted, with this grateful acknowledgement, from the Preface to Tertullian's works in *Corpus Christianorum* (Turnholt, 1953) and from the *Monitum* prefixed to Dr Borleffs' edition of the text in the second volume of that series.]

This work, under the title *De Carnis Resurrectione* or *De Resurrectione Mortuorum*, was preserved in three of the four collections in which Tertullian's works have come down to us. It is not, and apparently never was, contained in the ninth-century *codex Agobardinus*, now at Paris (B.N. 1622), though its companion *De Carne Christi* is in part contained there. The text as now constructed depends on these groups of authorities:

I   *Codex Trecensis* [T], formerly at Clairvaux and now at Troyes (523), the only extant representative of a collection of five treatises made apparently in the fifth century, perhaps (it is suggested) by Vincent of Lérins. This manuscript has comparatively recently come to light, having been discovered by Dom Wilmart in 1916. It is of the highest value, though not an unimpeachable witness, for the reconstruction of the text, frequently differing in detail (as was to be expected) from manuscripts of a different tradition. It was, however, carelessly written, many sentences and clauses being omitted by homoeoteleuton.

II A group of manuscripts, apparently derived at first or second hand from a codex (now lost) which was at Cluny in the eleventh century, and seems itself to have been derived from a collection of twenty-one treatises, made in Spain, perhaps under the direction of St Isidore, bishop of Seville (600–36). Its most important representatives are
   Codex Montepessulanus [M] (Montpellier H 54), of the eleventh century.
   Codex Paterniacensis [P] (Schlettstadt 439), also of the eleventh century.

> Codex Magliabechianus [F] (Florence, conv. soppr. I. vi. 9), dated 1426.
>
> Codex Magliabechianus [N] (Florence, conv. soppr. I. vi. 10), also of the fifteenth century.

The last two appear to be copies of two now lost manuscripts of the Cluny group, both of which were known to Beatus Rhenanus and were used by him in his first and third editions (1521, 1539).

III A group of manuscripts once existed, derived from a codex formerly at Corbey, containing five treatises of Tertullian and Novatian, *De Trinitate*, works collected apparently in the fifth century by some Montanist or Novatianist. No manuscripts of this group survive: but it appears that copies of it, which were formerly at Corbey and Cologne, were known to the Englishman John Clements, who communicated their readings to Pamelius. Mesnart also and Gelenius had access to codices of this family.

The present edition of the text follows that of Dr Borleffs as closely as possible, and its *apparatus criticus* is abbreviated from the very full information given by him concerning the manuscripts T, M, and P (already mentioned) and

> Codex Luxemburgensis [X] (Luxemburg 75), a fifteenth-century manuscript of composite origin containing twenty-one treatises. It usually agrees with M and P.

Dr Borleffs has himself collated or scrutinized these four manuscripts. Rightly, as it appears, he does not quote the readings of the two Florentine manuscripts, judging that they are well enough represented by Rhenanus, who used the books they were copied from. Like other modern editors, Dr Borleffs prefers the testimony of T except where it is manifestly impossible: in the present edition the same course is followed, but with some reserve. A list of manuscripts and editions appears at the head of the Latin text.

Q. SEPTIMII FLORENTIS TERTULLIANI
DE RESURRECTIONE CARNIS LIBER

SIGLA

T   *Codex Trecensis* [523] saec. xij.
M   *Codex Montepessulanus* [H 54] saec. xj.
P   *Codex Seledstadiensis* [88], olim *Paterniacensis* [439] saec. xj.
X   *Codex Luxemburgensis* [75] saec. xv.
R^1 Editio princeps Beati Rhenani quae Basiliae anno 1521 in lucem prodiit: qui Rhenanus et *P* usus est et Hirsaugiensibus quibusdam libris iam deperditis.
R^3 Editio tertia eiusdem Rhenani, Basiliae anno 1539 prolata.
R   Consensus harum editionum.
B   Editio Martini Mesnartii, Lutetiae anno 1545 prolata: qui Mesnartius et *T* et alio iam deperdito libro videtur usus esse.
C   Codex Iohannis Clementis Angli deperditus cuius lectiones citat Pamelius in sua editione.

Gel.   Editio Sigismundi Gelenii, Basiliae, 1550.
Pam. Editio Iacobi Pamelii, Antverpiae, 1579.
Iun.   Editio Francisci Iunii, Franekerae, 1597.
Rig.   Editio Nicolai Rigaltii, Lutetiae, 1634.
Urs.   Lectiones Fulvii Ursini a Rigaltio laudatae.
Oeh. Editio Francisci Oehler, Lipsiae, 1854.
Kroy. Editio Aemilii Kroymann, Vindobonae, 1906.
Eng. Coniecturae Augusti Engelbrecht, Kroymanno communicatae.
Brf.   Editio viri docti J. G. Ph. Borleffs, Turnholti, 1952: qui ipse codices *TMPX* denuo contulit, cuique grato animo accepta ea referimus quae in apparatu critico adnotanda censuimus.

Q. SEPTIMII FLORENTIS TERTULLIANI
DE RESURRECTIONE CARNIS LIBER

1 Fiducia Christianorum resurrectio mortuorum: illam credentes hoc sumus. hoc credere veritas cogit: veritatem deus aperit. sed 2 vulgus inridet, existimans nihil superesse post mortem: et tamen defunctis parentat, et quidem impensissimo officio pro moribus eorum, pro temporibus esculentorum, ut quos negant sentire quidquam etiam desiderare praesumant. at ego magis ridebo 3 vulgus tunc quoque cum ipsos defunctos atrocissime exurit, quos postmodum gulosissime nutrit, isdem ignibus et promerens et offendens. o pietatem de crudelitate ludentem! sacrificat an insultat cum crematis cremat? plane cum vulgo interdum et sapientes 4 sententiam suam iungunt. nihil esse post mortem Epicuri schola est: ait et Seneca omnia post mortem finiri, etiam ipsam. satis est 5 autem si non minor sententia Pythagorae, et Empedocles et Platonici, immortalem animam e contrario reclamant, immo adhuc proxime etiam in corpora remeabilem adfirmant, etsi non in eadem, etsi non in humana tantummodo, ut Euphorbus in Pythagoram, ut Homerus in pavum recenseantur. certe recidiva- 6 tum animae corporalem pronuntiaverunt, tolerabilius mutata quam negata qualitate, pulsata saltim licet non adita veritate. ita saeculum resurrectionem mortuorum nec cum errat ignorat.

2 Si vero et apud deum aliqua secta est Epicureis magis adfinis quam prophetis, sciemus quid audiant a Christo Sadducaei. Christo enim servabatur omnia retro occulta nudare, dubitata

1: 1 illam *TMX*: illa *P*.   hoc sumus *T* (*ut videtur*): sumus *ceteri*.
4 parentat *Kroy*.: parent. at *T*: parentant *MPX*.
5 eorum *libri*: sepultorum *Kroy*.
5, 6 negant...praesumant *TB*: negat...praesumat *MPX*.
13 sententia Pythagorae, et Emp. et Plat. *Trecensis testimonio fretus ita textum constituit Brf.*
17 re⟨dire⟩ censeantur *Eng. vix usitata sua felicitate.*
19 saltim *T*: salute *MPX* (*forsan recte*).

TERTULLIAN ON THE RESURRECTION OF THE FLESH

1 The resurrection of the dead is Christian men's confidence. By believing it we are what we claim to be. This belief the truth exacts: the truth is what God reveals. But the multitude mocks, reckoning that nothing remains over after death. Yet they offer sacrifices to the deceased, and that with most lavish devotion in accordance with their customs and the seasonableness of victuals, so as to create the supposition that those whom they deny to have any sensation are even conscious of being in need. I however shall with better reason mock at the multitude, especially on occasions when they savagely burn up those very deceased whom they presently supply with gluttonous meals, with the same fires both currying favour and provoking hostility. Thus does piety toy with cruelty. Is it sacrifice, or insult, to cremate to the cremated? Doubtless at times even philosophers conjoin their own judgement with the multitude. That there is nothing after death is Epicurus' doctrine: and Seneca affirms that after death all things come to an end, including death itself. But it is enough if the not younger judgement of Pythagoras, as well as Empedocles and the Platonics, make the contrary claim that the soul is immortal, yea more, assert that it is destined very soon afterwards to return into bodies, albeit not the same bodies, nor human bodies only, with the result that Euphorbus is reborn as Pythagoras, and Homer as a peacock. At least they have pronounced that the soul has a corporal recurrence (the alteration of its quality is more tolerable than the denial of it), knocking at truth's door though not entering into its house. Thus not even when it goes astray is the world ignorant of the resurrection of the dead.

2 If however even among God's people there is a sect more akin to the Epicureans than to the Prophets, we shall take cognizance of what Christ says to the Sadducees.[1] For to Christ it was reserved to lay bare all things formerly hidden, to give direction to things

[1] Cf. Matt. 22. 23–33.

dirigere, praelibata supplere, praedicata repraesentare, mortuorum certe resurrectionem non modo per semetipsum verum etiam in semetipso probare. nunc autem ad alios Sadducaeos praeparamur, 2 partiarios sententiae illorum: dimidiam agnoscunt resurrectionem, solius scilicet animae, ita aspernati carnem sicut et ipsum dominum carnis. nulli denique alii salutem corporali substantiae invident quam alterius divinitatis haeretici. ideoque et Christum aliter 3 disponere coacti, ne creatoris habeatur, in ipsa prius carne eius erraverunt, aut nullius veritatis contendentes eam secundum Marcionem et Basiliden, aut propriae qualitatis secundum heredes Valentini et Apellen. atque ita sequitur ut salutem eius sub- 4 stantiae excludant cuius Christum consortem negant, certi illam summo praeiudicio resurrectionis instructam si iam in Christo resurrexerit caro. propterea et nos volumen praemisimus de carne 5 Christi, quo eam et solidam probamus adversum phantasmatis vanitatem et humanam vindicamus adversus qualitatis proprietatem, cuius condicio Christum et hominem et filium hominis inscripserit. carneum enim atque corporeum probantes eum, 6 proinde et obducimus praescribendo nullum alium credendum deum praeter creatorem, dum talem ostendimus Christum in quo dinoscitur deus, qualis promittitur a creatore. obducti dehinc de deo carnis auctore et de Christo carnis redemptore, iam et de resurrectione carnis revincentur, congruente scilicet et deo carnis auctori et Christo carnis redemptori. hoc ferme modo dicimus 7 ineundam cum haereticis disceptationem: nam et ordo semper a principalibus deduci exposcit, ut de ipso prius constet a quo dicatur dispositum esse quod quaeritur. atque adeo et haeretici ex con- 8 scientia infirmitatis nunquam ordinarie tractant. certi enim quam laborent in alterius divinitatis insinuatione adversum deum mundi

2: 11 creatoris TB^{mg}: creator carnis *MPX*.
    13 heredes *T*: haereses *X vulgo*: *lectiones contaminant ceteri*.
    26 congruente *T*: congruenter *ceteri*: *quaeritur annon quae post* congruenter scilicet *scripta sunt omittere praestet*.
    32 laborent *T*: laborant *MPX*.

in doubt, to fill up things sampled, to make present the things that were preached of, certainly to prove the resurrection of the dead not only by himself but also in himself. Now however we arm ourselves against other Sadducees, who hold only part of the views of those former. Just so, they acknowledge half a resurrection, that is, of the soul alone, spurning the flesh as they also spurn even the Lord of the flesh. In fact the only people who envy the bodily substance its salvation are precisely these heretical upholders of a second deity. Consequently, forced to assign Christ also to a different dispensation lest he be considered to belong to the Creator, they have first gone astray in respect of his flesh, maintaining either, according to Marcion and Basilides, that it had no true existence, or, according to the successors of Valentinus, with Apelles, that it was of a quality of its own. And thus it follows that they shut the door against the salvation of that substance of which they deny that Christ is partaker: for they are aware that it is equipped with the strongest precedent of resurrection if already in Christ the flesh has risen again. For that reason I also have issued a preparatory volume On the Flesh of Christ, in which I both prove its substantiality as opposed to the emptiness of a phantasm, and vindicate its humanity as opposed to its having a special quality of its own, it being flesh of such condition as to have registered Christ as both Man and Son of Man. For while we prove that he is possessed of flesh and of body, we forthwith as by a precedent judgement forestall the possibility of belief in any other God but the Creator, inasmuch as we show that Christ, in whom God is discerned, is such a one as is promised by the Creator. Forestalled for the future as concerning God the author of flesh and Christ the redeemer of flesh, they shall next be refuted in respect of the resurrection of the flesh. Appropriately so. And after this fashion I affirm that one ought as a rule to enter upon disputation with heretics—for due order demands that deduction should always be made from first principles—that agreement should first be reached concerning him by whom one says the thing under enquiry has been ordained. And this is the reason why heretics also, from a consciousness of their weakness, never discuss things in due order. For, well aware what heavy weather they make when insinuating

omnibus naturaliter notum de testimoniis operum, certe et in sacramentis priorem et in praedicationibus manifestatiorem, sub obtentu quasi urgentioris causae, id est ipsius humanae salutis ante omnia requirendae, a quaestionibus resurrectionis incipiunt, quia durius creditur resurrectio carnis quam una divinitas. atque ita 9 tractatum viribus ordinis sui destitutum et scrupulis potius oneratum depretiantibus carnem paulatim ad alterius divinitatis temperant sensum ex ipsa spei concussione et demutatione. deiectus 10 enim unusquisque vel motus de gradu eius spei quam susceperat apud creatorem, facile iam declinatur ad alterius spei auctorem etiam ultro suspicandum: per diversitatem enim promissionum diversitas insinuatur deorum. sic multos inretitos videmus, dum ante de resurrectione carnis eliduntur quam de unione divinitatis elidunt. igitur quantum ad haereticos demonstravimus quo cuneo 11 ⟨oc⟩currendum sit a nobis. et occursum est iam suo quoque titulo: de deo quidem unico et Christo eius adversus Marcionem: de carne vero domini adversus quattuor haereses ad hanc maxime quaestionem praestruendam: uti nunc de sola carnis resurrectione ita et digerendum sit tanquam penes nos quoque incerta, id est penes creatorem—nam et multi rudes, et plerique sua fide dubii, et simplices plures, quos instrui dirigi muniri oportebit—quia ex hoc latere unio divinitatis defenditur: sicut enim negata carnis resurrectione concutitur, ita vindicata constabilitur. animae autem 12 salutem credo retractatu carere: omnes enim fere haeretici eam, quoquo modo volunt, tamen non negant. viderit unus aliqui Lucanus ne huic quidem substantiae parcens, quam secundum Aristotelem dissolvens aliud quid pro ea subicit, tertium quiddam resurrectur*us*, neque anima neque caro, id est non homo, sed ursus

---

34 manifestatiorem *T*: manifestiorem *MPX*.
46 elidunt *MPX*: instantur *T, unde Brf.* instigantur.
47 occurrendum *Gel.*: currendum *T*: decurrendum *MPX*.
51 penes nos quoque incerta *TB*: *alii alia*.
53 ex *T*: et *MPX*.
59 tertium *om. MPX*.
60 resurrecturus *Gel.*: resurrecturum *libri*.

a second deity in opposition to the God of the world, by nature known to all on the evidence of his works, and undoubtedly prior in the types and more manifest in the preachings, these people, under cover of what they say is a more pressing case—that is, of man's salvation demanding enquiry before all else—begin with questions on the resurrection, because it is harder to believe the resurrection of the flesh than the unity of the deity: and thus, having stripped the discussion of the strength of its proper sequence and burdened it instead with scruples which belittle the flesh, they step by step, as a result of the bankruptcy and depreciation of the hope, water it down into conformity with the mind of that other deity. For each several individual, cast down or thrust back from his stance on that hope which he had embraced in the sight of the Creator, thereafter is easily led away, without further suggestion from elsewhere, to surmise an author of the other hope. For by diversity of promises is suggested a diversity of gods. Thus we find many enmeshed, while they are first caused to crash in respect of the resurrection of the flesh, and afterwards crash in respect of the unity of the deity. So, as far as heretics are concerned, I have shown in what formation we must attack them: and the attack has already been made, under each one's docket, concerning the one only God and his Christ against Marcion, and concerning the Lord's flesh against four heresies, chiefly to pave the way for the present discussion: so that we have now to consider only the resurrection of the flesh, as though it were uncertain in our, that is the Creator's, sight. For there are many unlearned, and a number doubtful of their own faith, and not a few plain men, who will need to be equipped, guided, and protected, seeing that on this flank also the unity of the deity calls for defence. For just as its foundations are shaken by the denial of the resurrection of the flesh, so by the vindication of it they are made strong. The salvation of the soul I believe needs no discussion: for almost all heretics, in whatever way they accept it, at least do not deny it. We may leave to his own devices the one single solitary Lucan, who spares not even this entity, but in Aristotelian fashion disperses it and substitutes something else for it: for he expects to rise again as a third something, neither soul nor flesh, that is, not a man, but a bear

forsitan qua Lucanus. habet et iste a nobis plenissimum de omni 13
statu animae stilum: quam imprimis immortalem tuentes, solius
carnis et defectionem agnoscimus et refectionem cum maxime
adserimus, redactis in ordinarium materiae corpus si quae et alibi
pro causarum incursione praestricta distulimus. nam ut quaedam 14
praelibari sollemne est, ita et differri necesse est, dummodo et
praelibata suppleantur suo corpore et dilata reddantur suo nomine.

3 Est quidem et de communibus sensibus sapere in dei rebus, sed
in testimonium veri, non in adiutorium falsi, quod sit secundum
divinam, non contra divinam dispositionem. quaedam enim et
naturaliter nota sunt, ut immortalitas animae penes plures, ut deus
noster penes omnes. utar ergo et sententia Platonis alicuius pro- 2
nuntiantis, 'Omnis anima immortalis': utar et conscientia populi
contestantis deum deorum: utar et reliquis communibus sensibus
qui deum iudicem praedicant, 'Deus videt' et 'Deo commendo'.
at cum aiunt 'Mortuum quod mortuum' et 'Vive dum vivis' et 3
'Post mortem omnia finiuntur, etiam ipsa', tunc meminero et cor
vulgi cinerem a deo deputatum et ipsam sapientiam saeculi stulti-
tiam pronuntiatam, tunc si haereticus ad vulgi vitia vel saeculi
ingenia confugerit, 'Discede dicam ab ethnico, haeretice: etsi unum
estis omnes qui deum fingitis, dum tamen hoc in Christi nomine
facis, dum Christianus tibi videris, alius ab ethnico es: redde illi
suos sensus, quia nec ille de tuis instruitur: quid caeco duce niteris 4
si vides? quid vestiris a nudo si Christum induisti? quid alieno
uteris clipeo si ab apostolo armatus es? ille a te potius discat carnis

61 qua *Gel.*: quasi *T*: tanquam *MPX*.
63 agnoscimus et refectionem *om. MPX*.
64 quae *T*: qua *MPX*.
3: 9 vive dum *Gel.*: vividum *TB*^{mg}·: vivens dum *MPX*.
16 duce niteris *T*: duci inniteris *MP*, *forsan recte*.

perhaps, being a Lucanian. He also has from me a treatise Concerning the whole Status of the Soul. This I maintain is in a primary sense immortal, while I admit the defection of the flesh alone and make a special assertion of its refection, reducing to an orderly body of material all things that elsewhere I have postponed after touching upon them as each case arose. For as it is common practice for some things to be sampled beforehand, so must they of necessity be postponed, provided the things sampled be fully supplied in their own stock, and the things postponed be paid up in their own account.
3 Now it is possible even on the basis of popular ideas to be knowledgeable in the things of God, though for evidence of the truth, not in support of falsehood, to establish what is in accordance with the divine ordinance, not what is opposed to it. For some things are known even by nature, as is the immortality of the soul among many people and as is our God among all. Consequently I shall use the pronouncement of one Plato who declares, 'All soul is immortal':[1] I shall use also the private knowledge of the people ⟨of Israel⟩ when it calls to witness the God of gods: I shall use also other nations' popular ideas, which proclaim that God is judge, 'God sees', and 'I entrust it to God'. But when they say, 'What is dead is dead', and 'Live whilst thou livest', and 'After death all things come to an end, even death itself', then I shall remember that the heart of the multitude is reckoned by God as ashes,[2] and that the very wisdom of the world is declared foolishness:[3] then, if the heretic take shelter under the vices of the multitude or the devices of the world, I shall say, 'Depart from the gentile, O heretic: even though there is substantial unity among all you who fabricate a god, yet so long as you do this in Christ's name, so long as you regard yourself as a Christian, you are a different man from the gentile: give him back his own ideas, for neither does he equip himself with yours. Why, if you have sight, do you lean on a blind guide? Why, if you have put on Christ, do you accept clothing from one naked?[4] Why, if you have been armed by the apostle,[5] do you use another man's shield? Rather

[1] Plato, *Phaedrus*, 245 C. [2] Cf. Isa. 44. 20.
[3] Cf. 1 Cor. 1. 20; 3. 19. [4] Cf. Gal. 3. 27; Rom. 13. 14.
[5] Cf. Eph. 6. 13-17.

resurrectionem confiteri quam tu ab illo diffiteri: quia si et a
Christianis negari eam oporteret sufficeret illis de sua scientia non
de vulgi ignorantia instrui.' adeo non erit Christianus qui eam
negabit quam confitentur Christiani, et his argumentis negabit
quibus utuntur non Christiani. aufer denique haereticis quae cum
ethnicis sapiunt, ut de scripturis solis quaestiones suas sistant, et
stare non poterunt. communes enim sensus simplicitas ipsa
commendat et compassio sententiarum et familiaritas opinionum,
eoque fideliores existimantur quia nuda et aperta et omnibus nota
definiunt: ratio autem divina in medulla est, non in superficie, et
plerumque aemula manifestis.

4 Itaque haeretici inde statim incipiunt et inde praestruunt, dehinc
et interstruunt, unde sciunt facile capi mentes de communione
favorabili sensuum. an aliud prius vel magis audias ⟨tam⟩ ab
haeretico quam ab ethnico, et non protenus et non ubique con-
vicium carnis, in originem in materiam in casum, in omnem exitum
eius, immundae a primordio ex faecibus terrae, immundioris
deinceps ex seminis sui limo, frivolae infirmae criminosae molestae
onerosae, et post totum ignobilitatis elogium caducae in originem
terrae et cadaveris nomen, et de isto quoque nomine periturae in
nullum inde iam nomen, in omnis iam vocabuli mortem?
'Hancne ergo, vir sapiens, et visui et contactui et recordatui tuo
ereptam persuadere vis quod se receptura quandoque sit in integrum de corrupto, in solidum de casso, in plenum de inanito, in
aliquid omnino de nihilo, et utique redhibentibus eam ignibus et
undis et alvis ferarum et rumis alitum et lactibus piscium et

19 et a *MPX*: et *T*.
23 utuntur non Christiani *TC*: utitur non Christianus *MPX*.
4: 3 tam *add*. Urs.
    7–8 molestae onerosae *T*: onerosae molestae *MPX*.
    9 terrae *T*: terram *MPX*.
    11 ⟨ait⟩ vir sapiens *Kroy. Brf.*
    12 persuadere vis *TB*: persuadere *MP forsan recte* (*i.e.* persuaderis): persuadeare *X*.
    15 lactibus *GR*³: iactibus *MPXR*¹: retibus *T*.

let that man learn from you to confess the resurrection of the flesh than you from him to repudiate it: for even though there were cause for Christians to deny it, it were better for them to be equipped of their own knowledge, not of the multitude's ignorance.' Thus one cannot be a Christian who denies that resurrection which Christians confess, and denies it by such arguments as non-Christians use. In short, take away from heretics the ideas they have in common with the gentiles, and make them base their questionings on the scriptures alone, and they will not be able to stand. For popular ideas are commended by their very simplicity and by the agreeableness of their pronouncements and the familiarity of the thoughts, and are considered the more trustworthy in that they define things open and apparent and generally known: whereas divine reason is in the marrow, not on the surface, and is frequently in opposition to things as they seem.

4 For this reason heretics immediately begin operations and lay their foundations and afterwards erect their scaffolding with those materials by which they know it is easy for them to entice men's minds, the popularity of the ideas making things favourable for them. Is there anything a heretic says, which a gentile has not already said, and said more frequently? Is there not, forthwith and throughout, reviling of the flesh, attacks upon its origin, its material, its fate, its whole destiny, as being from its first beginning foul from the excrement of the earth, more foul thereafter because of the slime of its own seed, paltry, unstable, reproachable, troublesome, burdensome, and (following on the whole indictment of its baseness) fated to fall back into the earth from whence it came and to be described as a corpse, and destined to perish from that description too into no description at all from thenceforth, into a death of any and every designation? 'Do you then, as a philosopher, wish to persuade us that this flesh, when it has been ravished from your sight and touch and remembrance—that it is sometime to recover itself to wholeness out of corruption, to concreteness out of vacuity, to fullness out of emptiness, in short to somethingness out of nothingness, and that even the funeral pyre or the sea or the bellies of wild beasts or the crops of birds or the

ipsorum temporum propria gula? adeone autem eadem sperabitur 4
quae intercidit ut claudus et luscus et caecus et leprosus et paralyticus revertantur, ut redisse non libeat, ad pristinum: an integri, ut
iterum talia pati timeant? quid tum de consequentiis carnis? 5
rursusne omnia necessaria illi, et imprimis pabula atque potacula?
et pulmonibus natandum et intestinis aestuandum et pudendis non
pudendum et omnibus membris laborandum? rursus ulcera et 6
vulnera et febris et podagra et mors redoptanda? nimirum haec
erunt vota carnis recuperandae, iterum cupere de ea evadere.' et 7
nos quidem haec aliquanto honestius pro stili pudore: ceterum
quantum etiam spurciloquio liceat, illorum ⟨est⟩ in congressibus
experiri tam ethnicorum quam haereticorum.

5 Igitur quoniam et rudes quique de communibus adhuc sensibus
sapiunt, et dubii et simplices per eosdem sensus denuo inquietantur,
et ubique primus iste in nos aries temperatur quo carnis condicio
quassatur, necessario et a nobis carnis primum condicio munietur,
vituperatione laudatione depulsa: ita nos rhetoricari quoque
provocant haeretici, sicut etiam philosophari philosophi. futtile et 2
frivolum istud corpusculum, quod malum denique appellare non
horrent, etsi angelorum fuisset operatio ut Menandro et Marco
placet, etsi ignei alicuius extructio aeque angeli ut Apelles docet,
sufficeret ad auctoritatem carnis secundae divinitatis patrocinium:
angelos post deum novimus. iam nunc quisquis ille summus deus 3
haeretici cuiusque est, non immerito ab ipso quoque deducerem
carnis dignitatem a quo voluntas producendae eius adfuisset:
utique enim prohibuisset fieri quam fieri scisset, si fieri noluisset.
itaque et secundum illos aeque caro dei res: nihil operis non eius
est qui passus est esse. bene autem quod et plures et duriores 4
quaeque doctrinae totam hominis figulationem deo nostro cedunt.

16 temporum *om. MPX.*
23 redoptanda *MPX*: impeccanda *T* (*pro* imprecanda).
26 liceat, illorum *ita pungebam.*   est *hoc ordine addidi*: Kroy. *post* experiri.
5: 1 rudes quique petras *T.*
  3 primus *T Gel.*: imprimis *MPX.*
  5 vituperationem laudatione depellens *T.*
  13 eius *T*: ei *MPX.*
  15 itaque *T*: ita *MPX.*
  17 credunt *T.*

intestines of fishes or the peculiar gluttony of time itself will give it back again? And is this same flesh which has disappeared to be an object of hope simply that the lame and the one-eyed and the blind and the leprous and the palsied may revert, so as to wish they had not returned, to what they were before? Or are they to be whole, so as to be apprehensive of suffering the same things a second time? Then what of the appurtenances of the flesh? Will these all again be necessary to it, and particularly food and drink? And will it again have to breathe with lungs and heave in its intestines and be shameless with its private parts and have trouble with all its members? Must it again expect sores and wounds and fever and gout and death? In that case the hope of the recovery of the flesh will amount to just this, the desire to escape from it a second time.' Now I have expressed this somewhat more decently, out of respect for my pen: but how much licence is given even to foulspeaking, you may find out for yourselves in these people's discussions, whether they be gentiles or heretics.

5 Therefore since also all the unlearned still think in terms of popular ideas, and doubters and plain men through these same ideas are disquieted anew, and since in every case the first battering-ram poised against us is this by which the quality of the flesh is shaken, we too shall of necessity begin by providing the quality of the flesh with defence-works, routing the vilification of it by means of an encomium. Thus the heretics challenge us to displays of rhetoric, as philosophers do to exercises in philosophy. Though this trivial fragile body, which they are not afraid to call an evil thing, had been the handiwork of angels (as Menander and Marcus hold), though it had been fabricated by some fiery being, this too an angel (as Apelles teaches), the patronage of secondary deities would have sufficed for the dignity of the flesh: we do acknowledge angels—after God. So then, whichsoever each heretic's supreme god is, I should with complete justification deduce the nobility of the flesh from that god from whom had proceeded the will to produce it. For assuredly, when he knew it was being made, he would have forbidden it to be made if he had not desired it to be made. Thus according to them also the flesh no less belongs to a god. No part of a work can fail to belong to him who has

quantus hic sit satis nosti qui unicum credidisti. incipiat iam tibi caro placere cuius artifex tantus est. 'Sed et mundus iste, inquis, dei opus est, et tamen praeterit habitus mundi huius, apostolo quoque auctore, nec idcirco restitutio mundi praeiudicabitur quia dei opus est: et utique si universitas inreformabilis post decessum, quid portio?' plane, si portio universitati adaequatur. ad distantias enim provocamus. primo quidem, quod omnia sermone dei facta sunt et sine illo nihil, caro autem et sermone dei constitit propter formam, ne quid sine sermone—Faciamus enim hominem ante praemisit—et amplius manu propter praelationem, ne universitati compararetur—Et finxit inquit deus hominem—magnae sine dubio differentiae ratio, pro condicione scilicet rerum: minora enim quae fiebant eo cui fiebant, siquidem homini fiebant cui mox a deo addicta sunt. merito igitur, ut famula, iussu et imperio et sola vocali potestate universa processerant; contra homo, ut dominus eorum, in hoc ab ipso deo extructus est ut dominus esse possit dum fit a domino. hominem autem memento carnem proprie dici, quae prior vocabulum hominis occupavit. Et finxit deus hominem limum de terra: iam homo qui adhuc limus: Et insufflavit in faciem eius flatum vitae et factus est homo, id est limus, in animam vivam, et posuit deus hominem quem finxit in paradiso. adeo homo figmentum primo, dehinc totus. hoc eo commendarim uti quidquid omnino homini a deo prospectum

19 iste *om. MPX.*
21 auctore *MPX*: doctore *T.*
23 distantias *T*: distantiam *MPX.*
24 provocamur *T Brf.*
26–9 *ita pungebam, Kroymannum aliquatenus secutus.*
30 eo cui fiebant *om. T.*   homini *MPX*: propter hominem *T.*
36 limum de terra *MPX*: de limo terrae *T.*

permitted it to be. Observe moreover that the majority of the sects, especially all the more durable ones, concede the whole formation of man to our God. How great he is is sufficiently known to you who believe him the only one. Then let the flesh begin to find favour with you, in view of the greatness of its artificer. 'But', you reply, 'the world also is God's work, and yet, on no less authority than the apostle's, the fashion of this world passeth away,[1] and the fact that the world is God's work cannot be taken as a proof that it will be restored again: and in fact, if the whole universe is not to be reconstituted after its decease, why should a portion of it be?' Evidently it cannot, if the portion is equated with the whole. But I appeal to the differences between them: in the first place that all things were made by the word of God,[2] and without it was nothing, whereas the flesh came into being both by the word of God, for the sake of the general rule, so that nothing should exist without the word (for he had already said, *Let us make man*),[3] and besides this by his hand, for the sake of pre-eminence, lest it should be kept equal with the whole: *And God*, it says, *formed man*.[4] Without doubt this is a factor of great unlikeness, in proportion to the quality of the two objects: for the things which were made are inferior to him for whom they were made; and indeed they were made for man, to whom shortly afterwards God put them in subjection. Rightly therefore the whole universe of things, being servants, came into existence by behest and command and by the sole power of the voice: whereas man, being their lord, was for this very purpose constructed by God himself, that he might be capable of being a lord because made by the Lord. And remember that 'man' in the strict sense means the flesh, for this was the first possessor of the designation 'man': *And God formed man, clay from the earth*—already is he man who is still clay—*and breathed into his nostrils the breath of life, and man*—that is, the clay—*became a living soul*,[5] and God placed in paradise the man whom he had formed. Thus 'man' is first that which was formed, and afterwards is the whole man. This submission I would offer, so that you may understand that whatso-

[1] 1 Cor. 7. 31. [2] Cf. Joh. 1. 3. [3] Gen. 1. 26.
[4] Gen. 1. 27. [5] Gen. 2. 7, 8.

atque promissum est non soli animae verum et carni scias debitum, ut si non ex consortio generis certe vel ex privilegio nominis.

6 Persequar itaque propositum, si tamen tantum possim carni vindicare quantum contulit ille qui eam fecit, iam tunc gloriantem quod illa pusillitas limus in manus dei, quaecumque sunt, pervenit, satis beatus etsi solummodo contactus. quid enim si nullo amplius *2* opere statim figmentum de contactu dei constitisset? adeo magna res agebatur quod ista materia extruebatur. itaque totiens honoratur quotiens manus dei patitur, dum tangitur, dum decerpitur, dum deducitur, dum effingitur. recogita totum illi deum *3* occupatum ac deditum, manu sensu opere consilio sapientia providentia, et ipsa imprimis adfectione quae liniamenta dictabat: quodcumque enim limus exprimebatur, Christus cogitabatur homo futurus quod et limus, et sermo caro quod et terra tunc. sic *4* enim praefatio patris ad filium, Faciamus hominem ad imaginem et similitudinem nostram: et fecit hominem deus, id utique quod finxit: ad imaginem dei fecit illum, scilicet Christi. et sermo enim deus, qui in effigie dei constitutus non rapinam existimavit pariari deo. ita limus ille iam tunc imaginem induens Christi futuri in *5* carne non tantum dei opus erat sed et pignus. quo nunc facit ad infuscandam originem carnis nomen terrae ventilare ut sordentis ut iacentis elementi, cum et si alia materia excudendo homini competisset artificis fastigium recogitari oporteret qui illam et eligendo dignam iudicasset et tractando fecisset? Phidiae manus Iovem *6* Olympium ex ebore molitae adorantur: nec iam bestiae et quidem insulsissimae dens est sed summum saeculi numen, non quia elephantus sed quia Phidias tantus: deus vivus et deus verus quam-

41 soli *MPX*: solum *T*.
42 ut *del. Kroy.*: *sed quidni* et *rescribas*?
6: 6 quod *T*: quae *MP*: qua *XR*.
 9 ac deditum *X Gel.*: ac dedicatum *MP*: accedit e *T*.
 12 sermo caro *T*: caro sermo *MPXR*.
 16 pariari *R*[3] *ex variis et parum certis librorum testimoniis*.
 23 molitae adorantur *T Gel.*: molitur et adoratur *MPX*.

ever at all was provided and promised beforehand by God to man became a debt not to the soul only but also to the flesh, if not by kindred of origin surely at least by prior possession of the name.
6 So I shall follow out my project, if perchance I may but vindicate for the flesh as much as he conferred upon it who made it even then with cause for pride: because that paltry thing, clay, came into God's hands—whatever they may be—though it would have been blessed enough had it been no more than touched. For what if, by no further operation, it had at once taken form and fashion at the touch of God? So great was the matter in hand, the thing which was being constructed of that material: and so it as often receives honour as it is worked upon by God's hands, when touched, when broken off the lump, when kneaded, when moulded. Recollect that God was wholly concerned with it and intent upon it, with hand, mind, work, counsel, wisdom, providence, and especially with that affection which prescribed its features. For whatever expression the clay took upon it, the thought was of Christ who was to become man (which the clay was) and of the Word who was to become flesh (which at that time the earth was). For the Father had already spoken to the Son in these words, *Let us make man unto our own image and likeness. And God made man* (the same thing of course as 'formed'):[1] *unto the image of God* ('of Christ', it means) *made he him*. For the Word also is God, who being in the form of God thought it not robbery to be equal with God.[2] Thus that clay, already putting on the image of Christ who was to be in the flesh, was not only a work of God but also a token of him. What is the use now, with intent to sully the origin of the flesh, of flinging about the name of earth, as of a dirty ignoble element, when even though some other material had been to hand for the sculpturing of man, it were needful to bear in mind the dignity of the Artificer who both by choosing judged it worthy and by handling made it so? The hand of Phidias builds out of ivory the Olympian Jove, which is worshipped, being no longer the tusk of a wild beast, and a very stupid one at that, but this world's supreme divinity, not because the elephant is so great but because Phidias is: and could not the living God, the true God, by

---
[1] Gen. 1. 26, 27.   [2] Cf. Phil. 2. 6.

cunque materiae vilitatem nonne de sua operatione purgasset et ab omni infirmitate sanasset? an hoc supererit, ut honestius homo deum quam hominem deus finxerit? nunc et si scandalum limus, 7 alia iam res est. carnem iam teneo, non terram: licet et caro audiat, Terra es et in terram redibis, origo recensetur, non substantia revocatur. datum est esse aliquid origine generosius et 8 demutatione felicius: nam et aurum terra quia de terra, hactenus tamen terra est ex quo aurum, longe alia materia, splendidior atque nobilior, de obsoletiore matrice. ita et deo licuit carnis aurum de limi quibus putas sordibus excusato censu eliquasse.

7 Sed ne dilutior videatur auctoritas carnis quia non et ipsam proprie manus divina tractavit sicut limum, quando in hoc tractaverit limum ut postmodum caro fieret ex limo carni utique negotium gessit. sed adhuc velim discas quando et quomodo caro 2 floruerit ex limo. neque enim, ut quidam volunt, illae pelliciae tunicae quas Adam et Eva paradisum exuti induerunt, ipsae erunt carnis ex limo reformatio, cum aliquanto prius et Adam substantiae suae traducem in feminae iam carne recognoverit—Hoc nunc os ex ossibus meis et caro ex carne mea—et ipsa delibatio masculi in feminam carne suppleta sit, limo opinor supplenda si Adam adhuc limus. obliteratus igitur et devoratus est limus in carnem. 3 quando? cum factus est homo in animam vivam de dei flatu, vaporeo scilicet et idoneo torrere quodammodo limum in aliam qualitatem, quasi in testam ita et in carnem. sic et figulo licet 4 argillam temperato ignis adflatu in materiam robustiorem recorporare et aliam ex alia stringere speciem, aptiorem pristina et sui iam generis ac nominis. nam etsi scriptum est, Numquid argilla 5

34 obsoletiore *Gel.*: obsolentiore *libri*.
7: 8 cognoverit *T*.
13 vapore scilicet idoneo *Lat. Urs*.

his own operation have cleaned away any baseness of his material, and healed it of all infirmity? Or shall we have to suppose it more honourable for a man to have formed a god than for God to have formed man? For even if clay was an offence, it is now something else: it is flesh I now take hold of, not earth. Even though the flesh also hear it said, *Earth thou art and unto earth shalt thou return*,[1] it is its origin which is being recounted, not its substance which is being revoked. It has been made possible for a thing to be more noble than its origin, and richer by reason of change: for even gold is earth, because it is from the earth, yet it is no longer earth after it becomes gold, but another material by far, more resplendent and noble by contrast with the dullness of its origin. So also God was not precluded from smelting the gold of flesh from what you consider the foulness of clay, removing the reproach of its birth.

7 But lest the dignity of the flesh appear somewhat watered down because the divine hand did not actually touch it, as it had the clay, ⟨I answer that⟩ since it did touch the clay, with the intent that forthwith it should become flesh instead of clay, it by that very fact served the interests of the flesh. And moreover I would have you learn how and when flesh blossomed out of clay. For it cannot be the case, as some will have it, that those coats of skins which Adam and Eve put on when stripped of paradise,[2] were themselves a transforming of clay into flesh: for somewhat earlier Adam had already recognized in the female's flesh the offshoot of his own substance—*This is now bone out of my bones and flesh out of my flesh*[3] —and the transfusion from the male into the female was itself made good with flesh, though I suppose it would have had to be made good with clay if Adam had still been clay. Therefore the clay was blotted out and swallowed up into flesh. When? When man was made into a living soul by the breath of God,[4] a fiery breath, competent as it were to bake clay into a different quality, into flesh as though into earthenware. Thus also the potter may with a tempered blast of fire re-embody potter's clay into a firmer material, and out of one species extract another, more useful than the original, and now of its own kind and designation. For

[1] Gen. 3. 19.   [2] Cf. Gen. 3. 21.
[3] Gen. 2. 23.   [4] Cf. Gen. 2. 7.

dicet figulo, id est homo deo; et si apostolus In testaceis ait vasculis: tamen et argilla homo quia limus ante, et testa caro quia ex limo per adflatus divini vaporem. quam postea pelliciae tunicae, id est 6 cutes, superductae vestierunt: usque adeo, si detraxeris cutem nudaveris carnem. ita quod hodie spolium efficitur si detrahatur, hoc fuit indumentum cum superstruebatur. hinc et apostolus circumcisionem despoliationem carnis appellans tunicam cutem confirmavit. haec cum ita sint, habes et limum de manu dei 7 gloriosum, et carnem de adflatu dei gloriosiorem, quo pariter caro et limi rudimenta deposuit et animae ornamenta suscepit. non es 8 diligentior deo, uti tu quidem Scythicas et Indicas gemmas et rubentis maris grana candentia non plumbo non aere non ferro neque argento quoque oblaquees sed delectissimo et insuper operosissimo de scrobibus auro, vinis item et unguentis pretiosissimis quibusque vasculorum prius congruentiam cures, proinde perspectae ferruginis gladiis vaginarum adaeques dignitatem, deus vero animae suae umbram, spiritus sui auram, oris sui operam, vilissimo alicui commiserit capulo et indigne collocando utique damnaverit. collocavit autem, an potius inseruit et inmiscuit 9 carni? tanta quidem concretione ut incertum haberi possit utrumne caro animam an carnem anima circumferat, utrumne animae caro an anima adpareat carni. sed etsi magis animam invehi atque 10 dominari credendum est ut magis deo proximam, hoc quoque ad gloriam carnis exuberat quod proximam deo et continet et ipsius dominationis compotem praestat. quem enim naturae usum, 11 quem mundi fructum, quem elementorum saporem non per carnem anima depascitur? quidni? per quam omni instrumento

25 confirmavit *T Gel.*: affirmavit *MPX*.
27 non *TMPX*: num *Kroy. signo quoque interrogandi infra post* damnaverit *posito*.
31 vinis item *om. MPX*.

although it is written, *Shall the potter's clay say to the potter*[1]—that is, shall man say to God—, and although the apostle says, *In vessels of earthenware*,[2] yet man is called potter's clay because he was previously clay, and flesh is called earthenware because it was made of clay by means of the heat of the divine breathing. It was afterwards that coats of skins (that is, cuticle) were drawn on over it and clothed it: and the proof of this is, that if you strip off the skin you leave the flesh naked. Thus what today becomes spoil if it is stripped off, became a garment while it was being made a superstructure. Hence also the apostle, when he called circumcision a despoiling of the flesh,[3] affirmed that the skin is a coat. This being so, you have both clay glorious from God's hand, and flesh more glorious from God's breathing: and by this breathing the flesh at the same time laid aside the rudiments of clay and took upon it the adornments of soul. Your care for your property is not greater than God's: yet you mount Scythian and Indian gems, and the gleaming pearls of the Red Sea, neither in lead nor bronze nor iron nor even silver, but in choice gold carefully separated from its dross, while for all precious wines and ointments you first provide suitable vessels, and likewise for swords of perfect ironwork you make scabbards of equal dignity: and is it conceivable that God has consigned to some very cheap receptacle the reflection of his own soul, the breath of his own spirit, the workmanship of his own mouth, and has thus by giving it an unworthy lodging definitely brought about its damnation? But did he give it a lodging, or not rather entwine and commingle it with the flesh? Yes, in such close concretion that it may be considered uncertain whether the flesh is the vehicle of the soul or the soul the vehicle of the flesh, whether the flesh is at the service of the soul or the soul at the service of the flesh. Yet though it is more credible that the soul, as more akin to God, is the rider and the master, this also redounds to the glory of the flesh, that it both contains this soul which is God's kin, and puts it in possession of that selfsame mastery. For what enjoyment of nature, what fruition of the world, what savouring of the elements, does the soul feed upon except by means of the flesh? What think you? Through it as intermediary

[1] Rom. 9. 20.   [2] 2 Cor. 4. 7.   [3] Cf. Col. 2. 11.

45 sensuum fulta est, visu auditu gustu odoratu contactu: per quam divina potestate respersa est, nihil non sermone prospiciens vel tacite praemisso. et sermo enim de organo carnis est. artes per 12 carnem, studia ingenia per carnem, opera negotia officia per carnem, atque adeo vivere totum animae carnis est ut non vivere
50 aliud non sit animae quam a carne divertere. sic etiam ipsum mori carnis est, cuius et vivere. porro si universa per carnem subiacent 13 animae, carni quoque subiacent: per quod utaris, cum eo utaris necesse est. ita caro, dum ministra et famula animae deputatur, consors et coheres invenitur: si temporalium, cur non et aeter-
55 norum?

8 Et haec quidem velut de publica forma humanae condicionis in suffragium carnis procuraverim. videamus nunc de propria etiam Christiani nominis forma, quanta huic substantiae frivolae ac sordidae apud deum praerogativa sit. etsi sufficeret illi quod 2
5 nulla omnino anima salutem possit adipisci nisi dum est in carne crediderit: adeo caro salutis est cardo, de qua cum anima deo alligatur ipsa est quae efficit ut anima eligi possit a deo. sed et 3 caro abluitur ut anima emaculetur, caro unguitur ut anima consecretur, caro signatur ut et anima muniatur, caro manus imposi-
10 tione adumbratur ut et anima spiritu illuminetur, caro corpore et sanguine Christi vescitur ut et anima de deo saginetur. non possunt ergo separari in mercede quas opera coniungit. nam et 4 sacrificia deo grata, conflictationes dico animae, ieiunia et seras et aridas escas et adpendices huius officii sordes, caro de proprio suo
15 incommodo instaurat. virginitas quoque et viduitas et modesta in occulto matrimonii dissimulatio et una notitia eius de bonis carnis

46 prospiciens *T*: perficiens *MPX*.
49 vivere totum *T*: totum vivere *MPX*.
8: 5 est *om*. *T*.
    7 alligatur *X*: alligitur *MP*: aligitur *T*: allegitur *R*: allegatur *Brf.*   eligi *T*: allegi *R Brf.*: alligi *MP*: alligari *X*.   a deo *T*: om. *MPX*.
    13 dico carnis animae *MPX*, *manifesto errore*.

it is enriched by the whole apparatus of the senses, sight, hearing, taste, smell, touch. Through it it is aspersed with divine power, seeing it provides for nothing except by speech previously expressed, at least in silence: for speech also derives from the flesh as its organ. By the flesh are the manual arts, by the flesh are liberal and professional studies, by the flesh are activities, occupations, and services: and to such a degree does the whole of the soul's living belong to the flesh, that to the soul to cease to live is exactly the same thing as to retire from the flesh. Thus also dying itself belongs to the flesh, because to it living belongs. Moreover, if it is through the flesh that all things are subject to the soul, they are subject to the flesh as well: you must of necessity have for partner in your use of a thing the instrument by which you use it. Thus the flesh, while it is reckoned the servant and handmaid of the soul, is found to be its consort and coheir: if in things temporal, why not also in things eternal?

8 Thus far let it suffice me to have produced judgements in favour of the flesh as it were from the common law of human nature. We must next consider also from the private law of the Christian nation how great a prerogative this pitiful and squalid substance enjoys in the sight of God: though it would be sufficient for it that no soul can ever obtain salvation unless while it is in the flesh it has become a believer. To such a degree is the flesh the pivot of salvation, that since by it the soul becomes linked with God, it is the flesh which makes possible the soul's election by God. For example, the flesh is washed that the soul may be made spotless: the flesh is anointed that the soul may be consecrated: the flesh is signed ⟨with the cross⟩ that the soul too may be protected: the flesh is overshadowed by the imposition of the hand that the soul may be illumined by the Spirit: the flesh feeds on the Body and Blood of Christ so that the soul also may be replete with God. There is then no possibility of these, which the work associates, being divided in the wages. For those sacrifices also that are pleasing to God—I mean these conflicts of the soul, fastings, deferred and meagre food, and the squalor which accompanies this observance—the flesh initiates at its own proper inconvenience. Virginity besides, and widowhood, and the secret continent

deo adulantur. age iam, quid de ea sentis cum pro nominis fide in 5
medium extracta et odio publico exposita decertat, cum in
carceribus maceratur taeterrimo lucis exilio penuria mundi squalore
paedore contumelia victus, ne somno quidem libera, quippe ipsis
etiam cubilibus vincta ipsisque stramentis lancinata, cum iam et in
luce omni tormentorum machinatione laniatur, cum denique suppliciis erogatur, enisa reddere Christo vicem moriendo pro ipso, et
quidem per eandem crucem saepe, nedum per atrociora quoque
ingenia poenarum? ne illa beatissima et gloriosissima, quae potest 6
apud Christum dominum parere debito tanto, ut hoc solum debeat
ei quod ei debere desierit, hoc magis vincta quo absoluta.

9 Igitur, ut retexam, quam deus manibus suis ad imaginem dei
struxit, quam de suo adflatu ad similitudinem suae vivacitatis
animavit, quam incolatui fructui dominatui totius suae operationis
praeposuit, quam sacramentis suis disciplinisque vestivit, cuius
munditias amat, cuius castigationes probat, cuius passiones sibi
adpretiat, haecine non resurget, totiens dei res? absit, absit, ut 2
deus manuum suarum operam, ingenii sui curam, adflatus sui
vaginam, molitionis suae reginam, liberalitatis suae heredem,
religionis suae sacerdotem, testimonii sui militem, Christi sui
sororem, in aeternum destituat interitum. bonum deum novimus: 3
solum optimum a Christo eius addiscimus. qui dilectionem
mandat post suam in proximum, facit et ipse quod praecipit:
diligit carnem tot modis sibi proximam; etsi infirmam, sed virtus 4
in infirmitate perficitur; etsi imbecillam, sed medicum non
desiderant nisi male habentes; etsi inhonestam, sed inhonestioribus

17 adulantur *T*: adolantur *MP*: adolatur *X*: adolentur *Gel.*, *forsan recte*.
9: 4 praeposuit *MPX*: imposuit *T*.
 6 dei res *T*: dei *MPX*.
 12 praecipit *T*: praecepit *MPX*.

dissimulation of matrimony, and abstention from second marriages, are offered in sacrifice to God from the possessions of the flesh. Come now, what think you of the flesh when for the faith of the Name it is dragged into public and fights it out exposed to popular hatred, when it is tormented in prisons by loathsome exile from light, by lack of adornment, by squalor, filth, abusive food, free not even in sleep, since even on its bed it is chained, and is mangled even by its mattress—when next even in daylight it is rent by every contrivance of torture, when at length it is destroyed by execution, having striven to pay Christ back by dying for him, often enough by means of the same cross, not to mention also more dire devices of punishment? Yea, most blessed it is and most glorious, when it is able in the presence of Christ the Lord to meet so great a debt, so as to owe him naught but what it has ceased to owe him, so much the more bound as having been set free.

9 So then, to resume. The flesh, which God with his own hands constructed in God's image, which from his own breathing he made animate in the likeness of his own abounding life, which he set in authority over the denizens, the fruits, the dominion of his whole workmanship, which he has clothed with his own mysteries and doctrines, whose cleanliness he loves, whose discipline he approves, whose sufferings he counts precious to himself—shall this not rise again, so many times over a thing of God? God forbid, God forbid, that God should abandon to eternal destruction the work of his own hands, the product of his own skill, the receptacle of his own breath, the queen of his own creation, the heir of his generosity, the priest of his cult, the warrior of his testimony, the sister of his Christ. We know that God is good:[1] that he alone is supremely good we learn in addition from his Christ. He who enjoins love, first of himself, and afterwards towards one's neighbour,[2] himself also performs that which he commands. He loves the flesh, which in so many ways is his neighbour: weak though it be, yet strength is made perfect in weakness:[3] feeble, yet none know the need of a physician except such as are sick:[4] uncomely, yet upon uncomely things we bestow

[1] Cf. Matt. 19. 17; Luke 18. 19. [2] Cf. Matt. 22. 37.
[3] Cf. 2 Cor. 12. 9. [4] Cf. Luke 5. 31.

maiorem circumdamus honorem; etsi perditam, sed Ego inquit veni ut quod periit salvum faciam; etsi peccatricem, sed Malo mihi inquit salutem peccatoris quam mortem; etsi damnatam, sed Ego inquit percutiam et sanabo. quid ea exprobras carni quae 5
20 deum expectant, quae in deum sperant? honorantur ab illo quibus subvenit. ausim dicere, si haec carni non accidissent, benignitas gratia misericordia, omnis vis dei benefica, vacuisset.

10 Tenes scripturas quibus caro infuscatur: tene etiam quibus illustratur. legis cum quando deprimitur: adige oculos et cum quando relevatur. Omnis caro foenum: non hoc solum pronun- 2 tiavit Esaias, sed et Omnis caro videbĭt salutare dei. notatur in
5 Genesi dicens dominus, Non manebit spiritus meus super ipsos homines, quia caro sunt: sed et auditur per Ioelem, Effundam de spiritu meo in omnem carnem. apostolum quoque ne de uno 3 stilo noris quo carnem plerumque compungit: nam etsi negat habitare quidquam boni in carne sua, etsi adfirmat eos qui in carne
10 sint deo placere non posse, quia caro concupiscat adversum spiritum, et si qua alia ita ponit ut carnis non tamen substantia sed actus oneretur, dicemus quidem alibi nihil proprie carni exprobari oportere nisi in animae suggillationem quae carnem ministerio sibi subigit. verum interim et in illis litteris Paulus est cum stigmata 4
15 Christi in corpore suo portat, cum corpus nostrum ut dei templum vitiari vetat, cum corpora nostra membra Christi facit, cum monet tollere et magnificare deum in corpore nostro. itaque si igno- 5 miniae carnis resurrectionem eius expellunt, cur non dignitates

---

10: 3 relevatur *TR*: revelatur *MPX*.
  5 super ipsos homines *T*: in hominibus istis *MPX*.
  12 oneretur *Brf.*: honoretur *T*: inhonoretur *MPX vulgo*.

the greater comeliness:[1] lost, yet he says, *I am come to save that which is lost*:[2] sinful, yet he says, *I would rather have the saving of a sinner than his death*:[3] condemned, yet he says, *I will smite and I will heal.*[4] Why do you reprove the flesh for those attributes which look to God, which hope towards God? These are honoured by him, for to their rescue he came. I would boldly say: If the flesh had not had these disabilities, God's kindness, grace, mercy, every beneficent function of God's, would have remained inoperative.

10 You retain the scriptures by which the flesh is brought under a cloud: retain those also by which it is made glorious. You read when it is brought low: apply your eyes also whenever it is lifted up. *All flesh is grass*:[5] not this pronouncement alone did Isaiah make, but also, *All flesh shall see the salvation of God.*[6] The Lord is recorded in Genesis as saying, *My Spirit shall not abide upon these men, seeing they are flesh*:[7] but he is also heard, through Joel, saying, *I will pour forth of my Spirit upon all flesh.*[8] The apostle also you ought to know not from that single theme in which he frequently stigmatizes the flesh.[9] For though he says that in his flesh dwelleth no good thing,[10] though he affirms that those who are in the flesh cannot please God, because the flesh lusteth against the spirit[11]—and any other expressions he uses with the effect of accusing not indeed the substance but the activity of the flesh—I shall reply later on that no reproach ought in a particular sense to be brought against the flesh, but only for a reproof to the soul which subdues the flesh to menial service to itself. Enough for the present that Paul is also ⟨described⟩ in those scriptures as bearing in his body the marks of Christ,[12] as saying that our body, being the temple of God, must not be defiled,[13] as making our bodies the members of Christ[14], and admonishing us to uplift and magnify God in our body.[15] And so, if the ignominies of the flesh involve rejection of its resurrection, why shall not its dignities rather suggest its acceptance? For it is more consistent with God to restore to

[1] Cf. 1 Cor. 12. 23.   [2] Luke 19. 10.   [3] Ezek. 18. 23.
[4] Deut. 32. 39.   [5] Isa. 40. 6.   [6] Cf. Isa. 40. 5.
[7] Gen. 6. 3.   [8] Joel 2. 28.   [9] Cf. Rom. 7. 18.
[10] Cf. Rom. 8. 8.   [11] Cf. Gal. 5. 17.   [12] Cf. Gal. 6. 17.
[13] Cf. 1 Cor. 3. 16, 17.   [14] Cf. 1 Cor. 6. 15.   [15] Cf. 1 Cor. 6. 20.

potius inducent? quoniam deo magis congruit in salutem redigere
quod reprobarit interdum, quam in perditionem dedere quod etiam
probavit.

11 Hucusque de praeconio carnis adversus inimicos et nihilominus amicissimos eius. nemo enim tam carnaliter vivit quam qui negant carnis resurrectionem: negantes enim et poenam despiciunt et disciplinam. de quibus luculenter et paracletus per prophetidem 2 Priscam 'Carnes sunt et carnem oderunt'. quam si tanta auctoritas 3 munit quanta illi ad meritum salutis patrocinari possit, numquid etiam dei ipsius potentiam et potestatem et licentiam recensere debemus, an tantus sit qui valeat dilapsum et devoratum et quibuscumque modis ereptum tabernaculum carnis reaedificare atque restituere? an et aliqua nobis exempla huiusmodi sui iuris in 4 publico naturae promulgavit, ne qui forte adhuc sitiant deum nosse, qui non alia lege credendus est quam ut omnia posse credatur? plane apud philosophos habes qui mundum hunc 5 innatum infectumque defendant. sed multo melius quod omnes fere haereses natum et factum mundum adnuentes conditionem deo nostro adscribunt. igitur confide illum totum hoc ex nihilo 6 protulisse, et deum nosti fidendo quod tantum deus valeat. nam et quidam, infirmiores hoc prius credere, de materia potius subiacenti volunt ab illo universitatem dedicatam secundum philosophos. porro et si ita in vero haberetur, cum tamen longe alias 7 substantias longeque alias species ex reformatione materiae diceretur protulisse quam fuisset ipsa materia, non minus defenderem ex nihilo eum protulisse si ea protulerat quae omnino non fuerant. quo enim interest ex nihilo quid proferri an ex aliquo 8 dum quod non fuit fiat, quando etiam non fuisse nihil sit fuisse? sic et fuisse e contrario nonnihil est fuisse. nunc etsi interest tamen 9

20 reprobarit *MPX*: reprobat *T*.
11: 4–5 de quibus...oderunt *om. T*.
  6 meritum *MPX*: interitum *T Brf.* (*forsan recte*).
  10 restituere *MPX*: restruere *T*.
  11 promulgavit *Urs.*: promulgarit *TR*[3]: promulgaret *MPXR*[1].

salvation that of which he has perhaps for a time disapproved, than to surrender to perdition that of which he has even expressed his approval.

11 Thus far in commendation of the flesh against those enemies who are none the less its greatest friends. For no man lives so carnally as those who deny a carnal resurrection; for while denying the penalty they also despise the discipline. Concerning these the paraclete also expressly says, by Prisca the prophetess, 'Lumps of flesh they are, and the flesh they hate'. And now that the flesh is protected by warrants strong enough to establish its claim to be worthy of salvation, must we not also reckon up the power, the authority, the liberty of action of God himself, asking whether he is not great enough to be competent to rebuild and restore the tabernacle of the flesh after it has fallen down or been swallowed up or in whatsoever manner been dismantled? Or has he not published for us some instances of this his right, in the records of nature, lest any persons perchance be still athirst to know God, belief in whom is conditioned by belief that he can do all things? Certainly among philosophers you have such as claim that this world is unbegotten and uncreated: but it is much more to the point that almost all the sects, admitting that this world is begotten and created, ascribe its foundation to our God. Trust therefore that he has brought forth this everything out of nothing, and you will at once know God by trusting that God has so much power. Some indeed, too weak for this prior belief, will have it that the universe was constructed by him from subjacent material, according to the philosophers. Yet even if this were in fact the case, since the allegation would be that by the refashioning of the material he produced very different substances and very different species from the material itself, I should no less maintain that he brought them forth out of nothing, seeing he had brought forth things which had been in fact non-existent. For what does it matter whether a thing is brought forth out of nothing or out of something, so long as what was not comes into being, when even not to have been is to have been nothing? So also on the contrary, to have been is to have been something. As it is, although it does matter, yet I win approval in either case. For if out of nothing

utrumque mihi adplaudit. sive enim ex nihilo deus molitus est cuncta, poterit et carnem in nihilum prodactam exprimere de nihilo: sive de materia modulatus est alia, poterit et carnem quo-
30 cumque dehaustam evocare de alio. et utique idoneus est reficere 10 qui fecit, quanto plus est fecisse quam refecisse, initium dedisse quam reddidisse. ita restitutionem carnis faciliorem credas institutione.

12 Aspice nunc ad ipsa quoque exempla divinae potestatis. dies moritur in noctem et tenebris usquequaque sepelitur; funestatur mundi honor, omnis substantia denigratur: sordent silent stupent cuncta: ubique iustitium est, quies rerum: ita lux amissa lugetur.
5 et tamen rursus cum suo cultu cum dote cum sole eadem et 2 integra et tota universo orbi revivescit, interficiens mortem suam noctem, rescindens sepulturam suam tenebras, heres sibimet existens, donec et nox revivescat cum suo et illa suggestu. redaccen- 3 duntur enim et stellarum radii quos matutina succensio extinxerat,
10 reducuntur et siderum absentiae quas temporalis distinctio exemerat, redornantur et specula lunae quae menstruus numerus adtriverat. revolvuntur hiemes et aestates, verna et autumna, cum 4 suis viribus moribus fructibus. quippe etiam terrae de caelo disciplina est, arbores vestire post spolia, flores denuo colorare,
15 herbas rursus imponere, exhibere eadem quae absumpta sunt semina, nec prius exhibere quam absumpta. mira ratio: de 5 fraudatrice servatrix, ut reddat intercipit, ut custodiat perdit, interficit ut vivificet, ut integret vitiat, ut etiam ampliet prius decoquit, siquidem et uberiora et cultiora restituit quam extermi-
20 navit, re vera fenore interitu et iniuria usura et lucro damno. semel 6 dixerim, universa conditio recidiva est: quodcumque conveneris fuit, quodcumque amiseris erit: nihil non iterum est: omnia in

28 prodactam *T Oeh.*; productam *MPX*; perductam *Urs.*
29 modulatus *TXR*[1]: moderatus *MP*.
12: 4 quies rerum *deletum volunt Rig. Brf.*
9 succensio *TB*[mg.]: suggestio *MPX*.
18 interficit ut vivificet *T*: *om. MPX*.
21 conveneris *MPX*: cognoveris *TB*[mg.].

God has built up all things, he will be able also out of nothing to produce the flesh reduced to nothing: or if out of material he has contrived things other than it, he will be able also out of something other than it to recall the flesh, into whatsoever it may have been drained away. And certainly he who has made is competent to remake, seeing it is a greater thing to make than to remake, to give a beginning than to give back again. Thus may you believe that the restitution of the flesh is easier than its institution.

12 Look next at actual instances of divine power. Day dies into night and is on every side buried in darkness. The beauty of the world puts on mourning, its every substance is blackened. All things are squalid, silent, numb: everywhere there is vacation, cessation of business: such lamentation is there for the light that is lost. And yet again the same light, entire and whole, together with its adornment and endowment, together with the sun, revives for the whole world, slaying its own death, the night, stripping off its funeral-trappings, the darkness, becoming heir to its own self, until night also revive, herself also with her own appurtenance. For there is also a rekindling of the beams of the stars, which the lighting up of morning had put out; there is a returning home of constellations which have been abroad, which the dividing of seasons had removed; a refurbishing of the mirrors of the moon, which the date of the month had worn away; a revolution of winters and summers, of springs and autumns, with their own functions, fashions, and fruits. Moreover the earth also learns from heaven: to clothe the trees after their stripping, to colour the flowers anew, to dress itself in grass again, to bring to light the same seeds as have perished, and not to bring them to light until they have perished. A marvellous exchange: by defrauding she preserves, so as to give back she takes away, so as to guard she wastes, so as to make alive she slays, so as to make whole she corrupts, so that she may even multiply she first goes bankrupt, inasmuch as she restores things more abundant and more elegant than she has abolished, destruction verily being profit, injury interest, and loss gain. To put it in one word, the whole creation is recurrent. Whatsoever you are to meet with has been: whatsoever you are to lose will be. Nothing exists for the first time. All

statum redeunt cum abscesserint, omnia incipiunt cum desierint: ideo finiuntur ut fiant: nihil deperit nisi in salutem. totus igitur 7 hic ordo revolubilis rerum testatio est resurrectionis mortuorum: operibus eam praescripsit deus ante quam litteris, viribus praedicavit ante quam vocibus. praemisit tibi naturam magistram, 8 submissurus et prophetiam, quo facilius credas prophetiae discipulus ante naturae, quo statim admittas cum audieris quod ubique iam videris, nec dubites deum carnis etiam resuscitatorem quem omnium noveris restitutorem. et utique si omnia homini 9 resurgunt cui procurata sunt, porro non homini nisi et carni, quale est ut ipsa depereat in totum propter quam et cui nihil deperit?

13 Si parum universitas resurrectionem figurat, si nihil tale conditio signat, quia singula eius non tam mori quam desinere dicantur, nec redanimari sed reformari existimentur, accipe plenissimum atque firmissimum huius spei specimen, siquidem animalis est res, et vitae obnoxia et morti. illum dico alitem 2 orientis peculiarem, de singularitate famosum, de posteritate monstruosum, qui semetipsum libenter funerans renovat, natali fine decedens atque succedens, iterum phoenix ubi nemo iam, iterum ipse qui non iam, alius idem. quid expressius atque 3 signatius in hanc causam, aut cui alii rei tale documentum? deus etiam in scripturis suis, Et florebis enim inquit velut phoenix, id est de morte, de funere, uti credas de ignibus quoque substantiam corporis exigi posse. multis passeribus antestare nos dominus 4 pronuntiavit: si non et phoenicibus, nihil magnum. sed homines semel interibunt, avibus Arabiae de resurrectione securis?

23 omnia incipiunt cum desierint *TB*: *om. MPX*.
32 si non et carni *T, ut videtur, forsan recte*.
13: 4 atque firmissimum *om. T*.
 8 nemo iam *X*: iam nemo *MP*: nonne iam *T*.

things return to their estate after having departed: all things begin when they have ceased. They come to an end simply that they may come to be: nothing perishes except with a view to salvation. Therefore this whole revolving scheme of things is an attestation of the resurrection of the dead. God wrote down resurrection in works before he put it in writing, he preached it by acts of power before he told of it in words. He first gave you nature for a teacher, intending also to add prophecy, so that as previously a disciple of nature you might the more readily believe prophecy, might at once assent on hearing what you had already everywhere seen, and might not doubt that God is also a raiser up of the flesh when you knew that he is a restorer of all things. And further, if all things rise again for man, for whose benefit they are administered, and moreover not for man except as including the flesh, how could that flesh utterly perish, for the sake and for the benefit of which all things are kept from perishing?

13 If the universe is not a satisfactory parable of the resurrection, if the creation sets the seal on nothing of this sort, in that its single elements are alleged not so much to die as to cease to be, and are supposed not to be re-animated but to be re-formed, accept what is a very complete and unshakable example of this hope, seeing it is an animate creature, one subject to life and to death. I refer to that bird, the special property of the East, notable because there is only one of it at a time, portentous in respect of its progeny, the bird which renews itself while of its own will performing its own obsequies, deceasing and inheriting by a death which is a birth, phoenix again where just now there was none, once more himself who but now was not, another and the same. What more manifestly and with better attestation meets this case, what other fact has such a proof? God also says, in his own scriptures, *And thou shalt flourish like the phoenix*,[1] that is, out of death, out of burial, so that you may believe that the substance of the body can be exacted of the flames as well. Our Lord has declared that we are of more value than many sparrows:[2] if not also phoenixes, there is not much in it. But shall men die once for all, while birds of Arabia are assured of their resurrection?

[1] Ps. 92. 12.   [2] Cf. Matt. 10. 31.

14 Talia interim divinarum virium liniamenta non minus parabolis operato deo quam locuto, veniamus et ad ipsa edicta atque decreta eius, quo cum maxime divisionem istam materiae ordinamus. exorsi enim ab auctoritate carnis, an ea sit cui dilapsae 2 salus competat, dehinc prosecuti de potentia dei, an tanta sit quae salutem conferre dilapsae rei soleat, nunc si probavimus utrumque 3 velim etiam de causa requiras, an sit aliqua tam digna quae resurrectionem carnis necessariam et rationi certe omni modo debitam vindicet: quia subest dicere, etsi caro capax restitui, etsi divinitas idonea restituendi, sed causa restitutionis praeesse debebit. accipe 4 igitur et causam, qui apud deum discis tam optimum quam et iustum, de suo optimum, de nostro iustum. nisi enim homo deliquisset, optimum solummodo deum nosset ex naturae proprietate: at nunc etiam iustum eum patitur ex causae suae necessitate, tamen et hoc ipso optimum dum et iustum. et bono enim iuvando et 5 malo puniendo iustitiam exhibens utramque sententiam bono praestat, hinc vindicans istud inde remunerans illud. sed cum 6 Marcione plenius disces an hoc sit dei totum. interim talis est noster, merito iudex quia dominus, merito dominus quia auctor, merito auctor quia deus. hinc et ille nescio quis haereticorum 7 merito non iudex, non enim *dominus*: merito non dominus, non enim auctor: nescio iam si deus, qui nec auctor quod deus, nec dominus quod auctor. igitur si deo et domino et auctori con- 8 gruentissimum est iudicium in hominem destinare de hoc ipso an dominum et auctorem suum agnoscere et observare curarit an non, idque iudicium resurrectio expunget, haec erit tota causa immo

---

14: 3 istam *libri*: iustam *Kroy*.
   6 soleat *libri*: valeat *Kroy*.
  10 sed *T Gel.*: etsi *MPX*.
  14 suae *om. MPX*.
  21 dominus (*priore vice*) *R*: deus *libri*.
  22 quod deus *MPX*: quia deus *T*.

14 Such for the mean while being the broad outlines of those divine powers which God has wrought out in parables as well as expressed in speech, let us now come to his actual edicts and decrees, since this is the way we are at present arranging this division of our subject-matter. For we began with the dignity of the flesh, asking whether it is the kind of thing for which after collapse salvation is practicable: and thereafter we proceeded to treat of the power of God, whether it is great enough to be accustomed to confer salvation on a thing which has collapsed. Now, if we have proved both points, I would ask you to raise the question of purpose, whether there is one good enough to establish the resurrection of the flesh as necessary, and as indubitably in every way a debt to reason: because it is still possible to suggest that although the flesh be capable of restoration, and although deity be competent to restore it, for all that, restoration will need to have a purpose to justify it. Hear then of its purpose, you who are a disciple of God who is supremely good and also righteous, supremely good in respect of what is his, righteous in respect of what is ours. For if man had not become a delinquent he would have known God only as supremely good, by that nature which is properly his; but now he also experiences him as righteous, by the necessity of his own purpose, yet also supremely good precisely in this that he is also righteous. For while he displays righteousness by aiding that which is good and punishing that which is bad, both the sentences he gives are a tribute to the good, whether he is exacting vengeance of the one or rewarding the other. But in my books against Marcion you will learn more fully whether this is the whole of what God is. Meanwhile such is our—necessarily Judge because Lord, necessarily Lord because Maker, necessarily Maker because God. Hence also that—whatever you may call him—of the heretics is necessarily not judge, for he is not lord, necessarily not lord, for he is not maker, and I suppose then not god, seeing he is neither maker, which God is, nor lord, which a maker is. Therefore since it is most appropriate for one who is God and Lord and Maker to appoint for man judgement concerning precisely this, whether or not he has taken care to acknowledge and respect his Lord and Maker, and since the resurrection will bring that

necessitas resurrectionis, congruentissima scilicet deo destinatio iudicii. de cuius dispositione dispicias an utrique substantiae humanae diiudicandae censura divina praesideat, tam animae quam et carni: quod enim congruet iudicari, hoc competet etiam resuscitari. dicimus plenum primo perfectumque credendum iudicium dei, ut ultimum iam atque exinde perpetuum, ut sic quoque iustum dum non in aliquo minus, ut sic quoque deo dignum dum pro tanta eius patientia plenum atque perfectum: itaque plenitudinem perfectionemque iudicii nonnisi de totius hominis repraesentatione constare: totum porro hominem ex utriusque substantiae congregatione parere, idcircoque in utraque exhibendum quem totum oporteat iudicari, qui nisi totus non vixerit: qualis ergo vixerit talem iudicatum iri, quia de eo quod vixerit habeat iudicari. vita est enim causa iudicii, per tot substantias dispungenda per quot et functa est.

15 Age iam scindant adversarii nostri carnis animaeque contextum prius in vitae administratione ut ita audeant scindere illud etiam in vitae remuneratione: negent operarum societatem, ut merito possint etiam mercedum negare. non sit particeps in sententia caro si non fuerat et in causa: sola anima revocetur si sola decedit. at enim non magis sola decedit quam sola decucurrit illud unde decedit, vitam hanc dico. adeo autem non sola anima transigit vitam ut nec cogitatus, licet solos, licet non ad effectum per carnem deductos, auferamus a collegio carnis, siquidem in carne et cum carne et per carnem agitur ab anima quod agitur in corde. hanc denique carnis speciem, arcem animae, etiam dominus in

37 congregatione *MPX*: concretione *TB*^{mg}.
39 iudicatum iri *Brf.*: iudicaturi *MP*: iudicari *XR*: habeat iudicari *T*.
41 *quaero an scribendum* dispungendi.
15: 4 mercedum *T*: mercedem *MPX*.

judgement into actuality, this will be the whole purpose, yea the necessity, of the resurrection, such a provision of judgement as is most appropriate to God. And concerning the ordering of it you have to discern whether the divine censureship presides over the judgement of both the human substances, the flesh no less than the soul: for that which it is fitting should be judged, will with good reason also be raised up again. I affirm that God's judgement must be believed to be in the first place plenary and complete, as being by that time final, and thereafter everlasting, so that it may in this also be just as not being in any respect defective, and in this also worthy of God that in accordance with all his great patience it is plenary and complete: and that thus the plenity and completeness of judgement can be assured only by the production ⟨in court⟩ of the whole man—in fact that the whole man appears ⟨in court⟩ in the assemblage of both substances—and consequently he must be made present in both, seeing he needs to be judged as a whole, as assuredly he has not lived except as a whole. Therefore in that state in which he has lived, in that will he be judged, because he has to be judged in respect of his life as he has lived it. For life is the purpose of judgement, and this must be made complete in as many substances as it has employed in living.

15 Well now, let our opponents first sever the warp and woof of flesh and soul in life's administration, that then they may be bold enough to make such a severance also in life's remuneration: let them deny their association in workmanship, so as with good reason to be able also to deny it in wages. Let the flesh be no partner in the sentence, if it has not also been partner in the suit. Let the soul alone be recalled, if it alone has departed. It has however no more been alone in departure than it was alone in running that course from which it has departed, I mean this present life. So far is the soul from being alone in the conduct of life, that not even the thoughts, though only thoughts, though not by means of the flesh brought into effect, do we remove from the partnership of the flesh, seeing that it is in the flesh and in company with the flesh and by means of the flesh that that is wrought by the soul which is wrought in the heart. Indeed this portion of the flesh, the soul's

suggillatione cogitatuum taxat: *Quid cogitatis in cordibus vestris nequam?* et, *Qui conspexerit ad concupiscendum iam adulteravit in corde:* adeo et sine opere et sine effectu cogitatus carnis est actus. sed etsi in cerebro vel in medio superciliorum discrimine vel ubiubi philosophis placet principalitas sensuum consecrata est, quod ἡγεμονικόν appellatur, caro erit omne animae cogitatorium. nunquam anima sine carne est quamdiu in carne est: nihil non cum illa agit sine qua non est. quaere adhuc an cogitatus quoque per carnem administrantur qui per carnem dinoscuntur extrinsecus: volutet aliquid anima, vultus operatur indicium; facies intentionum omnium speculum est. negent factorum societatem cui negare non possunt cogitatorum. et illi quidem delinquentias carnis enumerant: ergo peccatrix tenebitur supplicio: nos vero etiam virtutes carnis opponimus: ergo et bene operata tenebitur praemio. et si anima est quae agit et impellit in omnia, carnis obsequium est. sed deum non licet aut iniustum iudicem credi aut inertem—iniustum si sociam bonorum operum a praemiis arceat, inertem si sociam malorum a suppliciis secernat—cum humana censura eo perfectior habeatur quo etiam ministros facti cuiusque deposcit, nec parcens nec invidens illis quominus cum auctoribus aut poenae aut gratiae communicent fructum.

16 Sed cum imperium animae obsequium carni distribuimus, prospiciendum est ne et hoc alia argumentatione subvertant, ut velint carnem sic in officio animae conlocare, non quasi ministram ne et sociam cogantur agnoscere. dicent enim ministros et socios habere arbitrium ministrandi atque sociandi, et potestatem suae voluntatis in utrumque, homines scilicet et ipsos: idcirco cum auctoribus merita communicare quibus operam sponte accommo-

---

12 suggillatione *T Gel.*: suggillationem *MPX*.
18 quamdiu in carne est *T Gel.*: *om. MPX*.
27 sed *om. MPX*.
30 quo *MPX*: quod *T Gel*.
16: 2 et hoc *T Pam.*: et ex hoc *MPX*.

citadel, our Lord himself censures in his castigation of thoughts: *Why think ye evil in your hearts?*[1] and, *Whoso looketh for the sake of lusting hath already committed adultery in his heart.*[2] Thus, apart from either deed or performance, thought is an activity of the flesh. But even if that headquarters of the senses, which is called ⟨in Greek⟩ *hegemonicon*, is established in the brain, or perhaps in the space between the eyebrows, or wherever philosophers decide, any and every thinking-house of the soul must be flesh. Never is soul apart from flesh, so long as it is in the flesh: it performs no act without it, for apart from it it does not exist. Can you still ask whether thoughts too are administered by means of the flesh, when by means of the flesh they are externally cognizable? Let the soul consider a matter: the countenance tells the tale, the face is a mirror of all intentions. Can they deny it association in things done, when they cannot deny it association in things thought of? And these are the very people who enumerate the delinquencies of the flesh: consequently, as a sinner it will be liable to punishment. We however set in opposition even the virtues of the flesh: consequently, having also done well, it will be liable to reward. And if it is the soul which gives leading and impulse to all acts, to the flesh belongs the obedience. But we ought not to think that God is either an unjust judge or an indolent one—unjust if he excludes from rewards an ally in good works, indolent if he shelters from penalties an ally in evil ones—when man's judgement is considered the more perfect in that it cites even the abettors of every act, neither sparing them nor envying them but that they may share with their principals the fruit either of penalty or of grace.

16 But when we assign empire to the soul and submission to the flesh, we must take precautions lest our opponents overturn even this by a further quibble, being content in this manner to place the flesh in the employment of the soul, not as a free servant, lest consequently they be forced to acknowledge it as an associate. For they will allege that servants and associates have free choice in service and association, with power over their own will in both directions, as being themselves also men, and that therefore they share the merits or demerits of those principals to whom of their

[1] Matt. 9. 4.   [2] Matt. 5. 28.

darint: carnem autem nihil sapientem nihil sentientem per 3 semetipsam, non velle non nolle de suo habentem, vice potius vasculi adparere animae, ut instrumentum non ut ministerium: itaque animae solius iudicium praesidere, qualiter usa sit vasculo 4 carnis, vasculum vero ipsum non esse sententiae obnoxium: quia nec calicem damnari si quis eum veneno temperarit, nec gladium ad bestias pronuntiari si quis eo latrocinium fuerit operatus. iam 5 ergo innocens caro ex ea parte qua non reputabuntur illi operae malae, et nihil prohibet innocentiae nomine salvam eam fieri. licet enim nec bona opera deputentur illi sicut nec mala, divinae tamen benignitati magis competit innocentes liberare: beneficos enim debet: optimi est autem etiam quod non debetur offerre. et 6 tamen calicem, non dico venenarium in quem mors aliqua ructuarit, sed frictricis vel archigalli vel gladiatoris aut carnificis spiritu infectum, quaero an minus damnes quam oscula ipsorum. nostris quoque sordibus nubilum vel non pro animo temperatum elidere solemus quo magis puero irascamur: gladium vero latro- 7 ciniis ebrium quis non a domo tota, nedum a cubiculo, nedum a capitis sui officio relegabit, praesumens scilicet nihil aliud se quam invidiam animarum somniaturum urguentium et inquietantium sanguinis sui concubinum? at enim et calix bene sibi conscius et de 8 diligentia ministri commendatus de coronis quoque potatoris sui inornabitur aut aspergine florum honorabitur, et gladius bene de bello cruentus et melior homicida laudem suam consecratione pensabit. 'Estne ergo et in vascula et in instrumenta sententiam 9 figere, ut dominorum et auctorum meritis et ipsa communicent?' et huic quoque argumentationi satisfecerim, licet ab exemplo vacet 10 diversitas rerum. omne enim vas vel instrumentum aliunde in

17 deputentur *T*: reputentur *MPX*.
18 beneficos enim debet, optimi est autem *TBX*: beneficus enim est atque optimus, debet autem *MP*.
21 frictricis *Gel.*: fictricis *MPX*: strictius *T*.
27 invidiam *T Rig.*: invidia *MPXR*[1]: inludia *R*[3].

own will they have lent their assistance; whereas the flesh, having no thoughts of its own, and no sensations, having of itself neither assent nor refusal, attends upon the soul rather in the guise of a receptacle, as a tool and not as a servant: and that thus the judgement is set in respect of the soul alone, as to how it has used its receptacle the flesh, while the receptacle itself is not liable to sentence, since neither is a cup condemned if someone has mixed poison in it, nor does a sword receive capital sentence if someone has committed highway-robbery with it. In that case, we reply, the flesh will be innocent, in so far as evil actions are not to be imputed to it, and there is nothing to prevent its being saved on the ground of innocence. For though good works be not imputed to it, as neither are evil, yet does it rather befit the kindness of God to absolve the innocent. Welldoers he must absolve: but it appertains to him who is supremely good to grant even more than he must. Moreover, as for the cup—I do not mean one that has held poison, one into which someone has spewed out his life, but one tainted with the breath of a witch or a sodomite or a gladiator or a hangman—I wonder if you would condemn it any less than those people's kisses. Even one that is clouded with our own filth or that is not mixed to our taste, we are wont to smash, to signify more clearly our annoyance with the pageboy. And as for the sword that is drunken with murders, is there anyone who will not expel it from his whole house, not to speak of his bed-chamber or his pillow-head, under the impression, I suppose, that his dreams could not help but be of the remonstrances of the souls which would oppress and disquiet one who had taken to his bed their own blood? On the other hand, a cup with a good conscience, which has been praised because of the servant's care, will also be adorned from the garland of him who drinks from it, or honoured by the strewing of flowers: and a sword nobly bloodied in war, a man-slayer of a better sort, will have its credit rewarded by consecration. 'Is it possible therefore to attach sentence even to receptacles and tools, that they too may share in the merits of their owners and principals?' I shall proceed to deal faithfully with this quibble also—though the facts are of a different kind and not fully met by the illustration. For any vessel or tool comes into use from

usus venit, extranea omnino materia a substantia hominis: caro autem, ab exordio uteri consata conformata congenita animae, etiam in omni operatione miscetur illi. nam etsi vas vocatur apud 11 apostolum, quod iubet in honore tractari, eadem tamen ab eodem homo exterior appellatur, ille scilicet limus qui prior titulo hominis incisus est, non calicis aut gladii aut vasculi ullius. vas 12 enim capacitatis nomine dicta est qua animam capit et continet, homo vero de communione naturae quae eam non instrumentum in operationibus praestat sed ministerium. ita et ministerium tenebitur iudicio, etsi de suo nihil sapiat, quia portio est eius quae sapit, non supellex. hoc et apostolus sciens, nihil carnem agere per 13 semetipsam quod non animae deputetur, nihilominus peccatricem iudicat carnem, ne eo quod ab anima videatur impelli, iudicio liberata credatur. sic et cum aliquas laudis operas carni indicit— 14 Glorificate, tollite deum in corpore vestro—certus et hos conatus ab anima agi, idcirco tamen et carni eos mandat quia et illi fructum repromittit. alioquin nec exprobratio competisset in alienam 15 culpae nec adhortatio in extraneam gloriae: et exprobratio enim et exhortatio vacarent erga carnem si vacaret et merces quae in resurrectione captatur.

17 Simplicior quisque fautor sententiae nostrae putabit carnem etiam idcirco repraesentandam esse iudicio quia aliter anima non capiat passionem tormenti seu refrigerii, utpote incorporalis: hoc enim vulgus existimat. nos autem animam corporalem et hic 2 profitemur et in suo volumine probavimus, habentem proprium genus substantiae ⟨ac⟩ soliditatis per quam quid et sentire et pati possit: nam et nunc animas torqueri foverique penes inferos, licet nudas, licet adhuc exules carnis, probabit Lazari exemplum. dedi 3

40 exterior appellatur *T Gel.*: appellatur exterior *MPX*.
50 et tollite *T*: inquit et tollite *Pam*.
17: 6 ac *addidit Eng*.
    8 probabit *MP*: probavit *TX Gel. Brf.* *l*azari *T*: lazari *MPX*: Eleazari Souter, *Brf*.

without, its material being entirely external to man's substance; whereas the flesh, being since its origin in the womb conceived and formed and brought to birth in company with the soul, is also in every operation commingled with it. For although in the apostle it is called a vessel, which he commands to be held in honour,[1] yet by the same apostle it is called the outer man,[2] being in fact that clay which first was engraved with the inscription 'man', not 'cup', or 'sword', or any sort of 'receptacle'. For it is called a vessel in view of the containership by which it contains and encloses the soul, but 'man' because of the community of nature which makes it in operations not a tool but a servant. So also, as a servant, it will be held to judgement, even though of itself it does no thinking, because it is the portion of that which thinks, not its chattel. The apostle, with this in mind, that the flesh does nothing of itself that is not imputed to the soul, none the less judges the flesh sinful,[3] lest because it seems to be set in motion by the soul it should be thought to have been set free of judgement. So also when he enjoins upon the flesh some works of praise—*Glorify and uplift God in your body*[4]—though aware that these activities are performed by the soul, yet he enjoins them on the flesh as well, just because he also promises it the fruits of them. Else neither would rebuke have appertained to it if it were a stranger to blame, nor behest if a foreigner to glory: for both rebuke and behest would have been void as regards the flesh if there had been a void also of the wages which are expected at the resurrection.

17 The more artless supporters of my opinion will think that another reason why the flesh will need to be brought under review at the judgement is that otherwise the soul would be incapable of experiencing torment or refreshment, as being incorporal: for such is the vulgar idea. I however both state here, and have proved in a treatise of its own, that the soul is corporal, having its own particular kind of substance and solidity by which it is capable both of perception and of suffering. For that even now souls are tormented or comforted among those below, though unclothed, and as yet exiles from the flesh, the instance of Lazarus[5]

---

[1] Cf. 1 Thess. 4. 4.   [2] Cf. 2 Cor. 4. 16.   [3] Cf. Rom. 8. 3.
[4] 1 Cor. 6. 20.   [5] Cf. Lk. 16. 25.

igitur adversario dicere, 'Ergo, quae habet corpulentiam propriam, de suo sufficiet ad facultatem passionis et sensus, ut non egeat repraesentatione carnis'. immo et eatenus egebit, non qua sentire quid sine carne non possit sed qua necesse est illam etiam cum carne sentire: quantum enim ad agendum de suo sufficit, tantum et ad patiendum. ad agendum autem minus de suo sufficit: habet enim 4 de suo solummodo cogitare velle cupere disponere, ad perficiendum autem operam carnis expectat. sic itaque ad patiendum 5 societatem carnis expostulat, ut tam plene per eam pati possit quam sine ea plene agere non potuit. et ideo in quae de suo sufficit, eorum interim sententiam pendit, concupiscentiae et cogitatus et voluntatis. porro si haec satis essent ad plenitudinem meritorum, ut 6 non requirerentur et facta, sufficeret anima ad perfectionem iudicii, de istis iudicanda in quae agenda sola suffecerat. cum vero 7 etiam facta devincta sint meritis, facta autem per carnem administrentur, iam non sufficit animam sine carne foveri sive cruciari pro operibus etiam carnis, etsi habet corpus, etsi habet membra, quae proinde illi non sufficiunt ad sentiendum plene quemadmodum nec ad agendum perfecte. idcirco pro quo modo egit, 8 pro eo et patitur apud inferos, prior degustans iudicium sicut prior induxit admissum, expectans tamen et carnem ut per illam etiam facta compenset cui cogitata mandavit. denique haec erit ratio in 9 ultimum finem destinati iudicii, ut exhibitione carnis omnis divina censura perfici possit: alioquin non sustineretur in finem quod et nunc animae decerpunt apud inferos, si solis animabus destinaretur.

18 Hucusque praestructionibus egerim ad muniendos sensus

24 animam *MPX*: anima *T* (*manifesto errore*).
25 etsi habet corpus *om. T*.
26 plene quemadmodum *T Gel.*: *om. MPX*.
33 animae *om. T*.

will prove. Thus I have left it possible for my adversary to say, 'In that case, having its own bodily constitution, it will of its own suffice for the faculty of suffering and perception, and so will have no need for the flesh to be brought up for judgement'. Nay rather, it will have need, not in the sense that without the flesh it is devoid of sensation, but that it is essential for it to have the flesh to share in its sensations. For in so far as of its own it suffices for acting, in so far does it also suffice for suffering. For acting however it is of its own less than sufficient: for of its own it has no more than thought, will, desire, determination, while for accomplishment it awaits the activity of the flesh. Likewise also for suffering it demands the alliance of the flesh, so as by means of it to be able as completely to suffer as without it it was unable completely to act. Consequently, of the things for which it is of its own sufficient, concupiscence and thought and will, it is in the mean time working off the sentence. Certainly if these things had been sufficient for the fullness of its deserts, so that deeds as well were not brought under inquisition, it would have wholly sufficed for the perfection of judgement that the soul should be judged concerning those matters for the doing of which it had itself sufficed. But since deeds also are bound by deserts, and deeds are effected through the flesh, it is evidently not sufficient for the soul without the flesh to be comforted or tormented for works which belong to the flesh as well, even though it has body, even though it has members, for they do not suffice it for completeness of sensation, any more than they do for perfection of action. Consequently, to the extent to which it has acted, to that extent it also suffers among those below, being the first to taste of judgement as it was the first to contract the fault, yet waiting for the flesh so that it may pay the penalty of its deeds besides by means of that flesh to which it has made its thoughts into commands. This in fact will be the reason for the judgement being appointed for the last end, namely, that by the presentment of the flesh it may be possible for the whole divine censure to be made complete. Otherwise the punishment of which souls even now have the foretaste among those below would not be reserved until the end, if it were designed for souls alone.

18 So far let it suffice me to have laid foundations for the protec-

omnium scripturarum quae carnis recidivatum pollicentur. cui cum tot auctoritates iustorum patrociniorum procurent—honores dico substantiae ipsius, tum vires dei, tum exempla earum, tum rationes iudicii et necessitates ipsius—utique secundum praeiudicia tot auctoritatum scripturas intellegi oportebit, non secundum ingenia haereticorum de sola incredulitate venientia, quia incredibile habeatur restitui substantiam interitu subductam, non quia aut substantiae ipsi inemeribile sit aut deo impossibile aut iudicio inhabile. plane incredibile, si nec praedicatum divinitus fuerit: 2 nisi quod etsi praedicatum id a deo non fuisset ultro praesumi debuisset, ut propterea non praedicatum quia tot auctoritatibus praeiudicatum. at cum divinis quoque vocibus personat, tanto 3 abest ut aliter intellegatur quam desiderant illa a quibus etiam sine divinis vocibus persuadetur. videamus igitur hoc primum, quonam 4 titulo spes ista proscripta sit. unum opinor apud omnes edictum dei pendet, RESURRECTIO MORTUORUM: duo verba expedita decisa detersa. ipsa conveniam, ipsa discutiam, cui se substantiae addicant. cum audio resurrectionem homini imminere, quaeram 5 necesse est quid eius cadere sortitum sit, siquidem nihil resurgere expectabit nisi quod ante succiderit. qui ignorat carnem cadere per mortem potest eam nec stantem nosse per vitam. sententiam 6 dei natura pronuntiat, Terra es et in terram ibis: et qui non audit videt: nulla mors non ruina membrorum est. hanc corporis sortem dominus quoque expressit cum ipsa substantia indutus, Diruite inquit templum istud et ego illud triduo resuscitabo: ostendit 7

18: 10 inhabile *T*: inhabitabile *MPX*.   praedicatum *TX*: praeiudicatum *MP* (*male*).
10–11 divinitus...etsi praedicatum *om. T*.
13 personat *TMPX*: personet *Rig.* (*sed haud opus erat*).
21 succiderit *MPX*: ceciderit *T*.

tion of the meaning of all the scriptures which promise the restoration of the flesh. Since this has the advocacy of so many competent authorities—I mean the dignities of the substance itself, the power of God, instances of that power, the reasons for judgement, and its implications—surely the scriptures will require to be understood in accordance with the precedent of all these authorities, and not in accordance with devices of heretics which proceed from mere unbelief; because the restitution of a substance withdrawn in destruction is considered incredible not because this is either beyond the deserts of the substance itself or beyond the power of God or without pertinence to the judgement. Incredible clearly it would be, had it not been divinely preached: except that even though that preaching had not been given by God, yet should we have needed to assume it of our own accord, as not having been preached simply because so many authorities had constituted a previous judgement in its favour. Yet since it resounds in divine words as well, it is so much the more impossible for it to be otherwise interpreted than those facts require which even without divine words are sufficiently persuasive.

Let us then first consider under what heading this hope has been promulgated. One divine edict, I suppose, is posted in the sight of all: THE RESURRECTION OF THE DEAD: two words, sharp, concise, and clear. These I shall confront, these I shall discuss, asking to which substance they assign themselves. When I am told that resurrection is man's destiny, I must needs ask what part of him it is whose lot it is to fall, since nothing will expect to rise again except that which has previously succumbed. Only one who is unaware that it is the flesh which falls by means of death, can be ignorant of it also standing up by means of life. The sentence of God is that which nature pronounces, *Earth thou art and into the earth shalt thou go.*[1] Even one who has not heard, sees it happen: all death is a collapse of the members. This destiny of the body the Lord also made manifest when, clothed with that very substance, he said, *Pull down this temple, and in three days I will raise it up again.*[2] He shows to what it appertains to be pulled down, to be thrown to the ground, to lie low, that to which it also appertains to be

---
[1] Gen. 3. 19. [2] Joh. 2. 19.

enim cuius sit dirui, cuius elidi, cuius et relevari et resuscitari—
quanquam et animam circumferret trepidantem usque ad mortem
sed non cadentem per mortem—quia et scriptura, De corpore
inquit suo dixerat. atque adeo caro est quae morte subruitur, ut 8
exinde a cadendo cadaver enuntietur. anima porro nec vocabulo
cadit, quia nec habitu ruit: atquin ipsa est quae ruinam corpori
infert cum efflata est, sicut ipsa est quae illud de terra suscitavit cum
inflata est. non potest cadere quae suscitavit ingressa: non potest
ruere quae elidit egressa. artius dicam: ne in somnum quidem cadit 9
anima cum corpore, ne tum quidem sternitur cum carne, sedenim
agitatur in somnis et iactitatur: quiesceret autem si iaceret, et iaceret
si caderet: ita nec in veritate mortis cadit quae nec in imagine eius
ruit. sequens nunc vocabulum 'mortuorum' aeque dispice cui 10
substantiae insideat. quanquam in hac materia admittamus interdum mortalitatem animae adsignari ab haereticis, ut si anima
mortalis resurrectionem consecutura est praeiudicium sit et carni
non minus mortali resurrectionem communicaturae, sed nunc
proprietas vocabuli vindicanda est suae sorti. iam quidem eo ipso 11
quod resurrectio caducae rei est, id est carnis, eadem erit et in
nomine mortui: quia caducae rei est resurrectio quae dicitur
mortuorum. sic et per Abraham patrem fidei, divinae familiari- 12
tatis virum, discimus: postulans enim Sarrae humandae locum de
filiis Heth, Date ergo inquit mihi possessionem sepulchri vobiscum
et humabo mortuum meum, carnem scilicet: neque enim animae
humandae spatium desiderasset, etsi anima mortalis crederetur,
etsi 'mortuus' dici mereretur. quodsi 'mortuus' corpus est,
corporum erit proprie resurrectio, cum dicitur 'mortuorum'.

    27 cuius et *libri*: eius et *Pam.* (*forsan recte*).
    31 enuntietur *T Gel.*: renuntietur *MPX*.
    37 somnis *libri*: *quaero an scribendum* somniis.
    43 communicaturae *libri*: *quaero an potius scribendum* communicatum iri.
    45–6 caducae...est resurrectio *om. T*.
    50 mortuum meum *T*: mortuam meam *MPX*.
    52 mortuus corpus *MPX*: corpus mortuum *T*.
    53 proprie *om. MPX*.

lifted up and raised again—though he also carried about with him a soul that was troubled even unto death,[1] yet which did not fall by means of death—because the scripture also says, *He had spoken of his body*.[2] And so truly is it the flesh that is overthrown in death, that thereafter it is described as *cadaver*, from *cadere*. The soul however has no name signifying falling, because in its proper habit it does not collapse: indeed it is it which, when expired, produces collapse in the body, just as it is it which, when it was breathed in, raised it up from the ground.[3] It cannot fall, seeing that by entering in it raised it up: it cannot collapse, seeing that by its exit it throws down. Let me speak more particularly: not even into sleep does the soul fall down along with the body, not even then is it laid supine along with the flesh: for in sleep it moves and stirs, whereas if it were lying down it would be quiet, and it would be lying down if it fell. Thus, as it does not collapse in the image of death, neither does it fall down in death's verity.

Now for the second word 'of the dead', distinguish no less clearly to which substance it adheres. Although in this matter I admit that at times mortality is ascribed by heretics to the soul—with the result that if mortal soul is to attain to resurrection there is a presumption that the flesh too, being no less mortal, will share in the resurrection—yet now the sole right to the term must be claimed for that which is entitled to it. At once then, by the very fact that resurrection appertans to a thing liable to fall, namely flesh, that same flesh will be indicated in the designation 'dead', because the resurrection which is described as 'of the dead' is the resurrection of a thing liable to fall. So also we learn through Abraham, the father of the faith, a close friend of God: for in demanding of the sons of Heth a place to bury Sarah he says, *Give me then the possession of a burying-place with you, and I will bury my dead man*,[4] the flesh of course: for he would not have wanted room to bury a soul, even if the soul were considered mortal, even if it merited being described as 'dead man'. But if 'dead man' is the body, the resurrection, since it is described as 'of the dead', will specifically be of bodies.

[1] Cf. Matt. 26. 38.
[2] Joh. 2. 21.
[3] Cf. Gen. 2. 7.
[4] Gen. 23. 4.

19 Et haec itaque dispectio tituli et praeconii ipsius, fidem utique defendens vocabulorum, illuc proficere debebit ut si quid diversa pars turbat obtentu figurarum et aenigmatum manifestiora quaeque praevaleant et de incertis certiora praescribant. nacti enim 2 quidam sollemnissimam eloquii prophetici formam, allegorici et figurati plerumque, non tamen semper, resurrectionem quoque mortuorum, manifeste adnuntiatam, in imaginariam significationem distorquent, adserentes ipsam etiam mortem spiritaliter intellegendam: non enim hanc esse in vero quae sit in medio, 3 discidium carnis atque animae, sed ignorantiam dei per quam homo mortuus deo non minus in errore iacuerit quam in sepulchro: itaque et resurrectionem eam vindicandam qua quis adita 4 veritate redanimatus et revivificatus deo, ignorantiae morte discussa, velut de sepulchro veteris hominis eruperit, quia et dominus scribas et pharisaeos sepulchris dealbatis adaequaverit: exinde ergo, resurrectionem fide consecutos, cum domino esse 5 quem in baptismate induerint. hoc denique ingenio etiam in 6 colloquiis saepe nostros decipere consueverunt quasi et ipsi resurrectionem carnis admittant: 'Vae, inquiunt, qui non in hac carne resurrexerit', ne statim illos percutiant si resurrectionem statim abnuerint. tacite autem secundum conscientiam suam hoc sentiunt, 'Vae qui non, dum in hac carne est, cognoverit arcana haeretica': hoc est enim apud illos resurrectio. sed et plerique, ab excessu 7 animae resurrectionem vindicantes, de sepulchro exire de saeculo evadere interpretantur, quia et saeculum mortuorum sit habitaculum, id est ignorantium deum, vel etiam de ipso corpore, quia et corpus vice sepulchri conclusam animam in saecularis vitae morte detineat.

20 Ob huiusmodi igitur coniecturas primam praestructionem

19: 4 de *om. T.*
   8 adserentes *T*: adseverantes *MPX.*
  12 vindicandam *MPX*: iudicandam *T.*
  17 quem in baptismate *T*: cum eum in baptismate *B*: cum baptisma *MPX.*
  19 *post* admittant *mirum in modum res a T turbatae sunt.*
20: 1 primam *libri*: primum *Souter, Brf.*

19 So then our inspection of the decree and of its contents, through our outright insistence that the terms mean what they say, must needs have the effect that, if our opponents cause trouble by the allegation of figures and enigmas, things more manifest in each case shall prevail, and things more certain lay down the law concerning the uncertain. For some people, taking hold upon a well-established usage of prophetic diction (which is frequently, though not always, allegorical and figurative) distort also the resurrection of the dead (though it is manifestly proclaimed) into an unreal signification, asserting that even death itself must be spiritually understood. For death, they say, is not really and truly this which is close to hand, the separation of flesh and soul, but ignorance of God, whereby man, being dead to God, lies low in error no less than in a tomb. So also, they add, the resurrection must be maintained to be that by which a man, having come to the truth, has been reanimated and revivified to God, and, the death of ignorance being dispelled, has as it were burst forth from the tomb of the old man:[1] because the Lord also likened the scribes and pharisees to whitened sepulchres.[2] Thereafter then, having by faith obtained resurrection, they are, they say, with the Lord, whom they have put on in baptism. In fact, by this device they are accustomed often enough to trick our people even in conversation, pretending that they too admit the resurrection of the flesh. 'Woe', they say, 'to him who has not risen again in this flesh', to avoid shocking them at the outset by a forthright repudiation of resurrection. But secretly, in their private thoughts, their meaning is, Woe to him who has not, while he is in this flesh, obtained knowledge of heretical secrets: for among them resurrection has this meaning. Also some, maintaining that the resurrection begins from the release of the soul, interpret 'come forth from the tomb' as 'escape from the world' (on the ground that the world is a habitation of dead men, that is, of men who know not God) or even 'escape from the body' (on the ground that the body, in the guise of a tomb, encloses and imprisons the soul in the death which is this world's life).

20 As against this kind of guesswork I shall push down their

[1] Cf. Eph. 4. 22; Col. 3. 9.   [2] Cf. Matt. 23. 27.

eorum depellam, qua volunt omnia prophetas per imagines contionatos: quando, si ita esset, ne ipsae quidem imagines distingui potuissent, si non et veritates praedicatae fuissent ex quibus imagines deliniarentur. atque adeo si omnia figurae, quid erit 2 illud cuius figurae? quomodo speculum obtendes si nusquam est facies? adeo autem non omnia imagines sed et veritates, nec omnia umbrae sed et corpora, ut in ipsum quoque dominum insigniora quaeque luce clarius praedicarentur. nam et virgo con- 3 cepit in utero non figurate, et peperit Emmanuelem, nobiscum deum [Iesum], non oblique: etsi oblique accepturum virtutem Damasci et spolia Samariae, sed manifeste venturum in iudicium cum presbyteris et archontibus populi. nam et tumultuatae sunt 4 gentes in persona Pilati, et populi meditati sunt inania in persona Israelis: adstiterunt reges terrae, Herodes, et archontes congregati sunt in unum, Annas et Caiaphas, adversus dominum et adversus Christum eius: qui et tanquam ovis ad iugulationem adductus est, 5 et tanquam agnus ante tondentem, scilicet Herodem, sine voce, sic non aperuit os suum, dorsum suum ponens ad flagella et maxillas ad palmas, et faciem non avertens a sputaminum iaculis: deputatus etiam inter iniquos, perfossus manus et pedes, sortem passus in vestimento et potus amaros et capitum inridentium nutus, triginta argenteis adpretiatus a proditore. quae hic figurae apud Esaiam, 6 quae imagines apud David, quae aenigmata apud Hieremiam, ne virtutes quidem eius per parabolas profatos? aut numquid nec oculi patefacti sunt caecorum, nec inclaruit lingua mutorum, nec manus aridae et genua dissoluta revaluerunt, nec claudi salierunt

11 deum *Pam.*: deus *T*: dominum *MPX*.   Iesum *om. T*.
18 sine *MPX*: et sine *T*.

primary scaffoldwork, that by which they claim that the prophets did all their preaching by means of pictures: for, if this had been the case, not even the pictures would have been recognizable, unless the verities had been first preached from which the pictures might be sketched out. And in fact, if all things are figures, what can that be of which they are figures? How can you hold out a mirror, if there is nowhere a face? But to such a degree were all things not pictures, but truths as well, nor all things shadows, but bodies as well, that in regard to the Lord himself all the more outstanding facts were preached more clearly than light. For it was not in a figure that the Virgin conceived in the womb, nor was it indirectly that she bore Emmanuel, God with us:[1] and if it was indirectly that he was to receive the strength of Damascus and the spoils of Samaria,[2] yet openly was he to come into judgement with the elders and princes of the people.[3] So too *the heathen raged*, in the person of Pilate, *and the peoples imagined vain things*, in the person of Israel: *the kings of the earth stood up*, Herod, *and the rulers were gathered together*, Annas and Caiaphas, *against the Lord and against his Christ*.[4] He was also brought as a sheep to the slaughter, and as a lamb before his shearer, Herod in fact; and was voiceless—*so he opened not his mouth*[5]—while he gave his back to smitings and his cheeks to the palms of hands, and turned not his face from missiles of spittings.[6] Also he was numbered among the transgressors,[7] was pierced in the hands and the feet, suffered the casting of lots upon his vesture, and bitter things to drink,[8] and the wagging of the heads of those that mocked,[9] when he had been priced at thirty pieces of silver by the traitor.[10] Are there any figures here in Isaiah, any pictures in David, any enigmas in Jeremiah? And these also prophesied of his miracles, again not by parables. Or were the eyes of the blind not made open, did not the tongue of the dumb speak plain, did withered hands and feeble knees not become strong again, did not lame men leap as an hart?[11] For although we

---

[1] Cf. Isa. 7. 14; Matt. 1. 23.   [2] Cf. Isa. 8. 4.
[3] Cf. Isa. 3. 14.   [4] Ps. 2. 1–2.   [5] Isa. 53. 7.
[6] Cf. Isa. 50. 6.   [7] Cf. Isa. 53. 12.   [8] Cf. Ps. 22. 16, 18.
[9] Cf. Ps. 22. 7.   [10] Cf. Zech. 11. 12; Matt. 27. 9.
[11] Cf. Isa. 35. 5, 6.

ut cervus? quae etsi spiritaliter quoque interpretari solemus 7
secundum comparationem animalium vitiorum a domino remedi-
atorum, cum tamen et carnaliter adimpleta sunt ostendunt prophetas in utramque speciem praedicasse, salvo eo quod plures voces
eorum nudae et simplices et ab omni allegoriae nubilo purae
defendi possunt: ut cum exitus gentium et urbium resonant, Tyri 8
et Aegypti et Babylonis et Idumaeae et Carthaginensium navium,
et cum ipsius Israelis plagas aut venias, captivitates restitutiones,
ultimaeque dispersionis exitum perorant. quis haec interpretabi- 9
tur magis quam recognoscet? res in litteris tenentur, litterae in
rebus leguntur. ita non semper nec in omnibus allegorica forma
est prophetici eloquii, sed interdum et in quibusdam.

21 Si ergo interdum et in quibusdam, inquies, cur non et in
edicto resurrectionis spiritaliter intellegendae? quoniam quidem
plurima ratio intercedit. primo enim quid facient tot alia instrumenta divina, ita aperte corporalem contestantia resurrectionem
ut nullam admittant figuratae significantiae suspicionem? et 2
utique aequum sit, quod et supra demandavimus, incerta de certis
et obscura de manifestis praeiudicari, vel ne inter discordiam
certorum et incertorum, manifestorum et obscurorum, fides dis-
sipetur, veritas periclitetur, ipsa divinitas ut inconstans denotetur.
tunc quod verisimile non est ut ea species sacramenti in quam fides 3
tota committitur, in quam disciplina tota conititur, ambigue
adnuntiata et obscure proposita videatur, quando spes resurrectionis, nisi manifesta de periculo et praemio, neminem ad huiusmodi praesertim religionem publico odio et hostili elogio
obnoxiam persuaderet. nullum opus certum est mercedis incertae, 4
nullus timor iustus est periculi dubii: et merces autem et periculum
in resurrectionis pendet eventu. sed et si temporalia et localia et 5

21: 1 inquies *Brf.*: iniquies *T*: inquis *MPX*.
13 huiusmodi *T*: eiusmodi *MPX*.
17 sed *TB*: *om*. *MPX*.

are wont to interpret these things spiritually as well, equating them with the diseases of the soul which the Lord healed, yet since they were also fulfilled in fleshly sort they show that the prophets preached in both forms, saving this, that most of their expressions can be claimed as bare and simple and clear of every mist of allegory, as when they cry aloud of the deaths of nations and cities, Tyre and Egypt and Babylon and Edom and the ships of Carthage, and when they make orations on Israel's own plagues and pardons, captivities and restorations, and the death of the final dispersion.[1] Is anyone disposed to interpret these, and not rather acknowledge them? Facts are contained in the writings: the writings are read in the facts. Thus the form of prophetic discourse is allegorical neither always nor in all places, but sometimes and in some places.

21 Well then, you ask, if 'sometimes and in some places', why are they not to be spiritually understood in the edict of the resurrection? Because, in fact, there is a high degree of difference. In the first place, what will become of all those other passages of divine scripture which so openly attest a corporal resurrection as to admit of no suspicion of a figurative signification? And indeed it would be equitable, as I have already postulated, that things uncertain should be prejudged by things certain, and things obscure by things manifest, at the least so that between the disagreement of things certain and things uncertain, of things manifest and things obscure, faith should not be frittered away, truth brought into danger, and God himself stigmatized as inconstant. Secondly, because it is not likely that that aspect of the mystery to which the whole faith is entrusted, on which the whole discipline is supported, should turn out to have been ambiguously announced and obscurely propounded, when the hope of resurrection, unless it were manifest in respect of peril and of reward, would persuade no one to a religion, particularly of this kind, which is the object of public hatred and hostile accusation. No work is certain, of which the wages are uncertain: no fear is well founded, of a peril which is in doubt. Yet both the wages and the peril depend on the issue of the resurrection. Moreover, if such open prophecy has launched

[1] Cf. Isa. 23, 24.

personalia dei decreta atque iudicia in urbes et gentes et reges tam
aperta prophetia iaculata est, quale est ut aeternae dispositiones eius
et universales in omne hominum genus lucem sui fugerint? quae
quanto maiora, tanto clariora esse deberent, ut maiora crederentur.
et puto deo nec livorem nec dolum nec inconstantiam nec leno- 6
cinium adscribi posse, per quae fere promulgatio maiorum
cavillatur.

22 Post haec ad illas etiam scripturas respiciendum esse dicemus
quae non sinunt resurrectionem, secundum animales istos, ne
dixerim spiritales, aut hic iam in veritatis agnitione praesumi aut
ab excessu statim vitae vindicari. cum enim et tempora totius spei 2
fixa sint sacrosancto stilo, nec liceat eam ante constitui, aeque non
licebit ita scripturas interpretari super illam ut possit ante constitui. in adventum opinor Christi vota nostra suspirant, in
saeculi huius occasum, ad diem domini magnum, diem irae et retributionis, diem ultimum et occultum nec ulli praeter patri notum,
et tamen signis atque portentis et concussionibus elementorum et
conflictationibus nationum praenotatum. evolverem prophetias 3
si dominus ipse tacuisset—nisi quod et prophetiae vox erant
domini—sed plus est quod illas suo ore consignat. interrogatus
a discipulis quando eventura essent quae interim de templi exitu
eruperat, ordinem temporum primo Iudaicorum usque ad
excidium Hierusalem, dehinc communium usque ad conclusionem
saeculi dirigit. nam posteaquam edixit, Et tunc erit Hierusalem 4
conculcata in nationibus donec adimpleantur tempora nationum—
adlegendarum scilicet a deo et congregandarum cum reliquiis
Israelis—inde iam in orbem et in saeculum praedicat secundum 5
Ioelem et Danielem et universum concilium prophetarum futura

19 aperta *libri*: aperte *Lat. Brf.*
22: 1 esse dicemus *T*: est *MPX*.
  5–7 aeque...ante constitui *T*: *om. MPX*.
  7 in saeculi *T Gel.*: *om.* in *MPX*.
  11 *quaero an legendum* praenotandum.
  12 prophetia vox erat *T*.
  18 conculcatui *MPX*.

God's temporal and local and personal decrees and judgements against cities and nations and kings, how can his eternal and universal ordinances against the whole human race have fled from the light that is themselves?[1] For the greater these are, the clearer they would need to be, so as to be believed to be the greater. And I suppose that to God one can ascribe neither envy nor guile nor cowardice nor the fear of displeasing, which are the usual reasons why the promulgation of great matters is wrapped up in subtilties.
22 Next I shall affirm that we must pay attention to those scriptures also which forbid us, after the manner of these soulful men—let me not call them spiritual—either to assume that the resurrection is already present in the acknowledgement of the truth, or to claim that it ensues immediately upon departure from this life. For just as the times of the hope as a whole are determined in the sacred page, and it is not permissible for it to be established earlier, so likewise it will not be permissible for the scriptures concerning it to be so interpreted as to allow it to be established earlier. Our prayers, I suppose, yearn for Christ's coming, for the sunset of this age, for the world also to pass away, at the great day of the Lord, the day of wrath and retribution, that last and secret day, known to none save the Father,[2] yet marked beforehand by signs and wonders and clashes of the elements and strifes of nations.[3] I should search the prophecies, if the Lord himself had kept silence—except that the prophecies too were the Lord's voice: but it matters more that he seals them with his own mouth. When asked by the disciples when those things would come to pass which he had just then hurled forth concerning the death of the Temple, he set in array the order of the times, first the Judaic until the destruction of Jerusalem,[4] and thereafter the general ones until the conclusion of the age.[5] For after he had declared, *And then shall Jerusalem be trampled down among the gentiles, until the times of the gentiles be fulfilled*[6]—that is, for them to be made God's elect, and gathered in with the remnants of Israel—from then on he preached against the world and the age,[7] in the manner of Joel and Daniel

[1] Cf. Isa. 13. 13; Zeph. 2. 1; Hos. 9. 7.
[2] Cf. Acts 1. 7.   [3] Cf. Luke 21. 7.   [4] Cf. Luke 21. 9–24.
[5] Cf. Luke 21. 25–8.   [6] Luke 21. 24.   [7] Cf. Luke 21. 25–6.

signa in sole et luna et in stellis, conclusionem nationum cum stupore sonitus maris, et motus refrigescentium hominum prae metu et expectatione eorum quae immineant orbi terrae. Virtutes 6 enim inquit caelorum commovebuntur, et tunc videbunt filium hominis venientem in nubibus caeli cum plurimo potentatu et gloria: ubi autem coeperint ista fieri emergetis et elevabitis capita vestra, quod redemptio vestra adpropinquaverit. et tamen adpro- 7 pinquare eam dixit, non adesse iam, et 'cum coeperint ista fieri', non 'cum facta fuerint', quia cum facta fuerint tunc aderit redemptio nostra, quae eousque adpropinquare dicetur, erigens interim et excitans animos ad proximum iam spei fructum. cuius 8 etiam parabola subtexitur tenerescentium arborum in caulem, floris et dehinc frugis antecursorem. Ita et vos, cum videritis omnia ista fieri, scitote in proximo esse regnum dei: vigilate ergo omni in tempore, ut digni sitis effugere omnia ista, et stetis ante filium hominis—utique per resurrectionem, omnibus ante transactis. ita etsi in agnitione sacramenti fruticat, sed in domini repraesentatione florescit atque frugescit. quis ergo dominum 9 tam intempestive tam acerbe excitavit iam a dextera dei ad confringendam terram secundum Esaiam, quae puto adhuc integra est? quis inimicos Christi iam subiecit pedibus eius secundum David, qua velocior patre, omni adhuc popularium coetu reclamante Christianos ad leonem? quis caelo descendentem Iesum talem conspexit qualem ascendentem apostoli viderunt, secundum angelorum constitutum? nulla ad hodiernum tribus ad tribum 10 pectora ceciderunt agnoscentes quem pupugerunt, nemo adhuc

---

22 conclusionem *MPX*: conclusione *T*: *frustra scribendum censuerunt Pam.* conlisionem, *Souter* concussionem.
26 caeli *om. T.*
30 quia cum facta fuerint *om. T.*
31 dicetur *T*: dicitur *MPX*.
38 fruticat *Pam.*: fructificat *T*: fructificasset *MPX*.
43 qua *T*: quasi *MPX*.

and the whole assembly of the prophets, that there shall be signs in the sun and the moon and the stars, constraint of nations, with perplexity at the roaring of the sea, and the emotions of men who wax cold through fear and expectation of the things that threaten the world. *For the powers of the heavens*, he says, *shall be shaken, and then shall they see the Son of Man coming in the clouds of heaven with great power and glory. But when these things begin to come to pass, ye shall look up and lift up your heads, because your redemption will have drawn nigh.*[1] Now he says it 'draws nigh', not 'is already present', and 'when these things begin to come to pass', not 'when they have come to pass', because when they have come to pass, then will our redemption be present, which until then will continue to be said to draw nigh, while meantime it lifts up and bestirs our minds towards that fruit of hope which is even now nigh at hand. Of this there is also appended a parable, of the trees which wax tender to form the bud which is the precursor of flower, and afterwards of fruit.[2] *So also ye, when ye have seen all these things come to pass, know ye that the kingdom of God is nigh at hand: watch therefore at every season, that ye may be worthy to escape all these things, and may stand before the Son of Man*[3]—evidently by means of the resurrection, when all those things have previously been accomplished. Thus, although in the acknowledgement of the mystery it comes to bud, yet it comes to flower and fruit at the Lord's actual presence. Who then in so untimely, so unripe, a sort, has summoned the Lord, now at the right hand of God, to shake terribly the earth, as Isaiah says,[4] when, I suppose, it is still intact? Who has already subdued Christ's enemies under his feet, as David says,[5] as though swifter than the Father, while still every assembly of the proletariat cries out for 'Christians to the lion'? Who has perceived Jesus coming down from heaven in like manner as the apostles saw him going up, according to the angels' decree?[6] Until this present day no tribe unto tribe have smitten their breasts,[7] recognizing him whom they pierced:[8] no one yet has welcomed

---

[1] Luke 21. 26–8; Dan. 7. 13.
[2] Cf. Luke 21. 29–31.   [3] Luke 21. 31, 36.   [4] Cf. Isa. 2. 19.
[5] Cf. Ps. 110. 1.   [6] Cf. Acts 1. 11.   [7] Cf. Zech. 12. 12.
[8] Cf. Zech. 12. 10.

excepit Heliam, nemo adhuc fugit antichristum, nemo adhuc
Babylonis exitum flevit: et est iam qui resurrexit, nisi haereticus? 11
50 exiit plane iam de corporis sepulchro etiam nunc febribus et ulceri-
bus obnoxius, et conculcavit iam inimicos etiam nunc luctari
habens cum mundi potentibus, et utique iam regnat etiam nunc
Caesari quae sunt Caesaris debens.

23 Docet quidem apostolus Colossensibus scribens mortuos fuisse
nos aliquando, alienatos et inimicos sensus domini, cum in operibus pessimis agebamus, dehinc consepultos Christo in baptismate,
et conresuscitatos in eo per fidem efficaciae dei qui illum suscitavit
5 a mortuis: Et vos, cum mortui essetis in delictis et praeputiatione 2
carnis vestrae, vivificavit cum eo, donatis vobis omnibus delictis: et
rursus, Si cum Christo mortui essetis ab elementis mundi, quomodo
quidam quasi viventes in mundo sententiam fertis? sed cum ita 3
nos mortuos faciat spiritaliter ut tamen et corporaliter quandoque
10 morituros agnoscat, utique et resuscitatos proinde spiritaliter
deputans aeque non negat etiam corporaliter resurrecturos.
denique, Si conresurrexistis, inquit, cum Christo, ea quae sursum 4
sunt quaerite, ubi Christus est in dextera dei residens: ea quae
sursum sunt sapite, non quae deorsum. ita animo ostendit
15 resurgere, quo solo adhuc possumus caelestia adtingere, quae non
quaereremus nec saperemus si possideremus. subicit etiam, Mortui 5
enim estis—scilicet delictis, non vobis—et vita vestra abscondita
est cum Christo in deo. sic et Iohannes, Et nondum, ait, mani- 6
festatum est quid futuri sumus: scimus quia si manifestatus erit

49 resurrexit *TX*: resurrexerit *MP*.
51 et conculcavit iam inimicos *om. T*.
23: 4 suscitavit *TP*: suscitaret *MX*: suscitarit *R vulgo*.
  5 in delictis *T Gel.*: *om.* in *MPX*.
  7 mortui essetis (*secunda vice*) *libri*: mortui estis *R vulgo* (*forsan recte*).
  12 conresurrexistis *Brf.*: cum resurrexistis *TX*: resurrexistis *ceteri*.
  17 vobis *T Pam.*: nobis *MPX*.

ON THE RESURRECTION 63

Elijah,[1] no one yet has fled from Antichrist,[2] no one yet has wept for the death of Babylon.[3] And is there any now who has risen again, except a heretic? He, to be sure, has already come forth from the sepulchre of the body, while even yet liable to fevers and boils, and has already trodden down the enemies, although even yet he has to wrestle with the rulers of the world:[4] and in fact he is now reigning, though he still has to pay to Caesar the things which are Caesar's own.[5]

23 The apostle indeed teaches, when writing to the Colossians, that we were at one time dead, alienated, and enemies of the mind of the Lord, when we were engaged in evil works,[6] but that afterwards we were buried together with Christ in baptism, and raised up together in him through faith in the effectual working of God who raised him from the dead:[7] *And you, when ye were dead in trespasses and the uncircumcision of your flesh, did he quicken together with him, having forgiven you all trespasses*:[8] and again, *If ye died with Christ from the elements of the world, how is it that, as though living in the world, some of you pass judgement?*[9] But since he in such sense makes us dead spiritually as yet to acknowledge that we shall also sometime die corporally, clearly, on the same principle, when he reckons us spiritually raised again he equally does not deny that we shall rise again corporally. *If*, he says in fact, *ye have risen again with Christ, seek those things which are above, where Christ is, sitting at the right hand of God: set your thoughts on the things which are above, not on those which are beneath.*[10] Thus he indicates a resurrection in mind, by which alone as yet we are able to reach up to heavenly things, things which we should neither be seeking nor setting our thoughts on if we were now in possession of them. He adds also, *For ye died*—'to trespasses' of course, not 'to yourselves'—*and your life is hid with Christ in God.*[11] Consequently that life, being hidden, is not yet within our grasp: and so also John says, *And it hath not yet been made manifest what we shall be: we know that if he shall have been made manifest we shall be like him.*[12] So far are we from being

[1] Cf. Mal. 4. 5.   [2] Cf. Apoc. 12. 6.   [3] Cf. Apoc. 18. 9.
[4] Cf. Eph. 6. 12.   [5] Cf. Matt. 22. 21.   [6] Cf. Col. 1. 21.
[7] Cf. Col. 2. 12.   [8] Col. 2. 13.   [9] Col. 2. 20.
[10] Col. 3. 1–2.   [11] Col. 3. 3.   [12] 1 John 3. 2.

similes ei erimus. tanto abest ut simus iam quod nescimus, utique scituri si iam essemus. adeo contemplatio est spei in hoc spatio per fidem, non repraesentatio, nec possessio sed expectatio. de qua spe et expectatione Paulus ad Galatas, Nos enim spiritu ex fide spem iustitiae expectamus: non ait 'tenemus': iustitiam autem dei dicit ex iudicio quo iudicabimur de mercede. ad quam pendens et ipse, cum Philippensibus scribit, Si qua inquit concurram in resurrectionem quae est a mortuis, non quia iam accepi aut consummatus sum. et utique crediderat, et omnia sacramenta cognoverat, vas electionis, doctor nationum: et tamen adicit, Persequor autem, si adprehendam in quo sum adprehensus a Christo. eo amplius, Ego me, fratres, nondum puto adprehendisse: unum tamen, oblitus posteriorum in priora me extendens secundum scopum persequor ad palmam incriminationis per quam concurrerem—utique in resurrectionem a mortuis, suo tamen tempore: sicut ad Galatas, Bene autem facientes ne taedeat, tempore enim suo metemus: sicut et ad Timotheum de Onesiphoro, Det illi dominus invenire misericordiam in illo die. in quem diem ac tempus et ipsi praecipit custodire mandatum immaculatum inreprehensibile in adparentiam domini Iesu Christi, quam suis temporibus ostendet beatus et solus potentator et rex regnantium, de deo dicens. de quibus temporibus et Petrus in Actis, Paeniteat itaque vos et respicite, ad abolenda delicta vestra, uti tempora vobis superveniant refrigerii ex persona dei, et mittat praedesignatum vobis Christum, quem oportet accipere caelos adusque tempora exhibitionis omnium quae locutus est deus de ore sanctorum prophetarum.

20 ei *TP*: eius *MX*.
25 iudicabimur *TB*: iudicabitur *MPX*.
26 resurrectionem *Gel.*: resurrectione *T*: resuscitationem *MPX*.
43 vobis *T Pam.*: nobis *MPX*.

already that which we know not: for we should certainly know it if we were it already. Thus in this part of the course there is a contemplation of the hope by means of faith, not its actual presence, and not the possession but the expectation of it. And of this hope and expectation Paul says to the Galatians, *For we by the Spirit look for the hope of righteousness as a result of faith.*[1] He does not say 'we hold': and by 'righteousness' he means the righteousness of God resulting from the judgement by which we shall be judged in respect of the reward: and on tenterhooks for this reward he himself, when writing to the Philippians, says, *If by any means I may arrive at the resurrection from the dead: not that I have already received it or am made perfect.*[2] And yet he had become a believer, and knew all mysteries, being a vessel of election, a doctor of the gentiles:[3] but he still adds, *But I follow after, if that I may apprehend that in which I have been apprehended by Christ.* More than that: *Brethren, I count not myself yet to have apprehended: one thing however, forgetting things behind, and stretching myself out to the things in front, I follow on after the mark towards* the palm of blamelessness which induced me to enter for the race[4]—evidently towards the resurrection from the dead, yet at its due time, as he says to the Galatians, *Be not weary of well-doing, for in due time we shall reap:*[5] as also to Timothy concerning Onesiphorus, *May the Lord grant him to find mercy in that day.*[6] And with a view to that day and time he instructs Timothy himself to keep the commandment unspotted, blameless, until the appearing of the Lord Jesus Christ, which at its due time he shall show, who is the blessed and only potentate, the King of kings—meaning God.[7] And of these times Peter also says in the Acts, *Repent ye therefore and look around, that your sins may be blotted out, so that times of refreshing may come upon you from the presence of God, and he may send Christ who before was appointed for you, whom the heavens must receive until the times of the delivery of all things which God hath spoken by the mouth of the holy prophets.*[8]

[1] Gal. 5. 5.
[2] Phil. 3. 11–12.
[3] Cf. Acts 9. 15; 1 Tim. 2. 7.
[4] Cf. Phil. 3. 12–14.
[5] Gal. 6. 9.
[6] 2 Tim. 1. 18.
[7] 1 Tim. 6. 14–15.
[8] Acts 3. 19–21.

24 Quae haec tempora, cum Thessalonicensibus disce. legimus enim, Qualiter conversi sitis ab idolis ad serviendum vivo et vero deo et ad expectandum a caelis filium eius, quem suscitavit a mortuis Iesum: et rursus, Quae enim spes nostra vel gaudium vel 2
5 exultationis corona quam ut et vos coram domino nostro Iesu Christo in adventu ipsius? item, Coram deo et patre nostro in adventu domini nostri Iesu Christi cum universis sanctis eius. de 3 quorum dormitione minus maerenda docens, simul et tempora resurrectionis exponit: Si enim credimus quod Iesus mortuus sit
10 et resurrexerit, sic et deus eos qui dormierunt per Iesum adducet cum ipso: hoc enim dicimus vobis in sermone dei, quod nos qui 4 vivimus, qui remanemus in adventum domini nostri, non praeveniemus eos qui dormierunt: quoniam ipse dominus in iussu et 5 in voce archangeli et in tuba dei descendet de caelo, et mortui in
15 Christo primi resurgent: deinde nos qui vivimus, qui ⟨relinqui- 6 mur,⟩ simul cum illis tollemur in nubibus obviam domino Christo in aerem, et ita semper cum domino erimus. quae vox archangeli, 7 quae tuba dei audita iam, nisi forte in cubiculis haereticorum? nam etsi tuba dei evangelicus sermo dici potest qui illos iam vocarit,
20 sed aut mortui erunt iam corporaliter ut resurrexerint, et quomodo vivunt? aut in nubibus erepti, et quomodo hic sunt? miserrimi revera, ut apostolus pronuntiavit, qui in ista tantum vita 8 sperantes habebuntur, excludendo, dum praeripiunt, quod post illam repromittitur, frustrati circa veritatem non minus quam
25 Phygellus et Hermogenes. et ideo maiestas spiritus sancti, 9 perspicax eiusmodi sensuum, et in ipsa ad Thessalonicenses epistula suggerit, De temporibus autem et temporum spatiis, fratres, non est necessitas scribendi vobis: ipsi enim certissime scitis quod dies 10 domini sicut fur in nocte ita adveniat: cum dicent 'Pax' et 'Tuta 11

24: 9 exponit dicens *P*.
   10 resurrexerit *MPX*: resurrexit *TB*.
   11 dei *TMPX*: domini *Pam*.
   15 relinquimur *addendum censebam*.
   16 domino Christo *T*: Christo *MPX*: domino *Brf*.
   23 excludendi *TC*.
   29 sicut fur in *T*: quasi fur *MPX*.   adveniat *T*: adveniet *MPX*.

ON THE RESURRECTION

24 What these times are, learn in company with the Thessalonians: for we read, *Even as ye turned from idols to serve the living and true God, and to wait for his Son from heaven, even Jesus,*[1] whom he raised from the dead. And again, *For what is our hope or joy or crown of rejoicing, but that ye also ⟨may be⟩ in the presence of our Lord Jesus Christ, at his coming?*[2] Again, *In the presence of our God and Father at the coming of our Lord Jesus Christ along with all his saints.*[3] And when teaching of their falling asleep, that it is the less to be sorrowed for, he also at the same time sets forth the times of the resurrection, saying, *For if we believe that Jesus died and rose again, so also them that are fallen asleep in Jesus will God bring forward with him. For this we say unto you in a word of God, that we who are alive, who remain behind until the coming of our Lord, shall not prevent those who are fallen asleep: because the Lord himself will descend from heaven with a rallying-cry and with the voice of the archangel and the trumpet of God, and the dead in Christ will be the first to rise again, and then we who are alive, who ⟨remain⟩, shall be lifted up along with them in the clouds to meet the Lord Christ in the air, and so shall we ever be with the Lord.*[4] What voice of an archangel, what trumpet of God, has yet been heard, except perhaps in the sleeping-places of heretics? For though the word of the gospel can be described as a trumpet of God, which has already called them, yet they must either have already corporally died so as to have risen again, and in what sense are they alive? or else have been snatched up in the clouds, and in what sense are they here? Truly most miserable are they,[5] as the apostle has declared, for they must be reckoned as hoping in this life only, because they shut out, while they snatch at it in advance, that boon which is promised after it, being frustrate concerning the truth no less than Phygellus and Hermogenes.[6] For this reason the majesty of the Holy Spirit, having discernment of thoughts of that sort, alleges also in the same epistle to the Thessalonians, *But concerning the times and the spaces of times, brethren, there is no need to write to you: for yourselves know most certainly that the day of the Lord so cometh as a thief in the night: when they shall say 'Peace', and 'All*

---

[1] 1 Thess. 1. 9–10.   [2] 1 Thess. 2. 19.   [3] 1 Thess. 3. 13.
[4] 1 Thess. 4. 14–17.   [5] Cf. 1 Cor. 15. 19.
[6] Cf. 1 Tim. 1. 19, 20; 2 Tim. 1. 15.

sunt omnia', tunc et illis repentinus insistet interitus. et in secunda pleniore sollicitudine ad eosdem, Obsecro autem vos, fratres, per adventum domini nostri Iesu Christi et congregationem nostram ad illum, ne cito commoveamini animo neque turbemini neque per spiritum neque per sermonem—scilicet pseudoprophetarum—neque per epistulam—scilicet pseudoapostolorum—acsi per nostram, quasi insistat dies domini: ne quis vos seducat ullo modo, quoniam nisi veniat abscessio primum—huius utique regni—et reveletur delinquentiae homo—id est antichristus—filius perditionis, qui adversatur et superextollitur in omne quod dicitur deus vel religio, uti sedeat in templo dei adfirmans deum se: nonne meministis quod cum apud vos essem haec dicebam vobis? et nunc quid teneat scitis, ad revelandum eum in suo tempore: iam enim arcanum iniquitatis agitatur: tantum qui nunc tenet teneat, donec de medio fiat—quis, nisi Romanus status, cuius abscessio in decem reges dispersa antichristum superducet?—et tunc revelabitur iniquus, quem dominus Iesus interficiet spiritu oris sui et evacuabit apparentia adventus sui: cuius est adventus secundum operationem satanae in omni virtute et signis atque portentis mendacii et in omni seductione iniustitiae his qui pereunt.

25 Etiam in Apocalypsi Iohannis ordo temporum sternitur, quem martyrum quoque animae sub altari ultionem et iudicium flagitantes sustinere didicerunt, ut prius et orbis de pateris angelorum plagas suas ebibat, et prostituta illa civitas a decem regibus dignos exitus referat, et bestia antichristus cum suo pseudopropheta certamen ecclesiae inferat, atque ita diabolo in abyssum interim religato primae resurrectionis praerogativa de soliis ordinetur, dehinc et igni dato universalis resurrectionis censura de libris

42 quid *TMP*: qui *XR*.
43 teneat *om. X Kroy. Brf.*
25: 5 bestia...pseudopropheta *om. T.*
7 relegato *Eng. Brf.*: sed *cf. Apoc. 20. 2.*   ordinetur: *quaero an scribendum* ordiatur.

*things are safe', then shall sudden destruction come upon them.*¹ And in the second epistle he speaks with more plenary carefulness to the same persons: *But I beseech you, brethren, by the coming of our Lord Jesus Christ and our gathering together unto him, that ye be not quickly shaken in mind, nor disturbed, either by spirit or by speech* (of false prophets, of course) *or by epistle* (of false apostles) *as if it were ours, as though the day of the Lord were here. Let no man seduce you in any way: because unless the disruption come first* (of this empire, he means) *and the man of delinquency be revealed* (that is, Antichrist), *the son of perdition, who opposeth and exalteth himself over everything that is called God or Worship, so as to sit in the Temple of God affirming that he is god—remember ye not that when I was with you I used to say these things to you? And now ye know what retaineth, that he may be revealed at his own time. For the secret of iniquity is already at work: only he who now retaineth, must retain, until he be taken out of the midst*²— who but the Roman state, whose disruption, being dispersed among ten kings, will bring in Antichrist?—*and then will the wicked one be revealed, whom the Lord Jesus will slay with the spirit of his mouth and will bring to naught by the presence of his coming—whose coming is according to the operation of Satan in all power and signs and lying wonders and in all the seduction of unrighteousness to them that are perishing.*³

25 Again in the Apocalypse of John the order of the times is laid down. This order, while beneath the altar they cry aloud for vengeance and judgement,⁴ the souls of the martyrs have learned to wait for, so that first the world may drink up its own plagues from the vials of the angels,⁵ and that harlot city may receive from the ten kings the death it deserves,⁶ and the beast Antichrist with his false prophet may bring conflict upon the church,⁷ and thus, the devil having for a season been bound in the abyss, the prerogative of the first resurrection may be set in order from the thrones,⁸ and thereafter, ⟨the devil⟩ having been given over to the fire,⁹ the censorial roll of the universal resurrection¹⁰ may be judged out of

---

¹ 1 Thess. 5. 1–3.   ² 2 Thess. 2. 1–7.   ³ 2 Thess. 2. 8–10.
⁴ Cf. Apoc. 6. 9–11.   ⁵ Cf. Apoc. 15. 7; 16. 1.   ⁶ Cf. Apoc. 17. 12.
⁷ Cf. Apoc. 19. 19–20.   ⁸ Cf. Apoc. 20. 2–4.
⁹ Cf. Apoc. 20. 9.   ¹⁰ Cf. Apoc. 20. 12.

iudicetur. cum igitur et status temporum ultimorum scripturae 3
notent et totam Christianae spei frugem in exodio saeculi collocent,
adparet aut tunc adimpleri totum quodcunque nobis a deo repromittitur, et vacat quod hic iam ab haereticis vindicatur, aut, si et
agnitio sacramenti resurrectio est, salva utique illa creditur quae in
ultimo praedicatur: et sequitur ut eo ipso quod haec spiritalis 4
vindicetur, illa corporalis praeiudicetur: quia, si nulla tunc adnuntiaretur, merito sola haec et tantummodo spiritalis vindicaretur:
cum vero et in ultimum tempus edicitur corporalis agnoscitur,
quia non et tunc spiritalis ⟨adnuntiatur. cur enim iterum⟩ 5
adnuntiaretur resurrectio eiusdem condicionis, id est spiritalis, cum
aut nunc eam deceret expungi sine ulla differentia temporum aut
tunc sub omni clausula temporum? ita nobis magis competit 6
etiam spiritalem defendere resurrectionem ab ingressu fidei qui
plenitudinem eius agnoscimus in exitu saeculi.

26 Unum adhuc respondebo ad propositionem priorem allegoricarum scripturarum, licere et nobis corporalem resurrectionem de
patrocinio figurati proinde eloquii prophetici vindicare. ecce 2
enim divina in primordio sententia terram hominem pronuntiando—Terra es et in terram ibis, secundum substantiam scilicet
carnis quae de terra erat sumpta et quae prior homo fuerat appellata,
sicut ostendimus—dat mihi disciplinam in carnem quoque interpretandi si quid irae vel gratiae in terram deus statuit, quia nec
proprie terra iudicio eius obnoxia est, quae nihil boni seu mali

---

10 exodio *Jun.*: exordio *libri.*
15 vindicetur illa corporalis *om. T.*
18 adnuntiatur cur enim iterum *suppl. Gel.*

the books. Since therefore the scriptures both note down the characteristics of the last times, and place the whole harvest of the Christian hope at the obsequies of the age, it is evident either that then is fulfilled the whole of what is promised us by God—and in that case that which is claimed here and now by the heretics is void —or else, if the acknowledgement of the mystery is also a resurrection, this belief is without prejudice to that other resurrection which is preached at the last, and it follows that, by the very fact that this one is claimed as spiritual, that other is already judged to be corporal: because if there had been no announcement of one for that time, this one might with good reason be claimed as the only one, and solely spiritual; but since it is also advertised ⟨as occurring⟩ at the last time, it is admittedly a corporal one, because for that time no spiritual one is announced. For why should there be a second announcement of a resurrection of the same character, a spiritual character, when it would be seemly for it to be completed either now without distinction of times, or else then at the whole conclusion of the times? Thus it befits us rather ⟨than them⟩ even to maintain that there is a spiritual resurrection at entrance into faith, seeing we recognize its plenitude at the end of the age.

26 One further answer I shall give to their prior allegation that the scriptures are allegorical, namely that we too have it no less in our power by the support of figurative prophetic diction to prove that the resurrection is corporal. For the primordial sentence of God, by declaring that man is earth—*Earth thou art and unto earth shalt thou go*,[1] according to the substance of the flesh of course, which was taken from the earth and first received the name of 'man', as I have shown—gives me the rule of interpreting with reference to the flesh whatsoever else of wrath or of grace God has determined with reference to the earth, for the reason that the earth is not in a strict sense exposed to his judgement, having committed nothing either of good or of evil. Cursed indeed is the earth because it has drunk blood:[2] but this itself is a metaphor for the flesh of the homicide. For even though the earth has to receive benefit or injury, this also is for man's sake, that he may receive benefit or injury by virtue of what befalls his dwelling-place, by

---

[1] Gen. 3. 19. [2] Cf. Gen. 4. 11.

admisit, maledicta quidem quod hauserit sanguinem, sed et hoc ipsum in figuram carnis homicidae. nam et si iuvari seu laedi habet 3 terra, id quoque propter hominem, uti ille iuvetur sive laedatur per consistorii sui exitus, quo magis ipse pensabit quae propter illum etiam terra patietur. itaque et cum comminatur terrae deus carni 4 potius comminari eum dicam, et cum quid terrae pollicetur carni potius polliceri eum intellegam, ut apud David, Dominus regnavit, exultabit terra—id est caro sanctorum, ad quam pertinet regni divini fructus—: dehinc subiungit, Vidit et concussa est terra, 5 montes velut cera liquefacti sunt a facie domini—caro scilicet profanorum—: Et videbunt enim eum qui confixerunt. atque 6 adeo, si simpliciter de terrae elemento utrumque existimabitur pronuntiatum, quomodo congruet et concuti et liquefieri eam a facie domini, quo supra regnante exultavit? sic et apud Esaiam, 7 Bona terrae edetis, bona carnis intellegentur, quae illam manent in regno dei reformatam et angelificatam et consecuturam quae nec oculus vidit nec auris audivit nec in cor hominis ascenderunt. alioquin satis vanum ut ad obsequium deus fructibus agri et cibariis 8 vitae huius invitet, quae etiam inreligiosis et blasphemis semel homini addicta conditione communicat, pluens super bonos et malos et solem suum emittens super iustos et iniustos. felix 9 nimirum fides, si ea consecutura est quibus hostes dei et Christi non modo utuntur verum etiam abutuntur, ipsam conditionem colentes adversus conditorem. bulbos et tubera in terrae bonis deputabis, domino pronuntiante ne in pane quidem victurum hominem? sic Iudaei terrena solummodo sperando caelestia 10 amittunt, ignorantes et panem de caelesti repromissum et oleum

26: 13 consistorii R^3 vulgo: consistoris TMP: consistore X.
17 exultabit T: exultavit MPX.
20 eum qui T: eum in quem MPX.
23 exultavit MPX: exultabit T.
26 ascenderunt TXR: ascendit MP.
36 caelesti MPX: caelis T.

so much the more as he himself must pay those penalties which the earth for his sake is to suffer. And so, even when God utters threats against the earth, I shall affirm that he is really threatening the flesh: and when he makes any promise to the earth, I shall understand that he is really making a promise to the flesh, as in David, *The Lord is king, the earth shall rejoice*[1]—that is, the flesh of the saints, to which pertains the fruition of the divine kingdom. Then he adds, *The earth saw it and was shaken, the mountains melted like wax from before the face of the Lord*[2]—this time the flesh of the ungodly: for also, *They shall look upon him who have pierced him.*[3] So much so, that if one suppose that both pronouncements were made, without metaphor, concerning the element of earth, how with consistency can it be shaken and be melted from before the face of the Lord, at whose reigning it has just now rejoiced? So also in Isaiah, *Ye shall eat the good things of the earth,*[4] we shall understand the good things of the flesh, which await it when in the kingdom of God it has been brought again into shape and made angelic, and is to obtain things which the eye hath not seen nor the ear heard, nor have they ascended into the heart of man.[5] Else it were somewhat vain that God should entice it to obedience with the fruits of the field and the victuals of this life which, by having once for all assigned the creation to man, he distributes even to the irreligious and blasphemous by making it to rain upon good men and bad and sending forth his sunshine upon just men and unjust.[6] A happy thing indeed faith is if it is to obtain things which the enemies of God and of Christ not only use but even abuse by worshipping the creation itself in opposition to the Creator.[7] Shall you reckon onions and truffles among the good things of the earth, when the Lord declares that not even by bread shall man live?[8] Thus the Jews, by hoping for earthly things and nothing more, lose the heavenly things, not knowing that even the bread that was promised is of the heavenly ⟨sort⟩,[9] the oil that of

[1] Ps. 97. 1.
[2] Ps. 97. 4–5.
[3] Zech. 12. 10; John 19. 37.
[4] Isa. 1. 19.
[5] Cf. 1 Cor. 2. 9.
[6] Cf. Matt. 5. 45.
[7] Cf. Rom. 1. 25.
[8] Cf. Deut. 8. 3; Luke 4. 4; Matt. 4. 4.
[9] Cf. John 6. 51.

divinae unctionis et aquam spiritus et vinum animae vigorantis ex vite Christo: sicut et ipsam terram sanctam Iudaicum proprie 11 solum reputant, carnem potius domini interpretandam quae 40 exinde et in omnibus Christum indutis sancta sit terra, vere sancta per incolatum spiritus sancti, vere lac et mel manans per suavitatem spei ipsius, vere Iudaea per dei familiaritatem: Non enim qui in manifesto Iudaeus, sed qui in occulto: ut et templum dei eadem 12 sit, et Hierusalem, audiens ab Esaia, Exsurge, exsurge, Hierusalem, 45 indue fortitudinem brachii tui, exsurge sicut in primordio diei, scilicet in illa integritate qua fuerat ante delictum transgressionis. qui enim in eam Hierusalem voces eiusmodi competent exhorta- 13 tionis et advocationis, quae occidit prophetas et lapidavit missos ad se et ipsum postremo dominum suum confecit? sed nec ulli 50 omnino terrae salus repromittitur, quam oportet cum totius mundi habitu praeterire. etiam si quis audebit terram sanctam paradisum 14 potius argumentari, quam et patrum dici capiat, Adae scilicet et Evae, proinde et in paradisum restitutio carni videbitur repromissa, quae eum incolare et custodire sortita est, ut talis illuc homo 55 revocetur qualis inde depulsus est.

27 Habemus etiam vestimentorum in scripturis mentionem ad spem carnis allegorizare, quia et Apocalypsis Iohannis, Hi sunt, ait, qui vestimenta sua non coinquinaverunt cum mulieribus, virgines scilicet significans et qui semetipsos castraverunt propter regna 5 caelorum. itaque in albis erunt vestibus, id est in claritate innubae 2 carnis. et in evangelio indumentum nuptiale sanctitas carnis agnosci potest. itaque Esaias, docens quale ieiunium dominus 3

37 aquam spiritus et vinum *C*: vinum spiritus et aquam *MPX*: aquam spiritus et *T*.
38 Christo *T*: Christi *MPX*.
42 dei *MPX*: fidei *T Brf*.
44 audiens...Hierusalem *om. T*.
47 qui *Eng.*: quae *libri*.

divine unction, the water that of the Spirit, and the wine that of the soul which receives strength from the vine which is Christ:[1] even as they reckon the holy land itself to be strictly the Jewish territory, though it ought rather to be interpreted as the Lord's flesh, so that flesh thenceforth also in all who have put on Christ is a holy land, truly holy through the indwelling of the Holy Spirit, truly flowing with milk and honey through the sweetness of his own hope,[2] truly Judaean through the familiar converse of God— *For he is not a Jew who is one openly, but who is one in secret*[3]—so that it is also the temple of God, and Jerusalem, to which Isaiah says, *Awake, awake, O Jerusalem, put on the strength of thine arm: awake as in the beginning of the day*[4]—that is, in that integrity in which it was before the sin of the transgression. For how can words of this kind of exhortation and invitation befit that Jerusalem which killed the prophets and stoned them that were sent unto her and at length actually slew her own Lord?[5] In fact to no earth at all is salvation promised, for it must pass away, along with the fashion of the whole world.[6] Even if any be bold rather to argue that the holy land is Paradise, which it is possible to say belongs also to the fathers (I mean Adam and Eve), it will be seen to follow that the promise of restoration to Paradise[7] was made to the flesh whose appointed task it was to inhabit and to keep it, to the end that man may be called back there in that same condition in which he was when driven out.

27 Also the mention of garments in the scriptures we have to allegorize with reference to the hope of the flesh, because the Apocalypse of John also says, *These are they who have not defiled their garments with women,*[8] meaning of course virgins and those who have made themselves eunuchs for the sake of kingdoms of heaven.[9] And thus they will be in white robes,[10] that is, in the glory of unwedded flesh. And in the gospel the wedding-garment can be recognized as sanctity of the flesh.[11] And so when Isaiah, teach-

[1] Cf. John 15. 1. [2] Cf. Exod. 3. 17. [3] Rom. 2. 28–9.
[4] Isa. 51. 9. [5] Cf. Matt. 23. 37; Luke 13. 34.
[6] Cf. 1 Cor. 7. 31. [7] Cf. Gen. 31. 3, 48. 21.
[8] Apoc. 14. 4; 3. 4. [9] Cf. Matt. 19. 12.
[10] Cf. Apoc. 3. 5. [11] Cf. Matt. 22. 11.

elegerit, cum subicit de mercede bonitatis, Tunc, inquit, lumen tuum temporaneum erumpet et vestimenta tua citius orientur: non subsericam utique nec pallium sed carnem volens accipi, ortum carnis resurrecturae de mortis occasu praedicavit. adeo 4 nobis quoque suppetit allegorice defensio corporalis resurrectionis. nam et cum legimus, Populus meus, introite in cellas promas quantulum donec ira mea praetereat, sepulchra erunt cellae promae, in quibus paulisper requiescere habebunt qui in finibus saeculi sub ultima ira per antichristi vim excesserint. aut cur 5 cellarum promarum potius vocabulo usus est et non alicuius loci receptorii, nisi quia in cellis promis caro salita et usui reposita servatur, depromenda illinc suo tempore? proinde enim et corpora medicata condimentis sepulturae mausoleis et monumentis sequestrantur, processura inde cum iusserit dominus. quod cum 6 ita intellegi congruat—ecquae enim ab ira dei cellariorum nos refugia servabunt?—hoc ipso quod ait, Donec ira praetereat, quae extinguet antichristum, post iram ostendit processuram carnem de sepulchro in quo ante iram fuerit inlata: nam et de cellariis non aliud effertur quam quod infertur, et post antichristi eradicationem agitabitur resurrectio.

28 Scimus autem sicut et vocibus ita et rebus prophetatum: tam dictis quam et factis praedicatur resurrectio. cum Moyses manum in sinum condit et emortuam profert, et rursus insinuat et vividam explicat, nonne hoc de toto homine portendit? siquidem trina 2 virtus dei per illa trina signa denotabatur cum suo ordine, primo diabolum serpentem quanquam formidabilem subactura homini, dehinc carnem de sinu mortis retractura, atque ita omnem sangui-

---

27: 10 subsericam *Gel.*: subscribam *MPX*: tunicam *T*: subuculam *B*.
    11 *a* resurrecturae *usque ad 28, l. 20* mortem occidens *per cod. T deficit.*
    22 ecquae *Oeh.*: et quae *MP*.

ing what kind of fast the Lord has chosen, added a reference to the wages of goodness and said, *Then shall thy light break forth betimes, and thy garments shall arise speedily*,[1] he wished these to be understood not as shirt or cloak but as the flesh, and preached of the dawning of the flesh which will rise again from the sunset of death. To this extent have we as well as they an allegory at our disposal to prove our case for a corporal resurrection. For also when we read, *O my people, enter into your larders for a little until my wrath pass by*,[2] the larders will be the sepulchres in which those will have to rest for a little who have deceased at the bounds of the age during the last wrath by the violence of Antichrist. Or else, why did he prefer to use the expression 'larders' and not that of some other place of storage, except that in larders flesh is kept which has been salted and put by for use, so as to be brought out from them in due time? For in like manner bodies also, having been treated with the spicery of burial, are laid aside in tombs and sepulchres so as to come forth from them when the Lord commands. And since this is appropriately understood in this sense—for can any taking of refuge in pantries preserve us from the wrath of God?—by the very fact that he says, *Until wrath pass by*,[3]—the wrath which will extinguish Antichrist—he indicates that after the wrath the flesh will come forth from the sepulchre into which it will have been brought before the wrath. For even from pantries nothing other is brought out than what is brought in, and it is after the uprooting of Antichrist that the resurrection will be set in motion.

28 We know moreover that prophecy has been delivered in facts no less than in words: the resurrection is preached by things done, as well as by things said. When Moses hides his hand in his bosom and brings it out dead, and again puts it in, and pulls it out alive, is he not making this a forecast concerning man as a whole?[4] In fact by that set of three signs[5] there was indicated, along with its due order ⟨of working⟩, the triple power of God, which will first subdue to man the devil the serpent, formidable though he be, and thereafter will withdraw the flesh from the bosom of death, and

[1] Isa. 58. 8.
[2] Isa. 26. 20.
[3] Isa. 26. 20.
[4] Cf. Exod. 4. 6–7.
[5] Cf. Exod. 4. 2–9.

nem exsecutura iudicio. de quo apud eundem propheten, Quo- 3
niam et vestrum, inquit deus, sanguinem exquiram de omnibus
bestiis, et de manu hominis et de manu fratris exquiram eum.
porro nihil exquiritur nisi quod reposcitur, nihil reposcitur nisi 4
quod et reddetur, et utique reddetur quod ultionis nomine repo-
scetur et exquiretur. neque enim vindicari poterit quod omnino
non fuerit: erit autem dum restituitur, uti vindicetur. in carnem
itaque dirigitur quicquid in sanguinem praedicatur, sine qua non
erit sanguis. caro suscitabitur, ut sanguis vindicetur. sunt et 5
quaedam ita pronuntiata ut allegoriae quidem nubilo careant,
nihilominus tamen ipsius simplicitatis suae sitiant interpretationem,
quale est apud Esaiam, Ego occidam et vivificabo. certe postea
quam occiderit vivificabit: ergo per mortem occidens per resurrectionem vivificabit. caro est autem quae occiditur per mortem: 6
caro itaque et vivificabitur per resurrectionem. certe si occidere
carni animam eripere est, vivificare, contrarium eius, carni animam
referre est, caro resurgat necesse est, cui anima per occisionem
erepta referenda est per vivificationem.

29 Igitur si et allegoricae scripturae et argumenta rerum et
simplices voces resurrectionem carnis quanquam sine nominatione
ipsius substantiae obradiant, quanto magis quae hanc spem in
ipsas substantias corporales speciali mentione determinant non
erunt ducendae in quaestionem? accipe Ezechielem: Et facta est, 2
inquit, super me manus domini et extulit me in spiritu dominus et
posuit me in medio campi: is erat ossibus refertus. et circumduxit 3
me super ea per circuitum et ecce multa super faciem campi et
ecce arida satis. et ait ad me, Fili hominis, si vivent ossa ista? et dixi, 4
Adonai domine tu scis. et ait ad me, Propheta in ossa haec et 5
dices, Ossa arida audite sermonem domini: haec dicit dominus 6

28: 21 occiditur TB^{mg}: occiderit *MPX*.
  23 eripere...animam *om. MPX*.
29: 3 obradiant *TC*: subradiant *MPX*.

then prosecute all blood with judgement. And of this God says, in the same prophet, *Because I will also require your blood of all beasts, and of the hand of a man and of the hand of a brother will I require it.*[1] Now requisition implies demand of what is due, and demand of what is due involves payment of debt, and in fact that will be paid as a debt which under the heading of vengeance will be demanded and required. For there will be no possibility of avenging that which has entirely ceased to exist: but that will exist, when brought again into being for the purpose of being avenged. And thus everything that is preached with reference to blood has a reference to flesh, for without flesh blood cannot be. The flesh will be raised again so that the blood may be avenged.

There are also some things stated in such form as to be free from the fog of allegory, yet which none the less thirst for an interpretation of their very literalness, as is that in Isaiah, *I will kill and will make alive.*[2] Evidently the making alive is subsequent to the killing. Consequently, as he kills by means of death, he will make alive by means of resurrection. But it is the flesh which is killed by means of death, and so it is the flesh also which will be made alive by means of the resurrection. Evidently if to kill is to take the soul away from the flesh, while to make alive, the contrary of it, is to bring the soul back to the flesh, the flesh must needs rise again, since to it the soul which was taken away by means of the killing is to be brought back again by means of the making alive.

29 Consequently, if both allegorical scriptures and the arguments of facts, as also plain words, though without naming the substance itself, throw light upon the resurrection of the flesh, how much more will it be impossible to call in question those scriptures which by mention of their several elements fasten this hope upon the corporal substances themselves. Hear Ezekiel: *The hand of the Lord,* he says, *came upon me and the Lord carried me out in the spirit and set me in the midst of the field: this was packed with bones. And he led me round and round over them, and behold they were many over the face of the field, and behold they were very dry. And he said unto me, Son of man, shall these bones live? and I said, O Lord Adonai, thou knowest. And he said unto me, Prophesy upon these bones and say, O dry bones,*

---

[1] Gen. 9. 5.   [2] Deut. 32. 39; cf. 1 Sam. 2. 6.

Adonai ossibus istis, Ecce ego adfero in vos spiritum et vivetis, et 7
dabo in vos *nervos* et reducam in vos carnes et circumdabo in vobis
cutem et dabo in vobis spiritum, et vivetis et cognoscetis quod ego
dominus. et prophetavi secundum praeceptum, et ecce vox dum 8
propheto et ecce motus, et accedebant ossa ad ossa: et vidi et ecce 9
super ossa nervi et caro ascendit et circumpositae sunt eis carnes, et
spiritus in eis non erat. et ait ad me, Propheta ad spiritum, fili 10
hominis, propheta et dices ad spiritum, Haec dicit dominus Adonai,
A quattuor ventis veni, spiritus, et spira in istis interemptis et
vivant. et prophetavi ad spiritum sicut praecepit mihi, et introivit 11
in ea spiritus et vixerunt et constiterunt super pedes suos, valentia
magna satis. et ait ad me, Fili hominis, ossa ista omnis domus 12
Israelis est: ipsi dicunt, Exaruerunt ossa nostra et periit spes nostra,
avulsi sumus in eis: propterea propheta ad eos, Ecce ego patefacio 13
sepulchra vestra et eveham vos de sepulchris vestris, populus meus,
et inducam vos in terram Israelis, et cognoscetis quod ego dominus 14
aperuerim sepulchra vestra et eduxerim vos de sepulchris vestris,
populus meus, et dabo in vobis spiritum et vivetis et requiescetis in 15
terra vestra, et cognoscetis quod ego dominus locutus sum et
fecerim, dicit dominus.

30 Hanc quoque praedicationem scio qualiter concutiant in allegoriae argumentationem, quia dicendo, Ossa ista omnis domus Israel est, imaginem ea fecerit Israelis et a propria condicione transtulit, atque ita figuratam esse, non veram, resurrectionis praedicationem: statum enim Iudaeorum deformari quodammodo emortuum et exaridum et dispersum in campo orbis: itaque et 2 imaginem resurrectionis in illum allegorizari, quia recolligi habeat et recompingi os ad os, id est tribus ad tribum et populus ad populum, et recorporari carnibus facultatum et nervis regni, atque ita de sepulchris, id est de habitaculis captivitatis tristissimis atque teterrimis, educi et refrigerii nomine respirari et vivere

13 nervos *Kroy*.: spiritum *MPX* (*deficit T*).
19 spiritum *MPX*: illum *T*.
28 aperuerim *TC*: aperui *MPX*.
29 in vobis *T*: vobis *MPX*.
30 sum *TMX*: sim *P*.
30: 11 respirari *MP*: respirati *X*: respirare *T Pam*.

ON THE RESURRECTION

hear the word of the Lord: thus saith the Lord Adonai to these bones, Behold I do bring spirit into you and ye shall live, and I will put sinews upon you and will bring back flesh upon you and I will surround you with skin and will put spirit in you and ye shall live and shall know that I am the Lord. And I prophesied according to the commandment, and behold a voice while I prophesied, and behold a movement, and bones came near to bones. And I saw, and behold over the bones there came up sinews and flesh, and flesh was laid about upon them, and spirit was not in them. And he said to me, Prophesy to the spirit, son of man, prophesy and say to the spirit, Thus saith the Lord Adonai, Come from the four winds, O spirit, and breathe in these slain, and let them live. And I prophesied to the spirit as he had commanded me, and the spirit entered into them and they lived and stood firm upon their feet, an exceeding great force. And he said unto me, Son of man, the whole house of Israel is these bones: they themselves say, Our bones are dried up and our hope is perished, we are made eunuchs among them. Therefore prophesy unto them, Behold I do open your sepulchres and will carry you out of your sepulchres, O my people, and will bring you into the land of Israel, and ye shall know that I the Lord have opened your sepulchres and brought you out of your sepulchres, O my people, and I will put spirit in you and ye shall live and shall be at rest in your land and shall know that I the Lord have spoken it and shall have done it, saith the Lord.[1]

30 I am aware in what fashion they weaken the force of this preaching also, arguing that it is an allegory, because in saying, *The whole house of Israel is these bones,*[2] he has made them an image of Israel and has transferred them from their proper condition: and that thus there is a figured and not a true preaching of resurrection, for there is delineated the Jewish state, which was in some sort dead and withered up, and scattered in the field of the world: and that consequently the image of resurrection is allegorized with reference to it, in that it has to be gathered again and recompacted bone to bone, that is, tribe to tribe and people to people, and to be re-embodied in the flesh of possessions and the sinews of kingdom, and thus to be brought out from its sepulchres, that is, the sorrowful and dismal habitations of captivity, and under the head of refreshment be made to breathe again and be alive thereafter in its

---
[1] Ezek. 37. 1–14. [2] Ezek. 37. 11.

exinde in terra sua Iudaea. et quid post haec? morientur sine 3
dubio. et quid post mortem? nulla opinor resurrectio si non haec
erit ipsa quae Ezechieli revelatur. sed enim et alias praedicatur
resurrectio: ergo et haec erit, et temere eam in statum Iudaicarum
rerum convertunt: aut si alia est illa quam defendimus, nihil mea
interest dum sit et corporum resurrectio sicut et rerum Iudaicarum.
denique hoc ipso quod recidivatus Iudaici status de recorporatione 4
et redanimatione ossuum figuratur, id quoque eventurum ossibus
probatur: non enim posset de ossibus figura componi si non id
ipsum ossibus eventurum esset. nam etsi figmentum veritatis in 5
imagine est, imago ipsa in veritate est sui: necesse est esse prius sibi
id quod alii configuretur. de vacuo similitudo non competit: de
nullo parabola non convenit. ita oportebit ossuum quoque credi 6
reviscerationem et respirationem qualis et dicitur, de qua possit
exprimi Iudaicarum rerum reformatio qualis adfingitur. sed magis 7
religiosum est veritatem de sua auctoritate et simplicitate defendi,
quam sensus divinae propositionis expostulat. si enim ad res
Iudaicas spectaret haec visio, statim revelato situ ossuum subiecis-
set, Ossa ista omnis domus Israelis est, et cetera deinceps. at cum 8
ostensis ossibus de propria spe eorum quid obloquitur, nondum
nominato Israele, et fidem temptat prophetae, Fili hominis si
vivent ossa haec?, ut et ille responderet, Domine tu scis, non
utique deus prophetae fidem de ea re temptasset quae futura non
esset, quam nunquam Israel audisset, quam credi non oporteret.
sed quoniam praedicabatur quidem resurrectio mortuorum, 9
Israel vero pro sua incredulitate diffidens scandalizabatur, et
aspiciens habitum senescentis sepulturae desperabat resurrec-

13 resurrectio *TX*: resuscitatio *MP*.
19 *et infra*: ossuum *MPX*: ossium *TR*.
23 id quod *T*: quo *MPX*.
27 de sua auctoritate et simplicitate *T*: de sua simplicitate et auctoritate *B*:
de suae veritate simplicitatis *MPX*.

own land of Judaea. And what after these things? Doubtless they will die. And what after death? No resurrection, I think, unless this is it which is revealed to Ezekiel. But resurrection is preached in other places besides: consequently this also will be one, and they are too bold in converting it into the state of the Jewish polity. Or if that whose case we are arguing is another one, it makes no difference to me so long as there is also a resurrection of bodies, as there is of the Jewish polity. In short, by this very fact that the reappearance of the Jewish state is figured by the re-embodiment and reanimation of bones, there is proof that this also will take place with bones: for it would not be possible for a parable to be devised from bones unless that same thing were also going to take place with bones. For although in an image there is a model of the truth, the image itself is in the truth which it is itself: that must of necessity exist first for itself, which is to be made a parable of something else. A similitude concerning vacuity has no application, and a parable concerning nullity has no pertinence. Thus we shall need to believe that there will be also a revisceration and reinspiration of bones, such as is described, so that it may be possible for there to be expressed by it such a reshaping of the Jewish polity as is modelled upon it. But it is more consonant with piety for the truth to have its case proved by its own authority and the plain meaning which the sense of the divine purpose demands. For if this vision had had in view the Jewish polity, immediately the location of the bones had been revealed he would have added, *The whole house of Israel is these bones*,[1] and the rest to follow. But since, having pointed out the bones, he makes some allusion to their own proper hope, not yet having mentioned Israel, and tests the prophet's faith, *Son of man, shall these bones live?*, so that he replied, *O Lord, thou knowest*[2]—God would certainly not have tested the prophet's faith concerning something that was not going to happen, which Israel had never heard of, which was no necessary object of belief. But inasmuch as the resurrection of the dead was indeed being preached, though Israel, faithless because of its unbelief, was offended and in view of the condition of the corpse now some time dead had given up hope of its resurrection, or else

---

[1] Ezek. 37. 11. [2] Ezek. 37. 3.

tionem, vel non in eam potius animum dirigebat sed in circum-
stantias suas, idcirco deus et prophetam qua et ipsum dubium
praestruxit ad constantiam praedicationis revelato ordine resurrectionis, et populo id credendum mandavit quod prophetae
revelavit, ipsos dicens esse ossa quae erant resurrectura qui non
credebant resurrectura. denique in clausula, Et cognoscetis, inquit,
quod ego dominus locutus sum et fecerim, id utique facturus quod
fuerat locutus, ceterum non id facturus quod locutus si aliter facturus quam locutus.

31 Plane si et populus allegorice mussitaret ossa sua arefacta et
spem suam perditam, dispersionis exitum querulus, merito
videretur et deus figuratam desperationem figurata promissione
consolatus. sed cum dispersionis quidem iniuria nondum populo
accidisset, resurrectionis vero spes apud illum saepissime cecidisset,
manifestus est de corporum interitu labefactans fiduciam resurrectionis: ita et deus eam restruebat fidem quam populus destruebat.
quanquam etsi aliqua praesentium rerum tunc conflictatione
maerebat Israel, non idcirco in parabola accipienda esset revelationis intentio sed in testationem resurrectionis, ut in illam spem
erigeret illos, aeternae scilicet salutis et necessarioris restitutionis, et
averteret a respectu praesentium rerum. ad hoc enim et alibi
prophetes, Exibitis—de sepulchris—velut vituli de vinculis soluti
et conculcabitis inimicos: et rursus, Gaudebit cor vestrum et ossa
vestra velut herba orientur—quia et herba de dissolutione et
corruptela seminis reformatur. in summa, si proprie in Israelis
statum resurgentium ossuum imago contenditur, cur etiam non
Israeli tantummodo verum et omnibus gentibus eadem spes
adnuntiatur et recorporandarum et redanimandarum reliquiarum

43 qui non credebant resurrectura *om. T.*
45 sum *T*: sim *MPX.*
47 quam locutus *om. MPX.*
31: 5 cecidisset *Gel.*: cecinisset *libri.*
15 velut herba *TB*^{mg.}: velociter *MPX.*

was directing its mind not towards it but rather towards its own circumstances, for this reason God forearmed the prophet, as though he too was in doubt, for steadfastness in preaching, by revealing the order of the resurrection, and commended to the people's belief that which he had revealed to the prophet, affirming that the bones which were to rise again were those very people who did not believe that the bones would rise again. Finally, at the conclusion, he says, *And ye shall know that I the Lord have spoken it and shall have done it*[1]—evidently intending to do that which he had spoken: whereas he would not have been intending to do that which he had spoken, if he had been intending to do it otherwise than he had spoken it.

31 Clearly, if it were in an allegory that the people ⟨of Israel⟩, bemoaning the death of dispersion, were whispering that their bones were dried up and their hope lost, we might reasonably have thought that God had consoled a figurative despair with a figurative promise. But since the damage of dispersion had not yet come upon that people, whereas the hope of resurrection had often collapsed among them, it is evident that on the ground that bodies perish they were making unstable their confidence of resurrection: and so God also was rebuilding that faith which the people were pulling down. And yet, even if Israel's mourning at that time was occasioned by some dismay at their present experiences, it would not follow that the purpose of the revelation must be understood as a parable, but as an attestation of the resurrection, so as to lift them up towards that hope (I mean of eternal salvation with its more indispensable restitution) and recall them from consideration of their present affairs. For to this effect the prophet also speaks elsewhere, *Ye shall go forth*—from the sepulchres—*as calves let loose from halters and ye shall tread down your enemies*:[2] and again, *Your heart shall rejoice and your bones shall come up like the grass*[3]— because the grass also is refashioned from the dissolution and corruption of the seed. To sum up: if the claim is that the figure of the resurrection of the bones applies to the state of Israel and it alone, why is it that not for Israel alone but for all the nations that same hope is proclaimed of the reincorporation and reanimation of their

---

[1] Ezek. 37. 14.   [2] Mal. 4. 2.   [3] Isa. 66. 14.

et de sepulchris exsuscitandorum mortuorum? de omnibus enim dictum est, Vivent mortui et exsurgent de sepulchris: ros enim qui a te, medela est ossibus eorum. item alibi, Veniet adorare omnis caro in conspectu meo, dicit dominus. quando? cum praeterire coeperit habitus mundi huius: supra enim, Quemadmodum caelum novum et terra nova quae ego facio, in conspectu meo, dicit dominus, ita stabit semen vestrum. tunc ergo et quod subiecit implebitur, Et exibunt—utique de sepulchris—et videbunt artus eorum qui impie egerunt, quoniam vermis eorum non decidet et ignis eorum non extinguetur, et erit satis conspectui omni carni—scilicet quae resuscitata et egressa de sepulchris dominum pro hac gratia adorabit.

32 Sed ne solummodo eorum corporum resurrectio videatur praedicari quae sepulchris demandantur, habes scriptum, Et mandabo piscibus maris et eructuabunt ossa quae sunt comesta, et faciam compaginem ad compaginem et os ad os. ergo, inquis, et pisces resuscitabuntur et ceterae bestiae et alites carnivorae ut revomant quos comederunt, quia et apud Moysen legis exquiri sanguinem de omnibus bestiis? non utique: sed idcirco nominantur bestiae et pisces in redhibitionem carnis et sanguinis quo magis exprimatur resurrectio etiam devoratorum corporum cum de ipsis devoratoribus exactio edicitur—puto autem huius quoque divinae potestatis documentum idoneum Ionam, cum incorruptus utramque substantiam, carnem atque animam, de alvo bestiae piscis evolvitur, et utique triduum concoquendae carni viscera ceti suffecissent quam capulum quam sepulchrum quam senium requietae atque conditae alicuius sepulturae—salvo eo quod et bestia feros in Christianum vel maxime nomen homines vel ipsos etiam iniquitatis angelos figuravit, de quibus sanguis exigetur per

---

20 exsuscitandorum *MX Gel.*: excitandorum *TP*.
22 medela est *Brf.*: medela *MPX*: medulla est *T*,
29 erit satis *TMPX*: erunt *Gel*.
32: 4 faciam *TB*^{mg}·: facient *MPX*.
  10–15 *parenthesim indicabam*.
  13, 14 ⟨tam⟩ viscera *Kroy*.: ⟨tam⟩ suffecissent *Urs*.
  16 homines *R*^{3}: hominis *libri*.

remains, along with the awakening of the dead from their sepulchres? For of them all it is said, *The dead shall live and shall arise from the sepulchres, for the dew which is from thee is healing to their bones.*[1] Also in another place, *All flesh shall come to worship in my sight, saith the Lord:*[2] when? When the fashion of this world begins to pass away. For he had first said, *Even as the new heaven and the new earth which I do make are in my sight, saith the Lord, so shall your seed stand.*[3] Then also will be fulfilled what he says next, *And they shall go forth*—surely from their sepulchres—*and look upon the ⟨severed⟩ limbs of those who have done wickedly, because their worm shall not fail, nor shall their fire be quenched, and it shall be enough for all flesh to see*[4]—that flesh, in fact, which having been raised again and come forth from the sepulchres will be worshipping the Lord for this grace.

32 But lest it should seem that the only resurrection preached is of those bodies which are consigned to sepulchres, you have it written, *And I will command the fishes of the sea and they shall spew up the bones that are consumed and I will bring joint to joint and bone to bone.*[5] In that case, you say, the fishes also will be raised up again, as will the other beasts and the carnivorous fowl, so as to vomit back those whom they have consumed: because in Moses you read that the blood is required of all beasts.[6] Not so: the beasts and fishes are mentioned in the restitution of flesh and blood solely for the clearer expression of the resurrection even of bodies devoured, in that exaction is decreed upon the very devourers—but I suppose that Jonah is a sufficient proof that God has this power as well,[7] when he is disembarked from the sea-monster's belly uncorrupt in respect of both substances, flesh and soul, and certainly the whale's entrails would have been more competent to digest the flesh in three days than would a coffin, a sepulchre, and the long age of some peaceful and embalmed burial—saving the fact that by beasts he has indicated in a figure men who are in an exceptional degree fierce against the Christian name, or even the very angels of iniquity, of whom the blood will be exacted by means of

[1] Isa. 26. 19.   [2] Isa. 66. 23.   [3] Isa. 66. 22.
[4] Isa. 66. 24.   [5] Enoch 61. 5.   [6] Cf. Gen. 9. 5.
[7] Cf. Jonah 2. 10.

ultionem pensandam. quis ergo discendi magis adfinis quam 5
praesumendi, et credendi diligentior quam contendendi, et divinae
potius sapientiae religiosus quam suae libidinosus, audiens aliquid
a deo destinatum et in carnes et cutes et nervos et ossa, aliud quid
haec commentabitur, quasi non in hominem destinetur quod in
istas substantias praedicatur? aut enim nihil in hominem destinatur, 6
non liberalitas regni, non severitas iudicii, non quodcunque
est resurrectio, aut, si in hominem destinatur, necesse est in eas
substantias destinetur ex quibus homo instructus est in quem
destinatur. illud etiam de argutissimis istis demutatoribus ossuum 7
et carnium et nervorum et sepulchrorum requiro, cur si quando in
animam quid pronuntiatur nihil aliud animam interpretantur nec
transfingunt eam in alterius rei argumentum, cum vero in aliquam
speciem corporalem quid edicitur omnia potius adseverant quam
quod nominatur. si corporalia parabolae, ergo et animalia: si non 8
et animalia, ergo nec corporalia. tam enim corpus homo quam et
anima, ut non possit altera species admittere aenigmata, altera
excludere.

33 Satis haec de prophetico instrumento. ad evangelicum nunc
provoco, hic quoque occursurus prius eidem astutiae eorum qui
proinde et dominum omnia in parabolis pronuntiasse contendunt
quia scriptum sit, Haec omnia locutus est Iesus in parabolis et sine
parabola non loquebatur ad illos, scilicet ad Iudaeos: nam et 2
discipuli, Quare aiunt in parabolis loqueris illis?, et dominus,
Propterea in parabolis loquor ad eos ut videntes non videant et
audientes non audiant, secundum Esaiam. quodsi ad Iudaeos in 3
parabolis, iam non ad omnes: si ⟨non⟩ ad omnes in parabolis, iam
non semper nec omnia parabolae, sed quaedam cum ad quosdam,
ad quosdam autem dum ad Iudaeos: nonnunquam plane et ad

26 instructus *T*: structus *MPX* (*forsan recte*).
33: 1 evangelicum *T*: evangelia *MPX*.
  6 illis *T*: *om. MPX*,
  9 ⟨non⟩ *add. R*³.

the penalty they will have to pay. Will any one then, who is nearer akin to learning than to guesswork, and more diligent of belief than of contention, who is rather in awe of the divine wisdom than rashly confident of his own, when he hears that God has appointed a certain destiny for flesh and skin and sinews and bones, invent some other meaning for these, as though that which is preached respecting these substances were not the destiny of man? For either man has no destiny, neither the citizenship of the kingdom nor the sternness of the judgement nor whatsoever the resurrection consists of, or else, if that is man's destiny, it must be the destiny of those substances which constitute man whose destiny it is. This also I ask of these cunning transmuters of bones and flesh and sinews and sepulchres: Why, whenever any pronouncement is made respecting the soul, do they refrain from interpreting soul as something else or from remoulding it into a proof of the other entity, yet when any decree is published respecting some constituent of the body assert that it is anything and everything except the thing named? If statements referring to the body are parables, so are those which refer to the soul: if those which refer to the soul are not, neither are those which refer to the body. For man is as much body as soul, and consequently it is impossible for one of his constituents to admit of enigmas while the other excludes them.

33 That is enough concerning the prophetic document. I now make my appeal to the Gospels, intending here also to confront first of all that same subtilty of those who, because it is written, *All these things spake Jesus in parables and without a parable spake he not unto them*,[1] namely the Jews, immediately claim that the Lord made all his pronouncements in parables. For the disciples also say, *Why speakest thou in parables?*[2] and the Lord answers, *Therefore speak I unto them in parables that seeing they may not see and hearing they may not hear*,[3] according to Isaiah.[4] But if to the Jews in parables, then not to all: if not to all in parables, then not always: and not all things are parables but only some things, when he speaks to some. But to some when to the Jews: sometimes evidently even to the

[1] Matt. 13. 34.   [2] Matt. 13. 10.
[3] Matt. 13. 13.   [4] Cf. Isa. 6. 9.

discipulos. sed quomodo referat scriptura considera: Dicebat 4
autem et parabolam ad eos. ergo et non parabolam dicebat: quia
non notaretur cum parabolam loquebatur si ita semper loquebatur.
etiam et nullam parabolam non aut ab ipso invenies edissertatam, 5
ut de seminatore in verbi administrationem, aut a commentatore
evangelii praeluminatam, ut iudicis superbi et viduae instantis ad
perseverantiam orationis, aut ultra coniectandam, ut arboris fici
dilatae in spem ad instar Iudaicae infructuositatis. quodsi nec 6
parabolae obumbrant evangelii lucem, tanto abest ut sententiae et
definitiones, quarum aperta natura est, aliter quam sonant sapiant.
definitionibus autem et sententiis dominus edicit sive iudicium sive
regnum dei sive resurrectionem. Tolerabilius erit, inquit, Tyro et 7
Sidoni in die iudicii: et, Dicite illis quod adpropinquaverit regnum
dei: et, Retribuetur tibi in resurrectione iustorum. si nomina 8
absoluta sunt rerum, id est iudicii et regni dei et resurrectionis, ut
nihil eorum in parabolam comprimi possit, nec ea in parabolas
compellentur quae ad dispositionem et transactionem et passionem regni Iudaici et resurrectionem praedicantur, atque ita
corporalia defendentur ut corporalibus destinata, id est non spiritalia
quia non figurata. nam et ideo praestruximus tam corpus animae 9
quam et carnis obnoxium esse mercedibus pro communi operatione pensandis, ne corporalitas animae occasionem subministrans
figurarum corporalitatem carnis excludat, cum utramque partici-
pem et regni et iudicii et resurrectionis oporteat credi. et nunc eo 10
pergimus uti corporalitatem carnalem proprie demonstremus a

15 etiam et *T*: et tamen *MPX*.
edissertatam *R*³: edisseratam *libri*.
28 compellentur *T*: compellantur *MPX*.
29 Iudaici *T*: iudicii *MPX*.   resurrectionem *T*: resurrectionis *MPX*.
mallem scripsisse regni ⟨et⟩ iudicii et resurrectionis.

disciples. But observe how the scripture relates it: *But he was speaking also a parable unto them.*[1] Consequently he used also to speak that which was not parable, for it would not have been noted when he did speak a parable if he was used always so to speak. Moreover you will not find any parable which is not either explained by him, like that of the sower regarding the administration of the word;[2] or else has light thrown on it beforehand by the compiler of the Gospel, like that of the proud judge and the persistent widow respecting perseverance in prayer;[3] or else is obviously to be surmised, like that of the figtree spared in hope, in the likeness of Jewish unfruitfulness.[4] But if not even parables becloud the light of the gospel, even less will statements and pronouncements, whose nature it is to be open, mean other than they sound. But it is by pronouncements and statements that the Lord propounds whether it be the judgement or the kingdom of God or the resurrection. *It will be more tolerable,* he says, *for Tyre and Sidon in the day of judgement*:[5] and, *Say unto them that the kingdom of God hath come nigh*:[6] and, *Thou shalt be recompensed at the resurrection of the just.*[7] If the names of the things, that is, 'judgement' and 'kingdom of God' and 'resurrection' have an evident meaning, so that nothing of theirs can be constrained into a parable, neither can those things be forced into parables which are preached respecting the establishment, the administration, the downfall, and the resurrection of the Jewish kingdom: and thus they will establish their claim to be corporal, as being destined for corporal beings, and in that case not spiritual, because not metaphorical. And it is for this reason that I have already proved that the body of the soul, as of the flesh, has owing to it rewards which will be paid for that which they have wrought in common, so that the corporeity of the soul may not, by supplying opportunity for metaphors, exclude the corporeity of the flesh, seeing we must believe that both the one and the other is a partaker of both kingdom and judgement and resurrection. And now I proceed with my purpose of proving that corporeity of the flesh is speci-

[1] Luke 18. 9.
[2] Cf. Matt. 13. 18–23.
[3] Cf. Luke 18. 1–5.
[4] Cf. Luke 13. 6–9.
[5] Matt. 11. 24.
[6] Matt. 10. 7.
[7] Luke 14. 14.

domino significari in omni resurrectionis mentione, salva animali quam et ipsam pauci receperunt.

34 In primis cum ad hoc venisse se dicit ut quod periit salvum faciat, quid dicis perisse? hominem sine dubio. totumne an ex parte? utique totum, siquidem transgressio, quae perditionis humanae causa est, tam animae instinctu ex concupiscentia quam
5 et carnis actu ex degustatione commissa, totum hominem elogio transgressionis inscripsit atque exinde merito perditionis implevit. totus itaque salvus fiet qui periit totus delinquendo, nisi si et ovis 2 illa sine corpore amittitur et sine corpore revocatur. nam si caro quoque eius cum anima, quod pecus totum est, humeris boni
10 pastoris advehitur, ex utraque utique substantia restituendi hominis exemplum est. aut quam indignum deo dimidium hominem 3 redigere in salutem, paene minus facere ⟨quam faciat homo⟩, cum etiam saecularium principum plena semper indulgentia vindicetur. diabolus validior in hominis iniuriam intellegetur totum eum
15 elidens, deus infirmior renuntiabitur non totum eum relevans? atquin et apostolus suggerit, ubi delictum abundaverit illic gratiam superabundasse. quomodo denique salvus habebitur qui poterit et 4 perditus dici? carne scilicet perditus, anima vero salvus, nisi quod iam et anima in perdito constituatur necesse est ut salva effici possit:
20 id enim salvum effici oportebit quod perditum fuerit. porro aut 5 recipimus animae immortalitatem, ut perdita non in interitum credatur sed in supplicium, id est in gehennam: et si ita est, iam non animam spectabit salus, salvam scilicet suapte natura per immortalitatem, sed carnem potius quam interibilem constat apud
25 omnes: aut si et anima interibilis, id est non immortalis, quod et 6 caro, iam et carni forma illa ex aequo proficere debebit proinde

---

34: 1 uti *MPX*.
   7 periit *Gel.*: perit *libri*.
   12 quam faciat homo *supplenda censebam*.
   14 intellegetur *Eng.*: intellegitur *libri*.
   18 dici *om. MPX*.
   20 aut *T*: autem *MPX*.
   23 suapte *Souter*: suaabte *T*: sua *ceteri*.

fically indicated by our Lord at every mention of the resurrection, without prejudice to the corporeity of the soul, which indeed few have admitted.

34 In the first place, when he says he has come for the purpose of saving that which has perished,[1] what do you allege has perished? Man, undoubtedly. In whole or in part? In whole, of course, seeing that the transgression which is the cause of man's perdition, having been committed alike by the prompting of the soul from concupiscence and by the act of the flesh from tasting, has involved the whole man in the indictment of transgression and consequently infected him with the guilt of perdition. As then he has totally perished by sinning, totally will he be saved, unless perchance that sheep gets lost without its body, and without its body is brought home.[2] For if its flesh along with its soul (and this is the whole animal) is carried on the good shepherd's shoulders, this is obviously a precedent of man's being restored in respect of both his substances. Else how unworthy of God, to bring half a man back to salvation, almost to do less ⟨than a man would do⟩, when even of this world's princes the indulgence is always claimed in full. Must the devil be understood to be more powerful for man's damage, as smashing the whole man down, and God be declared less powerful, as lifting less than the whole man up? And yet the apostle submits that where sin abounded, there grace did much more abound.[3] How indeed shall a man be considered saved when it will also be possible to say he has perished? Perished in the flesh, I mean, though saved in soul: except that now even the soul has to be classed with that which has perished, to make it possible for it to be saved: for that which is to be saved must needs be the same thing as has perished. But once more, either we accept the soul's immortality, so that its perdition may be believed to issue not in destruction but in chastisement, which means hell—and if that is so, then salvation will have in view not the soul, it being of its own nature safe through immortality, but rather the flesh, which all agree is destructible—or else, if the soul also is destructible (that is, not immortal) as the flesh is, that standing rule that

[1] Cf. Luke 19. 10. [2] Cf. Luke 15. 4–6.
[3] Cf. Rom. 5. 20.

mortali et interibili qua id quod perit salvum facturus est dominus. nolo nunc contentioso fune deducere hac an illac hominem perditio depostulet, dum utrimque eum salus destinet in ambas substantias peraequata. ecce enim, ex quacunque substantia hominem perisse praesumpseris, ex altera non perit: salvus ergo erit iam ex qua non perit, et salvus nihilominus fiet ex qua perit. habes totius hominis restitutionem, dum et quodcunque eius perit salvum facturus est dominus et quodcunque non perit utique non erit periturus. quid ultra de utriusque substantiae securitate dubitas, cum altera salutem consecutura sit, altera amissura non sit? et tamen adhuc sensum rei exprimit dominus, Ego dicens veni non ut meam sed ut patris qui me misit faciam voluntatem. quam? oro te. Ut omne quod dedit mihi, non perdam ex eo quidquam sed resuscitem illud in novissimo die. quid a patre Christus acceperat nisi quod et induerat? hominem sine dubio, carnis animaeque texturam. neutrum ergo eorum quae accepit perire patietur, immo nec quidquam utriusque, immo nec modicum: quodsi modicum caro, ergo nec carnem quia nec modicum, nec quidquam quia nec quidquam. atquin si non et carnem resuscitabit novissima die, iam non modicum patietur perire de homine, sed pro tanta dixerim parte prope totum. ingerens amplius, Hoc est patris voluntas, ut omnis qui aspicit filium et credit in eum habeat vitam aeternam, et suscitem illum novissimo die, plenitudinem exstruit resurrectionis: tribuit enim utrique substantiae per officia propriam mercedem salutis, et carni per quam filius aspiciebatur, et animae per quam credebatur. ergo, dices, illis erit promissa res a quibus Christus videbatur. sit plane ita, ut et ad nos eadem spes

---

29 utrimque *R*³: utrumque *libri*.
36 altera amissura non sit *om. MPX*.
43-4 quodsi...nec modicum nec quidquam *om. T*.
47 hoc *MPX*: haec *T*.
50 propria *Kroy., sed haud opus erat.*

the Lord is to save that which is perishing will in equity have to apply to the flesh which is certainly mortal and destructible. I have no mind at present to play tug-of-war as to whether perdition lays claim to man on this side or on that, so long as on both sides salvation points his way, equally balanced towards both his substances. For in respect of whichever substance you suppose man to have perished, in respect of the other he does not perish: and it must follow that he is saved already in that in respect of which he does not perish, while none the less he is to be brought to salvation in that in respect of which he does perish. There you have the restitution of the whole man, in that whatsoever of him perishes the Lord will bring to salvation, while whatsoever does not perish he is of course not going to destroy. How can you still suspect that either substance has anything to fear, when one of them is to attain to salvation, while the other is not going to lose it? Moreover the Lord again expresses the meaning of the matter when he says, *I am come not to do my own will but the Father's who hath sent me.*[1] What will, I ask you? *That of everything he hath given me I should lose nothing, but should raise it up at the last day.*[2] What had Christ received of the Father, if not that with which he had clothed himself, manhood undoubtedly, warp and woof of flesh and soul? Therefore he will suffer to perish neither of the things he has received, not even any part of either, not even a little bit. But if the flesh is a little bit, then not the flesh, because 'not even a little bit', nor any of it, because 'not even any part'. And besides, if he is not to raise the flesh up again at the last day, then it is not a little bit that he will suffer to perish from manhood but (in respect of so large a part I might say) almost the whole. When he adds further, *This is the Father's will, that every one that looketh upon the Son and believeth in him should have eternal life, and that I should raise him up at the last day,*[3] he builds up a resurrection with nothing left out: for to each substance by means of its functions he assigns its proper meed of salvation—to the flesh by means of which the Son was looked upon, and to the soul by means of which he was believed in. In that case, you will say, the promise was made to those persons by whom Christ was ⟨actually⟩ seen. Clearly let it be so,

---
[1] John 6. 38. [2] John 6. 39. [3] John 6. 40.

inde manaverit: nam si videntibus et idcirco credentibus fructuosa tunc fuerunt opera carnis atque animae, multo magis nobis: feliciores enim qui non vident et credent: quando et si illis negaretur carnis resurrectio, certe felicioribus competisset: quomodo enim felices si ex parte perituri?

35 Sed et praecipit eum potius timendum qui et corpus et animam occidat in gehennam, id est dominum solum, non qui corpus occidant animae autem nihil nocere possint, id est humanas potestates. adeo hic et anima immortalis natura recognoscitur, 2 quae non possit occidi ab hominibus, et carnis esse mortalitatem, cuius sit occisio, atque ita resurrectionem quoque mortuorum carnis esse, quae in gehennam nisi resuscitata non poterit occidi. sed quoniam et hic de interpretatione corporis quaestio cavillatur, 3 ego corpus humanum non aliud intellegam quam omnem istam struem carnis, quoquo genere materiarum concinnatur atque variatur, quod videtur, quod tenetur, quod denique ab hominibus occiditur. sic et parietis corpus non aliud admittam quam 4 caementa, quam saxa, quam lateres. si quis arcanum aliquod corpus inducit, ostendat revelet probet ipsum etiam esse quod occidatur ab homine, et de illo erit dictum. item si animae corpus opponitur 5 vacabit astutia: cum enim utrumque proponitur, corpus atque animam, occidi in gehennam, distinguitur corpus ab anima, et relinquitur intellegi corpus id quod in promptu est, caro scilicet, quae sicut occidetur in gehennam si non magis a deo timuerit occidi, ita et vivificabitur in vitam aeternam si maluerit ab hominibus potius interfici. proinde si quis occisionem carnis 6 atque animae in gehennam ad interitum et finem utriusque substantiae adripiet et non ad supplicium, quasi consumendarum non quasi puniendarum, recordetur ignem gehennae aeternum praedicari in poenam aeternam, et inde aeternitatem occisionis prop-

54 et idcirco credentibus *om. T.*
35: 2 deum *T (forsan recte).*
9 humanum *T:* hominis *MPX.*

provided the same hope has seeped down to us from them. For if at that time the acts of flesh and soul were fruitful to those who saw and consequently believed, much more so for us—for, *More blessed are they who do not see, and ⟨yet⟩ will believe*[1]—since even if to those the resurrection of the flesh were denied, it would certainly have been granted to such as are more blessed: for how could they be blessed if they were partly to perish?

35 Moreover his injunction is that he is rather to be feared who slays both body and soul in hell (that is, the Lord alone), not those who slay the body but can do the soul no harm (meaning human potentates).[2] Here then is an acknowledgement that the soul is immortal by nature, seeing it cannot be slain by men, and that mortality is of the flesh, which is what is slain, and that thus also the resurrection of the dead is of the flesh, for this will not be able to be slain in hell unless it is first raised up again. But, seeing that here also a captious question is raised concerning the interpretation of 'body', my understanding will be that a man's body is none other than all that structure of the flesh, of whatever sort of materials it is composed and diversified, that which is seen, is handled, that in short which is slain by men. So also the body of a wall I shall not admit to be any other than rubble, stones, and bricks. If anyone suggests some occult body, let him display it, reveal it, prove that it is even it that is slain by man, and the text shall refer to it. And again, if the soul's body is brought up ⟨against us⟩, the subtilty will fall flat. For as the proposition is twofold, that body and soul are slain in hell, body is distinguished from soul, and it remains for body to be understood as that which is obvious, flesh in fact, which just as it will be slain in hell if it has not rather feared being slain by God, so will it be made alive unto life eternal if it has preferred rather to be put to death by men. Further, if any man is going to force the slaying of flesh and soul in hell to mean the destruction and the end of both substances, not their chastisement (as though they were to be consumed, not as though they were to be punished) let him recollect that the preaching is that the fire of hell is eternal, for eternal punishment,[3] and thereafter let him acknowledge that eternity of slaying is rather to be feared than

---

[1] John 20. 29. [2] Cf. Matt. 10. 28. [3] Cf. Matt. 25. 46.

terea humanae ut temporali praetimendam: tunc et aeternas sub- 7
stantias credet quarum aeterna sit occisio in poenam. certe cum
post resurrectionem corpus cum anima occidi habeat a deo in
gehennam, satis de utroque constabit, et de carnali resurrectione et
30 de aeterna occisione. absurdissimum alioquin si idcirco resuscitata 8
caro occidetur in gehennam ut finiatur, quod et non resuscitata
pateretur: in hoc scilicet reficietur ne sit, cui non esse iam evenit.
eidem nos spei fulciens passerum quoque subiungit exemplum, 9
quod ex duobus non cadat alter in terram sine dei voluntate, ut et
35 carnem quae ceciderit in terram proinde credas resurgere posse per
eiusdem dei voluntatem. nam et si passeribus hoc non licet, sed 10
nos multis passeribus antistamus eo quod cadentes resurgamus,
quorum denique capillos capitis omnes numeratos adfirmans
salvos utique repromittit. perituros enim quae ratio in numerum 11
40 redegisset? nisi quia hoc est, Ut omne quod pater mihi dedit non
perdam ex eo quidquam, id est nec capillum, sicut nec oculum nec
dentem. ceterum unde erit fletus et dentium frendor nisi ex oculis 12
et ex dentibus, occiso scilicet etiam corpore in gehennam et
detruso in tenebras exteriores, quae oculorum propria tormenta
45 sunt?—si quis in nuptiis minus dignis operibus fuerit indutus, con-
stringendus statim manibus et pedibus, utpote qui cum corpore
resurrexerit. sic ergo et recumbere ipsum in dei regno et sedere in 13
thronis duodecim et adsistere ad dexteram tunc vel sinistram et
edere de ligno vitae corporalis dispositionis fidelissima indicia sunt.
36 Videamus nunc an et Sadducaeorum versutiam elidens nostram magis sententiam erexerit. causa opinor quaestionis fuit

28 a deo *T*: *om. MPX (forsan recte)*.
42-7 ceterum...resurrexerit: *quomodo interpungendae forent hae duae incisiones haud satis perspicuum fuit.*
45 operibus *libri*: opertibus *Kroy. (perperam).*
47 resurrexerit *Kroy.*: surrexerit *MPX*: resurrexit *T*.

man's slaying, precisely because the latter is temporal. Then also he will believe that those substances are eternal, seeing that the slaying of them for punishment is eternal. Certainly, since after the resurrection the body along with the soul is to be slain by God in hell, there will be sufficient agreement on both points, resurrection of the flesh no less than eternal slaying. Else would it be most absurd if the flesh, having been raised up again, is to be slain in hell for the express purpose of bringing it to an end, which is what would happen to it if it were not raised up again: in such a case it will be reconstituted with intent to terminate the existence of a thing which has already attained to non-existence. Giving us support for the same hope he also adds the instance of the sparrows,[1] that one out of two does not fall to the ground without God's will, so that you may likewise believe that the flesh also which has fallen to the earth can rise up again through the will of that same God. For although this is not permitted to sparrows, yet we are more valuable than many sparrows by the fact that when we fall we rise again:[2] and in fine, when he affirms that the hairs of our head are all numbered he at once promises their salvation.[3] For had they been going to perish, what accountancy would have reduced them to number? And surely this is the meaning of, *That of all which the Father hath given me I should lose nothing*,[4] that is, not even a hair, as neither an eye nor a tooth. Moreover, whence can come weeping and gnashing of teeth, if not from eyes and from teeth?[5] In fact, even when the body has been slain in hell and thrust down into outer darkness—and this is a torture particularly attaching to eyes —any one who at the marriage-feast is clothed in works less than worthy will at once be bound hand and foot,[6] which shows that he will have risen again with a body. So again that reclining at meat in the kingdom of God, and sitting on twelve thrones, and standing then at the right hand or the left, and eating of the tree of life,[7] are most trustworthy evidence of attitude of body.

36 Let us next consider whether, in the process of striking down the Sadducees' trickery, he has not established our judgement

[1] Cf. Matt. 10. 29. [2] Cf. Matt. 10. 31. [3] Cf. Matt. 10. 30.
[4] John 6. 39. [5] Cf. Matt. 8. 12, 25. 30. [6] Cf. Matt. 22. 13.
[7] Cf. Apoc. 2. 7.

destructio resurrectionis, siquidem Sadducaei neque animae neque carnis admittunt salutem et ideo, ex qua vel maxime specie resurrectionis fides labefactatur, ex ea argumentum problemati suo accommodaverunt, de carnis scilicet obtentu nupturae necne post resurrectionem, sub eius mulieris persona quae septem fratribus nupta in dubio habebatur cui eorum restitueretur. porro serventur 2 sensus tam quaestionis quam responsionis, et controversiae occursum est. si enim Sadducaei quidem respuebant resurrectionem, dominus autem eam confirmabat, et scripturarum ignaros increpans, earum scilicet quae resurrectionem praedicassent, et virtutis dei incredulos, idoneae utique mortuis resuscitandis, postremo sub- 3 iciens Quoniam autem mortui resurgunt, sine dubio et confirmando esse quod negabatur, id est resurrectionem mortuorum apud deum vivorum, talem quoque eam confirmabat esse qualis negabatur, utriusque scilicet substantiae humanae. neque enim si 4 nupturos tunc negavit ideo nec resurrecturos demonstravit: atquin filios resurrectionis appellavit, per eam quodammodo nasci habentes post quam non nubent sed resuscitati similes [enim] 5 erunt angelis, qua non nupturi quia nec morituri sed qua transituri in statum angelicum per indumentum illud incorruptibilitatis per substantiae, resuscitatae tamen, demutationem. ceterum nec quae- 6 reretur nupturi sive morituri necne rursus essemus si non eius vel maxime substantiae restitutio in dubium vocaretur quae proprie et morte et nuptiis fungitur, id est carnis. habes igitur dominum 7 confirmantem adversus haereticos Iudaeorum quod et nunc negatur apud Sadducaeos Christianorum, solidam resurrectionem.

36: 11 confirmabat *T*: confirmat *PX*: *de M dubitatur.*
    16 deum *TC*: dominum *MPX.*
    20 sed resuscitati *et quae sequuntur ita pungenda censuit Eng.*: enim (*in T deletum*) *restituit Brf., periodo post* resuscitati *facta. Quaero an scribendum fuerit* sed resuscitati ⟨virgines manebunt⟩: similes enim, *etc.*

instead. The purpose of the question, I suppose, was the pulling down of the resurrection, inasmuch as the Sadducees admit the salvation neither of soul nor of flesh: and consequently they contrived an argument applicable to their proposition from that aspect ⟨of human nature⟩ from which the faith of the resurrection is most plausibly weakened, under the pretext, that is, of the flesh, whether or not it will marry after the resurrection, in the person of the woman who, having been married to seven brothers, gave reason for doubt to which of them she should be restored.[1] Now let the purport of both question and answer be kept in mind, and the controversy has been met. For if, while the Sadducees rejected the resurrection, our Lord was affirming it, both when he rebuked them for ignorance of the scriptures (those which had preached the resurrection) and for disbelief in the power of God (which is certainly competent to raise the dead) and finally when he added, *But that the dead rise again*,[2] there is no doubt that by affirming the existence of that which was denied (that is, the resurrection of the dead in the presence of the God of the living)[3] he also affirmed that it is of a character such as was denied, is, in fact, of both the human substances. For if he said they would not then marry,[4] he gave thereby no indication that they will not rise again: indeed he called them sons of the resurrection,[5] for by it in a sort of way they have to be born: and after it they will not marry, but, having been raised again.... For they will be like the angels, in that they are not to marry because they are not to die, and also in that they are to pass over into angelic quality by virtue of that garment of incorruptibility, by virtue of a transmutation of substance, substance however raised up again. Else the question whether or not we are to marry or to die once more would not have been asked, if they had not been casting doubt upon the restitution of that substance which is specifically the subject of death and of marriage, that is, the flesh. Thus you have the Lord affirming as against the heretics of the Jews that which is now being denied among the Sadducees of the Christians, a complete and entire resurrection.

[1] Cf. Matt. 22. 23–33; Mark 12. 18–23; Luke 20. 27–38.
[2] Luke 20. 37.
[3] Cf. Matt. 22. 32.   [4] Cf. Luke 20. 36.   [5] Luke 20. 36.

37 Sic et si carnem ait nihil prodesse, ex materia dicti dirigendus est sensus. nam quia durum et intolerabilem existimaverunt sermonem eius, quasi vere carnem suam illis edendam determinasset, et ut in spiritum disponeret statum salutis, praemisit *Spiritus est qui vivificat*, atque ita subiunxit, *Caro nihil prodest*, sed ad vivificandum scilicet. exsequitur etiam quid velit intellegi 2 spiritum, *Verba quae locutus sum vobis spiritus sunt, vita sunt*: sicut et supra, *Qui audit sermones meos et credit in eum qui me misit habet vitam aeternam et in iudicium non veniet sed transiet de morte in vitam*. itaque sermonem constituens vivificatorem, 3 quia spiritus et vita sermo, eundem etiam carnem suam dixit quia et sermo caro est factus, proinde in causam vitae adpetendus, et devorandus auditu et ruminandus intellectu et fide digerendus. nam et paulo ante carnem suam panem quoque caelestem pro- 4 nuntiarat, urgens usquequaque per allegoriam necessariorum pabulorum memoriam patrum qui panes et carnes Aegyptiorum praeverterant divinae vocationi. igitur conversus ad recogitatus 5 illorum, quia senserat dispargendos, *Caro* ait *nihil prodest*. quid hoc ad destruendam carnis resurrectionem? quasi non liceat esse aliquid, quod etsi nihil prodest aliud tamen ei prodesse possit. spiritus prodest, vivificat enim: caro nihil prodest, mortificatur enim. itaque secundum nos magis conlocavit utriusque proposi- 6 tionem. ostendens enim quid prosit et quid non prosit, pariter illuminavit quid cui prosit, spiritum scilicet carni, mortificatae vivificatorem: *Veniet enim* inquit *hora cum mortui audient* 7 *vocem filii dei et qui audierint vivent*. quid mortuum nisi caro?

37: 1 sic et si *Gel.*: licet si *MPX*: licet sic *T*.
    4 et ut *T*: ut *P*.
    6 sed *om. T Gel. Brf*.
    9 transiet *libri*: transibit *Gel*.: *cave ne scribas* transiit.
    17 praeverterant *MPX*: praeposuerant *T*.

37 So again, if he says the flesh profiteth nothing,[1] the meaning must take direction from the context of that remark. For seeing that they regarded his speech as hard and unbearable,[2] as though he had really prescribed his flesh for them to eat, since his purpose was to assign the establishment of salvation to the Spirit, he first said, *It is the Spirit that quickeneth*,[3] and only then added, *The flesh profiteth nothing*—towards quickening, of course. He also proceeds to state how he wishes 'the Spirit' to be understood: *The words which I have spoken unto you are spirit and are life*:[4] as also previously, *He that heareth my discourses and believeth in him that hath sent me hath eternal life and shall not come into judgement but shall pass over from death into life*.[5] And so, when establishing discourse as the life-giver (because the Discourse is spirit and life), he also said that it is his flesh, because the Discourse also was made flesh, and consequently must be sought after for an ⟨efficient⟩ cause of life, both to be eaten by hearing and chewed over by the understanding and digested by faith. For a little earlier he had pronounced that his flesh is also heavenly bread,[6] forcing from all sides, by the allegory of essential food, the memory of their fathers who preferred the bread and flesh of the Egyptians to the divine vocation. Therefore, turning back to their secret thoughts (because he had perceived that these needed to be broken down) he said, *The flesh profiteth nothing*.[7] What has this to do with overthrowing the resurrection of the flesh? Is it not possible for a thing to exist which, although it profit nothing, yet can receive profit from something else? The Spirit profiteth, for he giveth life: the flesh profiteth nothing, for it is put to death. And so it is rather in accordance with our ⟨view⟩ that he has determined the relationship of them both. For while showing what is profitable and what is not profitable he no less threw light on what is profitable to what, namely the Spirit to the flesh, the Lifegiver to that which is put to death. For he says, *The hour will come when the dead shall hear the voice of the Son of God, and those that have heard shall live*.[8] What is the dead thing, if not the flesh? and what is the voice of

[1] Cf. John 6. 63.　[2] Cf. John 6. 60.　[3] John 6. 63.
[4] John 6. 63.　[5] John 5. 24.　[6] Cf. John 6. 51.
[7] John 6. 63.　[8] John 5. 25.

et quid vox dei nisi sermo? et quid sermo nisi spiritus, merito carnem resuscitaturus quod factus est ipse, et ex morte quam passus est ipse, et ex sepulchro quo inlatus est ipse? denique cum 8
30 dicit, Ne miremini, quod veniet hora in qua omnes qui in monumentis sunt audient filii dei vocem, et procedent qui bona fecerunt in vitae resurrectionem, qui mala in resurrectionem iudicii, nemo iam poterit aliud mortuos interpretari qui sunt in monumentis nisi corpora et carnem, quia nec ipsa monumenta aliud quam cada-
35 verum stabula: siquidem et ipsi homines veteres, id est peccatores, 9 id est mortui per ignorantiam dei, quos monumenta intellegendos argumentantur haeretici, de monumentis processuri in iudicium aperte praedicantur. ceterum quomodo de monumentis monumenta procedent?

38 Post dicta domini etiam facta eius quid sapere credamus, de capulis, de sepulchris, mortuos resuscitantis? cui rei istud? si ad simplicem ostentationem potestatis aut ad praesentem gratiam redanimationis, non adeo magnum aliquid illi denuo morituros
5 suscitare. enimvero si ad fidem potius sequestrandam futurae 2 resurrectionis, ergo et illa corporalis praescribitur de documenti sui forma. nec sustinebo dicentes idcirco tunc resurrectionem 3 animae soli destinatam in carne quoque decucurrisse quia non potuisset aliter ostendi resurrectio animae invisibilis nisi per visibilis
10 substantiae resuscitationem. male deum norunt qui non putant illum 4 posse quod non putant. et tamen sciunt potuisse, si instrumentum Iohannis norunt: qui enim animas adhuc solas martyrum sub altari quiescentes conspectui subdidit, posset utique et resurgentes oculis exhibere sine carne. at ego deum malo decipere non posse, 5
15 de fallacia solummodo infirmum, ne aliter documenta praemisisse

30 quod *MPX*: cum *T*.
33 sunt *T*: sint *MPX* (*forsan recte*).
38: 1 credamus *MPX*: debemus *T* (*manifesto errore*).
2 suscitantis *T*.
4 aliquid *om. MPX*.
5 suscitari *MPX* (*falso*).
8 carnem *MPX*.   praecucurrisse *MP(X)*.

God, if not the Discourse? and what is the Discourse, if not the Spirit, who with good reason will raise up the flesh, that thing which he himself was made, from the death which he himself suffered, from the sepulchre into which he himself was brought? Lastly, when he says, *Marvel not, because the hour will come in which all who are in the tombs will hear the voice of the Son of God and will come forth, those that have done good things into the resurrection of life, and those that have done evil things into the resurrection of judgement*,[1] no one will any longer be able to interpret the dead who are in the tombs as anything else than bodies and flesh, seeing that tombs themselves are nothing else than lodging-places for corpses. And indeed the 'old men'[2] themselves, that is, the sinners, those who are dead through ignorance of God, those who the heretics argue must be understood as tombs, it is openly stated in the preaching will come forth from the tombs for judgement. And yet how can tombs come forth from tombs?

38 We have considered the Lord's words. Now what should we take to be the purport of his deeds, when he raises up the dead from their coffins and sepulchres? For what purpose was that? If for mere display of power or for present grace of reanimation, it was not a very great thing for him to raise them up when they were to die once more. But if it was rather with intent to commit to safe keeping the faith of the resurrection which is to be, it follows that this too is prejudged as corporal in accordance with the pattern laid down by this proof of it. Nor shall I tolerate their saying that on those occasions the resurrection, which is intended for the soul alone, in its preliminary course reached as far as the flesh because the resurrection of the invisible soul could not have been made evident except by means of the raising up again of the substance which is visible. They know God badly who think him unable to do what they do not think him able to do. And yet they know he was able, if they know John's document: for God who subjected to view the souls, as yet bodiless, of the martyrs, which were at rest beneath the altar,[3] could certainly without flesh have made them evident to men's eyes as they rose again. But I prefer

[1] John 5. 28–9. [2] Cf. Eph. 4. 22; Col. 3. 9.
[3] Cf. Apoc. 6. 9.

quam rem disposuisse videatur—immo ne, si exemplum resurrectionis sine carne non valuit inducere, multo magis plenitudinem exempli sine eadem substantia exhibere non possit. nullum vero 6 exemplum maius est eo cuius exemplum est. maius est autem si animae cum corporibus resuscitabuntur in documentum sine corpore resurgendi, ut tota hominis salus dimidiae patrocinaretur, quando exemplorum condicio illud potius expeteret quod minus haberetur, animae dico solius resurrectionem, velut gustum carnis etiam resurrecturae suo in tempore. atque adeo, secundum 7 nostram veritatem, exempla illa mortuorum a domino suscitatorum commendabant quidem et carnis et animae resuscitationem, ne cui substantiae negaretur hoc donum. qua tamen exempla, eo minus aliquid edebant: non enim in gloriam nec in incorruptibilitatem sed in mortem aliam suscitabantur.

39 Quam Christus ediderit resurrectionem apostolica quoque instrumenta testantur: nam et apostolis nullum aliud negotium fuit, dumtaxat apud Israelem, quam veteris testamenti resignandi et novi consignandi et potius iam dei in Christo contionandi. ita 2 et de resurrectione nihil novi intulerant, nisi quod et ipsam in gloriam Christi adnuntiabant, de cetero simplici et nota iam fide receptam sine ulla qualitatis quaestione, solis refragantibus Sadducaeis: adeo facilius fuit negari in totum mortuorum resurrectionem quam aliter intellegi. habes Paulum apud summos 3 sacerdotes sub tribuno inter Sadducaeos et Pharisaeos fidei suae professorem: Viri, inquit, fratres ego Pharisaeus sum, filius Pharisaeorum, de spe nunc et de resurrectione iudicor apud vos—

16 immo ne, etc. *Oehlerum secutus ita pungebam*: ne si *MPX*: si nec *T* (*quam scripturam si acceperis mox* non *omittere oportebit*).
18 in eadem substantia *MPX*.
20 corporibus *T*: corpore *MPX*.
25 veritatem *TB*ᵐᵍ·: vero aestimationem *MPX*, *unde Leopoldus* veri aestimationem, *forsan recte*.
26 resurrectionem *MPX*.
27 qua *Oeh. Brf.*: quae *libri*.
39: 5 intulerant *TMPX*: intulerunt *C Brf.* (*sed haud opus erat*).

to think that God cannot tell lies, that he is weak in deception only, so that he should not give the impression of having provided proofs beforehand in one fashion and established the fact itself in another. Nay rather, if he had not power without flesh to submit a precedent of resurrection, even more so will he be unable without that same substance to bring into evidence the full effect which the precedent represented. But no precedent is greater than that of which it is a precedent: yet greater it is if souls along with body are to be raised up again for a proof of their rising again without body, with the result that man's complete salvation should be guarantee for the half of it: for the very nature of precedents called rather for that which might be considered smaller, I mean a resurrection of a soul alone, as it might be a foretaste of flesh which was also to rise again at its due time. And consequently, according to the truth as we see it, those precedents of dead persons raised by the Lord did indeed supply proof of the resuscitation of both flesh and soul, so that this boon might be denied to neither substance, while yet, as being precedents, they provided somewhat less than this: for those persons were raised up not for glory nor for incorruptibility, but so as to die once more.

39 Also the apostolic documents give evidence of what resurrection Christ has announced. For the apostles had no other task, at least in Israel, than the unsealing of the Old Testament and the sealing of the New, and now rather of preaching God in Christ. Thus even concerning the resurrection they introduced nothing new, except that the resurrection itself they proclaimed to the glory of Christ.[1] Apart from that it was already accepted in simple and acknowledged faith without any question as to its nature, the Sadducees alone objecting: so much easier was it for the resurrection of the dead to be totally denied than for a different construction to be put upon it. You have Paul as a professor of his own faith before the chief priests, under the chief captain, between the Sadducees and the Pharisees.[2] *Men and brethren*, he says, *I am a Pharisee and the son of Pharisees: of the hope now and of the resurrection am I judged before you*[3]—evidently a hope they shared—so that,

[1] Cf. Luke 24. 26. [2] Cf. Acts 23. 1–9.
[3] Acts 23. 6.

utique communi, ne, quia iam transgressor legis videbatur, de praecipuo fidei totius articulo, id est de resurrectione, ad Sadducaeos sapere existimaretur. ita quam nolebat videri rescindere fidem resurrectionis utique confirmabat secundum Pharisaeos, respuens negatores eius Sadducaeos. proinde et apud Agrippam 4 nihil se ait proferre citra quam prophetae adnuntiassent. ergo servabat resurrectionem quoque qualem prophetae adnuntiaverant. nam et de resurrectione mortuorum apud Moysen scriptum 5 commemorans corporalem eam norat, in qua scilicet sanguis hominis exquiri habebit. itaque talem praedicabat qualem et 6 Pharisaei susceperant et dominus ipse defenderat et Sadducaei, ne talem quoque crederent, in totum esse noluerant. sed nec Athenienses aliam intellexerant a Paulo portendi: denique inriserant, non 7 inrisuri omnino si animae solius restitutionem ab eo audissent: suscepissent enim vernaculae suae philosophiae frequentiorem praesumptionem. at ubi iam nationes praeconium resurrectionis 8 inauditae retro ipsa novitate concussit, et digna incredulitas rei tantae quaestionibus fidem torquere coepit, tunc et apostolus per totum paene instrumentum fidem huius spei corroborare curavit, et esse eam ostendens et nondum transactam et, de quo magis quaerebatur, corporalem et, quod insuper dubitabatur, non aliter corporalem.

40 Nihil autem mirum si et ex ipsius instrumento argumenta captantur, cum oporteat haereses esse: quae esse non possent si non et perperam scripturae intellegi possent. nactae denique haereses 2 duos homines ab apostolo editos, interiorem, id est animam, et exteriorem, id est carnem, salutem quidem animae, id est interiori

13 communi ne quia *T Gel.*: *om.* ne *MPX*.
32 eam *MPX*: iam *T* (*quod manifesto falsum*).
40: 3 nactae *Gel.*: natae *MPX*: hancte *T*.

since he was already thought a transgressor of the law, he might not in respect of the chief article of the whole faith, that is, the resurrection, be suspected of thinking with the Sadducees. Thus that faith of the resurrection which he would not seem to annul, he straightway affirmed in agreement with the Pharisees while rejecting those deniers of it, the Sadducees.[1] Likewise also before Agrippa he said he professed nothing beyond what the prophets had proclaimed: so it follows that he retained the resurrection also, in the form in which the prophets had proclaimed it. For when he reminded them that it was written in Moses concerning the resurrection of the dead, he recognized that it was corporal, one, that is, in which a man's blood will have to be required.[2] And so he preached it in such form as the Pharisees too had accepted and as the Lord himself had maintained, while the Sadducees, to avoid believing it in that form, had totally denied its existence. Nor did the Athenians understand that any other was envisaged by Paul.[3] In fact they mocked, which they would by no means have done if they had heard from him of the restitution of the soul alone: for they would have accepted it as a more common supposition of their native philosophy. But when the preaching of a resurrection previously unheard-of had shaken the gentiles by its very novelty, and condign unbelief of so great a matter had begun to torment the faith with questionings, thereupon the apostle also took care throughout almost his whole writings to confirm the faith of this hope, showing both that it exists and has not yet been accomplished, and (a matter that was more often brought into question) that it is corporal, and (a point which was further in doubt) that it is not corporal in some unusual sense.

40 Now no wonder if captious arguments are drawn even from the apostle's own writings, seeing there must needs be heresies,[4] and these could not exist unless it were also possible for the scriptures to be perversely understood. The heresies then, seizing upon the fact that the apostle has set forth two men, the inner, which is the soul, and the outer, which is the flesh,[5] have adjudged

[1] Cf. Acts 26. 22.
[2] Cf. Acts 26. 22; Gen. 9. 5.
[3] Cf. Acts 17. 32.
[4] Cf. 1 Cor. 11. 19.
[5] Cf. 2 Cor. 4. 16.

homini, exitium vero carni, id est exteriori, adiudicaverunt, quia scriptum est Corinthiis, Nam etsi homo noster exterior corrumpitur, sed interior renovatur die et die. porro nec anima per semet- 3 ipsam homo, quae figmento iam *homini* appellato postea inserta est, nec caro sine anima homo, quae post exilium animae cadaver inscribitur. ita vocabulum homo consertarum substantiarum duarum quodammodo fibula est, sub quo vocabulo non possunt esse nisi cohaerentes. porro apostolus interiorem hominem non 4 tam animam quam mentem atque animum intellegi mavult, id est non substantiam ipsam sed substantiae saporem, siquidem Ephesiis scribens in interiorem hominem habitare Christum, sensibus utique intimandum dominum significavit. denique adiunxit, Per fidem, 5 et In cordibus vestris, et In dilectione, fidem quidem et dilectionem non substantiva animae ponens sed conceptiva: In cordibus autem dicens, quae substantiva sunt carnis, iam et ipsum interiorem hominem carni deputavit quem in corde constituit. inspice nunc 6 quomodo exteriorem quidem hominem corrumpi allegarit, interiorem vero renovari die ac die, ne illam corruptelam carnis adfirmes quam ex die mortis in perpetuum defectura patiatur, sed quam in istius vitae spatio ante mortem vexationibus et pressuris, tormentis atque suppliciis, nominis causa experi*tur*. nam et homo 7 interior hic utique renovari habebit, per suggestum spiritus proficiens fide et disciplina die ac die, non illic, id est non post resurrectionem, ubi non utique die ac die renovari habebit sed semel ad summam. de sequentibus disce: Quod enim ad praesens est, inquit, 8 temporale et leve pressurae nostrae, per supergressum in supergressum aeternum gloriae pondus perficit nobis, non intuentibus quae videntur—id est passiones—sed quae non videntur—id est mercedes—: quae enim videntur temporalia sunt, quae vero non videntur aeterna sunt. pressuras enim et lacsuras, quibus corrum- 9

8 die et die *M*: *alii alia, ad eundem sensum.*
9 homini *Gel.*: homine *MPX*: hominis *T*.
22 allegarit *T Gel.*: allegaret *MPX*.
26 experitur *Kroy.*: experiretur *T*: experietur *MPX*.

salvation to the soul, the inner man, but destruction to the flesh, the outer man, on the ground that it is written to the Corinthians, *For although our outward man is decaying, yet our inward man is being renewed from day to day.*[1] Now the soul by itself is not man, for the thing formed ⟨by God⟩ was already called 'man' before the soul was threaded into it:[2] nor is flesh without soul man, for after the soul's exile it is enregistered as 'corpse'. Thus the term 'man' is so to speak a pin joining together two inter-threaded substances, and they cannot be described by this term except when they cohere. But the apostle would rather have 'inner man' understood not as soul but as mind and intelligence, that is, not as the substance itself but as a flavour of the substance: for in writing to the Ephesians that Christ should dwell in the inner man he meant that the Lord must be made intimate to their thoughts. In fact he added *By faith*, and *In your hearts*, and *In love*,[3] setting down faith and love not as pertaining to the substance of the soul but to its content, while by saying *In your hearts*, which are of the substance of the flesh, he had already assigned even the inner man to the flesh by locating it in the heart. Look now in what sense he has suggested that the outward man is decaying while the inner man is being renewed from day to day: and take care not to assert that the decay of the flesh is that which it suffers after the day of death so as to disappear for ever: rather was it that which, in the course of this life, before death and even unto death, it was suffering for the sake of the Name, by tribulations and distresses, tortures and executions. For the inner man also will here and now need to be renewed by the supply of the Spirit, progressing in faith and doctrine from day to day, not hereafter, not after the resurrection, when we are to be renewed certainly not from day to day but once and for all. Learn from what follows: *For our temporal and light affliction which is for the present perfecteth for us by surpassing unto surpassing an eternal weight of glory, while we look not at the things which are seen*—that is, the sufferings—*but at the things which are not seen*—that is, the wages—*for the things which are seen are temporal, but the things which are not seen are eternal.*[4] For the oppressions and the injuries by

[1] 2 Cor. 4. 16.   [2] Cf. Gen. 2. 7.
[3] Eph. 3. 16–17.   [4] 2 Cor. 4. 17–18.

pitur homo exterior, ut leves et temporales idcirco contemnendas adfirmat, praeferens mercedum aeternarum et invisibilium et gloriae pondus in compensationem laborum quos hic caro patiendo corrumpitur. adeo non illa est corruptio quam in perpetuum carnis interitum ad resurrectionem expellendam exteriori homini adscribunt. sic et alibi, Siquidem ait compatimur uti et conglorificemur: reputo enim non esse dignas passiones huius temporis ad futuram gloriam quae in nos habet revelari. et hic minora ostendit incommoda praemiis suis. porro si per carnem compatimur cuius est proprie passionibus corrumpi, eiusdem erit et quod pro compassione promittitur. atque adeo carni adscript*urus* pressurarum proprietatem, ut et supra, dicit, Cum venissemus autem in Macedoniam nullam remissionem habuit caro nostra: dehinc, ut et animae daret compassionem, In omnibus inquit compressi, extrinsecus pugnae—debellantes scilicet carnem—intrinsecus timor —adflictans scilicet animam. adeo etsi corrumpitur homo exterior, non ut amittens resurrectionem sed ut sustinens vexationem corrumpi intellegitur, et hoc non sine interiore. ita amborum erit etiam conglorificari sicut et compati: secundum collegia laborum consortia quoque decurrant necesse est praemiorum.

41 Eandem adhuc sententiam exsequitur remunerationes vexationibus praeferens: Scimus enim, inquit, quoniam etsi terrena domus nostri tabernaculi dissolvatur, habemus domum non manu factam aeternam in caelis: id est, pro hoc quod dissolvetur caro nostra per passiones, domicilium consecuturi sumus in caelis. meminerat evangelicae definitionis, Beati qui persecutionem passi fuerint propter iustitiam, quia illorum est regnum caelorum. non

46 adscripturus *Oeh.*: adscribitur ut *MPX*: adscribit *T.*
41: 1 ad hoc *MPX.*
   3 nostra *T.*
   6 passi fuerint *T*: patiuntur *MPX.*

which the outer man is brought to decay, as being light and temporal, he declares are for that reason to be despised, while he gives preference to the weight of the eternal invisible wages and of the glory, to compensate for the labours which the flesh here suffers and is brought to decay: so far is he from meaning such decay as these persons, with intent to discountenance the resurrection, ascribe to the outer man to the perpetual destruction of the flesh. So also he says in another place, *Forasmuch as we suffer together, that we may be also glorified together: for I reckon that the sufferings of this time are not worthy in respect of the future glory which is to be revealed towards us.*[1] Here also he shows that the inconveniences are less than their rewards. Further, if it is by the flesh that we suffer together, and it specially appertains to the flesh to be brought to decay by sufferings, to the flesh also will pertain that which is promised ⟨as a reward⟩ for suffering together. And in like manner, with the intention of ascribing to the flesh its particular share in afflictions, as he has already done, he says, *But when we were come into Macedonia our flesh had no release*: and afterwards, so as to grant to the soul the sharing of sufferings, he says, *In all things distressed: without were fightings*—those which battle down the flesh—*within was fear*[2]—that which afflicts the soul. Thus although the outer man is decaying, it is understood to be decaying not as being deprived of resurrection but as suffering vexation, and that not apart from the inner man. So it will appertain to both to be glorified together just as it does to suffer together: for association in profits must of necessity run in accordance with partnership in toil.

41 The apostle takes the same thought one step further when he says that the rewards are greater than the vexations. *For we know*, he says, *that though the earthly house of our tabernacle is being dissolved, we have a house not made by hand, eternal in the heavens*:[3] that is, in recompense for our flesh being dissolved by sufferings, we shall acquire a dwelling in the heavens. He remembered the gospel pronouncement, *Blessed are they that shall have suffered persecution for righteousness' sake, because theirs is the kingdom of heaven.*[4] He did

---

[1] Rom. 8. 17-18. [2] 2 Cor. 7. 5.
[3] 2 Cor. 5. 1.   [4] Matt. 5. 10.

tamen carnis restitutionem negavit si compensationem mercedis opposuit, cum ipsi compensatio debeatur cui dissolutio reputatur, scilicet carni: sed quia domum dixerat carnem, eleganter voluit et 3 in mercedis comparatione vocabulo domus uti, ipsi domui quae dissolvetur per passionem meliorem domum repromittens per resurrectionem. nam et dominus multas mansiones quasi domos apud patrem repromittit. quanquam et de domicilio mundi potest 4 intellegi, quo dissoluto aeterna sedes repromittatur in caelis, quia et quae sequuntur ad carnem manifeste pertinentia ostendunt priora non ad carnem pertinere: divisionem enim facit apostolus 5 cum subicit, Nam et in hoc gemimus, domicilium nostrum quod de caelo est superinduere desiderantes, siquidem et exuti non nudi inveniemur: id est, ante volumus superinduere virtutem caelestem aeternitatis quam carne exuamur. huius enim gratiae privilegium 6 illos manet qui ab adventu domini deprehendentur in carne et propter duritias temporum antichristi merebuntur compendio mortis per demutationem expunctae concurrere cum resurgentibus, sicut Thessalonicensibus scribit: Hoc enim dicimus vobis in 7 sermone domini, quod nos qui vivimus, qui remanemus in adventum domini, non praeveniemus eos qui dormierunt: quoniam ipse dominus in iussu et voce et tuba dei descendet de caelo: et mortui in Christo resurgent primi, dehinc nos cum ipsis simul rapiemur in nubibus obviam Christo et ita semper cum domino erimus.

42 Horum demutationem ad Corinthios reddit dicens, Omnes quidem resurgemus, non autem omnes demutabimur, in atomo, in momentaneo motu oculi, in novissima tuba: sed illi scilicet soli qui invenientur in carne: Et mortui, inquit, resurgent et nos demutabimur. hac ergo prius dispositione prospecta reliqua 2

17 non *libri*: omnino *Urs.*
19 superindui *MPX.*
26 in adventu *MPX*: ad adventum *T.*
28 in voce angeli *P.*
42: 1 omnes quidem resurgemus *om. T.*
   5 prospecta *libri*: perspecta *Kroy.* (*perperam*).

not however deny the restitution of the flesh when he set in opposition the recompense of the reward, since the recompense is owed to that same thing to which the dissolution is accounted, namely, the flesh. But in that he had called the flesh a house, he was content tastefully to use the term 'house' in comparing the reward also, promising to that very house which will be dissolved through suffering a better house by virtue of the resurrection. For the Lord also promises many mansions, as it were houses, at his Father's.[1] For all that, it can also be understood as our dwelling-place the world, as that when this is dissolved an eternal abode is promised in heaven, for as the things which follow manifestly apply to the flesh they show that what goes before does not apply to the flesh. For the apostle makes a change of subject when he adds, *For in this we groan, desiring to clothe ourselves with our dwelling which is from heaven, if so be that, even unclothed, we shall not be found naked*:[2] that is, we wish to clothe ourselves with the heavenly virtue of eternity before being divested of the flesh. For the special grant of this grace awaits those who at the Lord's coming are found in the flesh and because of the hardnesses of the times of Antichrist will be counted worthy, by the short-cut of a death accomplished by means of change, to complete their course along with those who rise again, as he writes to the Thessalonians: *For this we say unto you in a discourse of the Lord, that we who are alive, who remain until the coming of the Lord, shall not prevent those who have fallen asleep: for the Lord himself will descend from heaven with a rallying-cry and the voice and the trumpet of God, and the dead in Christ will rise again first: and thereafter, we along with them shall be caught up together in the clouds to meet Christ, and so shall we ever be with the Lord.*[3]

42 The change which these undergo he reports to the Corinthians, saying, *We shall all indeed rise again but we shall not all be changed, in a moment, in the twinkling of an eye, at the last trump*—not all, but those only, he means, who are found in the flesh: *And the dead*, he continues, *will rise again, and we shall be changed.*[4] Having therefore first taken note of this order of events you will then refer

[1] Cf. John 14. 2. [2] 2 Cor. 5. 2–3.
[3] 1 Thess. 4. 15–17. [4] 1 Cor. 15. 51–2.

revocabis ad superiorem sensum. nam cum adicit, Oportet etenim corruptivum istud induere incorruptelam et mortale istud induere immortalitatem, hoc erit illud domicilium de caelo quod gementes in hac carne superinduere desideramus, utique super carnem in qua deprehendemur, quia gravari nos ait qui simus in tabernaculo, quod nolimus exui sed potius superindui, uti devoretur mortale a vita, scilicet dum demutatur superinduendo quod est de caelis. quis enim non desiderabit dum in carne est superinduere immortalitatem, et continuare vitam lucrifacta morte per vicariam demutationem, ne inferos experiatur usque novissimum quadrantem exacturos? ceterum demutationem etiam post resurrectionem consecuturus est inferos iam expertus. abhinc enim iam definimus carnem omnimodo quidem resurrecturam, atque illam ex demutatione superventura habitum angelicum suscepturam: aut si in his solis qui invenientur in carne demutari eam oportebit ut devoretur mortale a vita, id est caro ab illo superindumento caelesti et aeterno, ergo qui mortui deprehendentur vitam non consequentur, privati iam materia et ut ita dixerim esca vitae, id est carne: aut necesse est recipiant eam et illi, ut et in ipsis mortale devorari possit a vita, si vitam sunt consecuturi. sed in mortuis, inquis, iam devoratum erit mortale istud. non utique in omnibus: quantos enim licebit vel pridianos inveniri, tam recentia cadavera ut nihil in illis devoratum videri possit? utique enim devoratum non aliud existimas quam interceptum, quam abolitum, quam omni sensui ereptum, quod comparere omni genere cessaverit. nec gigantum autem antiquissima cadavera devorata constabit quorum

18 illam *TC*: illa *MPX* (*falso*).
30 sensui *T*: sensu *MPX*.

what follows to the sense already indicated. For when he adds, *For this corruptible thing must put on incorruption, and this mortal thing must put on immortality*,[1] this will be that dwelling-place from heaven with which, while groaning in this flesh, we desire to be clothed upon, surely 'upon' the flesh in which we shall be found: because he says we who are in the tabernacle are burdened because we would not be unclothed but rather clothed upon, that the mortal thing may be swallowed up of life,[2] evidently while it is being changed by being clothed upon with that which is from heaven. For who will not desire, while still in the flesh, to be clothed upon with immortality, and to carry on his life without a break, having profited over death by a change substituted for it, so as not to experience the hell which will exact the uttermost farthing?[3] Otherwise he will have to acquire his change even after the resurrection, having first experienced hell. For from now on I pronounce that the flesh will certainly rise again, and that, as a result of the change which will supervene, it will take upon it angelic attire. Otherwise, if the flesh is to need to be changed in the case of those only who are found in the flesh, so that the mortal thing may be swallowed up of life,[4] that is, the flesh swallowed up by that heavenly and eternal overgarment, then those who are found dead either will not attain to life, being already deprived of the material and, so to speak, the food on which life can feed, that is, the flesh; or else it must needs be that these also receive it back, so that in them too, if they are to attain to life, it may be possible for the mortal thing to be swallowed up of life. 'But', you say, 'in the case of the dead, that mortal thing will already have been swallowed up.' Not indeed in them all. For it is conceivable that a good number will be found in the state of having died the day before, corpses so fresh that it can seem that nothing in them has been swallowed up. For in fact your supposition is that 'swallowed up' means nothing less than suppressed, abolished, removed from all sense-perception, a thing which in every way has ceased to make its presence felt. But no one will deny that even those very ancient corpses of the giants have not been swallowed up, for their

[1] 1 Cor. 15. 53.
[2] Cf. 2 Cor. 5. 4.
[3] Cf. Matt. 5. 26; Luke 12. 59.
[4] Cf. 2 Cor. 5. 4.

crates adhuc vivunt: diximus iam de isto alibi. sed et proxime in 8
ista civitate cum *odei* fundamenta tot veterum sepulturarum sacrilega collocarentur, quingentorum fere annorum ossa adhuc
35 succida et capillos olentes populus exhorruit. constat non tantum
ossa durare verum et dentes incorruptos perennare, quae ut semina
retinentur fructificaturi corporis in resurrectione. postremo etsi 9
tunc devoratum invenietur mortale in omnibus mortuis, certe a
morte, certe ab aevo, certe per aetatem, numquid a vita, numquid
40 a superindumento, numquid ab immortalitatis ingestu? porro 10
qui ⟨ab⟩ his ait devoratum iri mortale, ab aliis negavit: et utique
hoc a divinis viribus, non a naturalibus legibus perfici praestarique
conveniet. ergo cum a vita habeat devorari quod mortale est, id 11
exhiberi omnifariam necesse est ut devoretur, et devorari ut
45 demutetur: si ignem dicas accendi oportere, non potes id per quod
accenditur alibi necessarium adfirmare alibi non. sic et cum 12
infulcit, Siquidem exuti non inveniemur nudi, de eis scilicet qui
non in vita nec in carne deprehendentur a die domini, non alias
negavit nudos quos praedixit exutos nisi quia et revestitos voluit
50 intellegi eadem substantia qua fuerant spoliati: ut nudi enim 13
invenientur carne deposita vel ex parte discissa sive detrita—et hoc
enim nuditas potest dici: dehinc recipient eam, ut reinduti carne
fieri possint etiam superinduti immortalitatem: superindui enim
nisi vestito iam convenire non poterit.

43 Proinde cum dicit, Itaque confisi semper, et scientes quod
cum immoramur in corpore peregrinamur a domino: per fidem
enim ambulamus, non per speciem: manifestum est hoc quoque
non pertinere ad offuscationem carnis quasi separantis nos a

33 odei *Gel.*: hodie *MPXR*[1]: eo die *R*[3]: fodiunt *T*.
37 fruticaturi *Jun.* (*perperam*).
41 qui ab *Gel.*: quia *MP*: qui *TX*.
45 potes *R*: potest *libri*.
47 inveniamur *T*.
52 et dehinc *TC*.   carne *libri*: carnem *Gel*.
54 sine vestitu *T*.

skeletons still survive. I have already spoken of this elsewhere.[1] Moreover quite recently in this city, when the foundations of the Odeum were being laid, to the desecration of many ancient burials, the populace was aghast at bones almost five hundred years old, yet still moist, and hair still scented. All admit that not only do bones endure, but teeth also continue undecayed, and that both these are preserved, as it were seeds of a body which is to come to fruit at the resurrection. Finally, although in all the dead the mortal thing shall then be found to have been swallowed up,[2] certainly this will be by death, by time, by age, and surely not by life, by the overgarment, or by the bestowal of immortality. For by alleging that the mortal thing will be swallowed up by these, he denies that it will be swallowed up by the others: and obviously it will be appropriate for this to be accomplished by divine power, and not by the laws of nature. Consequently, as that which is mortal has to be swallowed up of life, it is on all counts necessary for it to put in an appearance in order to be swallowed up, and to be swallowed up in order to be changed. If you say that a fire has to be lighted, you cannot say that the means of its being lighted is in one case necessary and in another not. So also when he inserts, *If so be that unclothed we shall not be found naked*,[3] evidently speaking of those who will be overtaken by the day of the Lord not alive or in the flesh, he denies the nakedness of those he has just referred to as unclothed, for no other reason than that he would have them understood to be dressed again in the same substance of which they had been stripped. For they will be found as it were naked when the flesh has been laid aside or partly stripped off or worn away, for even this can be called nakedness: afterwards they will receive it back, so that being reclothed with flesh they may be able also to be clothed upon with immortality. For to be clothed upon can evidently only apply to one who is already dressed.

43 Likewise when he says, *Being therefore always confident, and knowing that while we are at home in the body we are on pilgrimage from the Lord, for we are advancing by faith, not by sight*,[4] it is evident that this too is not concerned with the vilifying of the flesh as though it

---

[1] Cf. *De Anima* 51.
[2] Cf. 2 Cor. 5. 4.
[3] 2 Cor. 5. 3.
[4] 2 Cor. 5. 6–7.

domino: et hic enim exhortatio fastidiendae vitae huius obvertitur, siquidem peregrinamur a domino quamdiu vivimus, per fidem incedentes non per speciem, id est spe non re. et ideo subiungit, Fidentes autem et boni ducentes magis peregrinari a corpore et immorari ad dominum, scilicet ut per speciem magis incedamus quam per fidem, per rem potius quam per spem. vides quam et hic corporum contemptum ad martyriorum praestantiam referat: nemo enim peregrinatus a corpore statim immoratur penes dominum nisi ex martyrii praerogativa, paradiso scilicet, non inferis, deversurus. defecerant autem apostolo verba ad significandum de corpore excessum, an ratione etiam nove loquitur? temporalem enim absentiam a corpore volens significare peregrinari nos ab eo dixit, quoniam qui peregrinatur etiam revertetur in domicilium. exinde iam ad omnes, Gestimus, inquit, sive peregrinantes sive immorantes placibiles esse deo: omnes enim manifestari nos oportet pro tribunali Christi Iesu. si omnes, et totos: si omnes, et interiores et exteriores, id est tam animas quam et corpora. Ut unusquisque, inquit, reportet quae per corpus secundum quae gessit, bonum sive malum. hoc iam quomodo legas quaero: quasi turbate enim per hyperbaton struxit: utrumne 'quae per corpus reportanda erunt' an 'quae per corpus gesta sunt'? sed et si 'quae per corpus reportanda sunt', corporalis indubitate resurrectio est: et si 'quae per corpus gesta sunt', per corpus utique pensanda sunt per quod et gesta sunt. ita totus hic a capite tractatus apostoli, tali clausula detextus qua carnis resurrectio ostenditur, secundum haec erit intellegendus quae cum clausula consonant.

43: 5-6 et hic enim...peregrinamur a domino *TB*: om. *MPX*.
    8 boni *T*: bonum *MPX*.
    17 revertetur *TMPX*: revertitur *Eng.* (*sed haud opus erat*).
    18 iam *T*: etiam *MPX*.
    20 si omnes (*altera vice*) *libri*: si totos *Gel. edd. sed vereor ut recte*.
    22 quod gessit *T*.
    24 instruxit *MPX*.
    26-7 reportanda sunt...per corpus (*priove vice*) om. *T*.

separated us from the Lord. For here also is brought to our attention an exhortation to despise this present life, inasmuch as we are in exile from the Lord as long as we live, advancing by faith and not by sight, that is, in hope and not in reality. And consequently he adds, *But being confident, and thinking it good rather to be on pilgrimage from the body and to be at home with the Lord,*[1] evidently so as to advance rather by sight than by faith, by reality rather than by hope. You see how here too he relates the belittling of bodies to the excellence of martyrdoms. For no one is at home with the Lord immediately on going into exile from the body except by the prerogative of martyrdom, in which case he will take up his lodging in paradise and not in hell. But was the apostle short of words to signify departure from the body, or had he a good reason for using a novel expression? Yes, it was because he would signify a temporary absence from the body, that he spoke of our being on pilgrimage from it, because one who is on pilgrimage will also return to his home. After that he says, now with reference to all, *We are eager, whether on pilgrimage or at home, to be pleasing to God: for we must all be presented before the judgement-seat of Christ* Jesus.[2] If all, then the whole: if them all, then both inner and outer man, that is, bodies no less than souls: *so that each one,* he says, *may receive back the things by means of the body according to what he hath done, a good thing or else an evil one.*[3] How, I ask, do you read this? For he has drawn it up as it were confusedly, by transposition of words. Does he mean the things which must be received back by means of the body, or the things which were done by means of the body? Now if he means the things which must be received back by means of the body, beyond doubt the resurrection is corporal: while if he means the things which were done by means of the body, by means of the body surely they must be recompensed, for by means of it they were performed. So, seeing the apostle's discussion is unravelled by the kind of conclusion in which the resurrection of the flesh is proved, the whole of it from its beginning will need to be understood in these terms, for they are in harmony with its conclusion.

[1] 2 Cor. 5. 8. [2] 2 Cor. 5. 9–10.
[3] 2 Cor. 5. 10.

44 Si enim adhuc ad superiora respectes unde mentio hominis exterioris et interioris inducta est, nonne et dignitatem et spem carnis integram invenies? cum enim de lumine quod illuxerit **2** deus in cordibus nostris ad illuminationem agnitionis gloriae suae in persona Christi, dicit habere nos thesaurum istum in testaceis vasis, scilicet in carne, utrumne quia testacea est secundum originem ex limo destruetur, an quia divini thesauri conditorium est extolletur? atquin si lumen ipsum dei illud verum quod est in **3** persona Christi vitam in se continet, eaque vita committitur cum lumine in carnem, peritura est in quam vita committitur? plane, si periturus et ipse thesaurus: perituris enim peritura creduntur, sicut veteribus utribus novum vinum. cum item subicit, Semper **4** mortificationem Christi Iesu circumferentes in corpore nostro, qualis ista res est, quae post dei templum iam et sepulchrum Christi potest dici? cur autem mortificationem domini circum- **5** ferimus in corpore? Ut et vita, inquit, manifestetur. ubi? In corpore. in quo? In mortali. ergo in carne, plane mortali secundum culpam sed et vitali secundum gratiam—vide quantam, ut in illa vita Christi manifestetur. in re ergo aliena salutis, in **6** substantia perpetuae dissolutionis, manifestabitur vita Christi aeterna iugis incorrupta, iam et dei vita? aut cuius temporis vita domini manifestabitur in corpore nostro? illa quidem quam vixit **7** usque in passionem, non modo apud Iudaeos in manifesto fuit verum etiam omnibus nunc gentibus prodita est. adeo eam significat quae portas adamantinas mortis et aeneas seras inferorum infregit, quae exinde iam nostra est. denique manifestabitur in **8** corpore. quando? post mortem. quomodo? dum resurgimus in

44: 7 conditorium *MPX*: vas *T*.
 8 dei *TB*: *om. MPX*.
 22 quam *CX*: qua *TMP*.

44 If you look back now at the preceding sentences, beyond the point at which the mention of outer and inner man was introduced,[1] shall you not find both the dignity and the hope of the flesh unimpaired? For when, speaking of the light which God has made to shine in our hearts unto the illumination of the knowledge of his glory in the person of Christ, the apostle says that we have this treasure in earthen vessels, that is, in the flesh,[2] is the flesh, because it is earthen, to be thrown down in accordance with its origin from mud, or not rather to be lifted up because it is a receptacle of divine treasure? Yea more, if that very light of God, that true light which is in the person of Christ, contains life in itself, and that life along with the light is deposited in flesh, is that flesh to perish in which life is deposited? Evidently so, if the treasure itself is to perish: for things entrusted to perishable things themselves perish, like new wine put in old wineskins.[3] When again he adds, *Always bearing about in our body the dying of Christ Jesus,*[4] what manner of thing is this, which can first be called the temple of God,[5] and then the sepulchre of Christ? But to what purpose do we bear about in the body the dying of the Lord? *So that the life also*, he says, *may be manifested*. Where? *In the body*. Which? *The mortal body*.[6] In the flesh then, which evidently is mortal according to guilt, but vital according to grace: and see how great a grace, that in it the life of Christ should be manifested. Can it then be that in a thing alien to salvation, a substance destined to perpetual dissolution, there shall be manifested that life of Christ which is eternal, perennial, incorruptible, which was from the first the life of God? Or what period of the Lord's life will be manifested in our body? That life indeed which he lived until his passion, was not only manifest among the Jews but has now also been published to all the gentiles. Therefore he means that which has broken down the adamantine gates of death and the brazen bolts of hell,[7] that life which from thenceforth has become ours. Once more, it is to be manifested in the body. When? After death. How? When we rise again in the body, as Christ did. For, so that no one may argue

[1] Cf. 2 Cor. 4. 16. [2] Cf. 2 Cor. 4. 6–7.
[3] Cf. Matt. 9. 17; Mark 2. 22; Luke 5. 37. [4] 2 Cor. 4. 10.
[5] Cf. 1 Cor. 3. 16. [6] 2 Cor. 4. 11. [7] Cf. Ps. 107. 16.

corpore, sicut et Christus. ne enim quis argumentetur nunc habere manifestari vitam Iesu in corpore nostro per disciplinam
30 sanctitatis et patientiae et iustitiae et sapientiae quibus domini vita floruit, providentissima apostoli intentio suggerit, Si enim nos qui 9 vivimus in mortem tradimur propter Iesum, ut et vita eius manifestetur in corpore nostro mortali: adeo defunctis nobis hoc ait futurum in corpore nostro. quodsi tunc, quomodo nisi resuscitato
35 eo? proinde et in clausula, Scientes ait quod qui suscitavit Iesum, 10 et nos suscitabit cum ipso: quia iam resurrexit a mortuis: nisi quia 'cum ipso' 'sicut ipsum' sapit. si vero sicut ipsum, non utique sine carne.

45 Sed et rursus alia caecitate in duos homines impingunt, in veterem et in novum, monente apostolo deponere nos veterem hominem qui corrumpitur per concupiscentias seductionis, renovari autem spiritu sensus et induere novum hominem qui secun-
5 dum deum conditus est in iustitia et religione veritatis, ut et hic ad duas substantias distinguendo, vetustatem ad carnem, novitatem ad animam, corruptionem perpetuam veteri defendant, id est carni. porro si secundum substantias, nec anima novus homo quia 2 posterior, nec caro ideo vetus quia prior: quantulum enim temporis
10 inter manum dei et adflatum? ausim dicere, etiam si multo prior 3 anima caro, eo ipso quod anima impleri se expectavit priorem eam fecit: omnis enim consummatio atque perfectio, etsi ordine postumat, effectu anticipat: magis illud prius est sine quo priora non possunt. si caro vetus homo, quando istud? a primordio? 4
15 atquin Adam novus totus, et ex novo vetus nemo. nam et exinde a benedictione geniturae caro atque anima simul fiunt sine calculo temporis, ut quae simul in utero seminantur, quod docuimus in commentario animae: contemporant fetu, coaetant natu: duos 5

    31 suggerit *T*: ingerit *MPX*.
    33 adeo *T Gel.*: ideo *MPX*.
    36 quia iam *et quae sequuntur ita pungebam*.   resurrexit *TMX*: resurrexerit *P*.
  45: 3 concupiscentias *T*: concupiscentiam *MPX*.
    7 defendat *MPX* (*manifesto errore*).
    10 flatum *T*.
    11 quam caro *TB* (*prorsus contra sensum scriptoris*).
    14 esse non possunt *T* (*ut videtur*).

that the life of Jesus has now to be manifested in our body by means of the discipline of holiness and patience and righteousness and wisdom, qualities in which the Lord's life came to flower, the apostle's very foresighted statement subjoins, *Forasmuch as we who live are being delivered to death for Jesus' sake, so that his life also may be manifested in our mortal body.*[1] Thus he means that this will come to pass in our body after we are dead. But if then, how, unless it has been raised again? Accordingly he also says, at the conclusion, *Knowing that he who hath raised up Jesus will also raise us up along with him,*[2] because he has already risen again from the dead: unless it is that 'along with him' means 'like him'. But if it means 'like him', then certainly not without flesh.

45 Yet once more, by another piece of blindness, they stumble up against two men, the old man and the new,[3] when the apostle enjoins us to put off the old man, who is being corrupted through the lusts of deceit, and to be renewed in the spirit of the mind and to put on the new man who according to God has been created in the righteousness and religion of the truth: so that here also, by making a distinction into two substances, ⟨assigning⟩ oldness to flesh and newness to soul, they may claim perpetual corruption for the old ⟨man⟩, that is, the flesh. Yet if the distinction is according to substances, neither is the soul the new man because it is later, nor is the flesh the old man because earlier. For how short a time was there between the hand of God and his breathing! I would be bold to say, Even if the flesh were much earlier than the soul, by the very fact that it waited for itself to be filled with soul it made the soul earlier. For every consummation and perfection, though subsequent in sequence, is previous in effect. A thing is earlier than earlier if without it earlier things cannot exist. If the flesh is the old man, when did it become so? From the beginning? Yet Adam was wholly new, and no man reverts back from new to old. For ever since the blessing of their procreation flesh and soul come into existence together,[4] without reckoning of time, as things which are simultaneously sown in the womb, as I have taught in my treatise On the Soul.[5] They are contemporaries at

[1] 2 Cor. 4. 11. [2] 2 Cor. 4. 14. [3] Cf. Eph. 4. 21–24.
[4] Cf. Gen. 1. 28. [5] Cf. *De Anima* 27.

istos homines, sane ex substantia duplici, non tamen et aetate, sic
20 unum edunt dum prior neutra est. citius est totos nos aut veteres
aut novos esse: qua enim alterum possumus esse, nescimus. sed 6
apostolus veterem hominem manifeste notat: Expone, enim inquit,
secundum pristinam conversationem veterem hominem, non
secundum alicuius substantiae senium. neque enim carnem prae-
25 cipit deponamus, sed quae et alibi carnalia ostendit, opera non
corpora accusans. de quibus et hic subicit, Deponentes mendacium 7
loquimini veritatem unusquisque ad proximum suum, quoniam
membra alterutrum sumus. irascimini autem et nolite delinquere: 8
sol non occidat super iracundiam vestram, neque dederitis diabolo
30 locum. qui furabatur iam non furetur, immo potius laboret 9
operando manibus, ut habeat impertire indigenti. omnis sermo 10
turpis non procedat ex ore vestro, sed qui sit optimus ad aedificationem fidei, ut gratiam audientibus praestet. et nolite contristare 11
spiritum dei sanctum, in quo signati estis in redemptionis diem.
35 omnis amaritudo et ira et clamor et blasphemia auferatur a vobis 12
cum omni malitia: estote autem in alterutrum benigni miseri- 13
cordes, donantes invicem sicut et deus vobis donavit in Christo.
igitur, qui carnem veterem hominem existimant cur non mortem 14
sibi properant ut vetere homine deposito praeceptis apostoli occur-
40 rant? nos enim, qui totam fidem in carne administrandam credi- 15
mus, immo et per carnem, cuius est et os ad proferendum optimum
quemque sermonem et lingua ad non blasphemandum et cor ad
non indignandum et manus ad operandum et largiendum, tam
vetustatem hominis quam novitatem ad moralem non ad sub-
45 stantialem differentiam defendimus. atque ita pariter agnoscimus 16
hominem qui secundum pristinam conversationem vetus fuerit,
eundem et corrumpi ita dictum secundum concupiscentias
seductionis quemadmodum et veterem secundum pristinam conversationem, non secundum carnem per interitum perpetuum,

20 *quaero an scribendum* et veteres et novos.
35 ira animi *T*.
47 concupiscentias *T*: concupiscentiam *MPX*.

conception, of one age at birth. They bring to birth as one these two men, certainly of double substance, though not of double age, since neither is the elder. It is easier to regard us as being wholly either old or new: for how we can be one without the other, we know not. But the apostle sets a clear mark upon the old man: for he says, *Put off the man who is old according to former conversation,*[1] not 'according to the decrepitude of some substance or other'. For he is not instructing us to put away the flesh, but those things which he elsewhere describes as carnal,[2] bringing accusation not against bodies but against works, of which also he adds here, *Putting away lying, speak the truth each man to his neighbour, for we are members one of another. But be ye angry and sin not: let not the sun go down upon your wrath, neither give place to the devil. Let him that stole steal no more, yea rather let him labour by working with his hands, that he may have to impart to him that is in need. Let no ugly speech proceed out of your mouth, but that which is best for the edifying of faith, that it may minister grace to the hearers. And grieve not the Holy Spirit of God, in whom ye are sealed unto the day of redemption. Let all bitterness and wrath and clamour and blasphemy be taken away from you, with all malice. But be kind one to another, merciful, forgiving one another, even as God hath in Christ forgiven you.*[3] Why then do these who regard the flesh as the old man not bring speedy death upon themselves, so that by putting off the old man they may hasten to meet the apostle's precepts? We however, in our belief that the whole faith must be administered in the flesh, and even through the flesh—for to it belongs the mouth for bringing forth every good speech, and the tongue for not blaspheming, and the heart for not being indignant, and the hands for working and for imparting—claim that both the oldness of man and his newness imply not a substantial but a moral difference. And thus no less do we acknowledge that the same man who was old according to his former conversation is said ⟨by the apostle⟩ to be corrupt according to the lusts of deceit in the same sense as ⟨he is called⟩ old according to his former conversation—not corrupt according to the flesh by a perpetual destruction, but rather, his flesh being

---

[1] Eph. 4. 22. [2] Cf. Gal. 5. 19.
[3] Eph. 4. 25–32.

50 ceterum salva carne tam salvum quam eundem, utpote vitiosam disciplinam, non corpulentiam, exutum.

46 Talem ubique apostolum recognoscas, ita carnis opera damnantem ut carnem damnare videatur, sed ne ita quis existimet ex aliorum vel cohaerentium sensuum suggestu procurantem. nam et 2 dicens eos qui in carne sunt deo placere non posse, statim de pravo
5 intellectu ad integrum revocat adiciens, Vos autem non estis in carne sed in spiritu. eos enim quos in carne esse constabat negando 3 in carne esse, in operibus carnis non esse monstrabat, atque ita illos demum deo placere non posse, non qui in carne essent sed qui carnaliter viverent, placere autem illos deo qui in carne positi
10 secundum spiritum incederent. et rursus corpus quidem ait 4 mortuum, sed propter delinquentiam, sicut spiritum vitam propter iustitiam: vitam autem morti opponens in carne constitutae, sine dubio illic et vitam repromisit ex iustitia ubi mortem determinavit ex delinquentia. ceterum frustra opposuit vitam morti ⟨si⟩ non est 5
15 illic ubi est ipsa cui eam opposuit, excludendae utique de corpore. porro si vita mortem de corpore excludit, non potest id perficere nisi illud penetret ubi est quod excludit. et quid ego nodosius, cum 6 apostolus absolutius? Si enim, inquit, spiritus eius qui suscitavit Iesum habitat in vobis, qui suscitavit Iesum a mortuis suscitabit et
20 mortalia corpora vestra propter inhabitantem spiritum eius in vobis: ut et si animam quis corpus mortale praesumpserit, cum 7 hoc et carnem negare non possit carnis quoque resuscitationem cogatur agnoscere secundum eiusdem status communionem. ex 8 sequentibus adhuc discas opera carnis damnari, non ipsam: Itaque,
25 fratres, ait, debitores sumus non carni ad vivendum ⟨secundum carnem⟩: si enim secundum carnem vixeritis futurum est ut moriamini, si vero spiritu carnis actus mortificaveritis vivetis. porro, ut 9

50 salva *Brf.*: salve *T*: om. *MPX, forsan recte.*
46: 14 si *add. R.*
    16 porro...de corpore *om. T.*
    17 illud *libri*: illuc *Latinius (forsan recte).*
    25–6 secundum carnem *add. Kroy.*

saved, both the same man and a saved man, seeing he has stripped himself not of his corporeity but of his vicious conduct.

46 You may find the apostle always like this, condemning the works of the flesh in such terms as to seem to condemn the flesh, yet by the provision of thoughts from elsewhere, or even from the same context, taking precaution that no one should so think. For when he says that those who are in the flesh cannot please God,[1] he immediately recalls us from corrupt to sound understanding by adding, *But ye are not in the flesh but in the Spirit.*[2] For by denying that those were in the flesh who it was evident were in the flesh, he indicated that they were not in the works of the flesh, and thus in fine that those who could not please God were not such as were in the flesh but such as lived in fleshly fashion; while those did please God who though located in the flesh were walking according to the Spirit. And again he says that the body indeed is dead—yet because of transgression, even as he says the Spirit is life because of righteousness.[3] But, when opposing life to the death which is situated in the flesh, there is no doubt that he promised life as a result of righteousness in the same sphere in which he decreed death as a result of transgression: else in vain did he oppose life to death, if it is not in the same sphere as that death to which he opposed it—evidently with the idea of its being expelled from the body. Now if life expels death from the body it can only do so by penetrating that in which that is which it expels. But why should I argue with such complexity, when the apostle speaks with less reserve? *For if,* he says, *the Spirit of him who raised up Jesus dwelleth in you, he who raised up Jesus from the dead will also raise up your mortal bodies because of his Spirit who dwelleth in you.*[4] So that even if someone has made up his mind that 'mortal body' means the soul, yet since he cannot deny that the flesh also is a mortal body, he is forced to acknowledge the raising up of the flesh as well, according as each of them shares that quality which the other has. From what follows, you may learn once more that it is the works of the flesh that are condemned, not the flesh itself. *Therefore, brethren,* he says, *we are debtors not to the flesh to live after the flesh: for if ye live*

---

[1] Cf. Rom. 8. 8.   [2] Rom. 8. 9.
[3] Cf. Rom. 8. 10.   [4] Rom. 8. 11.

ad singula quaeque respondeam, si in carne constitutis secundum spiritum tamen degentibus salus repromittitur, iam non caro
30 adversatur saluti sed operatio carnis: operatione autem carnis exclusa, quae causa est mortis, salva iam caro ostenditur, causa carens mortis. Lex enim, inquit, spiritus vitae in Christo Iesu 10 manumisit me a lege delinquentiae et mortis—certe quam praemisit habitare in membris nostris. ergo iam membra nostra legi mortis
35 non tenebuntur, quia nec delinquentiae, a quibus manumissa sunt. Quod enim invalidum erat legis, in quo infirmabatur per carnem, 11 misso deus filio suo in simulacro carnis delinquentiae et per delinquentiam, damnavit delinquentiam in carne—non carnem in delinquentia: neque enim domus cum habitatore damnabitur:
40 habitare enim peccatum dixit in corpore nostro. damnata autem 12 delinquentia caro absoluta est, sicut indemnata ea legi mortis et delinquentiae obstricta est. sic etsi sensum carnis mortem appellavit, dehinc et inimicitiam ad deum, sed non carnem ipsam. cui 13 ergo, dices, reputabitur sensus carnis si non substantiae ipsi? plane,
45 si probaveris aliquid carnem de suo sapere. si vero sine anima nullius est sensus, intelleges sensum carnis ad animam esse referendum, carni interdum deputatum quia propter carnem et per carnem administratur. et ideo habitare ait delinquentiam in 14 carne, quia et anima a qua delinquentia inducitur inquilina est
50 carnis, mortificatae quidem, sed non suo verum delinquentiae

  33 me *MPX*: te *TB* ⲙⲉ·.
  34 legi *T*: lege *MPX*.
  44 plane si *om. T*.
  47 propter carnem et *om. T Gel*.

after the flesh ye shall die: but if by the Spirit ye mortify the deeds of the flesh ye shall live.[1] So then, that I may reply to all the questions severally: if it is to those who are situated in the flesh but are dwelling according to the Spirit, that salvation is promised, in that case it is not the flesh, but the operation of the flesh, which is hostile to salvation. But when the operation of the flesh, which is the cause of death, has been expelled, the flesh is at once proved to be saved, since it is free from the cause of death: *For*, he says, *the law of the Spirit of life in Christ Jesus hath set me free from the law of transgression and death*[2]—evidently that law which he has already said dwells in our members.[3] Consequently our members will no longer be held to the law of death, because neither are they held to the law of transgression, from both which laws they have been set free. *For, that wherein the law was powerless, that in which it was being made weak through the flesh, God, having sent his own Son in the likeness of the flesh of transgression, and by means of transgression, hath condemned transgression in the flesh*[4]—not the flesh in the transgression, for neither is a house to be condemned along with its inhabitant. For he has said that sin is an inhabitant of our body.[5] But when the transgression was condemned the flesh was acquitted, just as, when transgression was uncondemned, the flesh was under bond to the law of death and transgression. Thus though he has described the mind of the flesh as death,[6] and consequently as enmity towards God, yet he does not so describe the flesh itself. To what then, you will ask, is the mind of the flesh to be accounted, if not to that substance itself? Evidently to it, if you prove that the flesh has any consciousness of its own. But if apart from the soul it has no mind, you must understand that the mind of the flesh is to be referred to the soul, though it is for a time accounted to the flesh because it is for the sake of the flesh and by means of the flesh that it is administered. And for this reason he says that transgression dwells in the flesh,[7] because the soul also, by which transgression is introduced, is an inmate of the flesh, and the flesh has indeed been put to death, not however on its own account but on account of

[1] Rom. 8. 12–13.   [2] Rom. 8. 2.   [3] Cf. Rom. 7. 23.
[4] Rom. 8. 3.   [5] Cf. Rom. 7. 17.   [6] Cf. Rom. 8. 6–7.
[7] Cf. Rom. 7. 17.

nomine. nam et alibi, Quomodo, inquit, etiam nunc velut 15
viventes in mundo sententiam fertis?—non ad mortuos scribens
sed ad eos qui desinere deberent mundialiter vivere.

47 Haec enim erit vita mundialis quam veterem hominem dicit
confixum esse Christo, non corporalitatem sed moralitatem.
ceterum si non ita accipimus, non est corporalitas nostra confixa,
nec crucem Christi caro nostra perpessa est, sed quemadmodum
5 adiecit, Ut evacuetur corpus delinquentiae, per emendationem
vitae, non per interitum substantiae: sicut ait, Uti hactenus
delinquentiae serviamus, ut et hac ratione commortui in Christo
credamus quod etiam convivemus illi. Sic, enim inquit, et vos 2
reputate mortuos quidem vos. cuinam? carni? non, sed
10 delinquentiae. ergo salvi erunt carni, viventes autem deo in
Christo Iesu, per carnem utique cui mortui non erunt, delinquentiae scilicet mortui, non carni. nam et adhuc ingerit, Ne ergo 3
regnaverit in corpore vestro mortali delinquentia ad obaudiendum
illi et ad exhibendum membra vestra arma iniustitiae delinquentiae:
15 sed exhibete vosmetipsos deo velut ex mortuis vivos—non velut
vivos sed velut ex mortuis vivos—et membra vestra arma iustititae.
et rursus: Sicut exhibuistis membra vestra famula immunditiae et 4
iniquitatis ad iniquitatem, ita et nunc exhibete membra vestra
famula iustitiae in sanctificium: cum enim servi essetis delinquen-
20 tiae liberi eratis iustitiae: quem ergo fructum habebatis super his de 5
quibus nunc confundimini? finis enim illorum mors. nunc vero 6
liberi facti a delinquentia, famulati autem deo, habetis fructum
vestrum in sanctificium, finem autem vitam aeternam: stipendia 7
enim delinquentiae mors, donativum autem dei vita aeterna in
25 Christo Iesu domino nostro. ita per totam hanc sensuum seriem 8
ab iniustitia et delinquentia membra nostra divellens, et iustitiae

47: 1 enim *om. T.*   quam *MPX*: qua *T.*
  2 mortalitatem *T (falso).*
  4 sqq. *forsan post* perpessa est *gravius interpungendum sit, levius autem post* interitum substantiae, *ut deinde legas sic* ait.
  8 credamur *T (forsan recte).*
  15–16 vivos non...ex mortuis vivos *om. T.*
  21 enim *T*: ergo *MPX.*
  25 per portam hanc sensuum seriemque *MPX (male).*

the transgression. For he says also in another place, *How, even now, as though living in the world, do ye pass judgement?*,[1] when he is not writing to dead men but to those who ought to be ceasing to live in worldly fashion.

47 It will be this worldly living which he calls the old man, who he says was crucified together with Christ,[2] not a corporal constitution but a moral character. Otherwise, if we do not so take it, our corporal constitution has not been crucified together, nor has our flesh suffered the cross of Christ; but as he has added, *That the body of transgression may be made void*,[3] by amendment of life, not by destruction of its substance, even so he says, *That henceforth we may not be in bondage to transgression*,[4] so that, having on this reckoning also died together with Christ, we may believe that we shall also be alive along with him. For he says, *Even so ye, reckon ye yourselves dead indeed*:[5] to what? to the flesh? No, but *to transgression*. Consequently they will be saved to the flesh, but alive to God in Christ Jesus, by means of the flesh surely to which they will not be dead, seeing they are dead to transgression, not to the flesh. For he adds yet once more, *Let not therefore transgression reign in your mortal body for you to obey it and to present your members to transgression as weapons of unrighteousness: but present yourselves to God as those that are alive from the dead*—not 'as those alive' but 'as those alive from the dead'—*and your members as weapons of righteousness*.[6] And again, *As ye have presented your members as servants of uncleanness and iniquity unto iniquity, so also now present your members as servants of righteousness unto sanctifying. For when ye were the slaves of transgression ye were free of righteousness. What fruit therefore had ye in respect of the things of which ye are now ashamed? For the end of those things is death. Now however, having been made free from transgression and become servants to God, ye have your fruit unto sanctifying, and the end everlasting life: for the wages of transgression is death, but God's gratuity is eternal life in Christ Jesus our Lord.*[7] Thus while throughout this whole sequence of thoughts he dissevers our members from unrighteousness and transgression and conjoins

[1] Col. 2. 20.   [2] Cf. Rom. 6. 6.   [3] Ibid.
[4] Ibid.   [5] Rom. 6. 11.   [6] Rom. 6. 11-13.
[7] Rom. 6. 19-23.

et sanctimoniae adiungens, et transferens eadem a stipendio mortis ad donativum vitae aeternae, carni utique compensationem salutis repromittit: cui nullam omnino competisset imperari propriam sanctimoniae et iustitiae disciplinam si non ipsius esset et praemium disciplinae, sed nec ipsum baptisma committi si per regenerationem non etiam restitutioni inauguraretur, hoc quoque apostolo ingerente: An ignoratis quod quicunque in Iesum tincti sumus in mortem eius tincti sumus? consepulti ergo illi sumus per baptisma in mortem, uti quemadmodum surrexit Christus a mortuis ita et nos in novitate vitae incedamus. ac ne de ista tantum vita putes dictum quae ex fide post baptisma in novitate vivenda est, providentissime adstruit, Si enim consati sumus simulacro mortis Christi, sed et resurrectionis erimus: per simulacrum enim morimur in baptismate, sed per veritatem resurgimus in carne, sicut et Christus: Ut sicut regnavit in morte delictum, ita et gratia regnet per iustitiam in vitam sempiternam per Iesum Christum dominum nostrum. quomodo 'ita', si non aeque in carne? ubi enim mors, ibi et vita post mortem, quia et vita ibi ante ubi postea mors. nam si regnum mortis nihil operatur quam carnis dissolutionem, proinde vitam contrariam morti contrarium oportet operari, id est carnis redintegrationem, ut sicut devoraverat mors invalescendo, ita et mortali devorato ab immortalitate audire possit, Ubi est mors aculeus tuus, ubi est mors contentio tua? sic enim et gratia illic superabundabit ubi et iniquitas abundavit: sic et virtus in infirmitate perficietur, quod periit salvum faciens, quod mortuum est vivificans, quod percussum est sanans, quod languit medicans, quod ereptum est redimens, quod famulatum est liberans, quod seductum est revocans, quod elisum est suscitans, et quidem de

34 *pro* tincti (*altera vice*), intincti *T*.

them to righteousness and holiness, transferring them also from the wages which is death to the gratuity which is life eternal, he evidently promises the flesh the recompense of salvation: for it would on no account have been fitting to demand of it any discipline of its own in holiness and righteousness unless to it also had pertained the prize of the discipline, nor for baptism itself to be entrusted to it if it were not also by means of regeneration being set on the way towards restitution: for the apostle makes this point as well, *Know ye not that whosoever we are that have been baptized into Jesus have been baptized into his death? Therefore we are buried together with him by means of baptism into death, so that even as Christ hath risen from the dead so we also should proceed in newness of life.*[1] And lest you should think that that is spoken only of this life which, starting from faith, must after baptism be lived in newness, with great precaution he adds, *For if we have been planted together by a likeness of Christ's death, we shall also belong to the resurrection.*[2] For by a likeness we die, in baptism; but in actuality we rise again, in the flesh, as Christ also did. *So that as the offence reigned in death, so also grace may reign through righteousness unto life everlasting through Jesus Christ our Lord.*[3] How 'so also', if not, no less than he, in the flesh? For where death was, there also is the life after death, because the life was first there where afterwards the death was. For if the reign of death has no other effect than the dissolution of the flesh, it logically follows that life, being contrary to death, must have the contrary effect, namely the redintegration of the flesh, to the end that as death had swallowed it up by gaining the mastery,[4] so also, the mortal thing being swallowed up by immortality, death may be in a position to be asked, *O death where is thy sting? O death where is thy striving?*[5] Thus then will grace superabound where also iniquity has abounded.[6] And thus also will strength be made perfect in weakness,[7] by saving what has perished, quickening what has died, healing what was smitten, curing what is sick, redeeming what was stolen, freeing what was enslaved, recalling what was led astray, raising up what was stricken down:[8] raising it even from

[1] Rom. 6. 3–4.   [2] Rom. 6. 5.   [3] Rom. 5. 21.
[4] Cf. Isa. 25. 8.   [5] 1 Cor. 15. 55.   [6] Cf. Rom. 5. 20.
[7] Cf. 2 Cor. 12. 9.   [8] Cf. Ezek. 34. 16.

terra in caelum, ubi nostrum municipatum Philippenses quoque ab apostolo discunt, unde et salutificatorem nostrum expectamus Iesum Christum, qui transfigurabit corpus nostrae humilitatis conformale corpori gloriae suae—sine dubio post resurrectionem, quia nec ipse Christus glorificatus est ante passionem. haec erunt 16 corpora nostra quae Romanos obsecrat exhibere hostiam vivam sanctam placibilem deo. quomodo 'vivam' si peritura sunt? quomodo 'sanctam' si profana sunt? quomodo 'placibilem' si damnata sunt? age nunc, quod ad Thessalonicenses ut ipsius solis 17 radio putem scriptum, ita claret, qualiter accipient lucifugae isti scripturarum? Ipse autem deus pacis sanctificet vos totos. non sufficit? sed et exsequitur, Et integrum corpus vestrum et anima 18 et spiritus sine querela conserventur in praesentia domini. habes omnem substantiam hominis saluti destinatam, nec alio tempore quam in adventu domini qui clavis est resurrectionis.

48 Sed caro, inquis, et sanguis regnum dei hereditate possidere non possunt. scimus hoc quoque scriptum, sed de industria distulimus hucusque, ut quod adversarii in prima statim acie obstruunt in ultima congressione prosterneremus, omnibus quaestionibus quasi auxiliis eius ante disiectis. sed et nunc expetent 2 praecedentia recognosci, ut et huic sensui sua origo praeiudicet. ut opinor, apostolus disposita ad Corinthios omni distinctione ecclesiasticae disciplinae, summam et sui evangelii et fidei illorum in dominicae mortis et resurrectionis demandatione concluserat, ut et nostrae spei regulam inde deduceret unde constaret. itaque 3 subicit: Si autem Christus praedicatur quod a mortuis resurrexit, quomodo quidam dicunt in vobis resurrectionem mortuorum non esse? quae si non est, nec Christus resurrexit. si Christus non 4 resurrexit, inanis est praedicatio nostra, inanis est et fides vestra.

66 et exsequitur *T*: sequitur *MPX*: et sequitur *Brf*.
48: 5 expetent *P*: expectent *TMX* (*manifesto errore*): expediet *vel* expedit Kellner, Eng. (*sed debuerant et* recognosci *in* recognoscere *mutare*).
14 inanis est et fides vestra *om. MPX*.

earth to heaven, where the Philippians also learn from the apostle that our citizenship is, *from whence also we look for our Saviour Jesus Christ, who will transfigure the body of our humility into conformity with the body of his glory*[1]—without doubt after the resurrection, seeing that even Christ himself was not glorified until after his passion. It will be these bodies of ours which he prays the Romans to present as a sacrifice, living, holy, well-pleasing to God.[2] How can the sacrifice be living, if the bodies are to perish? How holy, if they are inadmissible to sacred use? How well-pleasing, if they are damned? Come now, how will these shunners of the light of the scriptures understand that to the Thessalonians which I think is written as with a beam of the sun itself, so bright it is?—*And may the God of peace sanctify you wholly*. Is that not enough? Yet he proceeds, *And may your entire body and soul and spirit be preserved without complaint at the presence of the Lord*.[3] There you have the whole substance of man, with salvation for its destiny, and that at no other time than at the coming of the Lord, which is the key of the resurrection.[4]

48 But, you object, *Flesh and blood cannot obtain by inheritance the kingdom of God*.[5] I am aware that this also is written, but have purposely deferred it until now, with the intention of laying flat at the final assault the obstruction the enemy build up at the very first onset, after first knocking down all the questionings with which it has been as it were buttressed. But in this case also the context will call for review, so that this thought too may be controlled by the precedent of what it springs from. The apostle, I suppose, having set before the Corinthians the complete definition of the church discipline,[6] had bound up the sum-total of his own gospel and of their faith in his delivery of our Lord's death and resurrection, so as to derive the rule of our hope also from that whereon it might stand firm. And so he adds, *But if Christ is preached that he hath risen from the dead, how say some among you that there is not a resurrection of the dead? For if there is not, neither is Christ risen. If Christ is not risen, our preaching is void, your faith also is void*. We shall

[1] Cf. Phil. 3. 20, 21.
[2] Cf. Rom. 12. 1.
[3] 1 Thess. 5. 23.
[4] Cf. Apoc. 1. 18.
[5] 1 Cor. 15. 50.
[6] Cf. 1 Cor. 15. 1–8.

inveniemur etiam falsi testes dei, qui testimonium dixerimus quod resuscitaverit Christum quem non resuscitavit. nam si mortui non resurgunt nec Christus resurrexit: si Christus non resurrexit vana est fides vestra, quia adhuc in delictis vestris estis, et qui in Christo dormierunt perierunt. per haec cui nos rei credendae videtur extruere? resurrectioni, inquis, mortuorum quae negabatur. certe sub exemplo dominicae resurrectionis volens eam credi? certe, inquis. exemplum porro ex diversitate an ex parilitate componitur? utique, inquis, ex parilitate. quomodo autem Christus resurrexit, in carne an non? sine dubio si mortuum, si sepultum audis secundum scripturas, non alias quam in carne, aeque resuscitatum in carne concedis: ipsum enim quod cecidit in morte, quod iacuit in sepultura, hoc et resurrexit, non tam Christus in carne quam caro in Christo. igitur si ad exemplum Christi resurgemus qui resurrexit in carne, iam non ad exemplum Christi resurgemus si non in carne et ipsi resurgemus. Quia per hominem, inquit, mors, et per hominem resurrectio: ut separaret quidem auctores, mortis Adam Christum resurrectionis, eiusdem autem constitueret substantiae resurrectionem cuius et mortem per ipsorum auctorum in nomine hominis comparationem: si enim sicut in Adam omnes moriuntur ita et in Christo omnes vivificabuntur, carne vivificabuntur in Christo sicut in Adam carne moriuntur: unusquisque autem in suo ordine, scilicet quia et in suo corpore. ordo enim meritorum dispositorum nomine disponetur. merita autem cum corpori quoque adscribantur, ordo quoque corporum disponatur necesse est, ut possit esse meritorum. si autem et baptizantur quidam pro mortuis, videbimus an ratione. certe illa praesumptione hoc eos instituisse portendit qua alii etiam carni ut vicarium baptisma profuturum existimarent ad spem

26 concedis *libri*: concedes *Kroy*.
38 dispositorum *om. T Gel. (forsan recte)*.

be found even false witnesses of God, seeing we have borne witness that he hath raised Christ up again, when he hath not raised him up. For if the dead rise not again, neither is Christ risen again. If Christ is not risen again your faith is vain, because ye are yet in your sins, and those who have fallen asleep in Christ have perished.[1] To belief of what fact do you think he is by these means building us up? The resurrection of the dead, you reply, which was under denial. Surely desiring it to be believed by the example of the Lord's resurrection? Certainly, you say. Now is an example applied out of diversity or out of similarity? Evidently, you say, of similarity. Then how did Christ rise again? In the flesh, or not? Undoubtedly if you hear that he died, that he was buried, *according to the scriptures*,[2] and not otherwise than in the flesh, you must no less admit that he was raised again in the flesh: for that very thing which died in death, which lay down in burial, this it is which has also risen again, not so much Christ in the flesh as the flesh in Christ. Therefore if we are to rise again after Christ's example, and he rose again in the flesh—well, we shall not be rising again after Christ's example if we are not ourselves also to rise again in the flesh. *Since*, he says, *by man ⟨came⟩ death, by man ⟨came⟩ also the resurrection*,[3] so as to distinguish the two authors, Adam the author of death, Christ the author of the resurrection, and yet, by bringing together the authors under the name of 'man', to determine that the resurrection is of the same substance as the death was. For if *as in Adam all die, even so in Christ shall all be made alive*,[4] they will be made alive in Christ in the flesh, just as in Adam they die in the flesh. *But every one in his own order*,[5] because of course in his own body: for the order will be regulated in accordance with already regulated deserts. But since deserts are accounted to the body as well, so of necessity the order of the bodies must be regulated, to make it possible for the order of deserts to be. And again, *if some are baptized for the dead*,[6] we shall enquire whether this is with good reason. Certainly he suggests that they had instituted that custom on the assumption by which they supposed that vicarious baptism would be of benefit even to another flesh towards the hope

---

[1] 1 Cor. 15. 12–18.   [2] Cf. 1 Cor. 15. 3–4.   [3] 1 Cor. 15. 21.
[4] 1 Cor. 15. 22.   [5] 1 Cor. 15. 23.   [6] Cf. 1 Cor. 15. 29.

resurrectionis, quae nisi corporalis non alias in baptismate corporali obligaretur. quid et ipsos baptizari ait ⟨si mortui non resurgunt⟩, id est si non quae baptizantur corpora resurgent: anima enim non lavatione sed responsione sancitur. Quid et nos, inquit, omni hora periclitamur?—utique per carnem. Cotidie morior—utique periculis carnis, per quam et depugnavit ad bestias Ephesi, illas scilicet bestias Asiaticae pressurae de qua in secunda ad eosdem, Nolumus enim vos ignorare, fratres, de pressura nostra apud Asiam, quod super quam supra gravati sumus citra vires, uti et de vita haesitaremus. omnia haec, nisi fallor, eo enumerat ut nolens vanam credi carnis conflictationem indubitate velit credi carnis resurrectionem: vana enim habenda est conflictatio eius cuius nulla erit resurrectio. Sed dicet quis, quomodo resurgent mortui? quo autem corpore venient? iam hic de qualitatibus corporum disserit, an eadem ipsa an alia resumantur: sed cum eiusmodi quaestio posterior habeatur, sufficiet interim ex hoc quoque genere corporalem definiri resurrectionem, cum de qualitate corporum quaeritur.

49 Ventum est nunc ad carnem et sanguinem, ⟨cardinem⟩ revera totius quaestionis: quas substantias quali condicione exheredaverit apostolus a dei regno aeque de antecedentibus discere est. Primus, inquit, homo de terra choicus—id est limaceus, id est Adam: Secundus homo de caelo—id est sermo dei, id est Christus, non alias tamen homo, licet de caelo, nisi quia et ipse caro atque anima, quod homo, quod Adam. nam et supra novissimus Adam dictus, de consortio substantiae commercium nominis traxit, quia nec Adam ex semine caro, quod et Christus. Qualis ergo choicus tales

---

44 non alias *scribebam*: non nisi alias *MPX*: non nisi... corporali *om. T*.
45 quid *Gel.*: qui *MPX*: ut *T*. si mortui non resurgunt *addenda putabam*: post id est *inseruit Brf.* lavari: *utrovis modo claudicanti loco mederi possis*.
46 anima *T Gel.*: animae *MPX* (*forsan recte*).
52 super quam supra *MPX*: super quam *T* (*male*).
59 genere *T*: *om. MPX*.
49: 1 cardinem *supplevit Kroy*.
3 a dei regno *om. MPX*.

of resurrection, which, unless it were corporal, would not be bound up with a corporal baptism. He asks why they themselves also are baptized ⟨if the dead rise not⟩, that is, if the bodies that are baptized do not rise again? For the soul is sanctified not by the washing but by the profession of faith. *And why*, he asks, *stand we in jeopardy every hour?*[1]—evidently by virtue of the flesh. *I die daily*[2]—surely by the perils of that flesh by which he also fought with beasts at Ephesus,[3] meaning those beasts of the Asiatic affliction of which he speaks in the second epistle to the same people: *For we would not have you ignorant, brethren, of our affliction in Asia, that above measure we were burdened beyond our strength, so that we were in doubt even of life.*[4] All these experiences, if I mistake not, he recounts because he does not wish the strivings of the flesh to be believed to be in vain, and does wish the resurrection of the flesh to be believed with full assurance: for the striving of that of which there will be no resurrection must be held to be in vain. *But some man will say, How will the dead rise again, and with what body will they come?*[5] Here at last he discourses of the qualities of bodies, whether they be the same bodies, or others, that are resumed. But as this kind of question may be considered to come later, it shall suffice meanwhile that by this theme also the resurrection is defined as corporal, since it is with the quality of bodies that the discussion is concerned.

49 We have now reached 'flesh and blood', in very truth ⟨the hub⟩ of the whole enquiry. Under what conditions the apostle has disinherited these substances from the kingdom of God, we may no less than before learn from what precedes. *The first man*, he says, *is from the earth, choic*, that is, composed of mud, and this is Adam: *the second man is from heaven*,[6] that is, the Word of God, and this is Christ, who is, however, though from heaven, man in no other sense than that he is himself also flesh and blood, which man is, and Adam was. For he has already been described as the last Adam,[7] deriving his partnership in that name from community of substance, because Adam also was flesh without human generation, as

---

[1] 1 Cor. 15. 30.   [2] 1 Cor. 15. 31.   [3] Cf. 1 Cor. 15. 32.
[4] 2 Cor. 1. 8.   [5] 1 Cor. 15. 35.
[6] 1 Cor. 15. 47.   [7] Cf. 1 Cor. 15. 45.

et choici, et qualis caelestis tales et caelestes. substantia tales? an primo disciplina, dehinc et dignitate quam disciplina captavit? atquin substantia nullo modo separabuntur choici atque caelestes, semel ab apostolo homines dicti. si enim et Christus, solus vere caelestis, immo et supercaelestis, homo tamen qua caro atque anima, nihilo ex ista substantiarum condicione a choica qualitate discernitur, proinde et qui caelestes secundum illum non de substantia praesenti sed de futura claritate caelestes praedicati intellegentur: quia et retro, unde distinctio ista manavit, de dignitatis differentia ostensa est alia supercaelestium gloria, alia superterrenorum, et alia solis, alia lunae, alia stellarum, quia et stella a stella differt in gloria, non tamen in substantia. denique praemissa differentia dignitatis in eadem substantia et nunc sectandae et tunc capessendae, subiungit etiam exhortationem ut et hic habitum Christi sectemur ex disciplina, et illic fastigium consequamur ex gloria: Sicut portavimus imaginem choici, portemus etiam imaginem supercaelestis: portavimus enim imaginem choici per collegium transgressionis, per consortium mortis, per exilium paradisi. nam si et in carne *hic portatur* imago Adae, sed non carnem monemur exponere: si non carnem, ergo conversationem, ut proinde et caelestis imaginem gestemus in nobis, non iam dei, nec iam in caelo constituti, sed secundum liniamenta Christi incedentes in sanctitate et iustitia et veritate. atque adeo ad disciplinam totum hoc dirigit ut hic dicat portandam imaginem Christi in ista carne et in isto tempore disciplinae: 'portemus' enim praeceptivo modo dicens huic tempori loquitur in quo homo nulla alia sub-

---

14 immo et supercaelestis *om. T.*
17 intellegentur *X*: intelleguntur *TMP.*
18 distinctio *MPX*: destinatio *T.*
26 eam imaginem *T.*
28 si et *TMP*: et si *X Rig.*   hic portatur *Urs.*: sic putatur *MPX*: esse putatur *T.*
34 praeceptivo modo *MP*: *alii alia sed nihil ad rem.*

Christ is. Therefore, *As is the choic one, such are they also that are choic: as is the heavenly one, such are they also that are heavenly.*[1] Such in substance? Or such at first in discipline and afterwards in the dignity which has been the aim of the discipline? Yet even in substance choic men and heavenly can by no means be dissevered when once the apostle has described them as men. For even if Christ alone is truly heavenly, nay rather even more than heavenly, and yet is man, as being flesh and soul, and as far as this condition of the substances goes is in no degree distinguished from the choic quality, it follows that those who after his fashion are heavenly must be understood to have been declared heavenly not on the ground of their present substance but on the ground of their future splendour: because at the previous point from which that distinction derived it was shown that it is by difference of dignity that there is one glory of the more than heavenly and another of the more than earthly, and one glory of the sun, another of the moon, and another of the stars, seeing that star also differs from star in glory,[2] yet not in substance. Consequently, having premised that there is in the same substance a difference of the dignity which must now be sought after and hereafter will be attained, he adds also an exhortation for us even here to seek after Christ's attire by discipline, and there to attain to his altitude by glory: *As we have worn the image of the choic man, let us also wear the image of him who is more than heavenly.*[3] For we have worn the image of the choic man by partnership in transgression, by fellowship in death, by exile from paradise. For though it is in the flesh that here the image of Adam is worn, yet it is not the flesh we are enjoined to take off:[4] and if not the flesh, then it is the life and manners, so that we may thereby also wear in us the image of the heavenly, though we are not yet gods, not yet established in heaven, but according to the lineaments of Christ are proceeding in holiness and righteousness and truth. And to such a degree does he turn all this in the direction of discipline, that he says the image of Christ must be worn here, in this flesh, and in this time of discipline. For by saying 'let us wear', in the imperative mood, he speaks for this present time, in which

[1] 1 Cor. 15. 48. [2] Cf. 1 Cor. 15. 40–1.
[3] 1 Cor. 15. 49. [4] Cf. Eph. 4. 22.

stantia est quam caro et anima, ut etsi quam aliam, id est caelestem, substantiam haec fides spectat, huic tamen repromissa sit cui ad illam elaborare mandatur. cum igitur imaginem et choici et caelestis in conversatione constituat, illam eierandam hanc vero sectandam, dehinc adiungat Hoc enim dico (id est 'propter ea quae supra dixi':—coniunctio est 'enim', sensus supplementum antecedentibus reddens) quod caro et sanguis regnum dei hereditate possidere non possunt, nihil aliud intellegi mandat carnem et sanguinem quam supradictam imaginem choici: quae si in conversatione censetur vetustatis, conversatio autem vetustatis non capit dei regnum, proinde caro et sanguis non capiendo dei regnum ad conversationem rediguntur vetustatis. plane si numquam apostolus pro operibus substantiam posuit, nec hic ita utatur: si vero in carne adhuc constitutos negavit esse in carne, in operibus carnis negans esse, formam eius subruere non debes non substantiam sed opera substantiae alienantis a dei regno. quibus etiam ad Galatas manifestatis praedicere se et praedixisse profitetur quod qui talia agant regnum dei non sint in hereditate consecuturi, non portantes scilicet imaginem caelestis sicut portaverant choici, ideoque ex vetere conversatione nihil aliud deputandi quam caro et sanguis. nam et si subito in hanc definitionem erupisset apostolus eliminandi carnem et sanguinem a dei regno, sine ullius supra sensus praestructione, nonne duas istas substantias proinde veterem hominem interpretaremur carni et sanguini deditum, id est esui et potui, cuius sit dicere adversus fidem resurrectionis, Manducemus et bibamus, cras enim moriemur? et hoc enim infulciens apostolus

---

40 hoc enim dico, *etc.*; *huic loco (nisi forte Oehlerus melius intellexerat quam indicavit) primus videor lumen infudisse*: propterea coniunctio est est enim *P*: propterea coniunctio est enim *MX*: coniunctio est enim *T*.
47 vetustatis *R³*: veritatis *libri*.
53 in *om. T*.
59 interpretaretur *MPX* (*falso*).

man is no other substance than flesh and soul: so that, even if this faith has in view some other substance, that is, a heavenly one, even so this substance is promised to that which is enjoined to labour towards it. Since therefore he makes the image of the choic and of the heavenly a matter of life and manners, the former to be forsworn, the latter to be sought after, and afterwards adds, *For this I say*—that is, 'because of what I have just said', because 'for' is a conjunction which refers back the completion of the thought to what precedes—*that flesh and blood cannot obtain by inheritance the kingdom of God,*[1] he requires us to understand by 'flesh and blood' no other thing than the previously mentioned 'image of the choic man': and if this image has its origin in our 'former conversation', and the former conversation is incapable of the kingdom of God, it follows that flesh and blood, as not being capable of the kingdom of God, are reduced to 'former conversation'. Of course, if the apostle never has named a substance when he has meant its works, you may deny that he does so here.[2] But if he has said that men who were still actually in the flesh were not in the flesh, meaning that they were not in the works of the flesh, you must not break down his rule when he makes alien from the kingdom of God, not a substance, but the works of the substance. Also when he had made these matters clear to the Galatians,[3] he affirmed that he forewarned them and had forewarned them that those who do such things will not obtain by inheritance the kingdom of God, that is, while they were not wearing the image of the heavenly, as they had worn the image of the choic, and thus, as a result of their old life and manners, could be reckoned as none other than flesh and blood. For even if the apostle had suddenly broken forth into this pronouncement of the exclusion of flesh and blood from the kingdom of God, without the groundwork of any previous thought, should we not forthwith interpret these two substances as the old man, given up to flesh and blood, that is, to eating and drinking, the old man to whom it appertains to say, in opposition to the faith of the resurrection, *Let us eat and drink, for tomorrow we shall die*?[4] For by this interjection too the apostle has laid an accusation against

---

[1] 1 Cor. 15. 50.   [2] Cf. 2 Cor. 10. 3.
[3] Cf. Gal. 5. 21.   [4] 1 Cor. 15. 32.

carnem et sanguinem de fructibus ipsorum manducandi et bibendi suggillavit.

50 Sed et omissis huiusmodi interpretationibus carnis et sanguinis opera taxantibus, ipsas quoque substantias non aliter quam sunt intellectas licebit resurrectioni vindicare. non enim resurrectio 2 carni et sanguini directo negatur, sed dei regnum quod obvenit resurrectioni: est autem et in iudicium resurrectio. immo et confirmatur carnis resurrectio generalis cum specialis excipitur: dum enim in quem statum non resurgat edicitur, in quem resurgat subauditur. atque ita dum pro meritis distinctionem resurrectionis 3 opus substantiae non genus patitur, apparet hinc quoque carnem et sanguinem nomine culpae non substantiae arceri a dei regno, nomine tamen formae resurgere in iudicium quia non resurgant in regnum. adhuc dicam, Caro et sanguis regnum dei hereditate 4 possidere non possunt: merito sola et per semetipsa, ut ostenderet adhuc spiritum in illis necessarium. spiritus enim est qui vivificat in regnum dei, caro nihil prodest: prodesse tamen illi aliud potest, id est spiritus, et per spiritum opera quoque spiritus. resurgunt 5 itaque ex aequo omnis caro et sanguis in qualitate sua: sed quorum est adire regnum dei induere oportebit vim incorruptibilitatis et immortalitatis, sine qua regnum dei adire non possunt, antequam consequi eam possint. merito ergo caro et sanguis, ut diximus, sola regnum dei capere deficiunt. iam vero cum devorari habeat 6 corruptivum istud ab incorruptibilitate, id est caro, et mortale istud ab immortalitate, id est sanguis, post resurrectionem ex demuta-

50: 4 carni et sanguini directo *om. T.*
  14 in illis *T*: illis *Pam.*: illi *MPX.*
  16 resurgit *T* (*forsan recte*).
  18 est *om. MPX.*

flesh and blood in respect of the fruits of them, which are eating and drinking.

50 But, even if we leave out interpretations such as these, which censure the works of flesh and blood, it will be permissible to vindicate for the resurrection the substances themselves, understood as they actually are. For it is not resurrection which is in set terms denied to flesh and blood, but the kingdom of God, which is a concomitant of the resurrection, though there is also a resurrection unto judgement: rather, a general resurrection of the flesh is even confirmed by the very fact that a specific one is excepted. For while announcement is made into what state it does not rise again, one tacitly understands into what state it does rise again. And thus, while the work of the substance, not its genus, experiences in accordance with its merits a distinction in resurrection, it is evident from this besides that flesh and blood are kept out of the kingdom of God on account of guilt, not of substance, yet that on account of the general rule they do rise again to judgement, just because they do not rise again to the kingdom. I will add even this, that with good reason the apostle said that flesh and blood cannot obtain by inheritance the kingdom of God alone and by themselves,[1] so as to show once more that the Spirit in them was necessary. For it is *the Spirit that quickeneth* unto the kingdom of God: *the flesh profiteth nothing*.[2] But it can receive profit from something else, namely the Spirit, and through the Spirit the works of the Spirit as well. And so all flesh and blood, without distinction, do rise again in their proper quality; but those to whom it appertains to approach to the kingdom of God will, before they are able to obtain it, have to clothe themselves with that principle of incorruptibility and immortality without which they cannot approach to the kingdom of God. With good reason then, as I said, flesh and blood alone are too weak to be capable of the kingdom of God. Now however, since that corruptible thing, which is the flesh, has to be swallowed up by incorruptibility, and that mortal thing, which is the blood, by immortality,[3] in consequence of the change, after the resurrection, with good reason

[1] Cf. 1 Cor. 15. 50. [2] John 6. 63.
[3] Cf. 1 Cor. 15. 53–4.

tione, merito demutata ac devorata caro et sanguis regnum dei hereditate possidere possunt, non tamen non resuscitata. sunt qui 7 carnem et sanguinem Iudaismum velint accipi propter circumcisionem, alienum et ipsum a dei regno, quia et ille vetustati deputetur et hoc titulo iam et alibi ab apostolo denotetur, qui post revelatum in se filium dei ad evangelizandum eum in nationibus statim non rettulerit ad carnem et sanguinem, id est ad circumcisionem, id est ad Iudaismum, sicut ad Galatas scribit.

51 Sed pro omnibus iam stabit quod in clausulam reservavimus, etiam pro apostolo ipso, revera maximae inconsiderantiae revincendo si tam abrupte, ut quidam volunt, clausis quod aiunt oculis, sine distinctione, sine condicione, omnem passim carnem et sanguinem a regno dei extrusit, utique ab ipsa regia caelorum, cum illic adhuc sedeat Iesus ad dexteram patris, homo etsi deus, Adam novissimus etsi sermo primarius, caro et sanguis etsi nostris puriora, idem tamen et substantia et forma qua ascendit, talis etiam descensurus, ut angeli adfirmant, agnoscendus scilicet et eis qui illum convulneraverunt. hic sequester dei atque hominum 2 appellatus ex utriusque partis deposito commisso sibi, carnis quoque depositum servat in semetipso, arrabonem summae totius. quemadmodum enim nobis arrabonem spiritus reliquit, ita et a nobis arrabonem carnis accepit et vexit in caelum, pignus totius summae illuc quandoque redigendae. securae estote, caro et sanguis: 3 usurpastis et caelum et regnum dei in Christo: aut si negent vos in Christo, negent et in caelo Christum qui vobis caelum negaverunt. ita Nec corruptela, inquit, incorruptelam hereditati habebit: non 4 ut carnem et sanguinem existimes corruptelam, quando ipsa sint

---

28 ab apostolo *om. T.*
51: 8 puriora *XR*: priora *MP* (*falso*): purior* *T, unde Eng. Brf.* purior.   qua *libri*: quam *Kroy. Brf.*

can flesh and blood, when changed and swallowed up, obtain by inheritance the kingdom of God: not however without being raised again. There are some who, because of the circumcision, would have flesh and blood taken to mean Judaism, itself an alien from the kingdom of God, on the ground that it too is reckoned for oldness and that it is elsewhere stigmatized by this description by the apostle, who, after the revelation of the Son of God in him for preaching him among the gentiles, immediately conferred not with flesh and blood, that is, the circumcision, which is Judaism, as he writes to the Galatians.[1]

51 But this that I have reserved to the end will remain valid for all, even for the apostle himself, who would indeed have stood convicted of great lack of reflection if with such precipitancy as some allege, with his eyes shut as the saying is, he did, without distinction or condition, thrust out all flesh and blood in general from the kingdom of God and, in effect, from the very palace of heaven, when Jesus is even now sitting there at the right hand of the Father,[2] Man albeit God, the last Adam[3] albeit the primal Word, flesh and blood albeit purer than ours, yet, the same in both the substance and the form in which he ascended, in like manner also will descend, as the angels affirm,[4] recognizable in fact by those who have wounded him.[5] He, who in view of the deposit of both parties entrusted to him is designated joint-trustee of God and men,[6] preserves in himself the deposit of the flesh as an earnest of the whole sum.[7] For just as he has left to us the earnest of the Spirit, so he has received from us the earnest of the flesh and has carried it into heaven as a pledge that the whole sum will sometime be conveyed thither. Have no fear, flesh and blood: you have already in Christ taken seizin of heaven and of the kingdom of God. Else, if they deny that you are in Christ, let them, as they have denied heaven to you, deny also that Christ is in heaven. So he says, *Neither will corruption have for an inheritance incorruption*,[8] not wishing you to suppose that flesh and blood are corruption,

[1] Cf. Gal. 1. 16.
[2] Cf. Mark 16. 19.
[3] Cf. 1 Cor. 15. 45.
[4] Cf. Acts 1. 11.
[5] Cf. John 19. 37; Zech. 12. 10.
[6] Cf. 1 Tim. 2. 5.
[7] Cf. 2 Cor. 5. 5.
[8] 1 Cor. 15. 50.

potius obnoxia corruptelae, per mortem scilicet, siquidem mors est quae carnem et sanguinem non modo corrumpit verum etiam consumit: sed quoniam opera carnis et sanguinis non posse consequi regnum dei edixerat, quo magis hoc exaggeraret ipsi quoque corruptelae, id est morti cui carnis et sanguinis opera proficiunt, hereditatem incorruptelae ademit. nam et paulo post ipsius mortis quodammodo mortem expressit, Devorata est, dicens, mors in contentione: ubi est mors aculeus tuus? ubi est mors potentia tua? aculeus autem mortis delinquentia—haec erit corruptela: virtus autem delinquentiae lex—illa alia sine dubio quam constituit in membris suis militantem adversus legem animi sui, ipsam scilicet vim delinquendi contra voluntatem. nam et si supra novissimum inimicum mortem evacuari ait, hoc modo nec corruptela hereditatem incorruptelae consequetur, id est, nec mors perseverabit. quando et quomodo defectura? cum in atomo, in momentaneo oculi motu, in novissima tuba, et mortui resurgent incorrupti— qui hi nisi qui ante corrupti, id est corpora, id est caro et sanguis? Et nos demuta*bi*mur—de qua habitudine nisi in qua deprehendemur? Oportet enim corruptivum istud induere incorruptelam et mortale istud induere immortalitatem—quid mortale nisi caro? quid corruptivum nisi sanguis? ac ne putes aliud sentire apostolum, providentem sibi et ut de carne intellegas laborantem, cum dicit 'istud corruptivum' et 'istud mortale' cutem ipsam tenens dicit: certe 'istud' nisi de subiecto, nisi de comparenti, pronuntiasse non potuit: demonstrationis corporalis est verbum. aliud autem erit corruptivum aliud corruptela, et aliud mortale aliud mortalitas: aliud enim quod patitur, aliud quod pati efficit. ita

33 consequitur *MPX*.
37 demutabimur *Pam.*: demutamur *PX*.
38 incorruptelam et mortale istud induere *om. MPX*.
41 *post* apostolum *suspicatus erat Kroy.* adspice ipsum *intercidisse*.

seeing these are themselves the rather subject to corruption, through death in fact, since it is by death that flesh and blood are not only corrupted but even consumed; but seeing that he had declared that the works of flesh and blood cannot obtain the kingdom of God, with the intention of stressing this further he took away even from corruption itself, which is death, to which the works of flesh and blood are conducive, the inheritance of incorruption. For a little later he did in a sort of way describe the death of death itself, saying, *Death is swallowed up in striving: O death, where is thy sting? O death where is thy power?* Now *the sting of death is transgression*, and this is what corruption must mean. *And the strength of transgression is the law*,[1] doubtless that other law which he locates in his members, fighting against the law of his mind,[2] indeed that very faculty of transgressing in spite of the will. For as he has already said that the last enemy to be destroyed is death,[3] it is in this way that neither will corruption attain to an inheritance of incorruption, that is, neither will death survive. When and how will it expire? When *in a moment, in the twinkling of an eye, at the last trump*, even *the dead will rise again uncorrupted*—who are these but those who were formerly corrupted, that is, bodies, which means flesh and blood? *And we shall be changed*[4]—from what condition if not that in which we shall be found to be? *For this corruptible thing must put on incorruption and this mortal thing must put on immortality*[5]—what is a mortal thing if not the flesh, and what is a corruptible thing if not the blood? And lest you should think the apostle had anything else in mind,... taking forethought for himself and toiling for you to understand that the statement referred to the flesh: when he says 'this corruptible thing' and 'this mortal thing' he touches his skin while speaking. Certainly he could not have spoken the word 'this' except of something actually there and present to sight: it is a term expressing corporal demonstration. But a corruptible thing must needs be one thing, and corruption another: a mortal thing be one thing, and mortality another. For that which experiences is one thing, and that which causes the experience is another. So those

---

[1] 1 Cor. 15. 54–6. [2] Cf. Rom. 7. 23. [3] Cf. 1 Cor. 15. 26.
[4] Cf. 1 Cor. 15. 50–2. [5] 1 Cor. 15. 53.

quae patiuntur corruptelam et mortalitatem, caro scilicet et sanguis, ea necesse est patiantur et incorruptelam et immortalitatem.

52 Videamus iam nunc quo corpore venturos mortuos disputet. et bene quod erupit statim ostendere, quasi quis eiusmodi quaerat. Stulte, inquit, tu quod seminas non vivificatur nisi mortuum fuerit. hoc ergo iam de exemplo seminis constet, non aliam vivi- 2
ficari carnem quam ipsam quae erit mortua, et ita sequentia relucebunt. nihil enim adversus regulam exempli licebit intellegi, 3 ne, quia sequitur, Et quod seminas non corpus quod futurum est seminas, idcirco aliud resurrecturum corpus quam quod moriendo seminatur existimes. ceterum excidisti ab exemplo: nunquam 4
enim frumento seminato et in terra dissoluto hordeum erumpit, et non idipsum genus grani eademque natura et qualitas et forma. denique unde, si non idipsum? et corruptela enim ipsum est, dum ipsius est. non enim et suggerit quomodo non quod futurum est 5 corpus seminetur, dicens Sed nudum granum, si forte frumenti vel
alicuius eiusmodi: deus autem dat ei corpus prout vult—certe ei grano quod nudum seminari ait? certe, inquis. ergo salvum est 6 cui dare habet deus corpus. quomodo autem salvum est si nusquam est, si non resurgit, si non idipsum resurgit? si non resurgit salvum non est: si non est salvum accipere corpus a deo non potest. sed 7
enim salvum omni modo constat. ad quid ergo dabit illi deus prout vult corpus, habenti utique proprium corpus illud nudum, nisi ut iam non *nu*dum resurgat? ergo additicium erit corpus quod corpori superstruitur, nec exterminatur illud cui superstruitur, sed augetur. salvum est autem quod augetur. seritur enim solum- 8

52: 1 videamus *T*: videmus *MPX*.
    4 constet *MPX*: constat *T*.
    22 nisi ut iam non nudum *om. T*.   non nudum *R*³: nondum *MPX*.

things which experience corruption and mortality, namely flesh and blood, must of necessity also experience incorruption and immortality.

52 Let us next enquire with what body he contends the dead will come.[1] And it is well that he has burst at once into exposition, as though someone were asking that kind of question. *Thou fool,* he says, *that which thou sowest is not made alive except it have died.*[2] Upon this let there once be agreement, from the illustration of the seed, that the flesh which is made alive is none other than that which will have died, and then what follows will be crystal clear. For there will be no room for any interpretation which contradicts the rule laid down by the illustration: lest because there follows, *And that which thou sowest, thou sowest not that body which shall be,*[3] on that account you suppose a body will rise again which is not that which is sown in dying. But you have missed the point of the illustration. For never, when wheat is sown and dissolved in the earth, does barley force itself up, but only that same species of grain, and the same nature and quality and form. In fact, where does it come from if it is not the same? For even the corruption is the thing itself since it is a corruption of the thing itself. For does he not also suggest in what sense the body sown is not that which shall be, when he says, *But naked grain, it may chance of wheat or of something of that kind: but God giveth it a body according as he will?*[4]— 'giveth', surely, to that grain which he says is sown naked. Evidently, you say. In that case that grain is conserved to which God is to give a body. But how is it conserved, if it has ceased to exist, if it does not rise again, if it does not rise again as its own self? If it does not rise again it is not conserved: and if again it is not conserved it cannot receive a body from God. But it is obvious that it is certainly conserved. To what purpose then will God give it a body according as he wishes, when it has all the time that naked body which is its own, unless with the intention of its rising again not naked? Consequently there will be an additional body, which is built up over the body, and that over which it is built up is not abolished but increased. But a thing that is increased is conserved.

[1] Cf. 1 Cor. 15. 35.   [2] 1 Cor. 15. 36.
[3] 1 Cor. 15. 37.   [4] 1 Cor. 15. 37–8.

modo granum, sine folliculi veste, sine fundamento spicae, sine munimento aristae, sine superbia culmi: exsurgit autem copia feneratum, compagine aedificatum, ordine structum, cultu munitum, et usquequaque vestitum. haec sunt ei corpus a deo aliud, in 9 quod non abolitione sed ampliatione mutatur: et unicuique seminum suum corpus deputavit non suum, id est non pristinum, ut tunc et illud suum sit quod extrinsecus a deo acquirit. servi igitur 10 exemplo et conserva speculum eius carni, eandem credens fructificaturam quae sit seminata, ipsam etsi pleniorem, non aliam etsi aliter revertentem: accipiet enim et ipsa suggestum et ornatum qualem et illi deus voluerit superducere secundum merita. sine 11 dubio ad hoc dirigit, Non omnis caro eadem caro, non ad denegandam substantiae communionem sed praerogativae peraequationem, corpus honoris non generis in differentiam redigens. in 12 hoc et figurata subicit exempla animalium et elementorum: Alia caro hominis, id est servi dei qui vere homo est: Alia iumenti, id est ethnici de quo et propheta Adsimilatus est, inquit, homo irrationabilibus iumentis: Alia caro volatilium, id est martyrum qui ad superiora conantur: Alia piscium, id est quibus aqua baptismatis sufficit. sic et de supercaelestibus corporibus argumenta committit: 13 Alia gloria solis, id est Christi: Et alia lunae, id est ecclesiae: Et alia stellarum, id est seminis Abrahae: et Stella enim a stella differt in gloria...et corpora terrena et caelestia, Iudaeos scilicet et Christianos. ceterum si non figurate, satis vane mulorum et 14 milvorum carnes et corpora caelestium luminum apposuit humanis, non pertinentia ad condicionis comparationem sicut nec ad resurrectionis consecutionem. postremo, cum per haec dif- 15 ferentiam gloriae non substantiae conclusisset, Sic inquit et resurrectio mortuorum. quomodo? non de alio aliquo sed de sola

30 deputavit *Pam*: putavi *T*: putari *MPX*.
31 adquirunt *T*.
35 et *T*: *om. MPX*.
36 dirigit *T*: direxit *MPX*.
47 post in gloria *ea intercidisse suspicabar propter quae* Iudaeos, Christianos, accusative (*sic enim libri omnes*) *stare possent*: Iudaeus, Christianus, *R*³ *edd.*

For when sown it is merely grain, without the clothing of its husk or the foundation of its ear or the defences of its beard or the pride of its stalk: but when it rises up it has made interest by multiplication, is built up in compactness, is drawn up in rank, fortified with apparel, and clothed in every sense. These it has from God as another body into which it is changed not by destruction but by enlargement. And to every one of the seeds he has assigned its own body,[1] which is not its own, that is, not its original one, so that afterwards that one also is its own which it acquires from God from without. Obey then the illustration, and retain the reflection of it for the flesh, trusting that the identical flesh which has been sown will bear fruit, itself, though fuller, not another, though it return in another guise. For it too will receive such equipment and adornment as it pleases God to clothe it with according to its deserts. Doubtless it is with this intention that he says, *All flesh is not the same flesh*,[2] so as to deny not community of substance but equivalence of honour, bringing back the body into difference not of species but of rank. For this purpose he also adds the figurative illustrations of the beasts and the heavenly bodies. *There is one flesh of man*, that is, of the servant of God, who is truly a man: *another of cattle*, that is, the heathen, of whom the prophet also says, *Man is compared to irrational cattle*:[3] *another flesh of birds*, that is, of the martyrs, who strive towards higher things: *another of fishes*, those for whom the water of baptism suffices. So also he sets in contrast arguments concerning the supercelestial bodies: *There is one glory of the sun*, which is Christ: *and another of the moon*, the church: *and another of the stars*, the seed of Abraham: *for star also differs from star in glory . . . also earthly bodies and heavenly*, Jews in fact and Christians.[4] Otherwise, if not figuratively, it is idle enough that he has set the flesh of mules and kites, and the bodies of the celestial luminaries, by the side of human bodies, if they have no bearing either on comparison of condition or on attaining to the resurrection. Finally, having by this means proved difference of glory, not of substance, he says, *So also is the resurrection of the dead.*[5] How 'so'? Differing in no other respect but in glory alone. For once

[1] Cf. 1 Cor. 15. 38.   [2] 1 Cor. 15. 39.   [3] Ps. 49. 20.
[4] 1 Cor. 15. 41.   [5] 1 Cor. 15. 42.

gloria differens. rursus enim resurrectionem ad eandem sub- 16
stantiam revocans, et ad granum denuo spectans, Seminatur inquit
in corruptela resurgit in incorruptela, seminatur in dedecoratione
resurgit in gloria, seminatur in infirmitate resurgit in virtute,
seminatur corpus animale resurgit spiritale. certe non aliud 17
resurgit quam quod seminatur, nec aliud seminatur quam quod
dissolvitur humi, nec aliud dissolvitur humi quam caro: hanc
enim sententia dei elisit, Terra es et in terram ibis, quia et de terra
erat sumpta. hinc et apostolus concepit seminari eam dicere cum 18
redhibetur in terram, quia et seminibus sequestratorium terra est
illic deponendis et inde repetendis: ideoque et reconsignat impri-
mens, Sic enim scriptum est, ne aliud existimes seminari quam, In
terram ibis ex qua es sumptus. sic nec alterius quam carnis: sic enim
scriptum est.

53 Sed corpus animale animam quidam argumentantur, ut illum
a carne avocent recidivatum. porro cum constet fixumque sit illud
resurrecturum corpus quod fuerit seminatum, ad ipsius rei exhibitionem provocabuntur. aut ostendant animam seminatam post 2
mortem, id est mortuam, id est humi elisam disiectam dissolutam,
quod in illam decretum a deo non est: proponant corruptelam
eius et dedecorationem, infirmitatem, ut ipsius sit etiam exsurgere
in incorruptelam et in gloriam et in virtutem. sed enim in 3
Lazaro, praecipuo resurrectionis exemplo, caro iacuit in infirmitate, caro paene computruit in dedecorationem, caro interim
putuit in corruptionem, et tamen Lazarus caro resurrexit, cum
anima quidem, sed incorrupta, quam nemo vinculis lineis strin-
xerat, nemo in sepulchro collocarat, nemo foetere iam senserat,
nemo quadriduo viderat seminatam. totum habitum, totum 4
exitum Lazari omnium quoque caro hodie experitur, anima vero

61 sententiam deus *MPX* (*male*).
64 repetundis *TX*.
66 sic enim scriptum est *deletum volunt Kroy. Brf.*
53: 1 illum *C*: illam *TMP*: illa *X*.
    2 recidivatum *C*: recidivatam *TMPX*.

more, referring the resurrection to the same substance, and with his eye again on the grain of corn, he says, *It is sown in corruption, it rises again in incorruption; it is sown in dishonour, it rises again in glory; it is shown in weakness, it rises again in power; it is sown a body informed by soul, it rises again informed by spirit.*[1] Certainly nothing else rises again but what is sown, nothing else is sown but what is dissolved in the ground, and nothing else is dissolved in the ground but flesh. For it was this flesh which the sentence of God hurled down, *Earth thou art and unto earth shalt thou go,*[2] because from the earth it had been taken. Hence also the apostle had the idea of using the expression 'it is sown' when it is returned to the earth, because the earth is a repository for seeds, which have to be deposited in it and withdrawn from it again. And thus again he puts the seal on the matter when he insists, *For so it is written,*[3] that you may not think being sown means anything else than, 'Unto earth shalt thou go, from which thou wast taken': and so it refers to the flesh and nothing else, since so it is written.

53 But there are some who, so as to filch from the flesh that recurrence, argue that soul-informed body means soul. But since it is agreed and determined that that body will rise again which has been sown, they shall be challenged to produce ⟨as in court⟩ the article in dispute. Or else let them prove that a soul has been sown after death, that is, has died, has been cast to the ground, dismembered, dissolved, a sentence which God has not decreed against it: let them set before us its corruption and dishonour, its weakness, so that it may appertain to it to rise up also to incorruption and glory and power. For in Lazarus, the pre-eminent instance of resurrection,[4] it was the flesh which lay down in weakness, the flesh which all but decayed into dishonour, the flesh which meanwhile stank to corruption: and yet as flesh Lazarus rose again—along with the soul indeed, but that soul uncorrupt, which no one had bound with linen bands, no one had placed in a sepulchre, no one had perceived to be stinking, no one had seen buried four days before. Everything that Lazarus was, everything that happened at his death, all men's flesh even today experiences,

[1] 1 Cor. 15. 42–4. [2] Gen. 3. 19.
[3] 1 Cor. 15. 45. [4] Cf. John 11.

nullius. in qua ergo stilus apostoli comparet, de qua eum loqui constat, ea erit et corpus animale cum seminatur, et spiritale cum suscitatur. nam ut ita intellegas manum adhuc porrigit, aeque de eiusdem scripturae auctoritate factum retexens primum hominem Adam in animam vivam. si Adam homo primus, caro autem homo ante animam, sine dubio caro erit facta in animam: facta porro in animam, cum esset corpus, utique animale corpus est facta. quid eam appellari velint quam quod per animam facta est, quam quod ante animam non fuit, quam quod post animam non erit nisi cum resurgit? recepta enim anima rursus animale corpus efficitur, ut fiat spiritale: non enim resurgit nisi quod fuit. ita unde carni competit corpus animale dici, inde animae nullo modo competit. caro enim ante corpus quam animale corpus: animata enim postea, facta est corpus animale. anima vero etsi corpus, tamen quia ipsa est corpus non animatum sed animans potius, animale corpus non potest dici, nec fieri quod facit. alii enim accedens facit illud animale: non accedens autem alii quomodo se facit animale? sicut ergo ante animale corpus caro recipiens animam, ita et postea spiritale induens spiritum. hunc ordinem apostolus disponens, in Adam quoque et in Christo eum merito distinguit ut in capitibus distinctionis ipsius. sed cum et Christum novissimum Adam appellat, hinc eum recognosce ad carnis, non ad animae, resurrectionem omnibus doctrinae viribus operatum. si enim et primus homo Adam caro non anima, qui denique in animam vivam factus est, et novissimus Adam Christus ideo Adam quia homo,

20 vivam *TX*: viventem *MP*.
30 animatum *Rig.*: animata *libri*.   animans *T Gel.*: anima *MPX*.
31, 32 accedens (*bis*) *T*: accidens *MPX*.
38–49 *ita pungebam*.
39 vivam om. *TMX Brf*.

but so does no man's soul. That flesh then in which the apostle's pen is in evidence, concerning which it is agreed he is speaking, that it must be which is both soul-informed body when it is sown, and spirit-informed when it is wakened up. For he again lends you a hand towards understanding it so when, no less on the authority of the same scripture, he recalls that the first man, Adam, was made into a living soul.[1] If Adam is the first man, and the flesh was man before the soul was, without doubt it must be the flesh which was made into a soul. And then, being made into a soul, since it was already a body, of course it had become a soul-informed body. What would they have it called but that which it has become by means of the soul, that which it was not before it received the soul, that which after the soul has departed it will not be, except when it rises again? For when it has received back the soul it is again made a soul-informed body, so that it may become a spirit-informed one: for nothing rises again but what has already been. Thus the very reason which makes it possible for the flesh to be termed soul-informed body, makes it totally impossible for the soul to be so called. For the flesh was body before it was soul-informed body; but afterwards, having become animate, it has become a soul-informed body: whereas the soul, although it is a body, yet as it is not an animate body but rather an animating one, cannot be termed a soul-informed body, nor can it become that which is the effect of its own action. For when it accrues to some other thing it makes that other thing soul-informed; but if it does not accrue to some other thing, how can it make itself soul-informed? As therefore the flesh is first a soul-informed body when it receives the soul, so also it is afterwards a spirit-informed body when it clothes itself with spirit. When the apostle sets out this sequence he rightly makes it a matter of distinction in Adam's case as also in Christ's, for these are as it were the heads from which the distinction arises. And since he also calls Christ the last Adam,[2] from this you must acknowledge that he has wrought with all his powers of doctrine for the resurrection not of the soul but of the flesh. For if the first man Adam was flesh and not soul, and afterwards was made into a living soul, and the last Adam, Christ, is Adam because

[1] Cf. 1 Cor. 15. 45. [2] Cf. ibid.

ideo homo quia caro non quia anima, atque ita subiungit, Non 13
primum quod spiritale sed quod animale, postea quod spiritale,
secundum utrumque Adam, ecquid tibi videtur corpus animale et
corpus spiritale in eadem carne distinguere, cuius distinctionem in
45 utroque Adam, id est in utroque homine, praestruxit? ex qua enim 14
substantia pariant inter se Christus et Adam—scilicet ex carne,
licet et ex anima: sed carnis nomine homo uterque sunt: prior
enim caro homo—ex illa et ordinem admittere potuerunt ut alter
primus alter novissimus homo, id est Adam, deputarentur.
50 ceterum diversa in ordinem disponi non possunt, de substantia 15
dumtaxat: de loco enim aut tempore aut condicione forsitan possint. hic autem de substantia carnis primus et novissimus dicti
sunt, sicut et rursus primus homo de terra et secundus de caelo:
quia etsi de caelo secundum spiritum, sed homo secundum carnem.
55 itaque cum carni conveniat ordo in utroque Adam, non animae, 16
ut primus homo in animam vivam novissimus in spiritum vivi-
ficantem distincti sunt, aeque distinctio eorum carni distinctionem
praeiudicavit, ut de carne sit dictum, Non primum quod spiritale
sed quod animale, postea quod spiritale, atque ita eadem sit et 17
60 supra intellegenda, et quae seminetur corpus animale et quae
resurgat corpus spiritale, quia non primum quod spiritale sed quod
animale, quia primus Adam in animam novissimus Adam in
spiritum: totum de homine, totum de carne quando de homine.
quid ergo dicemus? nonne et nunc habet caro spiritum ex fide, ut 18
65 quaerendum sit quomodo corpus animale dicatur seminari?
plane accepit hic spiritum caro, sed arrabonem, animae autem non

    43 ecquid *Gel.*: et quid *MPX*: et quod *T*.
    57 sunt *T*: sint *R*.
    66 spiritum caro *T*: spiritum ex fide ut quaerendum sit quomodo corpus animale dicatur seminari: plane accepit et hic spiritum caro *MPX*.

he is man, and man because he is flesh and not because he is soul—and thus he adds, *That was not first which is spirit-informed but that which is soul-informed, and afterwards that which is spirit-informed,*[1] according to the two Adams—does he not seem to you to be making this distinction of soul-informed body and spirit-informed body within the same flesh, seeing he has previously built up this distinction in both Adams, that is, in both men? For in respect of what substance Christ and Adam are one another's peers, namely the flesh—albeit the soul too, yet it is on account of the flesh that both of them are man, for flesh is the prior man—in respect of this it has been possible for them to be set in sequence, so that one should be reckoned the first, and the other the last, man or Adam. Now opposites cannot be arranged in sequence, in respect of substance at any rate: though in respect of place and time and circumstances perhaps they can. But here they are termed the first and the last in respect of the substance of flesh—even as again the first man is from the earth, while the second is from heaven—because although he is from heaven according to the Spirit, yet he is Man according to the flesh. And so, since in both Adams the setting in sequence applies to the flesh, not to the soul, as they are distinguished, the first man into a living soul, the last into a life-giving Spirit, no less does the distinction between the two Adams constitute a previous judgement that the distinction belongs to the flesh: and in consequence, the statement, *That was not first which is spirit-informed but that which is soul-informed, and afterwards that which is spirit-informed,* applies to the flesh, and so the flesh again must be understood above to be that which is both sown a soul-informed body and rises again a spirit-informed body, because that was not first which is spirit-informed but that which is soul-informed, because the first Adam was made into a soul and the last Adam into a spirit.[2] All of it concerns man, and all of it concerns flesh since it concerns man. What then shall we say? Does not the flesh even now have the Spirit, by faith,[3] so that we have to enquire in what sense it is said to be sown a soul-informed body? It is true that even here and now the flesh has received the Spirit, but as an

[1] 1 Cor. 15. 46. [2] Cf. 1 Cor. 15. 44.
[3] Cf. Gal. 5. 5.

arrabonem sed plenitudinem. itaque etiam propterea, maioris 19
substantiae nomine animale corpus nuncupata est in qua seminatur,
futura proinde per plenitudinem spiritus insuper spiritale, in qua
resuscitatur. quid mirum si magis inde vocata est unde conferta
est quam unde *re*spersa est?

54 Ita de vocabulorum occasionibus plurimum quaestiones sub-
ornantur, sicut et de verborum communionibus. nam quia et
illud apud apostolum positum est, Uti devoretur mortale a vita,
caro scilicet, devorationem quoque ad perditionem scilicet carnis
adripiunt, quasi non et bilem et dolorem devorare dicamur, id est
abscondere et tegere et intra nosmetipsos continere. denique cum 2
et illud scriptum sit, Oportet mortale hoc induere immortalitatem,
ostenditur quomodo mortale devoretur a vita, dum indutum
immortalitate absconditur et tegitur et intus continetur, non dum
absumitur et amittitur. ergo et mors, inquis, salva erit cum fuerit 3
devorata. ideo discerne pro sensibus communionem verborum, et
integre intelleges. aliud enim mors et aliud mortale: aliter itaque
devorabitur mors et aliter mortale. mors non capit immortalitatem, mortale autem capit. denique et scriptum est quod necesse 4
est mortale hoc induere immortalitatem. quomodo ergo capit?
dum devoratur a vita. quomodo devoratur a vita? dum recipitur
et redigitur et includitur in ipsam. ceterum mors merito in interitum devoratur quia et ipsa in hoc devorat. Devoravit, inquit, 5
mors invalescendo: et ideo devorata est in contentionem: Ubi est
mors aculeus tuus? ubi est mors contentio tua? proinde et vita,

    68 qua *TMPX*: quo *Urs*.
    69 qua *TMP*: que *X*: quo *Urs*.
    70 vocitata *MPX*.
    71 respersa *Gel.*: responsa *T*: dispersa *MPX*.
54: 10 absumitur *TX*: adsumitur *MP*.
    12 intelleges *T Gel.*: intellegis *MPX*.   aliter itaque...aliter mortale *om.*
    MPX.
    15 est *T*: sit *MPX*.
    16 quomodo devoratur a vita *om. MPX*.

earnest; but of the soul it has received not an earnest but the fullness. And thus even for that reason, on account of the major substance, it has received the name of soul-informed body, and in that substance it is sown; but in due course it will become, through the fullness of the Spirit, a spirit-informed body besides, and in that fullness it is raised up again. What wonder is it if it has received its name from that which has filled it throughout rather than from that which has bedewed it from without?

54 Questionings frequently have their material supplied not only by the contexts in which expressions are used, but also by equivocal terms. For because this saying too is found in the apostle, *That the mortal thing*—that is, the flesh—*may be swallowed up by life*,[1] they seize upon 'swallowed up' also as indicating destruction—of the flesh, of course—as though we were not also said to swallow up anger and sorrow, that is, to hide them and cover them up and confine them within ourselves. And in fact, since this too is in scripture, *This mortal thing must put on immortality*,[2] we are shown in what manner the mortal thing is swallowed up by life, namely by being clothed with immortality and thus hidden and covered by it and confined within it, not by being consumed and lost. In that case, you reply, death too will be saved when it has been swallowed up. Distinguish then the equivocal terms in accordance with their meanings, and you will understand aright. For death is one thing, and the mortal thing is another; and so death will be swallowed up in one manner, and the mortal thing in another. Death is not capable of immortality: the mortal thing is capable of it. In fact it is also written that this mortal thing must put on immortality.[3] How then is it capable of that? By being swallowed up by life. How is it swallowed up by life? By being received and brought back and enclosed within it. Death however is inevitably swallowed up into destruction, seeing that its own swallowing up has this effect: *Death*, he says, *swallowed it up by prevailing*,[4] and consequently it was itself swallowed up unto striving. *O death, where is thy sting? O death, where is thy striving?*[5] It follows that life also, the enemy of death, will through striving

[1] 2 Cor. 5. 4. [2] 1 Cor. 15. 53.
[3] Cf. 1 Cor. 15. 53.   [4] Isa. 25. 8.   [5] 1 Cor. 15. 55.

mortis scilicet aemula, per contentionem devorabit in salutem quod per contentionem suam devoraverat mors in interitum.

55 Quanquam igitur resurrecturam carnem probantes hoc ipso non aliam resurrecturam probemus quam de qua agitur, tamen singulae quaestiones et causae earum proprios quoque flagitant congressus, licet aliunde iam caesae. interpretabimur itaque 2
5 plenius et vim et rationem demutationis, quae ferme subministrat alterius carnis resurrecturae praesumptionem, quasi demutari desinere sit in totum et de pristino perire. discernenda est autem 3 demutatio ab omni argumento perditionis: aliud enim demutatio aliud perditio. porro non aliud, si ita demutabitur caro ut pereat.
10 peribit autem demutata, si non ipsa permanserit in demutatione quae exhibita fuerit in resurrectione. quemadmodum enim perit 4 si non resurgit, ita et si resurgit quidem verum in demutatione subducitur, aeque perit: aeque enim non erit ac si non resurrexerit. et quam ineptum si in hoc resurgit ut non sit, quae potuit non
15 resurrexisse ne esset, quia non esse iam coeperat. non miscebuntur 5 omnino diversa, mutatio atque perditio, operibus utique diversa: perdit haec, illa mutat. quomodo ergo quod perditum est mutatum non est, ita quod mutatum est perditum non est. perisse enim est in totum non esse quod fuerit: mutatum esse 6
20 aliter esse est. porro dum aliter est, idipsum potest esse. habet enim esse quod non omnino perit: mutationem enim passum est, non perditionem. atque adeo potest et demutari quid et ipsum esse 7 nihilominus, ut et totus homo in hoc aevo substantia quidem ipse sit multifariam tamen demutetur, et habitu et ipsa corpulentia
25 et valetudine et condicione et dignitate et aetate, studio negotio artificio, facultatibus sedibus legibus moribus, nec quicquam

22 suam *Jun.*: tuam *MPX*: *om. T Gel. Brf.*
55: 12 demutationem *MPX*.
 15 ne esset *Brf.*: necesse est *MPX*: necesse *R¹*: nec esse *R³* (*forsan recte*).
 21 omnino *om. MPX*.

swallow up unto salvation that which through its own striving death had swallowed up unto destruction.

55 So then, although by proving that the flesh will rise again we thereby prove that the very same flesh will rise again as is under discussion, yet each several expression of doubt, along with the purpose it has in view, demands its particular confrontation, although already defeated with other weapons. And so I shall interpret more fully the force and implication of 'change', since it is this that generally speaking suggests the assumption that it is another flesh that will rise again, the allegation being that to be changed is totally to cease to exist, to be destroyed in respect of what originally was. But change must be distinguished from everything that argues destruction: for change is one thing, and destruction is another. But it will not be another if the flesh is to be changed in such a sense as to be destroyed. It will however be destroyed when changed, if it does not during the change remain itself, that same flesh which will have been brought into view at the resurrection. For just as it is destroyed if it does not rise again, so, even if it rises, yet is abstracted during the change, it is no less destroyed: for it will no less cease to be than if it had not risen again. And how pointless it is for it to rise again for the express purpose of not existing, when it was possible for it not to have risen again so as not to exist, because it had already begun being non-existent. There is no possible means of combining the opposites, change and destruction, which are directly opposite in their effects. The latter destroys, the former changes. As then that which is destroyed is not changed, so that which is changed is not destroyed. For to be destroyed is for a thing, which has existed, totally to cease to exist: to be changed is to continue to exist, in another form. But while it exists in another form it can continue to be itself: for it possesses an existence which is not totally destroyed, since it has undergone change, not destruction. And, for a proof that a thing can be changed and none the less be itself, the man as a whole does during this life in substance remain himself, yet changes in various ways, in outward aspect and in the very constitution of his body, in health and circumstances and honour and age, in occupation, business, craft, in means, abode, laws, and

tamen amittat hominis, nec ita alius efficiatur ut cesset idem esse, immo nec alius efficiatur sed aliud. hanc formam demutationis 8 divina etiam documenta testantur. mutatur Moysi manus, et quidem ad instar emortuae exsanguis et exalbida et frigida: sed et recepto calore et refuso colore eadem caro et sanguis est. mutatur postea et facies eiusdem incontemplabili claritate: sed Moyses erat proinde qui non videbatur. sic et Stephanus angelicum iam 9 fastigium induerat: sed non alia genua in lapidatione succiderant. dominus quoque in secessu montis etiam vestimenta luce muta- 10 verat, sed liniamenta Petro agnoscibilia servaverat: ubi etiam Moyses et Helias, alter in imagine carnis nondum receptae, alter in veritate nondum defunctae, eandem tamen habitudinem corporis etiam in gloria perseverare docuerant. de quo exemplo instructus 11 et Paulus, Qui transfigura*b*it, inquit, corpus humilitatis nostrae conformale corpori gloriae suae. quodsi et transfigurationem et conversionem in transitum substantiae cuiusque defendis, ergo et Saul in alium virum conversus de corpore suo excessit, et ipse 12 Satanas, cum in angelum lucis transfiguratur, qualitatem suam amittit. non opinor. ita et in resurrectionis eventu mutari converti reformari licebit cum salute substantiae.

56 Etenim quam absurdum, quam vero et iniquum, utrumque autem quam deo indignum, aliam substantiam operari aliam mercede dispungi, ut haec quidem caro per martyria lanietur, alia vero coronetur, item e contrario haec quidem caro in spurcitiis volutetur, alia vero damnetur. nonne praestat omnem semel 2 fidem a spe resurrectionis abducere quam de gravitate atque iustitia dei ludere—Marcionem pro Valentino resuscitari—quando neque 3

    28 efficiatur *C*: efficitur *TMPX*.
    39 docuerant *T*: docuerunt *MPX*.
    40 transfigurabit *Pam.*: transfiguravit *TMPX*.
    41 quodsi et *T*: quod et si *MPX*.
    42 transitum *MPX*: transitu *T*.
56: 1 iniquum *TC*: ethnicum *MPX*.
    3 mercede *XR³*: mercedem *TMPR¹*.
    3–4 per martyria…quidem caro *om. T*.
    7 *ita pungebam.*

morals, yet loses nothing of his manhood, nor is so made into someone else as to cease to be himself: in fact he is not made into someone else but into something else. To this law of change the divine documents also bear witness. Moses' hand is changed, and in fact is bloodless, white, and cold, as though quite dead;[1] but yet, as its heat returns and its colour flows back, it is the same flesh and blood. Afterwards again, his face is changed, with glory it was impossible to gaze upon:[2] yet it was still Moses who was veiled from sight. So also Stephen was clothed with angelic excellence, but it was the same pair of knees that bent to the stoning.[3] The Lord also, at his withdrawal into the mountain, exchanged his garments for light, yet preserved the features recognizable by Peter:[4] and there also Moses and Elijah, the one in the reflection of flesh he had not yet received back again, the other in the verity of flesh which had not yet died, taught us that for all that the outward appearance of the body continues the same even in glory. And so Paul, equipped with this example, says, *Who shall change the body of our humility to be conformed to the body of his glory.*[5] But if you claim that transfiguration and conversion amount to the removal of each several substance, in that case when Saul was converted into another man[6] he withdrew from his own body, and Satan himself, when transfigured into an angel of light,[7] loses his proper quality. I think not. Thus also, when the resurrection takes effect, it will be possible to be changed, converted, and reformed, while the substance remains unimpaired.

56 For how absurd, and moreover how unjust, and on both grounds how unworthy of God, for one substance to do the work and another to be checked off with the wages, this flesh being butchered in martyrdom while another receives the crown, and, the other way round, this flesh wallowing in foulnesses while another receives damnation. Is it not better to dissociate the whole faith from the hope of the resurrection than to play tricks with the gravity and righteousness of God? Or for Marcion to be brought to life again instead of Valentinus? For it is not credible that either

---

[1] Cf. Exod. 4. 6–7.   [2] Cf. 2 Cor. 3. 7.
[3] Cf. Acts 7. 59–60.   [4] Cf. Matt. 17. 2–8.   [5] Phil. 3. 21.
[6] Cf. 1 Sam. 10. 6.   [7] Cf. 2 Cor. 11. 14.

mentem neque memoriam neque conscientiam hominis hodierni
credibile sit aboleri per indumentum illud mutatorium immortalitatis et incorruptelae, vacaturo scilicet emolumento et fructu
resurrectionis et statu divini utrobique iudicii? si non meminerim 4
me esse qui merui, quomodo gloriam deo dicam? quomodo
canam illi novum canticum, nesciens me esse qui gratiam debeam?
cur autem solius carnis demutatio excipitur, non et animae simul,
quae in omnibus praefuit carni? quale est ut eadem anima quae 5
in hac carne totum vitae ordinem decucurrit, quae in hac carne
deum didicit et Christum induit et spem salutis seminavit, in alia
nescioqua metat fructum? nae illa gratiosissima caro, cui gratis
vita constabit. quodsi non et anima mutabitur, iam nec animae
resurrectio est: nec ipsa enim resurrexisse credetur si non alia
resurrexerit.

57 Hinc iam illa vulgaris incredulitatis argutia est. si, inquiunt,
ipsa eademque substantia revocatur cum sua forma linea qualitate,
ergo et cum insignibus suis reliquis: itaque et caeci et claudi et
paralytici, et ut quis insignis excesserit ita et revertetur. quid nunc 2
et si ita? dedignaris tantam gratiam qualiscumque a deo consequi?
non enim et nunc animae solius admittens salutem dimidiatis
hominibus eam adscribis? quid est credere resurrectionem, nisi
integram credere? si enim caro de dissolutione reparabitur, multo
magis de vexatione revocabitur. minoribus maiora praescribunt. 3
cuiuscumque membri detruncatio vel obtusio nonne mors membri
est? si universalis mors resurrectione rescinditur, quid portionalis?
si demutamur in gloriam, quanto magis in incolumitatem? vitiatio 4
corporum accidens res est, integritas propria est. in hac nascimur.
etiam si in utero vitiemur, iam hominis est passio: prius est genus

9 amoveri *T*.
57: 10 cuiusque *T Brf*.

the mind or the memory or the conscience of the man who today is, is abolished by reason of that festal garment of immortality and incorruption, since in that case the revenue and usufruct of resurrection, and the stability of divine judgement upon both substances, would be ineffective. If I do not remember that it is I whose the deserts are, how shall I give glory to God? How shall I sing to him the new song,[1] if I am unaware that it is I from whom thanks are due? But why is it change of the flesh alone that receives special treatment, and not change of the soul as well, seeing it has in all things been in command of the flesh? How comes it that the same soul which in this flesh has run the whole of life's race, the same which in this flesh has learned of God and put on Christ and sowed the seed which is the hope of salvation, should reap its harvest in I know not what other flesh? Highly favoured indeed is that flesh to which life will be awarded without its deserving. But if the soul too is not to be changed, there is then no resurrection of the soul either: for it too will not be credited with having risen again, if it is not another when it has risen.

57 Next we have that well-known subtilty of vulgar unbelief: 'If', they suggest, 'the very same substance is recalled to existence, along with its own shape, outline and quality, then it retains also the rest of its distinguishing marks: and so the blind and lame and palsied—and however one was marked at his decease, so will he also return.' Well now, even if so, are you too proud, in whatever state, to obtain so great a grace from God? For even now, by admitting the salvation of the soul alone, are you not assigning that salvation to man reduced to half? What is belief in the resurrection, unless believing it entire? For if the flesh is to be restored from dissolution, much more will it be recalled from discomfort. Greater things prescribe the rule for the lesser. Is not the amputation or the crippling of any member the death of that member? If general death is rescinded by resurrection, what of partial death? If we are changed into glory, how much more into health. The defects that accrue to bodies are an accident: their integrity is a property. In the latter we are born. Even if we are crippled in the womb, this happens to one who is already man: the species is there

[1] Cf. Ps. 96. 1; Apoc. 5. 9.

quam casus. quomodo vita confertur a deo, ita et refertur: quales 5
eam accipimus, tales et recipimus. naturae non iniuriae reddimur:
quod nascimur, non quod laedimur, revivescimus. si non integros 6
deus suscitat, non suscitat mortuos. quis enim mortuus integer,
etsi integer moritur? quis incolumis qui exanimis? quod corpus
inlaesum cum interemptum, cum frigidum, cum expallidum, cum
edurum, cum cadaver? quando magis homo debilis, nisi cum
totus? quando magis paralyticus, nisi cum immobilis? ita nihil
aliud est mortuum resuscitari quam integrum fieri, ne ex ea parte
mortuus adhuc sit ex qua non resurrexerit. idoneus deus reficere 7
quod fecit. hanc suam et potestatem et liberalitatem satis iam in
Christo spopondit: immo et ostendit non tantum resuscitatorem
carnis verum etiam redintegratorem. atque adeo et apostolus, Et 8
mortui, inquit, resurgent incorrupti: quomodo, nisi integri qui
retro corrupti tam vitio valetudinis quam et senio sepulturae? nam 9
et supra utrumque proponens, oportere et corruptivum istud
induere incorruptelam et mortale istud immortalitatem, non itera-
vit sententiam sed differentiam demandavit: immortalitatem enim
ad rescissionem mortis, incorruptelam ad obliterationem corruptelae dividendo, alteram ad resurrectionem alteram ad redintegrationem temperavit. puto autem et Thessalonicensibus omnis
substantiae integritatem repromisit. itaque nec in posterum time- 10
buntur corporum labes: nihil poterit admittere integritas vel conservata vel restituta, ex quo illi etiam si quid amiserat redditur.
praescribens enim adhuc easdem passiones obituram carnem si 11
eadem resurrectura dicatur, naturam adversus dominum suum
temere defendis, legem adversus gratiam impie adseris, quasi deo
minus liceat et mutare naturam et sine lege servare. quo ergo

26 *immo et, etc., ita pungebam, conservata librorum MSS. scriptura* resuscitatorem, redintegratorem, *ubi ablativa scripserant Kroy. Brf.*
37 amittere *Rig. Brf.* (*sed haud opus erat*).
41 deo *T*: domino *MPX*.

before the accident. As life is given us by God, so also is it given again: as we were when we received it, so are we also when we receive it back. Our restoration is a gift to nature, not to injury: we live again as what we are born, not as what damage makes us. God is not raising the dead, if he does not raise them up entire: for what dead man is entire, even if he is entire when he dies? Who is in health, that has ceased to breathe? What body is uninjured when it is dead, cold, pallid, stiff, a corpse? When is a man more weak, than when he is wholly weak? When is he more palsied, than when he is motionless? Thus for a dead man to be raised again is precisely the same as for him to be made entire: otherwise he will still be dead, to the extent to which he has not risen again. God is competent to remake that which he has made. That this power and this generosity are his, he has already given pledges in Christ: nay more, he has set him in evidence not only as one who raises up the flesh again, but also as one who makes it whole. And consequently the apostle also says, *And the dead shall rise again uncorrupted.*[1] How so, unless entire, though previously corrupt by damage to health no less than by long abiding in their burying-place? For previously also, when he made the double statement that this corruptible thing must put on incorruption and this mortal thing must put on immortality,[2] he was not merely repeating the sentence, but was giving expression to a difference: for by assigning immortality to the rescinding of death, and incorruption to the obliteration of corruption, he made the one apply to resurrection and the other to redintegration. And I suppose even to the Thessalonians he promised integrity of the whole substance.[3] And so not even for the future will corporal defects be a matter of fear. Integrity, whether preserved or restored, will be capable of incurring no harm from the time when even what it had lost is given back to it. For when you postulate that the flesh, if it be said that it will be the same flesh when it rises again, will again meet with the same misfortunes, you rashly take up the cause of nature against its Lord, you impiously conduct a defence of the law against grace, as if it were not feasible for God both to change nature and to preserve it,

[1] 1 Cor. 15. 52.   [2] Cf. 1 Cor. 15. 53.
[3] Cf. 1 Thess. 5. 23.

legimus, Quae impossibilia apud homines possibilia apud deum: et, Stulta mundi elegit deus ut sapientia mundi confundat? oro te, 12
si famulum tuum libertate mutaveris, quia eadem caro atque anima permanebunt quae flagellis et compedibus et stigmatibus obnoxiae retro fuerant, idcircone illas eadem pati oportebit? non opinor: atquin et vestis albae nitore et anuli aurei honore et patroni nomine ac tribu mensaque honoratur. permitte hanc et deo potestatem 13 per vim illius demutationis condicionem non naturam reformandi, dum et passiones auferuntur et munitiones conferuntur. ita manebit quidem caro etiam post resurrectionem eatenus passibilis qua ipsa, qua eadem, et tamen impassibilis quia in hoc ipsum manumissa a domino ne ultra pati possit.

58 Iocunditas, inquit Esaias, aeterna super caput eorum: nihil aeternum nisi post resurrectionem: Aufugit, inquit, dolor et maeror et gemitus ab illis. proinde et Iohanni angelus, Et delebit deus 2 omnem lacrimam ab oculis eorum: utique ex isdem oculis qui retro fleverant quique adhuc flere potuissent si non omnem lacrimae imbrem indulgentia divina siccasset. et rursus, Deus enim 3 delebit omnem lacrimam ab oculis eorum, et mors hactenus: igitur et corruptela hactenus, proinde per incorruptelam fugata quemadmodum mors per immortalitatem. si dolor et maeror et 4 gemitus ipsaque mors ex laesuris et animae et carnis obveniunt, quomodo auferentur nisi cessaverint causae, scilicet laesurae carnis atque animae? ubi casus adversi apud deum, ubi incursus infesti 5 apud Christum? ubi daemonici impetus apud spiritum sanctum, iam et ipso diabolo cum angelis suis ignibus merso? ubi necessitas, aut quod dicitur fortuna vel fatum? quae resuscitatis plaga post

53 qua (*bis*) *MPX*: quia *T*.   quia *MPX*: qua *T Gel*.
58: 2 inquit *om. T*.
6 siccaret *MPX*.
12 deum *TC*: dominum *MPX*.   ubi (*altera vice*) *T*: aut ubi *MPX*.

without any law ⟨to control him⟩. In such a case what is the meaning of, *Things which are impossible with men are possible with God*,[1] and, *God hath chosen the foolish things of the world so that he may confound the world's wise things?*[2] I ask you, if you have changed your servant's status by setting him free, is it true that, because his flesh and soul will remain the same as were formerly subject to stripes and shackles and brandings, they will therefore have to continue to suffer them? I trow not. Rather is he honoured with the splendour of a white garment and the dignity of a gold ring, and with his patron's name and tribe and hospitality. Allow God also this right to reshape condition, not nature, by virtue of that mutation, while the possibility of injury is withdrawn and protection conferred. Thus the flesh will indeed remain, even after the resurrection, to that extent passible to which it is itself and the same self, while yet impassible in that it has received its freedom from its Lord, with the express intent that it should not be capable of suffering any more.

58 *Everlasting joy*, says Isaiah, *upon their head*. There is nothing everlasting until after the resurrection. *Sorrow and mourning and sighing*, he says, *hath fled away from them*.[3] Likewise also the angel to John, *And God shall wipe away every tear from their eyes*[4]—evidently the same eyes as had formerly wept, as would still have been capable of weeping unless divine indulgence had dried up every shower of a tear. And again, *For God shall wipe away every tear from their eyes, and there shall be no more death*:[5] and therefore no more corruption, since it will have been driven away by incorruption precisely as death will have been by immortality. If sorrow and mourning and sighing, and death itself, arise from injuries to soul and flesh, how shall they be removed unless their causes, the injuries of flesh and soul, have ceased? What room is there for adverse accidents in the presence of God? What room for hostile attacks in the presence of Christ? What room for demonic assaults in the presence of the Holy Spirit, after the devil himself along with his angels has been drowned in the fires?[6] What room for necessity or for what is called fortune or fate? What stripes for

[1] Matt. 19. 26.   [2] 1 Cor. 1. 27.   [3] Isa. 35. 10.
[4] Apoc. 7. 17.   [5] Apoc. 21. 4.   [6] Cf. Apoc. 20. 10.

veniam, quae reconciliatis ira post gratiam? quae infirmitas post virtutem, quae imbecillitas post salutem? quod vestimenta et 6 calciamenta filiorum Israelis quadraginta illis annis indetrita et inobsoleta manserunt, quod et in ipsis corporibus unguium et capillorum facilia crementa habilitatis et dignitatis iustitia defixit ne etiam enormitas corruptelae deputaretur, quod Babylonii ignes 7 trium fratrum nec tiaras nec sarabara quanquam Iudaeis aliena laeserunt, quod Ionas devoratus a belua maris in cuius alvo 8 naufragia de die digerebantur triduo post incolumis exspuitur, quod hodie Enoch et Helias, nondum resurrectione dispuncti 9 quia nec morte functi, qua tamen de orbe translati et hoc ipso iam aeternitatis candidati, ab omni vitio et ab omni damno et ab omni iniuria et contumelia immunitatem carnis ediscunt: cuinam fidei testimonium signant nisi qua credi oportet haec futurae integritatis esse documenta? figurae enim nostrae 10 fuerunt, apostolo auctore, quae scripta sunt ut et deum potentiorem credamus omni corporum lege, et carnis magis utique et conservatorem cuius etiam vestimenta etiam calciamenta protexit.

59 Sed futurum inquis aevum alterius est dispositionis et aeternae: igitur huius aevi substantiam non aeternam diversa possidere non posse. plane, si homo propter dispositionem futuram, et non dispositio propter hominem. sed enim apostolus 2 scribens, Sive mundus sive vita sive mors sive futura sive praesentia, omnia vestra sunt, eosdem constituit heredes etiam futurorum. nihil tibi largitur Esaias dicens Omnis caro foenum, et alibi Et videbit omnis caro salutare dei: exitus, non substantias, distinxit.

18 illis *om. T.*
20 incrementa *T.*
21 corruptela *MPX.*
32 et (*post* utique) *om. T Brf.*
59: 8 dei *MPX:* domini *T.*

those raised up again, after their pardon? What wrath for those reconciled, after grace? What weakness after strength? What feebleness after healing? That the clothes and shoes of the children of Israel were neither worn out nor became old those forty years; that in their bodies too due measure of comfort and propriety kept down the easy growth of nails and hair, lest even their immoderation should be accounted corruption;[1] that the Babylonian fires injured neither the hats nor the trousers of the three brethren, though these are garments foreign to the Jews;[2] that Jonah, though swallowed up by the beast of the sea in whose belly wrecked ships were daily digested, is spewed out unhurt three days later;[3] that today Enoch and Elijah, not yet made perfect by resurrection, because they have not yet experienced death, yet being translated from the world and by this very fact now candidates of eternity, are acquiring immunity of the flesh from every fault and every loss and every injury and insult;[4] to what faith do these facts bear witness except that by which we must needs believe that these are proofs of future integrity? For, on the apostle's authority, they were figures of us,[5] and have been written so that we may believe that God is both more powerful than any law concerning bodies, and that he is by so much the more also the preserver of the flesh in that he has protected even its clothes and its shoes.

59 But, you object, the age to come is of another, an eternal dispensation: and so the substance of this world, which is not eternal, cannot obtain possession of its opposites. Evidently so, if man was made for the sake of the future dispensation, and not that dispensation for the sake of man. But when the apostle writes, *Whether the world or life or death or things future or things present, all are yours*,[6] he appoints the same persons heirs even of things future. Isaiah gives you no support. When he says, *All flesh is grass*,[7] and elsewhere, *And all flesh shall see the salvation of God*,[8] he has made a distinction of destinies, not of substances. For who denies that the

[1] Cf. Deut. 8. 4.
[2] Cf. Dan. 3. 27.
[3] Cf. Jonah 2. 10.
[4] Cf. Gen. 5. 24; 2 Kings 2. 11.
[5] 1 Cor. 10. 11.
[6] 1 Cor. 3. 22.
[7] Isa. 40. 6.
[8] Cf. Isa. 40. 5.

quis enim iudicium dei non in sententia duplici statuit salutis et 3
poenae? omnis igitur caro foenum quae igni destinatur, et omnis
caro videbit salutare domini quae saluti ordinatur. ego me scio
neque alia carne adulteria commisisse, neque nunc alia carne ad
continentiam eniti. si quis est bina pudenda circumferens, potest 4
iam et demere foenum carnis immundae et solam sibi reservare
quae visura sit domini salutare. sed cum idem prophetes etiam 5
nationes ostendat nunc deputatas velut pulverem et salivam, nunc
speraturas et credituras in nomen et in brachium domini, numquid
et de nationibus fallimur, et aliae quidem sunt crediturae aliae in
pulverem deputatae, ex diversitate substantiae? sed et Christus 6
intra oceanum, et de isto caelo quod nobis incubat, verum lumen
nationibus obfulsit: et ipsi Valentiniani hic errare didicerunt: nec
alia erit forma nationum credentium nisi quae et non credentium,
de carne de anima. sicut ergo easdem nationes non genere sed 7
sorte distinxit, ita et carnes, quae in ipsis nationibus una substantia
est, non materia sed mercede disiungit.

60 Ecce autem, ut adhuc controversiam exaggerent carni, maxime
eidem, de officiis quoque membrorum argumentantur, aut et ipsa
dicentes permanere debere cum suis operibus et fructibus, ut
eidem corpulentiae adscripta, aut quia constet decessura esse officia
membrorum corpulentiam quoque eradunt, cuius scilicet perseverantia credenda non sit utique sine membris, quia nec membra
credenda sint sine officiis. quo enim iam, inquiunt, spelunca haec 2
oris et dentium statio et gulae lapsus et compitum stomachi et
alvei gurges et intestinorum perplexa proceritas, cum esui et potui

---

11 domini *MPX*: *om. T*: dei *Pam.* (*sed licuit scriptori quasi in transitu et hic et infra prophetae verba interpretari*).
20 incubat *TR*³: incumbat *PXR*¹: incumbit *M.*
25 disiunxit *MPX.*
60: 5 eradunt *Brf.*: eradant *libri.*

judgement of God stands in the double sentence of salvation and penalty? So all flesh is grass, which is destined to the fire: and all flesh shall see the salvation of God, which is ordained to salvation. I for my part am aware that it was not with some other flesh that I committed adulteries, and that it is not now with some other flesh that I am striving towards continence. If there is any man who is carrying about two sets of privy members, he can even now strip off the grass which is impure flesh and reserve to himself that flesh alone which is to see the salvation of our Lord. But when the same prophet shows that the nations also are at one time reckoned as dust and spittle, and are at another time to hope and to believe in the name and the arm of the Lord, do we make any mistake about the nations? And is it because of diversity of substance that some are to believe, while others are reckoned for dust? No, for even Christ shone forth as the true light of the nations,[1] within the ocean, and from this sky which broods over us: and these very Valentinians have here learned to go astray: nor will there be some other fashion of the nations which believe, but only that which is theirs who do not believe, of flesh, and of soul. As then he has distinguished, not in species but in destiny, nations which are the same, so also the kinds of flesh, which in these nations is one substance, he has opposed to one another not in material but in reward.

60 But see: so that they may still pile up controversy for the flesh, and in particular for the flesh in its own identity, they argue also about the functions of its members, either alleging that they ought to continue for ever in their own activities and effects, as being appurtenances of that identical bodily constitution; or else, because it is agreed that the functions of the members will cease, they cancel the bodily constitution as well, seeing its continuance is, they say, not credible without the members, as neither are the members credible without their functions. For to what purpose from thenceforth, they ask, this cave of the mouth and guardroom of the teeth and precipice of the throat and crossways of the gullet and cesspool of the belly and intricate length of the intestines, when there is to be no occasion for eating and drinking? To what

[1] Cf. John 1. 9.

locus non erit? quo huiusmodi membra admittunt subigunt devolvunt dividunt digerunt egerunt, quo manus ipsae et pedes et operarii quique artus, cum victus etiam cura cessabit? quo 3 renes conscii seminum, et reliqua genitalium utriusque sexus, et conceptuum stabula et uberum fontes, decessuro concubitu et fetu et educatu? postremo quo totum corpus, totum scilicet vacaturum? ad haec ergo praestruximus non oportere committi 4 futurorum atque praesentium dispositiones, intercessura tunc demutatione: et nunc superstruimus officia ista membrorum necessitatibus vitae huius eo usque consistere donec et ipsa vita transferatur a temporalitate in aeternitatem, sicut animale corpus in spiritale, dum mortale istud induit immortalitatem et corruptivum istud incorruptelam. et ipsa autem liberata tunc vita a necessitati- 5 bus, liberabuntur et membra ab officiis: nec ideo non erunt necessaria: licet enim officiis liberentur, sed iudiciis detinentur ut quis referat per corpus prout gessit. salvum enim hominem tribunal 6 dei exigit: salvum vero sine membris non licet, *etenim* ex quorum non officiis sed substantiis constat, nisi forte et navem sine carina sine prora sine puppi sine compaginis totius incolumitate salvam adseverabis. et tamen navem, procella dissipatam vel carie disso- 7 lutam, redactis et recuratis omnibus membris eandem saepe conspeximus etiam titulo restitutionis gloriantem: de dei artificio et arbitrio et iure torquebimur? porro si dives dominus et liberalis, 8 adfectui aut gloriae suae praestans solam navis restitutionem, hactenus eam voluerit operari, idcirco tu negabis necessariam illi compaginem pristinam ut exinde iam vacaturam, cum soli saluti navis sine operatione conveniat? igitur hoc tantummodo discere 9

21 induet *Pam.*
24 detinentur *Löfstedt*: desinentur *T*: retinentur *MPX*.   quis *libri*: quisque *Oeh. Brf.*
26 etenim *scribebam*: enim *MP*: alii alia.

purpose do members like these take in, break up, swallow down, divert, digest, eject? To what purpose the hands and the feet and all the muscles by which men work, when even thought for food is to cease? To what purpose the loins, privy to the seed, and the rest of the reproductive organs of both sexes, with the lodgements of conception and the fountains of the breasts, when cohabitation and childbearing and nurture are to pass away? In short, to what purpose the whole body, when it is to be wholly inactive? Now it was with this in view that we laid down as foundation that it is not reasonable for the ordinances of future things and things present to be brought into conflict, seeing that the change will by then intervene: and so now we add as superstructure that those functions of the members do by the necessities of this life remain until, and only until, the life itself be transferred from temporality to eternity, even as the soul-informed body will be transferred to spirit-informed, when this mortal thing puts on immortality and this corruptible thing incorruption. But when life itself has been delivered from necessities the members also will be delivered from their functions: but they will not for that reason be unnecessary. For though they be delivered from their functions, yet are they retained for judgements, that every man may receive through his body according as he hath done. For God's judgement-seat demands a man in full being: in full being however he cannot be without the members, for of their substances, though not their functions, he consists—unless perchance you are going to affirm that a ship is in full being without keel, without stem, without stern, without the integrity of its whole structure. Yet even a ship, broken by storm or fallen to pieces by decay, we have often seen, when all its members have been replaced and rehabilitated, boasting of its sameness even by the inscription 'restored': are we to be anxious about God's craftsmanship and authority and rights? Besides, if a rich and generous owner, while granting to his private sentiment or his public reputation the boon of the ship's restoration and that alone, has expressed the wish for it to work no more, will you say that it has no need of its original structure, from now on to be inactive, since thus it beseems the bare salvation of a ship without work to do? This then and this alone it suffices for us to

sufficit, an deus hominem saluti destinando carnem destinarit, an eandem velit denuo esse. quam non debebis ex futura membrorum vacatione praescribere denuo esse non posse: licet enim esse quid
40 denuo et nihilominus vacare. nec potest autem dici vacare si non sit. atenim si sit, poterit et non vacare: nihil enim apud deum vacabit.

61 Sed accepisti, homo, os ad vorandum atque potandum: cur non potius ad eloquendum, ut a ceteris animalibus distes? cur non potius ad praedicandum deum, et etiam hominibus antistes? denique Adam ante nomina animalibus enuntiavit quam de
5 arbore decerpsit, ante etiam prophetavit quam voravit. sed 2 accepisti dentes ad macellum corrodendum: cur non potius ad omnem hiatum et rictum tuum coronandum, cur non potius ad pulsus linguae temperandos, ad vocis articulos offensione signandos? denique et edentulos et audi et vide, ut honorem oris et
10 organum dentium quaeras. forata sunt inferna in viro et in 3 femina, nimirum qua libidines fluitent: cur non magis qua potu*um* deflux*us* colentur? est adhuc feminis intus quo semina congerantur: an quo sanguinis onera secedant quem pigrior sexus discutere non sufficit? dicenda enim et haec, quatenus quae volunt et 4
15 quorum volunt et qualiter volunt officia membrorum ludibriose de industria suffundendae resurrectionis oblatrant, non recogitantes ipsas prius causas necessitatis tunc vacaturas, cibi famem et potus sitim et concubitus genituram et operationis victum. sublata enim morte neque victus fulcimenta ad subsidia vitae neque generis
20 subparatura gravis erit membris. ceterum et hodie vacare intestinis 5 et pudendis licebit: quadraginta diebus Moyses et Helias ieiunio functi solo deo alebantur: iam tunc enim dedicabatur, Non in pane

37 pro an (*priore vice*) cum *Kroy. Brf.*   deus *T*: dominus *MPX*.
61: 11 potuum defluxus *scribebam*: potu de fructu *T*: defluxura *MPX*: potuum defruta *Gel*.
17 cibi *R*: ibi *MP*: ubi *X*: om. *T*.

know, whether God, in designing man for salvation, has included the flesh in that design, whether he will have it exist anew in its own identity. And you will have no right, on the ground that the members will in future be inactive, to deny the possibility of its existing anew: for it is feasible for a thing to exist anew and none the less be inactive. But it cannot be said even to be inactive, if it does not exist. Moreover, if it exist, it will be possible for it also not to be inactive: for in God's presence nothing can be inactive.

61 But, my friend, you have had given you a mouth for eating and drinking: why not rather for speaking, to make you different from the rest of animals? Why not rather for praising God, to make you superior even to men? In fact Adam pronounced names for the animals before he plucked of the tree: he was even a prophet before he was an eater. But, you say, you have had teeth given you for gnawing flesh-meat: why not rather for a crown to all your yawning and gaping? Why not rather for modifying the strokes of the tongue, for making the articulations of the voice significant by tripping them up? In fact, listen to and look at men without teeth, that you may find out the need for the adornment of the mouth and the instrumentality of the teeth. The lower parts in man and in woman are perforated—so that there, you say, the lusts may be in motion: why not rather that the excreta may be filtered? Also women have within them a place where the seed may be garnered: why not where there may be a diversion of the overplus of the blood which the less energetic sex has not the strength to throw off? For even this must be spoken, in that these, in their zeal for putting the resurrection to shame, wantonly rail as they will at what functions they will of what members they will, not considering that then the very causes of necessity will first be inoperative, of food hunger, and of drink thirst, and of cohabitation child-bearing, and of labour livelihood. For when death has been taken away, neither the supports of livelihood for the preservation of life, nor the replenishment of the race, will be a burden to the members. Moreover even today it will be possible for the intestines and the genitals to be inoperative. Moses and Elijah, fasting for forty days, were nourished on God alone:[1] for

---

[1] Cf. Exod. 24. 18; 1 Kings 19. 8.

vivet homo sed in dei verbo. ecce virtutis futurae liniamenta. nos 6
quoque, ut possumus, os ⟨a⟩ cibo excusamus, etiam sexum a congressione subducimus. quot spadones voluntarii, quot virgines Christi maritae, quot steriles utriusque naturae infructuosis genitalibus structi! nam si et hic iam vacare est et officia et emolumenta 7 membrorum temporali vacatione, ut in temporali dispositione, nec homo tamen minus salvus est, proinde homine salvo, et quidem magis tunc ut in aeterna dispositione, magis non desiderabimus quae iam hic non desiderare consuevimus.

62 Sed huic disceptationi finem dominica pronuntiatio imponet: Erunt, inquit, tanquam angeli: si non nubendo quia nec moriendo, utique nec ulli simili necessitati succidendo corporalis condicionis, quia et angeli aliquando tanquam homines fuerunt edendo et bibendo et pedes lavacro porrigendo: humanam enim induerant superficiem salva intus substantia propria. igitur si angeli, facti 2 tanquam homines, in eadem substantia spiritus carnalem tractationem susceperunt, cur non et homines, facti tanquam angeli, in eadem substantia carnis spiritalem subeant dispositionem, non 3 magis sollemnibus carnis obnoxii sub angelico indumento quam angeli sollemnibus spiritus sub humano, nec ideo non permansuri in carne quia non in sollemnibus carnis, cum nec angeli ideo non et in spiritu permanserint quia non et in sollemnibus spiritus? denique 4 non dixit, 'erunt angeli', ne homines negaret, sed 'tanquam angeli', ut homines conservaret: non abstulit substantiam, cui similitudinem attribuit.

63 Resurget igitur caro, et quidem omnis, et quidem ipsa, et quidem integra. in deposito est ubicunque apud deum per

24 a cibo *Brf.*: cibo *MPX*: ab osse *T*.
26 maritae *T*: maritatae *MPX*.
29–30 nec homo...aeterna dispositione *om. T*.
62: 1 imponit *MPX*.
13 in spiritu *TB*: spiritu *MX*: *hiat P*.
63: 2 deum *TP*: dominum *MX*.

even as early as that was authorization given to, *Not in bread shall a man live, but in the word of God.*[1] There you have the outline-sketch of virtue to be. We also, as we are able, give the mouth release from food, and even withdraw sex from copulation. How many voluntary eunuchs are there, how many virgins wedded to Christ, how many barren of both sexes equipped with genitals that bear no fruit. For if even here and now it is possible for both the functions and the emoluments of the members to be inactive with a temporal inactivity, as in a temporal dispensation, while for all that the man is none the less in full being, it follows that when the man is in full being, and the more so then, as in an eternal dispensation, the more shall we not feel the need for things which here and now we have accustomed ourselves not to feel the need of.

62 But the Lord's pronouncement shall conclude this discussion: *They will be*, he says, *like angels.*[2] If in not marrying, because also not dying, evidently also in submitting to no similar necessity of their corporal constitution: because angels also have at times been as men, eating and drinking and holding out their feet to be washed: for they had clothed themselves with a human exterior, while preserving within their proper substance.[3] Therefore if angels, made like men, did in the same substance of spirit admit of carnal handling, why should not men also, made like angels, enter, in the same substance of flesh, upon a spiritual dispensation, being, under their angelic clothing, no more tied to the usages of the flesh than the angels then, under human clothing, were tied to the usages of the spirit: not precluded from continuing in the flesh because they do not also continue in the usages of the flesh, since neither did the angels fail to continue in the spirit because they did not continue in the usages of the spirit? Moreover, he did not say, 'They will be angels', so as not to deny their manhood, but 'like angels', so as to conserve their manhood: he did not deprive them of their substance when he added to it a similarity.

63 So then the flesh will rise again, all of it indeed, itself, entire. Wherever it is, it is on deposit with God through the faithful trustee of God and men,[4] Jesus Christ, who will pay back both God

[1] Deut. 8. 3; cf. Matt. 4. 4; Luke 4. 4. [2] Matt. 22. 30.
[3] Cf. Gen. 18. 4–8. [4] Cf. 1 Tim. 2. 5.

fidelissimum sequestrem dei et hominum Iesum Christum, qui et homini deum et hominem deo reddet, carni spiritum et spiritui
5 carnem, qui utrumque iam in semetipso foederavit, sponsam sponso et sponsum sponsae comparavit. nam et si animam quis 2 contenderit sponsam, vel dotis nomine sequetur animam caro: non erit anima prostituta, ut nuda suscipiatur a sponso: habet instrumentum, habet cultum, habet mancipium suum carnem: ut
10 collactanea comitabitur. sed caro est sponsa, quae in Christo Iesu 3 spiritum sponsum per sanguinem passa est. huius interitum quem putas, secessum scias esse. non sola anima seponitur: habet et caro secessus suos interim, in aquis in ignibus in alitibus in bestiis. cum in 4 haec dissolvi videtur, velut in vasa transfunditur. si etiam ipsa vasa
15 defecerint, cum de illis quoque effluxerit in suam matricem terram, quasi per ambages resorbebitur, ut rursus ex illa repraesentetur Adam auditurus a domino: Ecce Adam factus est tanquam unus ex nobis: vere tunc compos mali quod evasit, et boni quod invasit. quid, anima, invides carni? nemo tam proximus tibi, quem post 5
20 deum diligas: nemo magis frater tuus quam quae tecum etiam in deo nascitur. tu potius illi exorare debueras resurrectionem: per te, 6 si forte, deliquit. sed nihil mirum si odisti cuius auctorem quoque respuisti, quam et in Christo aut negare aut mutare consuevisti, proinde et ipsum sermonem dei qui caro factus est vel stilo vel
25 interpretatione corrumpens, arcana etiam apocryphorum superducens, blasphemiae fabulas. atenim deus omnipotens, adversus 7 haec incredulitatis et perversitatis ingenia providentissima gratia sua effundens in novissimis diebus de suo spiritu in omnem carnem, in servos suos et ancillas, et fidem laborantem resurrectionis
30 carnalis animavit et pristina instrumenta manifestis verborum et

---

5 qui *T*: *om. MPX*.
16 resorbetur *MPX*.
17 quasi unus ex nobis factus est *MPX*.
20 deum *T*: dominum *MPX*.
23 consuevisti *Brf.*: consuevistis *T*: consuesti *MPX*.

to man and man to God, spirit to flesh and flesh to spirit. He has already made an alliance of both in himself, has brought the bride to the bridegroom and the bridegroom to the bride. For even if one shall claim that the soul is the bride, the flesh will go with the soul, at least in the name of dowry: the soul must be no prostitute, to be taken up by the bridegroom without assets. She has her chattels, her raiment, her serving-maid, the flesh: it will accompany her as a foster-sister. But it is the flesh which is the bride, for in Christ Jesus it has taken the Spirit for bridegroom by means of blood.[1] What you regard as its death you must know is a retirement. It is not the soul alone which is laid aside. The flesh also has meanwhile its places of retirement, in water, in fire, in birds, in beasts: when it seems to be dissolved into these it is being as it were poured out into vessels. If the vessels themselves fail, when it has flowed out from them also into its own place of origin, the earth, it will be as it were drawn in again by indirect ways, so that out of the earth that one may once more be brought into view who from the Lord will receive the name of Adam—*Behold Adam is become as one of us*[2]—truly then with knowledge of the evil which he has escaped, and of the good which he has entered into. Why, O soul, dost thou envy the flesh? No one is so much thy neighbour for thee to love next after God: no one is more thy brother than this which along with thee is even born in God. Thou more than others oughtest to have craved resurrection for it: it was through thee it sinned, if it did sin. But no wonder if thou hate that flesh, whose Author thou hast also rejected, that flesh which even in Christ thou art wont either to deny or to change, at the same time corrupting, at least with pen or comment, the very Word of God who was made flesh, as well as foisting in apocryphal mysteries, fables of blasphemy. But yet God Almighty, while in these last days, against these devices of unbelief and frowardness, by his most provident grace he pours forth of his Spirit upon all flesh, upon his servants and handmaids,[3] has also put life into the struggling faith of the resurrection of the flesh, and has by clear lights upon words and meanings purged the original documents of all

[1] Cf. Exod. 4. 25.   [2] Gen. 3. 22.
[3] Cf. Joel 2. 28.

sensuum luminibus ab omni ambiguitatis obscuritate purgavit. nam quia haereses esse oportuerat ut probabiles quique mani- 8 festentur, hae autem sine aliquibus occasionibus scripturarum audere non poterant, idcirco pristina instrumenta quasdam
35 materias illis videntur subministrasse, et ipsas quidem isdem litteris revincibiles. sed quoniam nec dissimulare spiritum sanctum 9 oportebat quominus et huiusmodi eloquiis superinundaret quae nullis haereticorum versutiis semina subspargerent, immo et veteres eorum caespites vellerent, idcirco iam omnes retro ambigui-
40 tates et quantas volunt parabolas aperta atque perspicua totius sacramenti praedicatione discussit per novam prophetiam de paracleto inundantem. cuius si hauseris fontem, nullam poteris 10 sitire doctrinam, nullus te ardor exuret quaestionum: resurrectionem quoque carnis usquequaque potando refrigeraberis.

35 illis *om. MPX.*
42 paraclito *TX.*
44 refrigeraberis *Leopold*: refrigerabis *libri.*

darkness of ambiguity. For because there must needs have been heresies,[1] that those who were approved might be made manifest, and heresies could have had no boldness apart from a few opportunities of the scriptures, therefore the original testaments are seen to have furnished them certain materials, though these themselves are capable of correction by the same scriptures. But since also it was not right for the Holy Spirit to dissemble, but rather to superabound with the kind of utterances which should not unwittingly sow seed for heretics' trickery, nay rather should pull up their old growths, therefore he has, by the new prophecy pouring in from the Paraclete, dispelled all former ambiguities, and what they will have it are parables, by an open and clear preaching of the whole mystery: and if you drink his fountain, you will be athirst for no doctrine, no heat of questionings will scorch you, and you will also be refreshed with draughts of the resurrection of the flesh wheresoever you turn.

[1] Cf. 1 Cor. 11. 19.

NOTES AND COMMENTARY

TITLE

The usual title of this work is *De Resurrectione Carnis*. The Troyes MS. has *De Resurrectione Mortuorum*, which is accepted by Dr Borleffs. The latter title might be justified by the first words of the treatise, and by the citation from the *regula fidei* in §18. But throughout the work the subject of debate is not the dead as such, but the flesh. Tertullian's adversaries would have been prepared to admit the resurrection of the dead, in their own interpretation of that phrase: it was the resurrection of the flesh which they denied, and it is precisely that which Tertullian defends. So that possibly the older title should stand.

In Greek and in Latin the words for 'flesh' have a less exclusively materialistic sound than this word has in English. In those languages 'body' (σῶμα, *corpus*) originally meant a dead body, and hardly ever succeeded in losing all sense of inertness and lifelessness: whereas 'flesh' (σάρξ, *caro*) envisages the presence, actual or potential, of an animating soul. 'Flesh', in fact, signifies the material, tangible, visible element of that human nature which Christ redeemed not in part but wholly: and in that sense the term is used in the Apostles' Creed and, if not in the title of this treatise, certainly throughout the work.

CHAPTER I

The resurrection of the dead is an essential article of Christian faith. The general public regard this as ridiculous, supposing (in spite of their own religious observances in honour of the dead) that death is the end of everything. In this they have the support of certain of the philosophers. Other philosophers, of earlier date, suppose that the soul is immortal: and some of them profess that after death it returns again to inhabit another body. Thus even in its errors the gentile world is not altogether ignorant of the resurrection of the dead.

NOTES AND COMMENTARY 189

1 **fiducia,** confidence, is the moral effect of *fides*, faith or the faith, on the inner conviction and godward relation of those who possess it. It represents St Paul's πεποίθησις in such texts as 2 Cor. 3. 4, πεποίθησιν δὲ τοιαύτην ἔχομεν διὰ τοῦ Χριστοῦ πρὸς τὸν θεόν (Lat. vg. *fiduciam*). Cf. *Apol.* 39 (in a description of the content and purpose of Christian worship): *certe fidem sanctis vocibus pascimus, spem erigimus, fiduciam figimus, disciplinam praeceptorum nihilominus inculcationibus densamus*: from which it would appear that *fides* is the formal content of the faith, while *fiducia* is the Christian's personal trust in Christ. Cf. also *De Carne Christi* 3, *quantum ad fiduciam reputas*, etc.

1 **illam credentes hoc sumus** (*T*), 'So long as we believe this we are the Christians we profess to be', is at first sight almost too good to be true. But cf. *Adv. Hermog.* 3, *itaque ex quo deus potestatem suam exercuit in eam faciendo ex materia, ex illo materia dominum deum passa demonstrat hoc illum tam diu non fuisse quamdiu fuit hoc*, 'proves that God was not the lord of matter during all the period in which he was its lord'. Of the older readings, *illam credentes sumus* (*MX*) could only mean 'while we believe it we exist': *illa credentes sumus* (*PR*) could mean 'by it we are believers', for the substantive use of the present participle is fairly frequent, e.g. *De Carne Christi* 18, *in credentes eius*.

2 **veritas** is the whole content of the faith as summarized in the *regula veritatis*, assumed to be of divine revelation communicated by Christ to the apostles, and by them to the Church: cf. *De Praesc. Haer.* 13, and elsewhere.

4 **parentat.** Greeks and Romans alike regarded their dead as in some sense gods (of a minor and somewhat ineffective sort) and at certain times offered in the neighbourhood of their burial-places the sacrifices known as *inferiae* or *parentalia*. See, e.g., Virgil, *Aeneid* v. 77, where Aeneas, on a later visit to his father's burial-mound, pours on the ground two bowls of wine, two of new milk, and two of the blood drawn from the animals sacrificed,

scattering also dark-red flowers. At Rome, on the funeral of a great man, there was a distribution of flesh-meat (*visceratio*) as well as gladiatorial shows. Suetonius (*D. Jul.*) says that Caesar gave a public show (*munus*) and a feast, in memory of his daughter the wife of Pompey—a *munus* never previously offered in the case of a woman. Cremation was the traditional Greek and Roman method of disposing of the dead. But it appears from tombs which have been excavated (among others from those uncovered beneath the crypt of St Peter's about 1945) that during the second century burial had begun to displace cremation, at least among the wealthy lower classes (many of whom would be freedmen of Levantine extraction) and that the newer custom became widespread during the third and fourth centuries. Tertullian seems to have been unaware of the change that was taking place during his own lifetime.

11 **Epicuri schola est.** *Schola* stands by metonymy for *doctrina* or *sententia*. Ritter and Preller (427*b*) quote from an epistle of Epicurus (*ap.* Diog. Laert. x. 125): τὸ φρικωδέστατον οὖν τῶν κακῶν ὁ θάνατος οὐθὲν πρὸς ἡμᾶς, ἐπειδήπερ ὅταν μὲν ἡμεῖς ὦμεν ὁ θάνατος οὐ πάρεστιν, ὅταν δ' ὁ θάνατος παρῇ τόθ' ἡμεῖς οὐκ ἐσμέν. So Tertullian, *De Anima* 42, *quanquam Epicurus vulgari satis opinione negarit mortem ad nos pertinere: quod enim dissolvitur, inquit, sensu caret, et quod sensu caret nihil ad nos*: an argument which Tertullian thus criticizes: *dissolvitur autem et caret sensu non ipsa mors sed homo qui eam patitur: at ille ei dedit passionem cuius est actio: quodsi hominis est pati mortem dissolutricem corporis et peremptricem sensus, quam ineptum ut tanta vis ad hominem non pertinere dicatur.* So also *De Test. An.* 1: *consiste in medio anima, seu divina et aeterna res es secundum plures philosophos,...seu minime divina quoniam quidem mortalis, ut Epicuro soli videtur.* On the subject in general cf. Cicero, *Disp. Tusc.* 1.

12 **Seneca.** Cf. *De Anima* 42: *multo coactius* ('much more briefly' = *coartius*) Seneca, *Post mortem ait omnia finiuntur, etiam ipsa,* quoted also by Lactantius as from *De Immatura Morte.* The sentiment is not uncommon: e.g. *Troades,* 397 *sqq.*: *post mortem nihil est, ipsaque mors nihil,* | *velocis spatii meta novissima...mors*

individua est, noxia corpori | nec parcens animae (where *individua* apparently means 'indiscriminate').

13 non minor sententia, 'the much older doctrine'. Tertullian transfers to the philosophers the criterion which he and others habitually apply to Christian doctrine, *id esse verum quodcumque primum*. Ritter and Preller (§88) observe that the doctrine of metempsychosis is the best known of all the doctrines of the Pythagorean school, and that which is on the best of evidence ascribed to Pythagoras himself: but they cite no authorities except a jocular epigram of Xenophanes and a general reference to Ovid, *Metam.* xv. 60-478. There is a similar lack of seriousness in Tertullian, *Apol.* 48, *age iam, si qui philosophus adfirmet, ut ait Laberius de sententia Pythagorae, hominem fieri ex mulo, colubram ex muliere,...nonne consensum movebit*, etc. See *De Anima* 28 sqq. for an argument against the veracity of Pythagoras, and a suggestion that he *Platoni auctor est de animarum recidivatu revolubili semper ex alterna mortuorum atque viventium suffectione*. Here again, and ibid. 54, the names of Pythagoras, Empedocles, and Plato are associated: *omnes ferme philosophi qui immortalitatem animae, qualiterqualiter volunt, vindicant*. For Euphorbus see *De Anima* 31, and for Homer, ibid. 33, *pavum se meminit Homerus, Ennio somniante: sed poetis nec vigilantibus credam...damnatus est igitur Homerus in pavum, non honoratus*.

13 Empedocles appears to have held that some of mankind, himself among them, are δαίμονες οἵ τε μακραίωνος λελάχασι βίοιο, degraded from their estate for some misdemeanour, and fated to pass through all ranks of being, while earth, sea, and sky refuse them a lodging: at length, when they have expiated their crime, they become men of note, prophets, soothsayers, physicians, and great captains, and eventually attain to the stature of gods, taking their place along with the others as benefactors of mankind. It does not, however, appear that all mankind enjoyed this kind of immortality. Empedocles himself professed to remember being a boy, then a girl, a shrub, a bird, and a fish. See the extracts in Ritter and Preller, §§ 181, 182. Hence the slaughter of animals was a crime, and the eating of their flesh is cannibalism: ibid. §§ 183,

184. So Tertullian, *De Anima* 32: *Thamnus et piscis fui, inquit: cur non magis et pepo, tam insulsus, et chamaeleon tam inflatus? plane ut piscis, ne aliqua sepultura conditiore putresceret, assum se maluit in Aetnam praecipitando,* etc.

The doctrines of Plato are too well known to need illustration. The later Platonics appear to have inclined to the more fanciful views of Pythagoras and Empedocles, but without the crudities associated with them.

On this passage as a whole see *De Test. An.* 4 (in an apostrophe to the soul), *iam nunc quod ad necessariorem sententiam tuam spectat, quantum et ad ipsum statum tuum tendit, adfirmamus te manere post vitae dispunctionem et expectare diem iudicii proque meritis aut cruciatui destinari aut refrigerio, utroque sempiterno: quibus sustinendis necessario tibi substantiam pristinam eiusdemque hominis materiam et memoriam reversuram, quod et nihil mali ac boni sentire possis sine carnis passionalis facultate, et nulla ratio sit iudicii sine ipsius exhibitione qui meruit iudicii passionem. ea opinio Christiana, etsi honestior multo Pythagorica, quae te non in bestias transfert, etsi plenior Platonica, quae tibi etiam dotem corporis reddit, etsi Epicurea gravior, quae te ab interitu defendit, tamen propter suum nomen* [sc. *Christianum*] *soli vanitati et stupori et, ut dicitur, praesumptioni deputatur.*

14 immo adhuc proxime. Oehler has a note that this phrase means 'approaching our own Christian doctrine'. I doubt this: I suspect it means that the philosophers mentioned thought that souls return into other bodies very shortly after death.

17 recenseantur, are entered for a second time on the censor's register. Cf. (in a slightly different sense) *Adv. Marc.* v. 17 (quoting Eph. 1. 10), *recapitulare, id est ad initium redigere vel ab initio recensere,* 'to refer things back to their origin or even to retrace them from their origin': where Tertullian does less than justice to ἀνακεφαλαιώσασθαι, though (as the context shows) he is quite clear that the *initium* is Christ.

19 pulsata saltim, etc. Perhaps 'knocking at Truth's door, though not entering into her house': but *adita veritate* occurs again in § 19 as used by heretics for acceptance of their particular tenets.

MPX have *pulsata salute*, 'knocking at Salvation's door though not entering into Truth's house', which is attractive: though the question of 'saving faith' hardly arises at this point, or indeed (except by implication) anywhere in this treatise.

CHAPTER II

On the chance of there being Christians who, like the Epicureans, totally deny any sort of resurrection, we shall in due course take note of our Lord's answer to the Sadducees. Meanwhile we take up arms against those half-Sadducees who admit a resurrection of the soul alone, despising the flesh because they have already rejected the God who made the flesh. Consequently their doctrine of Christ is different from ours: they either, with Marcion and Basilides, deny that his flesh had any reality at all, or else, with the Valentinians and Apelles, they claim that it had a special non-human quality of its own. Thus they are emboldened to deny the salvation of the flesh which they deny that Christ assumed. This I have discussed in my previous treatise *On the Flesh of Christ*, in which, by proving the verity and reality of Christ's flesh, I have shown the impossibility of there being any god besides the Creator: for the Christ of the Gospels is precisely such a one as was promised in the Old Testament, which these people admit contains the words of the Creator. Our next task will be to prove the resurrection of the flesh which God made and which Christ has redeemed.

This is the only satisfactory way of dealing with heretics, namely to ascertain first what manner of God has ordained that matter which is under discussion. The heretics reverse this order. They know the difficulty involved in the introduction of a second god besides the God revealed in creation and in the Scriptures: so they claim that the more pressing questions are those connected with man's salvation, and begin by discussing the resurrection. Having then suggested the impossibility of the flesh being saved, they proceed to the supposition of a god who is not the maker of the flesh: and by this reversed order of argument they overturn the faith of not a few.

I however insist on discussing matters in their proper order.

I have already in my books against Marcion proved that there is one God only, and that Christ belongs to him: and in my book on the flesh of Christ I have countered four heresies. My present task is, for the benefit of the unlearned and the doubtful, to discuss the resurrection of the flesh as though it were still an open question: in so doing I shall also be defending the unity of God. The salvation of the soul I imagine needs no defence: some have strange views about it, but no one actually denies it, except perhaps a certain Lucanus, who has borrowed his ideas from Aristotle: and he has already been answered in my book on the whole status of the soul. Our belief is that the soul is immortal, but that the flesh suffers destruction and is afterwards restored.

I now gather into formal shape matters which I have discussed elsewhere as occasion arose: for it is a common enough practice to give a foretaste of things which will afterwards be produced in full.

2 sciemus: i.e. in §36. The Sadducees said there was no resurrection, Matt. 22. 23; Luke 20. 27: nor angel nor spirit, Acts 23. 8. 'Spirit' here no doubt means human spirit, that which in modern English is commonly called soul. If there is no soul to rise, and the body does not rise, there is no resurrection at all: which was the Sadducees' position. The Pharisees admitted both 'spirit' and resurrection: and it appears, from Martha's words at John 11. 24, that some such hope was popularly current: οἶδα ὅτι ἀναστήσεται ἐν τῇ ἀναστάσει ἐν τῇ ἐσχάτῃ ἡμέρᾳ.

3 Christo enim servabatur, etc. That is, there were indications in the Old Testament of the resurrection, as of other Christian doctrines, as will be shown in the course of this treatise; but until Christ threw clear light upon them their full import was capable of escaping notice. Christ proved the resurrection of the dead both *per semetipsum*, by his words and by his acts of raising the dead, and *in semetipso*, by his own rising from the dead.

6 praeparamur, 'we are arming ourselves': the military metaphor is continued later in this chapter, *quo cuneo occurrendum sit*.

7 partiarios sententiae illorum, 'professing part of their doctrine', explained a little later by *ita dimidiam agnoscunt resurrec-*

tionem. Cf. *Adv. Marc.* III. 16, *cum partiariis erroris tui Iudaeis,* which means that the Jews rejected Christ, as (though unaware of it) Marcion did, though they did not, like him, reject the Creator. So, in a rather different but kindred sense, ibid. I. 24, *pluribus vero pereuntibus quomodo perfecta defenditur bonitas, ex maiore parte cessatrix, paucis aliqua, pluribus nulla, cedens perditioni, partiaria exitii:* i.e. such goodness would be incompletely good, surrendering some to perdition, and so, in part, a cause of destruction. The references to these passages in Lewis and Short should be corrected in the light of the previous part of that article, from which it appears that a *partiarius colonus* is not a smallholder who shares with another, but one who pays his rent with a part of his produce: the reference to Appuleius should read 5. 156.

10 aliter disponere. *Dispositio* means 'ordinance', i.e. something more fundamental than law, inherent in the constitution of nature itself: and *alia dispositio* would be so radically other that it would have to be regarded as dependent upon the will of some other god. So the present expression (a pregnant form for *aliter dispositum credere*) means 'regard Christ as appertaining to some other god'. All the four sects here mentioned claimed that the God and Father of our Lord Jesus Christ is not the same as the Creator, the God of the Old Testament, but that Christ's purpose was to rescue from the Creator such of mankind, or so much of the divine elements entangled in mankind, as were capable of being saved. Marcion's views are well known: he opposed a *deus bonus et optimus* to a Creator who was merely just. Basilides said that the world was created by the angels who inhabited the 365th sphere from the original centre of all being: *esse autem principem eorum eum qui Iudaeorum putatur esse deus*: and that the unbegotten and unnamable father sent his first-begotten Mind, who is known as Christ, to deliver believers in him from the power of the angels, the world-makers (Irenaeus, *Haer.* I. 19. 2). The Christ of the Valentinians, and apparently of Apelles, was a kind of composite being, generated in part within the pleroma of the deity, whose function was to rescue the divine elements entangled in humanity from the power of the semi-divine Demiurge or Creator who had, through his ignorance of the unknowable deity, bungled into the fabrication of the world and of man: so Irenaeus, *Haer.* I. 5; IV. 51. 2, *ipsum autem qui fecit omnia defectionis sive labis fructum esse dicunt*. Tertullian consistently, throughout his controversy with these people, claims the title Creator for the Father of our Lord Jesus Christ (as Irenaeus does with the title Demiurge) and dismisses the various forms of superior god which they professed as (what they were) merely idolatrous freaks of human fancy. Their various theories as to the non-existence, or non-humanity, of the flesh of Christ are discussed at length in *De Carne Christi*: Marcion and Basilides said it was empty phantasm or mere pretence (so *phantasmatis vanitatem*, below): the Valentinians and Apelles said it was *propriae qualitatis* (so below, *qualitatis proprietatem*), condensed either from celestial elements or from some semi-celestial matter.

14 atque ita sequitur, etc. All these speculators regarded matter as the work of some inferior, bungling or malicious, deity, and neither worthy nor capable of salvation. Salvation in their view meant rescue from the control of the creator. Tertullian uses the word in a Christian sense, of moral and spiritual health restored by Christ in this world, in expectation of a permanent place in the divine economy of the world to come. He also insists that this salvation, of the flesh as of the soul, is wrought by Christ not by any merely external act of superficial disentanglement, but by his having taken human nature to himself, and healed it. From which it follows (in reverse) that if Christ's flesh was not truly human, then human flesh is not saved, *sequitur ut eius substantiae salutem excludant cuius Christum consortem negant*.

15 consors signifies not partaker or sharer, but joint-possessor. The Son and the Holy Spirit (*Adv. Prax.* 3) are *consortes substantiae patris*, not that they share it between them or with him, but that each is it in full. This is the regular classical use: cf. Tacitus, *Ann.* I. 3, *collega imperii, consors tribuniciae potestatis*, where (as was the invariable custom with Roman magistracies) the power was not shared between two colleagues, but each possessed it entire. So here, Tertullian does not say that Christ shares our flesh with us, but that he possesses it whole, as we do.

NOTES AND COMMENTARY

20 condicio is almost synonymous (in some of their senses) with *conditio, natura, status, qualitas*, but differs from them in that it envisages them in actual or potential external relationships. So *Adv. Marc.* I. 3, *quae erit iam condicio ipsius summi magni?...non erit iam summum magnum eversa condicione et ut ita dixerim lege quae summo magno nihil sinit adaequari.* The quality of Christ's flesh is to be *solida*, its status is to be *humana*, and these, in relation to our flesh, are its *condicio*: and this *condicio* has justified Christ's enrolment or registration (in the Scriptures, as it were in a censorial list) as *homo* and *filius hominis*.

24 qualis promittitur is construed with *Christum*, not with *deus*. This is the argument worked out at length *Adv. Marc.* III, where it is shown that the Christ of the Gospels corresponds in all respects with the Christ promised in the Old Testament, which Marcion admits is the scripture of the Creator: consequently Christ belongs to the Creator, and there is no need to invent a second supposedly superior god.

24 obducti, 'shut out', seems to be an extension of the poetical use of *obducere*, 'shut up', for which cf. Lucan, *Pharsalia* v. 69, *multosque obducta per annos | Delphica fatidici reserat penetralia Phoebi.*

26 congruente scilicet, etc. The clause seems tautologous, and makes the end of the sentence very ugly. The words occur, however, with slight variations, in all the MSS., and it might be risky to omit them. Reading *congruente* with *T* (where the others have *congruenter*) the sentence will construe: 'the resurrection of the flesh is consonant with God's creation of it and Christ's redemption of it'. Rigaltius read *congruenter scilicet: et hoc ferme modo*, etc., and this may be correct.

27 hoc ferme modo, etc. The question whether theology is a deductive or an inductive science was not in those precise terms raised by Tertullian. But it was in his mind, and his implied answer is that it is both the one and the other, but that there are false and misleading forms of each. He dislikes *argumentatio*, and perhaps never uses this word, or its corresponding verb, of argument of which he approves: so *Adv. Hermog.* 3, *argumentari tibi* *videor?* Deductive argument of which he disapproved was such as was drawn from an *a priori* notion of God, without support in, or contrary to the data of, the Scriptures. There was also inductive argument (of which he here expresses disapproval), which seized upon some detail on which it was easy to suggest difficulties to the popular mind, and worked up from that to a false notion of God or of the scope and method of redemption. His own procedure was partly deductive (so here, *deduci*) in that it used for first principles the traditional rule of the faith and the data of Scripture: but also inductive in that it used the data of Scripture as a means of discovering the truth, while insisting that any doctrine propounded as truth must be in accord with scriptural facts. Moreover, in regard to those facts and their interpretation, a few superficially apparent exceptions must not be allowed to subvert the general testimony of the whole, nor must later evidence be allowed to clash with earlier: cf. *Adv. Prax.* 20, and my note. Words also must be understood in their true and natural sense, and statements conditioned by their context must be interpreted in accordance with it: *Adv. Hermog.* 19: *Adv. Marc.* IV. 19, *ita semper haeretici aut nudas et simplices voces coniecturis quo volunt rapiunt, aut rursus condicionales et rationales simplicitatis condicione dissolvunt.*

30 atque adeo, etc. *Adeo* stands for *ideo*, as often. For *conscientia* as esoteric or unavowed knowledge cf. *Adv. Prax.* 13, *si ex conscientia qua scimus dei nomen et domini et patri et filio et spiritui convenire deos et dominos nominaremus, extinxissemus faces nostras*, etc.: or for knowledge true but unarticulated, *Adv. Val.* 3, *si qui ex alia conscientia venerit fidei* (where *fidei* is genitive). Cf. also *De Carne Christi* 3, where *satis erat illi inquis conscientia sua* refers (as above) to knowledge privately held; but *cum iniuria conscientiae suae* and *adversus conscientiam suam* approach to the meaning of conscience as a moral guide or personal *censor morum*.

32 adversum deum mundi. The expression *deus mundi* seems to have been used by Marcion and the Valentinians (perhaps having in mind 2 Cor. 4. 4, ὁ θεὸς τοῦ αἰῶνος τούτου—where Souter wrongly prints a capital letter) for the Creator as contrasted with their supposed superior god. This exactly suits

Tertullian's purpose: he insists that the only God there is is he who is known in and through the world, *omnibus naturaliter notum*. *Sacramenta* seem here to be Old Testament historical narratives which are types of Christ, while *praedicationes* are the prophetic statements concerning him: *priorem* will mean that the Creator was, so to speak, first on the spot, and *manifestatiorem* that he is more clearly in evidence. Elsewhere (e.g. below, §§ 22, 25, *agnitio sacramenti*) *sacramentum* seems to mean the Christian faith, but not without the implication of the profession of it at baptism.

35 **quasi urgentioris causae.** *Causa* here has the sense of a case to be discussed or pleaded in court, for which see Lewis and Short s.v. II. E. The judicial metaphor is continued in *a quaestionibus resurrectionis incipiunt*, 'inquisitions on the resurrection': though *quaestiones*, as well as meaning judicial enquiries, suggests also the idea of doubt.

36 **quia durius creditur, etc.** *Durus*, meaning *difficilis*, is not quoted by Lewis and Short: the adverb here has apparently taken the same development as the English 'hard', 'hardly' (= *difficulter*). The manifest difficulties of the doctrine of the resurrection, often hinted at by the apologists, made it a convenient starting-point (as it still is) for those who would undermine more central articles of the faith. There was a certain lack of candour in the suggestion that this, since it concerns man's salvation, is a more urgent matter: its attraction really is that, being more within the competence of uninstructed minds, it is an easier matter on which to make plausible objections. These objections having made their impression, it was hardly necessary for the objector to introduce openly the notion of a second god: monotheism was at that date not so firmly established that the suspicion could not occur (as Tertullian says) *etiam ultro*.

40 **concussio,** meaning 'blackmail', is well attested: the word is sufficiently rare, and I suspect it here means bankruptcy, *decoctio*: but below, *concutitur* is opposed to *constabilitur*, and at § 22 we have *concussionibus elementorum* for 'signs in the sun and the moon and the stars' (Luke 21. 25). *Demutatio* is even more uncommon, but since its general meaning is 'change for the worse' it can here

continue the financial metaphor and stand for depreciation of coinage, an inevitable accompaniment of public bankruptcy.

41 de gradu eius spei. *Gradus* is the stance taken by a wrestler or a boxer, or the position taken up by opposing armies: cf. *Adv. Prax.* 8, *hic mecum gradum fige*, and frequently.

45 elidunt (*MPX*), understood in a reflexive sense, makes a good enough contrast in sense and sound with the passive *eliduntur*, and except for the variant of *T* (*instantur*, which is itself meaningless) need never have been suspected (though in fact it was). Possibly, but not probably, the original word (something like *instantur*) has been lost: but Dr Borleffs' proposal of *instigantur* will hardly serve, for (1) this word does not mean 'push down' or 'make unsteady', but 'urge on' or 'encourage': and (2), as Tertullian has just said that the suspicion of a second god arises *ultro*, the passive is wrong and *elidunt*, even if not original, gives the required meaning.

50 ita et digerendum, etc. The sentence, thus written by Mesnart, is now supported by *T* (*dirigendum*). *Digerere* for 'discuss' or 'consider' is apparently unparalleled, but seems a fairly easy development from the Virgilian *ita digerit omina Calchas*, 'interprets'. *Penes nos*, in our church, as it might be *penes creatorem*, 'in God's house'.

52 nam et multi, etc. Kroymann rightly marks this clause as parenthetic: *quia ex hoc latere* explains the earlier part of the sentence, *nunc de sola carnis*, etc. The military metaphor is continued in the words *instrui, dirigi, muniri, ex hoc latere*, as well as *defenditur*: *concutitur* could refer to the undermining of an edifice, but *constabilire* according to Lewis and Short is only used figuratively, of arguments, not of buildings.

56 retractatu carere. Borleffs, following van der Vliet, adds *posse*: which is unnecessary, for Tertullian was quite capable of making *carere* mean 'have no need of'.

58 Lucanus, according to Ps.-Tert., *Adv. Omn. Haer.*, was a follower and disciple of Marcion, and his doctrine agreed with Marcion and Cerdo. Hippolytus, *Haer.* VII. 37, writes to the same effect: Origen, *c. Cels.* II. 27, and Epiphanius, *Haer.* 43, evidently had no certain knowledge of him: nor apparently did Tertullian know very much. G. Salmon (in *D.C.B.*) thinks he may have been a Marcionite teacher at Rome after the death of Marcion. **Aristotle,** *De Anima* II. 1 (page 412 b) and elsewhere (see the citations in Ritter and Preller, §414) reaches the conclusion that ψυχή ἐστιν ἐντελέχεια ἡ πρώτη σώματος φυσικοῦ δυνάμει ζωὴν ἔχοντος: and again, καλῶς ὑπολαμβάνουσιν οἷς δοκεῖ μήτ' ἄνευ σώματος εἶναι μήτε σῶμά τι ἡ ψυχή. It would follow that the soul perishes with the body, or at least gradually fails as the body decays. Hippolytus, *Haer.* I. 20, says that whereas Plato had said that soul was immortal, Aristotle says that it remains a short time and afterwards it too disappears, along with that fifth more subtle substance of which he postulates the existence beside the four elements. This is partly in accordance with what might be expected: but cf. Aristotle, *De Anima* II. 1 (page 413 a), ὅτι μὲν οὖν οὐκ ἔστιν ἡ ψυχὴ χωριστὴ τοῦ σώματος, ἢ μέρη τινὰ αὐτῆς εἰ μεριστὴ πέφυκεν, οὐκ ἄδηλον· ἐνίων γὰρ ἡ ἐντελέχεια τῶν μερῶν ἐστιν αὐτῶν· οὐ μὴν ἀλλ' ἔνιά γε οὐθὲν κωλύει, διὰ τὸ μηθενὸς εἶναι σώματος ἐντελεχείας. ἔτι δὲ ἄδηλον εἰ οὕτως ἐντελέχεια σώματος ἡ ψυχὴ ὥσπερ πλωτὴρ πλοίου—i.e. is, at least in theory, separable from it. It is to be observed that Tertullian says no more than that Lucanus copied Aristotle in 'dissolving the soul' (i.e. in saying that it ceases to exist after death): *aliud quid pro ea subicit* does not refer to Aristotle but only to Lucanus. What this third thing was is not stated: Tertullian merely remarks that if it was neither soul nor body it was not human. The reference to the bear is a mere jibe: one should not deduce from it that Lucanus taught metempsychosis: its only point is that (according to Varro, *L.L.* IV: Stephanus, p. 26) *ursus* is a word of Lucanian origin—*ursi Lucana origo, vel unde illi, nostri ab ipsius voce,* whatever this may mean.

61 de omni statu, etc. This cannot be the extant work *De Anima,* which, so far from being directed against Lucanus, does not even mention him. For *stilus* by metonymy for *opus conscriptum,* cf. §22, *tempora totius spei fixa sunt sacrosancto stilo.*

202 NOTES AND COMMENTARY

67 suo corpore is apparently a mercantile term for the whole consignment, as distinguished from the samples: *suo nomine*, a banking term, 'its own account'.

CHAPTER III

It is permissible for Christian teachers to claim the support of popular ideas so long as these are in accordance with the truth and not in opposition to it. The immortality of the soul, and the unity of God, are, as common speech shows, convictions naturally implanted in the human mind. But there are other common expressions which need to be rejected: and if heretics use them as evidence I shall rebuke them on the ground that while claiming to be Christians they are following blind guides and are learning falsehood from those whom they ought to be teaching the truth. No one can be a Christian who denies what Christians affirm: and in fact the heretics, if deprived of gentile support and compelled to prove their case on Christian terms, are incompetent to maintain it. Moreover, popular ideas are only justified if they are concerned with plain and certain facts: but Christian doctrine deals with more recondite matters, and is sometimes the opposite of what seems evident.

1 de communibus sensibus sapere. *Sensus* has a whole range of meaning, from sense-perception to mental impression or, as here, commonly held views or opinions: the connexion no doubt was that the latter are general inductions from the former. The reference in Oehler's Index (s.v. *sensuum fallacia*) to *De Anima* 17 is misleading: Tertullian is there defending the trustworthiness of the five senses against the attacks of Academics, while criticizing in passing the Epicurean defence of them.

3 quaedam enim, etc. For these see the work *De Testimonio Animae naturaliter Christianae*, itself an expansion of a few pregnant sentences in *Apology* 17 and 47. So also *De Carne Christi* 12, [*anima*] *nihil adhuc de deo discens deum nominat: nihil adhuc de iudicio eius admittens deo commendare se dicit: nihil magis audiens quam spem nullam esse post mortem et bene et male defuncto cuique imprecatur.*

5 Platonis alicuius: so above, *aliqui Lucanus*: *De Carne Christi* 12, *in Lazaro aliquo*: ibid. 14, *aliqui Gabriel et Michael*: from which it would appear that the indefinite pronoun indicates neither defective knowledge nor a pretended lack of interest, but only that it is not Tertullian's present intention to go into any exact detail about them. The reference is to Plato, *Phaedrus*, p. 245 E *sqq.*, where ψυχὴ πᾶσα ἀθάνατος is set down as a thesis to be proved. The proof is as follows: τὸ γὰρ ἀεικίνητον ἀθάνατον: only that which moves itself, and consequently does not exhaust itself, never ceases moving and becomes ἀρχὴ κινήσεως to other things that move. But the ἀρχή is unoriginate, for if it were set in motion by something else it would not be an ἀρχή. Since it is unoriginate it is also indestructible: else all things would along with it cease to move and to exist. So then, as that which sets itself in motion is proved to be immortal, we shall not be wrong if we say that the soul's οὐσία τε καὶ λόγος is of this character. A body which is set in motion from without is ἄψυχον: one moved from within is ἔμψυχον, for it is of the nature of soul to move things from within. And since soul is the only thing that moves itself, it follows that soul must be ἀγένητόν τε καὶ ἀθάνατον. But, it appears from what follows, ψυχή to Plato is a very different thing from what Tertullian means by *anima*: cf. ibid. p. 246 B, ψυχὴ πᾶσα παντὸς ἐπιμελεῖται τοῦ ἀψύχου, πάντα δὲ οὐρανὸν περιπολεῖ, ἄλλοτ' ἐν ἄλλοις εἴδεσι γιγνομένη, κτέ. But Tertullian is basing no argument on Plato's views: he merely remarks that this is the kind of support he is prepared to accept from non-Christians.

25 simplicitas ipsa commendat. Cf. *Adv. Marc.* II. 21, *sed plus est si de absolutis revincamini, simplicitate veritatis, non curiositate*. *Simplicitas* often indicates the literal as opposed to the figurative sense of Scripture: *Adv. Marc.* IV. 24, *salva simplicitate scripturae*: *De Carne Christi* 13, *in Christo vero invenimus animam et carnem simplicibus et nudis vocabulis editas*. So it would seem that in the present passage, and elsewhere, *simplicitas* has a secondary sense, of 'clarity'.

28 ratio divina. *Ratio* has the following meanings: (1) manner or method: *Scorp.* 1, the scorpion's tail *hamatile spiculum in summo* *tormenti ratione stringit*: *De Carne Christi* 14, *sed et angelum, aiunt, gestavit Christus: qua ratione? qua et hominem.* (2) A reason or explanation offered or demanded: differing from *causa* in that it denotes the precedent cause or process of thought which led to the action, whereas *causa* is the final cause or purpose: *Adv. Marc.* I. 29, *et si habendi iam modus ponitur, quem quidem apud nos spiritalis ratio paracleto auctore defendit unum in fide matrimonium praescribens,* etc.: *De Corona* 4, *si legem nusquam reperio, sequitur ut traditio consuetudini morem hunc dederit, habiturum quandoque apostoli auctoritatem ex interpretatione rationis* (i.e. the apostle's exposition in 1 Cor. 11. 2–16 of the reasons why women ought to be veiled): *De Orat.* 13, *cum scrupulosius percontarer et rationem requirerem*: so also apparently *Adv. Marc.* IV. 19, *voces conditionales et rationales,* and *conditione rationali*. (3) Reason itself, as the fundamental truth deriving (so to speak) from the thoughts of God: as here, *ratio divina,* and *Adv. Prax.* 5, where *ratio* is the λόγος or eternal thought of God, the *sermo* with which God as it were converses with himself. See also *Adv. Marc.* I. 23, where *ratio* and its derivatives recur throughout: *sicut naturalia, ita rationalia esse debere in deo omnia: exigo rationem bonitatis* (i.e. 'in what sense God's goodness is derivative from his inmost thought') *quia nec aliud quid bonum haberi liceat quod non rationaliter bonum sit, nedum ut ipsa bonitas* (i.e. divine goodness) *irrationalis deprehendatur.* Hence, a little later, *nego rationalem bonitatem dei Marcionis iam hoc primo, quod in salutem processerit hominis alieni.* The whole chapter is important.

CHAPTER IV

Basing their argument on considerations by which they think they can entrap the popular mind, these heretics throughout this discussion make a violent attack upon the flesh, on the baseness of its origin, the foulness of its constituents, its burdensomeness during life, and its dispersal after death. They ask whether it is reasonable to suppose that after dispersal it can again be brought together as a living body. They suggest that the maimed and diseased will regret their return, while even the sound and whole will dread future ill-health or mutilation. Will the flesh, they ask, again need food and drink, and again exercise its natural functions? If so, its dearest hope will be for a second dissolution. For decency's sake I have moderated their language: how far they can go in indecency the actual writings of both gentiles and heretics abundantly prove.

The subject is raised again in § 60, but from the slightly different point of view of those who are prepared to admit the resurrection, but of a body deprived of its natural substance or its natural members.

1 praestruunt...interstruunt. Cf. *De Carne Christi* 1, *unde illi destruunt carnis vota inde nobis erunt praestruenda*. At *Apol.* 47, *antiquitas praestructa divinae litteraturae*, the metaphor from building-works, or the throwing up of defence-works, is almost forgotten. So also *Adv. Marc.* IV. 39, *nullam hic poteris interstruere distinctionem*.

2 de communione favorabili sensuum, an echo of § 3, *de communibus sensibus*. *Sensus* here are apparently impressions or opinions of a superficial nature unsupported by reason. Oehler (Index, s.v. *communio*) is not quite correct in his suggestion that *communio sensuum* is equivalent to *communes sensus*: the verbal noun has a collective force, and indicates that the opinions in question are such as his adversaries share with others, in this case the general public: which gives the adversaries a certain advantage in argument (*favorabili*). *Communio* seems to mean 'possession in common': e.g. *Adv. Marc.* IV. 10, *nominum communio simplex si forte videri potest*, 'that two men possess the same name (e.g. Joshua and our Lord) may perhaps have no special significance', but as concerns an appellation, like 'son of man' in Daniel, *difficile est ut et ipsa concurrat super nominis communionem*. So, § 46 below, Tertullian says that if anyone claims that 'mortal body' in Romans 8 means the soul, then he must admit the possibility of the flesh too being 'quickened', *secundum eiusdem status communionem*, because in that case flesh and soul share the same status, both of them being 'body' and possessing corporal attributes. So also § 52: St Paul says *non omnis caro eadem caro, non ad denegandam substantiae communionem*, 'not so as to deny that all flesh is the same in substance', *sed praerogativae peraequationem*, 'but so as to indicate difference of honour', *honoris non generis in differentiam redigens*.

3 **tam ab haeretico.** *Tam*, inserted by Ursinus, seems to be necessary to balance the *quam* which follows: which otherwise would respond to *magis*.

7 **ex seminis sui limo.** Scriptorem nostrum, vel eos potius qui hic vapulant haeretici, non ad eum limum ex quo deus ab initio figularat hominem suspicor spectare, sed ad seminis ipsius viscidam naturam.

11 **hancne ergo...evadere.** These sentences are evidently put into the mouth of a supposed objector. Kroymann inserts *ait*, making *vir sapiens* nominative. This may be right, though there could be some doubt whether Tertullian would, even in irony, have dignified his opponent by that title: so that it may be preferable to let *vir sapiens* be vocative, and ironical in the mouth of the objector.

19 **de consequentiis carnis.** *Consequentia* is not in Lewis and Short and, as far as Oehler's Index shows, occurs only here.

21 **pulmonibus natandum:** an apparently unparalleled use of *natare*, though it may stand: if any alteration were necessary I should prefer *nitendum*, 'pant'. *Non pudendum* is in all the MSS., except that *non* is crossed out in *T*: it need not be suspected: the evident meaning is *impudenter insolescendum*.

26 **illorum est in congressibus.** So I wrote in my copy of Oehler many years ago. *Illorum* evidently goes with *congressibus*, not with *spurciloquio*. Kroymann has *experiri est*: Borleffs *est experiri*: both of which are ugly. *Congressibus* would more naturally refer to verbal discussions than to written works. Irenaeus and others frequently mention that heretics despise the body and thus contradict their own salvation, though without any strictures on *spurciloquium*, unless perhaps there is a hint of this at Irenaeus, *Haer.* I. 15, *ipsi sui accusatores amarissimi et falsi testes existentes*.

CHAPTER V

Because the simple and the unlearned are disquieted by this incessant canvassing of the indignity of the flesh, our first concern must be to establish its honour. Even though it had been fabricated by angels, as some heretics allege, the secondary divinity of its creators would have been a sufficient warrant of its dignity—the more so as we should have to suppose that it was made by the will, or not against the will, of whatever supreme god the various sects envisage. But since it is the work of our one only God, his greatness answers for its nobility. 'But', they object, 'the whole world is God's handiwork, and the apostle says that the fashion of this world passeth away, and makes no suggestion that it will afterwards be reconstituted.' We reply that there are points of difference: first, that the world was made by God's spoken word alone, whereas the flesh was made both by the spoken word, for the sake of the general rule, and also, for the sake of pre-eminence, by God's actual handling. Rightly so: for as the world was made for man's sake, and to him God put it in subjection, man received special treatment in accordance with his lordship which was to be. Moreover 'man' in this context means the flesh: for while it was still clay of the earth, before God breathed the soul into it, it was already described as 'man', and the whole of what God has in view for mankind belongs not to the soul only, but to the flesh which first received that title.

This is the first of a series of illustrations of the dignity of the flesh: the subject is continued in the following chapters.

1 **rudes quique, etc.** So *Adv. Prax.* 3, *simplices enim quique, ne dixerim imprudentes et idiotae, quae maior semper credentium pars est.* T adds *petras* after *quique*: apparently some reader once mistook *rudes* for *rudera*, and made a marginal note which has crept into the text. *Temperatur*, for *libratur*, appears to be without parallel: at *Ad Nat.* I. 12, *grano piperis sub terra temperato*, the meaning seems to be 'retained', unless perchance Tertullian has invented a new verb *temporare*.

3 **carnis condicio:** see notes on §§ 2, 3. If *condicio* is the quality of an object as affected by its outward relationships, the outward relationships here envisaged may be the public estimate of it, and 'reputation' would be the right translation. So below, *auctoritas carnis* will mean its value in popular, or other, esteem.

8 **Menander,** according to Irenaeus, *Haer.* I. 17, was a disciple of

Simon of Samaria: which would place him in the first century. Both Irenaeus and Hippolytus (*Philos.* VIII. 27) say that his doctrine of creation is like that of Saturnilus. He says that there is one Father, unknown to all, and that he made angels, archangels, powers, and authorities. Seven of the angels made the world and all that is in it. Man also is their handiwork: for there appeared from the seat of power (ἀπὸ τῆς αὐθεντίας) a certain 'image of light', which they were unable to apprehend, because it immediately withdrew again upwards. So they exhorted themselves, saying, Let us make man after the image and likeness. This they did: but the thing formed (τοῦ πλάσματος) was, through the angels' inefficiency (ἀδρανές), unable to stand upright, but crawled like a worm. So the superior power (ἡ ἄνω δύναμις) took pity on him because he had been made in its likeness, and sent a spark of life which lifted the man up and caused him to live. After death this spark of life will return upwards to its kindred, while the rest of man's constituents will dissolve into that of which they were made.

8 Marcus, according to Irenaeus (*Haer.* I. 7) and Hippolytus (*Philos.* VI. 39), was of Gallic origin. He constructed a cosmology compounded of gematry and the Pythagorean theory of numbers. Irenaeus remarks that it is strange that the process of creation should have been conditioned by the peculiar characteristics of the Greek alphabet. Oehler here has a note that no one except Tertullian ascribes to Marcus a doctrine of creation by angels.

9 Apelles was a disciple and corrector of Marcion: so *De Carne Christi* 1. He appears to have been still alive in Rome in the last decade of the second century. Tertullian says, *De Praesc. Haer.* 33, that according to Apelles a certain fiery angel of the supreme god, thinking highly of himself (*gloriosum*), became the god of the law and of Israel: at *De Anima* 23 it is said that according to Apelles this angel had by the enticement of terrestrial food drawn souls down from their celestial abode and fabricated sinful flesh to clothe them. Hippolytus, *Philos.* VII. 38, says that Apelles agreed with Marcion that there is a good god, and added that the creator

NOTES AND COMMENTARY 209

of all is the just god: the God who spoke to Moses is a third, and he is made of fire (πύρινος): there is also a fourth, who is the cause of evil: and these four gods are angels. Hippolytus may have got this information from another source deriving from a more esoteric teaching which Apelles could have given to a select few: it seems inconsistent with the more general view given by Tertullian.

10 secundae divinitatis patrocinium is of course ironical: Tertullian was well aware (*Adv. Hermog.* 7) that *divinitas gradum non habet, utpote unica...minor se nunquam poterit esse.*

11 angelos post deum novimus. This is less compromising than Justin, *Apol.* 1. 6, ἐκεῖνόν τε [τὸν θεὸν] καὶ τὸν παρ' αὐτοῦ υἱὸν ἐλθόντα...καὶ τὸν τῶν ἄλλων ἑπομένων καὶ ἐξομοιουμένων ἀγαθῶν ἀγγέλων στρατόν, πνεῦμά τε τὸ προφητικὸν σεβόμεθα καὶ προσκυνοῦμεν, which is corrected, perhaps consciously and deliberately, by Athenagoras, *Suppl.* 10, λέγοντες θεὸν πατέρα καὶ υἱὸν θεὸν καὶ πνεῦμα ἅγιον...καὶ οὐκ ἐπὶ τούτοις τὸ θεολογικὸν ἡμῶν ἵσταται μέρος, ἀλλὰ καὶ πλῆθος ἀγγέλων καὶ λειτουργῶν φαμεν, κτέ.

11 iam nunc quisquis, etc. The gnostic teachers for the most part alleged that their creator made the world in ignorance: by which apparently they meant not that he was ignorant of what he was doing but that he was without knowledge of the 'supreme god' or of anything higher than himself: cf. *Adv. Val.* 19, 20. It is Tertullian's own idea that the superior power cannot have been ignorant of what was going on below, and that his acquiescence in it amounted to permission.

16 plures et duriores quaeque doctrinae would not include gnosticism in any of its forms. They might, on Tertullian's interpretation of the matter, include Marcionism: for Tertullian stedfastly refuses to admit the existence of Marcion's 'good god'. The Nazarenes also and the Ebionites ascribed creation to the one only God. But could their doctrine be described as *durior*? And how are they *plures*? Possibly what Tertullian means is that the doctrine of the catholic church is both more extensive and more durable than all the others. On *durus* see a note on §2: there seems to be no parallel to its present use as equivalent to *durabilis*, though this can be justified as an extension of a common use of *durare*: e.g. Virgil, *Georg*. II. 100, *totidem durare per annos*.

20 praeterit habitus, etc. I Cor. 7. 30. It does not occur to Tertullian to reply that the apostle does not say that this world is passing away, but that its σχῆμα, man's occupations while in it, are transitory experiences.

23 ad distantias provocamus. So we must surely read: the passive (*T*) is meaningless, and the verb can hardly be deponent. At *De Anima* 9 *illud trifariam distantivum* means the three dimensions of a solid body: at *Ad Nat*. I. 15 *distat* (=*differt*) is Oehler's conjecture, which may be right: cf. Quintilian, *Inst. Orat*. VI. 4. 21, *personis modo distat*, 'differs only in respect of the persons encountered'. So that *distantiae* here is apparently a synonym for *differentiae* in the next sentence.

24 primo quidem marks the first of a series of differences, which however is not completed in the same form. Here we have (1) that at the creation there was a difference between the rest of the world and the forming of man, and (2) that the difference in God's method of creation was justified and required by the intended superiority of man over the rest of creation. Also, arising out of the creation narrative, the flesh by itself has the name of 'man', and therefore enjoys the dignities referred to. The subject is continued in the following chapters.

36 qui adhuc limus. It appears from the context that *adhuc* means not 'until now' but 'still'.

42 ut si non, etc. *Ut* may well stand, though Kroymann removes it: if grammatical justification is needed for it, *debeatur* is to be understood: but that is to make too much of a trifle. *Ex consortio generis* would mean 'because flesh and soul alike have God for their originator': the caveat *si non* is needed because there is a difference between God's handling and his breathing. *Ex privilegio nominis* means that the possession by the flesh of the name of 'man' more than compensates for that difference: for it has the prior right to that name and has at least an equal expectation of its prerogatives.

CHAPTER VI

Human flesh is the more honourable because of the care and affection which God spent upon its formation,'in the knowledge that Christ was sometime to assume it: for the clay was not only God's handiwork, but also an earnest of the flesh of Christ. The quality of the material is of no account in comparison with the greatness of the Artificer. A sculptor, himself a man, has ennobled an animal's tusk into this world's supreme god: the living and true God can surely, by his handling of it, ennoble any material whatsoever. Gold was once earth, and is not despised: nor need flesh be despised because God has made it out of clay.

3 **manus dei, quaecunque sunt.** Tertullian will not here complicate his argument by expounding this expression. Elsewhere he gives the usual interpretation: *Adv. Hermog.* 45, *sermone eius caeli confirmati sunt et spiritu ipsius universae virtutes eorum: hic est dei dextera et manus ambae per quas operatus est atque* [forsan *ea quae*] *molitus est.* So Irenaeus, *Haer.* IV, *praef.* 3, *homo est autem temperatio animae et carnis qui secundum similitudinem dei formatus est et per manus eius plasmatus est, hoc est per filium et spiritum sanctum quibus et dixit Faciamus hominem*: ibid. IV. 31. 1; V. 1. 3, 28. 3.

11 **Christus cogitabatur homo futurus.** Tertullian, in this comment on Genesis 1. 26, insists on the important fact that, whatever has been the origin of human flesh, there is in human nature such kinship with, or likeness to, the divine that it was possible for God, by an act of humility indeed, but without degradation, to take upon himself human flesh and a human soul. The scriptural expression 'image and likeness' cannot mean that man was made in imitation of some physical shape which God already possessed: nor does Tertullian say this.[1] He does say that what the Creator

---

[1] It cannot even be supposed that the sacred text was ever intended to mean that. Apart from any question of divine inspiration, and supposing the commonly accepted analysis of the sources of Genesis to be correct, the post-exilic priestly writer to whom the critics ascribe this section would be the last person to think that God possesses body, parts, or passions.

had in mind was to give to human flesh such a shape and constitution as it would not be impossible or unseemly for God the Son in the fullness of time to assume: and the 'image and likeness' which was to be copied was not, in Tertullian's view, that of the Son in his divine nature, but that which the Son would assume at the Incarnation. This is no doubt true as far as it goes, though Origen denies it, preferring the possibility of moral assimilation to God and mental apprehension of his invisible attributes: *De Princ.* IV. iv. 10 (37), [*scriptura*] *dicit ad imaginem dei factum esse hominem: in quo et manifeste divinae imaginis cognoscuntur indicia, non per effigiem corporis quae corrumpitur sed per animi prudentiam, per iustitiam, per moderationem, per virtutem, per sapientiam, per disciplinam, per omnem denique virtutum chorum, quae cum in deo insint per substantiam in homine possunt esse per industriam et per imitationem dei* [quoting Luke 6. 36, Matt. 5. 48]...*unde et consanguinitatem quandam per hoc habere videntur ad deum, et...potest tamen etiam rationabilis mens proficiens a parvis ad maiora et a visibilibus ad invisibilia pervenire ad intellectum perfectiorem.* If this also seems too little, the reason may be that it attributes too much to human industry and imitation, and too little to the grace of God. But *consanguinitas quaedam ad deum* gives the necessary clue: for interpreted in its deepest sense this could mean that human nature taken as a whole has such kinship with the divine as to be receptive of God's grace and capable of divine converse, being not unsuitable for the eternal Son to take into the unity of his own Person, and competent by God's grace of a heavenly destiny. Origen also distinguishes between the image and the likeness: *De Princ.* III. vi. 1, *hoc ergo quod dixit, Ad imaginem dei fecit illum, et de similitudine siluit, non aliud indicat nisi quod imaginis quidem dignitatem in prima conditione percepit, similitudinis vero ei perfectio in consummatione servata est.* In what follows, industry and imitation again confuse the issue. Not the least trouble about such an anticipation of Pelagianism is that it is derogatory to human nature, just because it fails to reckon fully with divine grace.

16 pariari deo, here and *Adv. Marc.* v. 20, is in part due to Rhenanus: in the latter place the only extant MS. has *parari deo*,

NOTES AND COMMENTARY   213

which is manifestly wrong. Here the MSS. vary: *T* has *paria deo*
which seems to represent the Greek, τὸ εἶναι ἴσα θεῷ. At *Adv.
Prax.* 7 we have *esse se aequalem deo*. In all three places ἁρπαγμόν is
represented by *rapinam*, which is what the word naturally means:
but nowhere does Tertullian explain or comment on it. Is it
possible that by this unusual expression, and the strange use of ἴσα
(instead of ἴσος or ἴσον), St Paul was referring to the Old Testament theophanies in which the Son, because he is by nature and
right (ὑπάρχων) in the form of God, did not regard it as ἁρπαγ-
μός (may we say?) presumption, to present himself to the patriarchs as God (ἴσα θεῷ)? Heliodorus, *Aethiopica* VII. 20, makes
ἅρπαγμα a synonym of ἕρμαιον, which may perhaps justify the
R.V. translation 'a prize': though even so there is a difference,
for in Heliodorus the 'godsend' is still to be grasped, whereas in
St Paul the 'prize' (if this translation is correct) is something
which Christ Jesus already possessed, but which he was content
to appear to forgo.

23 **molitae adorantur** (making *manus* plural) is from Gelenius,
now supported by *T*. *Manus* can undoubtedly mean 'handiwork':
Martial, v. 39. 3, *Praxitelis manum Scopaeque*: and in the plural, for
several works of art, Virgil, *Aen.* I. 455, *artificumque manus inter se
operumque laborem | miratur*. But the use of the plural for a single
work of art is at least unusual, and the transition from *molitae*, 'the
hands wrought', to *adorantur*, 'the handiwork is worshipped', is
abrupt and ugly—which may have tempted some copyist to write
molitur et adoratur. In any case, the subject of the rest of the sentence
is *Iuppiter Olympius*, and we must punctuate with a colon after
adorantur. Tertullian borrows this remark from Theophilus, who
says (*Ad Autol.* II. 3) that at Pisa Zeus is ὁ κλέων ἕως τοῦ δεῦρο
τὰς χεῖρας Φειδίου.

29 **licet et caro audiat**, etc. *Et* (omitted by *T*) is better retained—'even though, now flesh, it is still addressed as earth (Gen.
3. 19) this is but to recall its origin, not to deny that it is what it is.'
Oehler's Index cites three examples of *revocare = rescindere,
infirmare*, none of them precisely like this present. A closer parallel
would be Tacitus, *Ann.* XIII. 26, *ut adversus male meritos* [*libertos*]

revocandae libertatis ius patronis daretur. *Substantia* is what a thing is, not what it is made of: the text of Gen. 3. 19 refers back to the *materies* but does not deny the *substantia*.

32 hactenus...terra est, etc. *Hactenus* for *haud amplius* is sufficiently common, but apparently peculiar to Tertullian: *De Praesc. Haer.* 11, the importunate widow *ubi audita est hactenus institit*, 'no longer persisted'. The natural sequence to *hactenus* in its more usual sense would (in the present passage) be *donec aurum fiat*: Tertullian's use of the word requires him to write *ex quo aurum (est)*.

34 de obsoletiore matrice, 'the dullness from which it is derived': so *De Anima* 53, *corpus istud Platonica sententia carcer...animam consaepto suo obstruit et obscurat...unde illi velut per corneum specular obsoletior lux rerum est*. *Census*, as often, means 'recorded origin', with a remote reference to the censorial roll.

CHAPTER VII

It is false to allege that flesh cannot claim the honour of having passed through God's hands, on the ground that it was clay and not flesh which was actually touched by them: for the honour done to the clay was communicated to the flesh which the clay became. And incidentally, the change from clay into flesh took place, as the Scripture clearly shows, not (as some say) when Adam and Eve were clothed with coats of skins on their expulsion from Paradise, but when the breath of God as it were baked the clay into flesh. The coats of skins are the skin, which was put on later. So then you have clay, glorious from God's hands, and flesh more glorious from God's breathing. And this is as it should be, since that precious jewel, the soul, needed a suitably noble vessel to contain it: or rather, the flesh is not a mere receptacle of the soul, but the two are thoroughly intertwined and mingled together. Also it is by means of the flesh that the soul enjoys all its honours and exercises all its functions: so that whatever pre-eminence the soul possesses is shared by the flesh.

1 dilutior...auctoritas: cf. *De Anima* 24, *animam longe infra deum expendimus quod natam eam agnoscimus ac per hoc dilutioris divinitatis et exilioris felicitatis, ut flatum non ut spiritum.*

5 **ut quidam volunt.** These are Valentinians, who apparently treated the Creation narrative as an allegory. Cf. *Adv. Val.* 24, *molitus enim mundum Demiurgus ad hominem manus confert et substantiam ei capit non ex ista inquiunt arida quam nos unicam novimus terra... sed ex invisibili corpore materiae illius scilicet philosophicae...: figulat ita hominem Demiurgus et de afflatu suo animat.* So far man is *choicus et animalis, ad imaginem et similitudinem factus*: but in fact, they say, he is *quadruplex res*, and *carnalem superficiem postea aiunt choico supertextam, et hanc esse pelliceam tunicam obnoxiam sensui*. The fourth element was *semen spiritale*, which Achamoth derived from her mother Sophia and communicated, unknown to him, to her son Demiurgus, who himself, again without knowing it, had along with his breathing passed it on into the choic body. It is this alone which, *feturatum in corpore materiali* [sc. *choico*] *velut in utero, et adultum illic, idoneum inveniretur suscipiendo quandoque sermoni perfecto*. All this Tertullian has copied with very little alteration from Irenaeus, *Haer.* I. I. 10, ὑλικός being represented by *choicus*, and ψυχικός by *animalis*: ὕστερον δὲ περιτεθεῖσθαι λέγουσιν αὐτῷ τὸν δερμάτινον χιτῶνα, τοῦτο δὲ τὸ αἰσθητὸν σαρκίον εἶναι λέγουσιν. Hippolytus, *Philos.* VI. 34, is not directly dependent on Irenaeus, though in general agreement with him: but in the text as it stands (there are some gaps) there is no reference to Gen. 3. 21. On this subject Tertullian's habitual common sense has failed him: by what seems to be a temporary aberration he suggests that Adam and Eve in Paradise had flesh with no skin, and that they first acquired skin after their expulsion: so below, *quam* [sc. *carnem*] *pelliciae tunicae, id est cutes, superductae vestierunt*. Gen. 3. 21 evidently means precisely what it says, that God provided the exiles with clothes.

8 **recognoverit** (*MPX*) would seem to be correct: *cognoverit* (*T*) would have the same sense as at Gen. 4. 1, a form of cognition which Tertullian (and many others) would not admit took place before the Fall: so *De Carne Christi* 17 (at the end).

9 **delibatio** is quoted by Lewis and Short only from the Digest and from Tertullian: it occurs at Rom. 11. 16 (Lat. vg.) for ἀπαρχή. Here it means the space left by the removal of a rib from

Adam (Gen. 2. 21), which God filled up with flesh—indicating that it was flesh which had been taken out, along with the rib.

13 vaporeo, the MS. reading, altered by Latinius and Ursinus to *vapore*, is rightly restored by Borleffs: its meaning is not 'steamy' but 'hot': and *vapor* below (*per adflatus divini vaporem*) means 'heat'. This is the regular meaning of the word in Lucretius, whose work, whether at first or at second hand, was certainly known to Tertullian: see H. Hagendahl, *Latin Fathers and the Classics* (Gothenburg, 1958).

15 recorporare and its derivatives are only found in Tertullian and in the fifth-century medical writer Caelius Aurelius, who could have learned them from him. Here it apparently means *transcorporare*, a word which does not appear to exist. *Stringere* here seems to have the same meaning as in the common phrase *gladium stringere*, 'draw' or 'extract'.

19 argilla homo, etc. Subject and predicate are inverted in these two sentences: 'man is called clay...and his flesh is called an earthen vessel'. Cf. a similar inversion *De Carne Christi* 13, *si caro anima est...si anima caro est....*

24 despoliationem carnis: Col. 2. 11, ἐν τῇ ἀπεκδύσει τοῦ σώματος τῆς σαρκός, Lat. vg. *in exspoliatione corporis carnis*, which (Tertullian fails to observe) refers to spiritual circumcision. *Spolium* in classical writers means (1) the skins of animals (not men) when stripped off: (2) armour stripped off a defeated enemy: and so (3) other spoils of battle.

26 gloriosum...gloriosiorem. A. J. Vermeulen, *The Semantic Development of Gloria in Early-Christian Latin* (Nijmegen, 1956), produces evidence that *gloria* does not acquire the modern sense of 'glory' or come to be the regular representative of δόξα until the late fourth century. If that is the case (but I suspect there are exceptions, of which the present is one) the only remaining meaning here would be 'competent, or more competent, to speak well of itself', by direct derivation from *gloriari*, as in Plautus: which seems very unnatural, especially in view of *ad gloriam carnis*, below.

NOTES AND COMMENTARY 217

27 non es diligentior deo. This, the MS. reading, may well stand, and there is no need for Kroymann's alteration of *non* to *num*, or his query after *damnaverit*. Tertullian often writes *non* for *nonne*: but this would give the opposite to the right sense here, and the sentence must be treated as a statement, not a question. Scythian emeralds (*smaragdi*) are mentioned by Pliny, *H.N.* 38. 5, *nullis maior austeritas aut minus vitii*: ibid. 36. 6, from India come marble and pearls: ibid., *gemmiferi amnes sunt Acesinus et Ganges, terrarum autem maxime India*: ibid. 37. 2, rock crystal: 37. 6, opals, *India sola et horum est mater*. There are notices of Indian precious stones in Dionysius, *Orbis Descriptio*, 1103 *sqq.*, with the comment of Eustathius and the Latin paraphrase of Priscian, 980 *sqq*. *Mare rubens* is apparently the Arabian Gulf: *grana candentia* can hardly mean anything but pearls (Lewis and Short, s.v. *granum*, do not quote this sense).

34 animae suae umbram, 'the reflection of his own soul'. If this is anything more than a rhetorical exaggeration, it raises the question how God can be supposed to have a soul. The following notes in Oehler's Index seem to promise something, but the reference numbers are in both cases false: *Adv. Marc.* IV. 37, *anima primi hominis ex materia dei*: *De Carne Christi* 24 should be *De Res. Carn.* 7, *animam carni ut magis deo proximam dominari*. *Apol*. 17, *novit* [*anima*] *sedem dei vivi ab illo* [sc. *caelo*], *et inde descendit*, may mean that the soul came down from heaven (as Origen thought): but again, in Tertullian this would be mere rhetoric, for his constant conviction is that the individual soul is engendered of the two parents, by natural descent from the soul of the first man: *De Anima* 27, possibly referred to below, §45, *quae simul in utero etiam seminantur, quod docuimus in commentario animae*. This primal soul Tertullian says was created in Adam by the divine inbreathing: so here, *spiritus sui auram*.

39 adpareat, 'stands in obedience to' or 'attends upon'.

45 per quam divina potestate, etc. This sentence, with those that follow, refers to natural human faculties, *publica forma humanae condicionis* (§8): the question of special grace, in a Christian sense, is treated in the following chapter. *Respergere* in classical

Latin usually conveys a sense of defilement, e.g. *sanguine manus respersa*. Here perhaps there is an anticipatory reference to baptism, and the meaning may be that, even on the natural plane, the soul through the flesh as intermediary possesses in some small or diminished degree faculties akin to the divine, and in particular that of foresight, at which it arrives by a kind of unspoken speech: for (*Adv. Prax.* 5, *vide cum tacitus tecum ipse congrederis ratione*, etc.) reasoning is a kind of unspoken speech, a silent conversation of the thinker with himself. Actual speech is a physical act done by, or through, a bodily organ—*sermo enim de organo carnis est*—and Tertullian suggests that for that reason even unspoken speech must be regarded as a bodily act. Lucretius had arrived at a similar conclusion, but from different premisses.

47 artes: studia ingenia: opera negotia officia: a rhopalic construction common in Tertullian, e.g. *De Carne Christi* 1, *caro: veritas et qualitas: an fuerit et unde et cuiusmodi fuerit*—which in that place is a further argument in favour of the traditional text.

49 vivere totum animae: this *animae* seems to be genitive: that which follows is certainly dative.

53 ministra in classical Latin seems always to occur in a religious context. *Si temporalium*, etc. is of course a begging of the question, or would be so, except that Tertullian immediately goes on to discuss the position here assumed as possible.

CHAPTER VIII

On the specifically Christian plane the prerogatives of the flesh are no less notable. By its mediation in the sacraments the soul obtains salvation. It is the flesh in the first instance which accomplishes works of abstinence and self-denial. And finally it is the flesh which suffers for Christ's sake the discomforts of confessorship and the torments of martyrdom.

1 forma is a plan or pattern, and so comes to mean a rule of law, the classical *formula* (Lewis and Short, s.v. *forma*, B. 2–5). In Tertullian it often, as here, approaches the sense of law in general:

so that *publica forma*, as it were *ius gentium*, is brought into contrast with *propria Christiani nominis forma*, as it might be the *ius civile*, the special law of the Christian people. *Nomen* here stands for nation, as in the common phrases *nomen Romanum, nomen Latinum*.

4 praerogativa, as an adjective, at first meant the tribe or century which had the right of being first asked to vote: then, as a substantive, the preferential right to vote, and consequently 'precedence' or 'superiority'. Pliny, *H.N.* 37. 9, *adeo decoris praerogativa* (in precious stones) *in nomine facta est*: this is the only classical example of 'superiority' quoted by Lewis and Short, but the word in this sense is common in Tertullian, e.g. *infra*, §25, *resurrectionis praerogativa*, the 'first resurrection' of Apoc. 20. 5: §29, *ex martyrii praerogativa*, the martyrs are taken straight to Paradise, not *ad inferos*: §52, St Paul says 'All flesh is not the same flesh', *non ad denegandam substantiae communionem sed praerogativae peraequationem, corpus honoris non generis in differentiam redigens*.

6 caro...cardo, a play on words which cannot be reproduced in English: Kroymann, with good effect, repeats it at §49.

6 de qua cum anima, etc. The Luxemburg MS. (*X*) has *deo alligatur*: *MP* also have *deo*, but the impossible verb *alligitur*: *T* has *a deo* and the equally impossible verb *aligitur*. Rhenanus printed *allegitur*, 'is chosen', or 'elected', with *allegi* towards the end of the sentence. This seems tautologous, and it would be more in Tertullian's manner to play upon different words of similar sound: the same objection applies to *alligari* (*X*), and to another impossible word *alligi* (*MP*). At the end of the sentence *a deo* is in *T* alone. It seems best to accept *deo alligatur*, 'is linked with God', from *X* and *eligi possit a deo* 'can become one of God's elect' from *T*, though *allegi* (Rhenanus, Borleffs) would do equally well. Dr Borleffs also prints *a deo allegatur* which, if the verb is indicative, can only mean 'is sent on a mission'. A further difficulty is *de qua* which, whatever verbs we have chosen, seems to stand for *per quam*.

7 sed et caro, etc. With these four sentences compare *De Baptismo* 4–8. There is first a blessing of the water, *invocato deo: supervenit enim statim spiritus de caelis et aquis superest sanctificans eas* *de semetipso et ita sanctificatae vim sanctificandi combibunt.* So *caro abluitur* (here) refers to the washing with this water, which conveys forgiveness of sins (*ut anima emaculetur*) and restitution to God, into the similitude of him (sc. Adam) who was formerly in the image of God. Next *caro unguitur*, the unction follows, having its ancient precedent in the anointing of priests (*ut anima consecretur*), and by virtue of which we are called Christians (i.e. anointed ones). *Caro signatur* has nothing corresponding to it in *De Baptismo*, but evidently refers to a signing with the cross, which in later times (see the Roman baptismal office, and the English service of 1549) came earlier, at the making of a catechumen. *Caro manus impositione adumbratur* refers to an imposition of the hand *per benedictionem, advocans et invitans spiritum sanctum* (so here, *ut et anima spiritu illuminetur*). It appears that Baptism was also known as φωτισμός: cf. Heb. 6. 4; 10. 32, and Justin, *Apol.* 1. 61, καλεῖται δὲ τοῦτο τὸ λουτρὸν φωτισμός, ὡς φωτιζομένων τὴν διάνοιαν τῶν ταῦτα μανθανόντων (which is not the real reason): so here, *illuminetur*.

13 conflictationes animae will be a reference to Isa. 58. 5, 'a day for a man to afflict his soul', Lat. vg. *per diem affligere hominem animam suam. Carnis*, rightly rejected by Borleffs, does not appear in Oehler's text or apparatus.

16 matrimonii dissimulatio. There are not a few references in antiquity to unconsummated marriages: perhaps 1 Cor. 7. 25–38 refers to an early example; and possibly Heb. 13. 4, τίμιος ὁ γάμος ἐν πᾶσι, καὶ ἡ κοίτη ἀμίαντος (which is a statement, as in English A.V., not a command as in R.V.), as well as 1 Cor. 7. 1–7, contains a warning of the possible selfishness of the practice.

16 una notitia eius: cf. *Ad Uxorem*, and *De Monogamia*: second marriages, after the death of one partner, were frowned upon, until Zephyrinus and Callistus at Rome allowed some relaxation, of which Tertullian and Hippolytus disapproved.

17 adulantur would naturally mean 'fawn' or 'flatter', and would require the accusative *deum*: if Tertullian wrote it, he certainly meant it for *adolentur*, which should possibly be substituted for it (so Gelenius). Quintilian, IX. 3. 1, observes that in his day people said *huic non hunc adulari*.

19 penuria mundi is strangely translated by Souter 'absence of people': Tertullian was writing Latin, not French, and *mundus* (like κόσμος) means 'adornment' or even cleanliness, or merely 'dress'.

26 ut hoc solum debeat, etc. This sentence is to some extent rhetorical, and it might be a mistake to reduce it to pedestrian fact. What it seems to mean is that the martyr has paid the debt, or met the obligation, he owes to Christ, yet is still in debt to him to the extent of continuing to owe what Christ has remitted (*ei debere desierit*), and is so much the more Christ's bondman because he has been set free, i.e. by Christ's act of redemption. That is, having spoken of martyrdom as the paying up of a debt, Tertullian dislikes that idea and guards himself by saying that the debt to Christ can never be repaid, for remission itself entails continued and continuous indebtedness.

CHAPTER IX

The flesh belongs to God so many times over that it is inconceivable that it should not rise again, but be left to eternal destruction. God, being good, follows his own precept of loving one's neighbour, for the flesh is his neighbour: and thus, as many texts of Scripture prove, he provides the remedies for its several infirmities. These are the very infirmities our adversaries object to: yet they are a necessary field for the exercise of God's goodness.

1 quam deus, etc. *Deus* is God the Father: *dei* five words later is God the Son, for it was in the image of what the Son was to be as Man that God created Adam in the beginning: cf. *supra*, §6, *Christus cogitabatur homo futurus, quod et limus, et sermo caro, quod et terra tunc.*

7 ingenii sui curam. *Cura* for a literary work occurs in Tacitus, and apparently not elsewhere: *Annals* IV. 11, *cura nostra*, 'this present work': the transition to mean any piece of work is not great.

9 Christi sui sororem seems without parallel, and can hardly be defended. It might have been thought to derive from Cant.

Sal. 5. 1, *soror mea sponsa*, except that Tertullian, like others, interprets this allegory of Christ and the Church; cf. *Adv. Marc.* IV. 11, *hanc [ecclesiam] sponsam Christus sibi etiam per Salomonem ex vocatione gentium arcessit*... *Veni sponsa de Libano*.

CHAPTER X

As there are Scriptures by which the flesh is brought under a cloud, there are others also which speak of it with honour. As for the apostle's strictures on the flesh, I shall at a later stage claim that these have reference to the soul, which has used the flesh as its servant. Meanwhile we observe that in other places the apostle speaks with honour of the body: and it is more consistent with the goodness of God to save that of which he sometimes disapproves than to let that perish of which he has at other times expressed approval.

3 omnis caro. Perhaps to avoid complicating the argument, Tertullian omits to notice that this expression (three times) has no specific reference to the flesh as a constituent of human nature, but is a Hebraism signifying humanity as a whole, *totum genus humanum*.

5 super ipsos homines (*T*) may be what Tertullian wrote: *in hominibus istis* (*MPX*) will then be a scribal correction from LXX ἐν τοῖς ἀνθρώποις τούτοις (Lat. vg. *in homine in aeternum*).

12 oneretur is Dr Borleffs' conjecture, extracted from the impossible reading of *T*: the other MSS. and editions have *inhonoretur*, which comes to much the same thing. In Tertullian *onerare* often means 'accuse' or 'blame' or 'reprove': e.g. *De Spect.* 26, *cum oneraretur immundus spiritus*, 'was rebuked': *Adv. Marc.* I. 22, *illum voluit oneratum*, 'held to blame'. The natural meaning also occurs, e.g. *Adv. Marc.* IV. 27, *quod onerarent alios importabilibus oneribus*.

13 suggillatio, with the verb *suggillare*, naturally means 'bruising', but is quoted once or twice from Livy in the sense of 'insult': so Tertullian, *Apol.* 11, *suggillatio est in caelo* [= *in caelum*] *vestra iustitia*, 'an insult to heaven': also, in the sense of 'accuse', 'reprove', *Adv. Marc.* v. 4, *physicae superstitionis suggillabat errorem*: and so here, 'reproof'.

20 reprobarit (*MPX*) needs no alteration: the subjunctive dissociates Tertullian from his opponents' suggestion that God has disapproved of the flesh: 'has perhaps disapproved' is all he will allow.

CHAPTER XI

Having proved that the flesh is worthy of restoration, we have now to consider whether God has the ability to restore it. Of this he has given sufficient indications in natural phenomena. Whatever the philosophers say, almost all Christian sects agree with us that God made the world, either (as some allege) out of pre-existent material, or (as is more correct to say) out of nothing. Yet creation out of pre-existent material is (for our present argument) tantamount to creation out of nothing: and I claim that God, who created flesh, whether out of nothing or out of pre-existent matter, is competent to remake it out of dissolution: for it is an easier thing to remake than to make.

2 nemo tam carnaliter, etc. *Carnaliter* is not infrequently in contrast with *spiritaliter* without being in opposition, and in such a case carries no sense of reprehension: e.g. *De Carne Christi* 20, *uti virgo esset regeneratio nostra spiritaliter, ab omnibus inquinamentis sanctificata per Christum, virginem et ipsum etiam carnaliter ut ex virginis carne*: *De Exhort. Cast.* 5, *et carnaliter in Adam et spiritaliter in Christo*. But the sense of moral reprehension also occurs, e.g. *De Anima* 11 (in a comment on Isa. 42. 5), *populo in terra incedenti, id est in carne carnaliter agenti*: and so here.

4 de quibus luculenter, etc. This is perhaps Tertullian's earliest indication of an inclination towards Montanism: *De Carne Christi*, which immediately preceded the present work, has no mention of that movement. There is a further recommendation of its revelations and its elucidations of scriptural ambiguities at the end of the present work, §63. The sentence before us is not in *T*, and was no doubt deliberately excised: §63 would have been harder to remove, and has been allowed to stay.

The Montanist movement began in Phrygia about the last quarter of the second century. Montanus claimed to be the recipient of a new and final revelation, that of the Paraclete promised by our Lord. He had as his companions or supporters two women, Prisca and Maximilla, who also claimed to be the recipients of divine revelations. These, so far as they have been preserved, do not seem to have been of any great interest, their religious content being as impoverished as the Latin in which it is expressed. Tertullian however seems to have thought they were of some value, though he was apparently attracted to the movement more by the newly enforced rigour of its disciplinary system than by any specific theological doctrine which he can have learned from it: in fact, he claims that in all points it supports the traditional faith—and, in the form in which Montanism reached Africa, that appears to be true. Other quotations from the Montanist book of prophecies are to be found at *De Pudicitia* 21, *potest ecclesia donare delictum, sed non faciam ne et alia delinquant* (a saying attributed to Montanus' paraclete): *De Exhort. Cast.* 10, *purificantia enim concordat, et visiones vident, et ponentes faciem deorsum etiam voces audiunt manifestas, tam salutares quam et occultas* (attributed to Prisca, and introduced by her statement that *sanctus minister sanctimoniam noverit ministrare*): *De Fuga* 9, *De Anima* 35, on the advantage of not fleeing so as to escape martyrdom.

5 **quam si tanta, etc.** *Ad interitum salutis* (*T* alone) is so unlikely a reading for any copyist or editor to have invented, that we must at least enquire if it will make sense. The connection of thought would seem to be that if the flesh is as powerful for destruction as the deniers of the resurrection allege, then we must argue in reply that God is no less powerful for salvation (*an tantus sit* standing for *annon tantus sit*: and so later with *an et aliqua*). But even so, *auctoritas munit* is hardly an expression which Tertullian (or any other controversialist) would apply to the view of his adversaries: and it seems possible that we should continue to read *meritum*, the connection of thought being that if the flesh has such a strong claim to salvation as we have alleged, surely it is not necessary (*numquid*) for us to raise the question whether (1) God is strong

enough to save, and (2) has given in nature itself certain examples of his right to do so. *Potentia* seems to mean God's inherent power: *potestas*, his control over creation: *licentia*, his moral right to exercise control: *sui iuris* (below) the laws or principles by which his control is exercised. *Tabernaculum reaedificare* is perhaps a reminiscence of Amos 9. 11 (= Acts 15. 16): for 'tabernacle' meaning the human body see 2 Cor. 5. 1, 4 (σκῆνος) and 2 Pet. 1. 13 (σκήνωμα).

10 an et aliqua, etc. If we delete the query after *restruere* and make what follows continue the previous clause, it will be possible to retain *promulgarit* (*TR*³). *Publicum* is cited by Lewis and Short from Varro, *De Re Rustica* 2. 11. 10 in the sense of public archives: this may be the meaning here, though possibly we need something less secret than archives, of the nature of a public noticeboard. *Sitiant* (from *TMPXR*¹) is correct: the word occurs also elsewhere as a substitute for *desiderare*: e.g. §28, *sitiant interpretationem*: Ursinus' conjecture *nesciant* is therefore unnecessary.

14 omnes fere haereses here apparently means almost all the philosophic sects, for most of the Christian heresies, gnostic, Marcionite, and others, erred on precisely this point. The philosophers, though pagan, by attributing creation to God, were, the suggestion is, in effect if not in intention, acknowledging our God, *deo nostro adscribunt*. On the question of creation out of subjacent matter, which Tertullian here abstains from discussing, see the treatise *Adversus Hermogenem*.

CHAPTER XII

Nature, which is God's handiwork, presents on all sides examples of life after death. These examples God has provided, with the express intention that we, having seen resurrection in act, should the more readily believe when we are told of it in words. Moreover, if all things rise again for man's sake, and man's flesh has the enjoyment of them, how can it be that flesh itself should utterly perish?

This theme would probably now be regarded as at best a not very apposite illustration: the ancients apparently thought it had some value as an argument, for it continually recurs. Tertullian had already used it in *Apology* 48 (for which see the Introduction, page xiii), and it occurs, either copied from him or copied by him, in Minucius Felix, *Octavius* 34: *vide adeo quam in solacium nostri resurrectionem futuram omnis natura meditetur: sol demergit et nascitur, astra labuntur et redeunt, flores recidunt et revivescunt, post senium arbusta frondescunt, semina nonnisi corrupta revirescunt: ita corpus in saeculo ut arbores in hiberno: occultant virorem ariditate mentita.* But it is much older than either: Tertullian apparently derived the idea (though he enriches the expression of it) from Clement of Rome, *Epistle* I. 24, κατανοήσωμεν, ἀγαπητοί, πῶς ὁ δεσπότης ἐπιδείκνυται διηνεκῶς ἡμῖν τὴν μέλλουσαν ἀνάστασιν ἔσεσθαι, ἧς τὴν ἀπαρχὴν ἐποιήσατο τὸν κύριον Ἰησοῦν Χριστὸν ἐκ νεκρῶν ἀναστήσας: day and night declare the resurrection: so of the seed sown in the earth, ἅτινα πεσόντα εἰς τὴν γῆν ξηρὰ καὶ γυμνὰ διαλύεται· εἶτ' ἐκ τῆς διαλύσεως ἡ μεγαλειότης τῆς προνοίας τοῦ δεσπότου ἀνίστησιν αὐτά, καὶ ἐκ τοῦ ἑνὸς πλείονα αὔξει καὶ ἐκφέρει καρπόν. There follows an account of the phoenix, also copied by Tertullian. Theophilus, *Ad Autolycum* I. 13, has rather more than Clement and less than Tertullian, but with the significant phrase, ταῦτα δὲ πάντα ἐνεργεῖ ἡ τοῦ θεοῦ σοφία, εἰς τὸ ἐπιδεῖξαι καὶ διὰ τούτων ὅτι δυνατός ἐστιν ὁ θεὸς ποιῆσαι τὴν καθολικὴν ἀνάστασιν ἁπάντων ἀνθρώπων, and with a further reply to the supposed objection that all this is the work of natural causes—natural causes themselves are the work of God.

4 quies rerum may, as Rigaltius suggests, be a gloss on *iustitium*, but it is attested by all the MSS., and must probably be retained: moreover it makes a better ending of the sentence.

9 succensio (TB^{mg}) is to be preferred: *suggestio* (MPX) could be due to some copyist who thought the other word could only mean 'irritation'.

10 quas temporalis distinctio, etc. *Quas*, if it is correct, must be a cognate accusative, for the seasonal division had not taken away the absences, but had caused them: but it is tempting to read

NOTES AND COMMENTARY 227

quae (sc. *sidera*). The reference is, of course, to the apparent annual procession of the constellations: e.g. Orion in the spring runs into daylight, but reappears in autumn.

13 **viribus,** 'functions', is apparently here a true plural: as below, *viribus praedicavit,* 'by acts of power'.

15 **eadem...semina** has an implied reference to 1 Cor. 15. 36.

22 **in statum redeunt.** As *stare* often approaches the meaning of *esse, status* here means almost 'their proper being'.

CHAPTER XIII

An actual example of resurrection is the phoenix, which rises again from its own death, an example to which Scripture itself makes reference.

For an account of the fable or myth of the phoenix see a long note by J. B. Lightfoot, *Clement of Rome,* vol. II, pp. 84 *sqq.* The earliest reference to this bird is apparently in Hesiod, frag. 171 (Rzach), where the only thing remarked on is the length of the bird's life. The story appears in one form (not of the bird's rebirth, but of its burying its sire) in Herodotus, II. 73, who had, according to Porphyry, taken it from Hecataeus (see a note by How and Wells). Pliny, *H.N.* x. 2, quotes Manilius, who apparently first brought the story to Rome: but still there is nothing about a resurrection from ashes. Nor is there in Tacitus, *Ann.* VI. 28, who says that the bird appeared in Egypt A.D. 34, and that the common story is that the phoenix, when its years are complete and death approaches, *suis in terris struere nidum eique vim genitalem adfundere ex qua fetum oriri: et primam adulto curam sepeliendi patris, neque id temere sed sublato myrrhae pondere temptatoque per longum iter, ubi par oneri par meatui sit, subire patrium corpus inque Solis aram perferre atque adolere. haec incerta et fabulosis aucta: ceterum aspici aliquando in Aegypto eam volucrem non ambigitur.* This is still substantially the story as Herodotus tells it, with the same expression of disbelief. Clement of Rome, *Ep.* I. 25, has a slightly different story, that the older bird when near his end makes a nest or ark of spices, into which he

15-2

enters and dies. When his body corrupts, a worm is bred out of the fluid, which grows up and sprouts wings. When it is strong enough it carries the ark, with its progenitor's bones within it, as far as Heliopolis, where it places them on the altar and so departs. Still there is no mention of the new bird rising from the ashes of the old, nor is there, at least expressly, here in Tertullian: though the sentence which follows, *uti credas de ignibus quoque substantiam corporis exigi posse* (referring not to the phoenix but to human bodies) might easily be read in that sense. Celsus apparently (*ap.* Origen, *Contra Cels.* IV. 98. 1) accepted the story, and Lightfoot gives further references to Cyril of Jerusalem, Ambrose, Rufinus and *Apost. Cons.*, where the story is accepted, and to Eusebius of Caesarea, Gregory Nazianzen, and Augustine, who reject it.

11 et florebis, etc. Psalm 92. 12 (LXX. 91. 13), δίκαιος ὡς φοίνιξ ἀνθήσει, where φοίνιξ means the palm-tree, as the sequence shows, ὡς ἡ κέδρος ἡ ἐν τῷ Λιβάνῳ πληθυνθήσεται. It seems unlikely that Tertullian was unaware of this.

CHAPTER XIV

We have so far proved on general principles that the flesh is capable of restoration and that God is competent to restore it: we must now consider God's statements of his intention to do so. But first we have to ask whether there is a sufficient purpose which demands that the flesh should be restored: and we answer that God, being both good and just, must needs exercise both his goodness and his justice, the one and the other no less in punishment than in reward, in accordance with man's present acknowledgement of him as God and Creator and Lord. But judgement will not be perfect unless it is passed upon man in his completeness, through the reassemblage of both the substances, flesh and soul, in which he has lived the life that is to be judged.

2 edicta atque decreta. An *edictum* was a statement by a judge or magistrate of the general principles on which he proposed to administer the law: a *decretum* was a decision by competent authority on some particular point. The latter part of this chapter contains several legal expressions: e.g. *causa*, a case in court (but this word also occurs with other meanings: see a note below): *sententiam praestat*, gives sentence: *repraesentatio*, production in court: *parere*, to appear in court, or answer a summons: *adhibere*, to present in court: *iudicium expungere vel dispungere*, to conclude a case.

3 divisionem istam. Kroymann's conjecture *iustam* is at first sight attractive: he makes a similar suggestion, equally attractive (*iustis quaestionibus*), at *De Carne Christi* 11. But *istam* goes closely with *cum maxime* (which means, as often, 'at this present moment') so as to mean 'this section of our argument'. Kroymann's *valeat* for *soleat* (accepted by Borleffs) is equally attractive, and apparently wrong: for the reference is to the preceding chapters in which it has been shown that God is accustomed, in the works of nature, to do things which prove that his power is great enough (*potentia... tanta sit*) to accomplish resurrection.

7 de causa requiras. *Causa* here, as regularly in Tertullian when it refers to causation, means the final cause or purpose, while *ratio* means the antecedent thought or preliminary reasoning: cf. *De Carne Christi* 6, *comparent velim et causas*, and ibid. 10, *passim*: so below, *tota causa immo necessitas resurrectionis*. But below (line 14), *ex causae suae necessitate* and perhaps (line 40) *vita est enim causa iudicii*, with §15 (line 4), *non sit particeps in sententia caro si non fuerit et in causa*, the word has the legal sense of a case in court.

17 cum Marcione, etc. The reference is to *Adv. Marc.* II, where it is proved that reason requires that God should be both good and just, and should have also other attributes, such as omnipotence and omniscience, which Marcion expressly or by implication had denied.

20 hinc et ille, etc. *Non enim dominus* (so Rhenanus for MSS. *deus*) is manifestly required by the sequence of thought. In the next sentence *quia deus* (*T* alone: *MPX, quod*) makes nonsense of the argument, and must be due to confusion with *quia deus* two lines above.

27 congruentissima...destinatio iudicii: the sentence should be punctuated as in the text: *congruentissima destinatio* go together, as an echo of *congruentissimum est destinare*, above:

congruentissima can hardly (as Dr Borleffs' punctuation suggests) be appositional to *causa* and *necessitas*.

36 totum porro hominem, etc. *Congregatione* (*MPX* and the first hand of *T*) is the better attested word: though *concretione* is the sort of word Tertullian might have written. But the sentence means, 'But the whole man's appearance in court involves the assemblage of both substances, and seeing the whole man has to be judged (for it is only as a whole man that he has lived) he must of necessity be presented in court in both substances'. The sentence is somewhat confused, but not really tautologous. *Iudicatum iri* is Dr Borleffs' brilliant emendation.

40 vita est enim, etc. Another difficult sentence. *Causa* seems to have its legal sense, and the first five words perhaps mean, 'Life is the case up for judgement'. The remainder would be easier if we could read *dispungendi*: but the words will just construe if we are allowed to treat *functa est* as passive: 'that case will have to be completed in as many substances as the life has been lived in'. This is by no means convincing: the removal of *per* from before *quot* (making *quot* ablative and *functa est* deponent) would ease matters not a little.

CHAPTER XV

Flesh and soul can only be separated in life's rewards if they are separable in the course of it. Such separation is manifestly impossible, since all the soul's activities are made effective through the flesh, and the heart (or the brain, or whatever may be the headquarters of thought) is itself flesh. Moreover, even secret thoughts not yet brought to effect show themselves upon the countenance. As our opponents rehearse the delinquencies of the flesh, we claim that for these it ought to be punished: for our part we tell of its virtues, for which it ought to be rewarded. If God fails in either respect, he is either unjust or indolent, both of which are, even on human principles, inconceivable.

2 scindere illud. *Illud* must here be a cognate accusative, 'make that division': so also possibly, but not so clearly, *decucurrit illud*, below.

5 **in causa** here, by contrast with *in sententia*, means 'in the suit', and this may have some bearing on *causa iudicii* (§ 14 *ad fin.*) where the meaning suggested is 'the case to be judged'.

12 **suggillatio** in the sense of justifiable reproof is not quoted in Lewis and Short. Tertullian is rather fond of the word: e.g. *De Carne Christi* 24, *in suggillatione haereticorum*. See a note on §10, line 13.

16 **quod ἡγεμονικόν appellatur.** The Stoics regarded this, as they regarded all real things, as of corporal constitution, comparing it to an originally white paper on which the soul proceeds to write down all its experiences—perceptions, memories, thoughts, desires, and so forth. Ritter and Preller (§485) quote from the doxographers: οἱ στωικοί φασιν· ὅταν γεννηθῇ ὁ ἄνθρωπος ἔχει τὸ ἡγεμονικὸν μέρος τῆς ψυχῆς ὥσπερ χάρτην εὔεργον εἰς ἀπογραφήν· εἰς τοῦτο μίαν ἑκάστην τῶν ἐννοιῶν ἐναπογράφεται. Cicero, *De Nat. Deor.* II. 11. 29, represents a Stoic disputant as applying the concept to nature in general and every part of it: *omnem enim naturam necesse est, quae non solitaria sit neque simplex, sed cum alio iuncta atque conexa, habere aliquem in se principatum, ut in homine mentem...principatum autem id dico quod Graeci ἡγεμονικόν vocant, quo nihil in quoque genere nec potest nec debet esse praestantius. ita necesse est illud etiam in quo sit naturae principatus esse omnium optimum omniumque rerum potestate dominatuque dignissimum.* J. B. Mayor, in a note on the above, quotes Sextus IX. 119, καὶ μὴν ἐν παντὶ πολυμερεῖ σώματι καὶ κατὰ φύσιν διοικουμένῳ ἔστι τι τὸ κυριεῦον· καθ' ὃ καὶ ἐφ' ἡμῶν ἢ ἐν καρδίᾳ τοῦτο τυγχάνειν ἀξιοῦται ἢ ἐν ἐγκεφάλῳ ἢ ἐν ἄλλῳ τινὶ μέρει τοῦ σώματος. He also refers to Cicero, *Disp. Tusc.* I. 20, *Plato triplicem finxit animum, cuius principatum, id est rationem, in capite sicut in arce posuit,* and cites from Diogenes Laertius, VII. 159, the definition, ἡγεμονικὸν εἶναι τὸ κυριώτατον τῆς ψυχῆς, ἐν ᾧ αἱ φαντασίαι καὶ αἱ ὁρμαὶ γίγνονται καὶ ὅθεν ὁ λόγος ἀναπέμπεται· ὅπερ εἶναι ἐν καρδίᾳ. The concept was of primary importance in Stoic ethics, the word frequently occurring in Marcus Aurelius: e.g. XII. 14, if the course of the world is φυρμὸς ἀνηγεμόνευτος, ἀσμένιζε, ὅτι ἐν τοιούτῳ κλύδωνι αὐτὸς ἔχεις ἐν σαυτῷ τινα νοῦν ἡγεμονικόν. Later Christian writers saw the obvious connection

with Ps. 51. 12 (50. 14 LXX), πνεύματι ἡγεμονικῷ στήρισόν με. For further discussion of the philosophers' views see *De Anima*, especially §14, where ἡγεμονικόν as *principale* is distinguished from λογικόν as *rationale*: *cogitatorium* also recurs in the same context. Also ibid. 25.

CHAPTER XVI

To say that the soul commands and the flesh obeys does not mean that the flesh, as a mere instrument, is exempt from praise and blame. If our adversaries raise this point, we reply, first, that if that were so, the flesh would be innocent and on that account it would behove the goodness of God to save it: secondly, that in practice it is not true that instruments are exempt from approval or disapproval: but thirdly, that the flesh is not an instrument or tool acquired by the soul from without, for since the very moment of conception the two are intimately entwined together, and (according to the narrative of the creation) the flesh has the prior right to the title 'man'. It is true that the apostle refers to the body as a vessel: but this is because it contains the soul, to which it ministers as a servant, not as a tool. Moreover the apostle speaks of 'sinful' flesh, showing that it is not exempt from blame: he also commands us to glorify God in our body, thus indicating that the flesh is not devoid of praise.

2 ut velint carnem, etc. Kroymann would, without any need, read *secus* for *sic*: Borleffs retains *sic*, but I suspect is wrong in suggesting that it means *ea argumentatione*. The key to the sentence is in *velint*, which means 'consent', not 'wish' (which would be *cupiant*, or in Tertullian's language *gestiant*). The adversaries might assent to our previous argument, and be content to place the flesh in the employment of the soul *sic* (i.e. in terms of *imperium* and *obsequium*), yet proceed to overthrow us by a further argument which claims that the flesh is not a free servant but a tool, and so is not answerable to judgement.

9 vice potius vasculi: for *vice* meaning not 'instead of' but 'as equivalent to' cf. §19, *vice sepulchri*: *Apol.* 17, *vice rebellantium* *ergastulorum*, 'after the manner of rebellious slaves': ibid. 48, *aulaei vice*, 'after the manner of a drop-curtain'.

13 si quis eum veneno temperarit, like *mors aliqua ructuarit*, below, can hardly be defended grammatically: but there are examples of this kind of case transference in Virgil, whose authority is good enough to cover any irregularity. *Ructuare* (found also in Augustine) seems to be the correct African spelling.

26 praesumens scilicet, etc. *Scilicet* dissociates Tertullian from the superstitious fears of the present sentence: and (one might have hoped) from the ill-temper of the sentence before it. *Invidiam* (*T Rig.*) is probably correct, though the ablative (*MPXR*¹) would not be impossible: *inludia* (*R*³) seems to be no more than a clever guess. *Invidia* means 'reproach' as *De Orat.* 5, *clamant ad dominum invidia animae martyrum*.

32 estne ergo...communicent should be marked as a supposed interruption by the opponents. They admit the prevalence of the practices and superstitions just mentioned, but ask whether on that account the weapons of crime are brought into court and condemned. Apparently they were not. Roman law, it appears, knew nothing about *deodanda*. Tertullian consents to answer this objection, though under protest, for the cases are not parallel, since the body is not an instrument.

38 vas vocatur, etc. 1 Thess. 4. 4, τὸ ἑαυτοῦ σκεῦος κτᾶσθαι ἐν ἁγιασμῷ καὶ τιμῇ, and perhaps 2 Cor. 4. 7, ἔχομεν δὲ τὸν θησαυρὸν τοῦτον ἐν ὀστρακίνοις σκεύεσιν. The former text is taken by some commentators, both ancient and modern, to mean τὴν ἰδίαν γαμετήν, and in view of 1 Pet. 3. 7, ὡς ἀσθενεστέρῳ σκεύει τῷ γυναικείῳ ἀπονέμοντες τιμήν, this view is possibly, though not probably, correct: for σκεῦος can never have been more than a vulgarism for γαμετή, and the use of the word here is inconsistent with the honour which St Paul enjoins.

42 capacitatis nomine. *Capacitas* in this sense of 'containership' is Ciceronian: e.g. *Disp. Tusc.* 1. 25. 61, *utrum capacitatem aliquam in animo putamus esse quo tanquam in aliquod vas ea quae meminimus infundantur*?

45 quia portio est eius. *Portio* in Novatian frequently stands for *pars*, and that may be the case in Tertullian, though never quite certainly. It seems safe to say that *portio* (as here) means something more close than a mere possession, though not actually a part: for the flesh is on no showing a part of the soul, though it may be regarded as inalienably attached to it, as a sort of dower. Cf. *Adv.Prax.* 9, *pater enim tota substantia est, filius vero derivatio totius et portio*: and my note.

46 hoc et apostolus sciens, etc. The comma should follow *sciens*, or *hoc* will be left out of syntax: in fact it anticipates *nihil... deputetur*.

47 peccatricem iudicat carnem. The reference is apparently to Rom. 8. 3, for which see again in §46, where the form given is *in simulacro carnis delinquentiae*: and to Rom. 7. 20, again referred to in §46, *habitare enim peccatum dixit in corpore nostro*. See also *De Carne Christi* 16, where Tertullian combats the view that 'likeness' indicates unreality: and to the same effect *Adv. Marc.* v. 14, where he reads *in similitudinem carnis peccati*, as also at *De Pud.* 17.

50 glorificate, tollite, etc. *Tollite* (or *portate*) seems not to be represented in any Greek manuscript, though evidently the variants stem from a Greek original. Chrysostom, *Hom. in Corinth.* I. 18 (page 153 E) has δοξάσατε δὴ ἄρατε τὸν θεὸν ἐν τῷ σώματι ὑμῶν καὶ ἐν τῷ πνεύματι, ἅτινά ἐστι τοῦ θεοῦ (where the anarthrous position of ἄρατε seems to indicate an interpolation, not indeed in the text of Chrysostom, but in his copy of the apostle): Lat. vg. *glorificate et portate deum in corpore vestro*.

CHAPTER XVII

It must not be supposed that the flesh has to rise again because souls apart from flesh are incapable of sensation: the example of the Rich Man and Lazarus proves otherwise. Nor on the other hand may it be assumed that because soul without flesh is capable of sensation, there will be no need for the flesh to be brought to judgement. Soul by itself is capable only of desire, thought, and will, and for these in the meantime it pays the penalty: but for acts which soul has wrought by means of the flesh, the flesh in company with the soul must be judged. This is the reason why judgement is deferred until the last end.

On this subject Tertullian makes three assumptions or perhaps deductions: first, that soul, because it is of corporal constitution, is even apart from the flesh capable of sensation, or inversely that the fact that soul is capable of sensation proves it to be of corporal constitution: secondly, that it is a fact, attested by Scripture and by the new prophecy, that the souls of the deceased do in the meantime *apud inferos* have a foretaste of the rewards and penalties due to them at the judgement: and thirdly, that for the fullness of these they have to await the resuscitation of their flesh. Tertullian's statement of these points, or at least the first two of them, is no doubt coloured by his Stoic metaphysic, which conversion to Christianity had not in this respect caused him to modify: but his facts, apart from their colouring, are of Christian origin and are part of his grasp of the Christian faith as a coherent whole.

The general Stoic principle is stated *De Carne Christi* 11, *omne quod est corpus est sui generis: nihil est incorporale nisi quod non est*: so that even God, being real, is (not 'has') a body, *Adv. Prax.* 7, *quis enim negabit deum corpus esse?* The soul however 'has' a body (*De Carne Christi* 11, *habente igitur anima invisibile corpus*) and 'is' a body, so that it would be a violation of reason to suppose that while soul exists, *corpus tamen non sit quicquid est anima*. The subject is discussed at length *De Anima* 5 *sqq.*, ending with an account of a revelation reported by a woman visionary of a soul in bodily shape, of the colour of fog, but gleaming, *color aërius et lucidus*. This view of the matter is capable of causing some confusion, which however it is easy enough to resolve: *Adv. Marc.* v. 15, a comment on 1 Thess. 5. 23, *nam et animam posuit et corpus, tam duas res quam diversas: licet enim et animae corpus sit aliquod suae qualitatis, sicut et spiritus, cum tamen et corpus et anima distincte nominantur, habet anima suum vocabulum proprium, non egens communi vocabulo corporis: id relinquitur carni, quae non nominata proprio communi utatur necesse est*: so that flesh, no less than soul and spirit, is to be conserved at the day of Christ.

On the question of the soul's experience of torment or comfort immediately after death, it seems at first sight as if Tertullian's views had undergone some development. At *Apol.* 48 he says that at the judgement *necessario idem ipse qui fuerat exhibebitur... ideoque repraesentabuntur et corpora, quia neque pati quicquam potest anima sola sine materia stabili, id est carne, et quod omnino de iudicio dei pati debent animae non sine carne meruerunt intra quam omnia egerunt*: and to the same effect *De Test. Animae* 4, *quod et nihil mali ac boni sentire possis sine carnis passionalis facultate, et nulla ratio sit iudicii sine ipsius exhibitione qui meruit iudicii passionem*. But in these places he is addressing himself to pagans, and his purpose is to prove the moral necessity of the resurrection, not to go into details such as would unduly complicate his argument, and to the mind of an unbeliever would partly stultify it. For Christian readers he bases himself on Scripture: e.g. *Adv. Marc.* v. 34, commenting on the parable of Dives and Lazarus, he says that there is a region of the nature of Elysian fields, and *eam itaque regionem sinum dico Abrahae, etsi non caelestem, sublimiorem tamen inferis, interim refrigerium praebituram animabus iustorum, donec consummatio rerum resurrectionem omnium plenitudine mercedis expungat*. So also, in controversy with the heathen, *Apol.* 47, *si paradisum nominemus, locum divinae amoenitatis recipiendis sanctorum spiritibus destinatum, maceria quadam igneae illius zonae a notitia orbis communis segregatum, Elysii campi fidem occupaverunt*.

At *De Anima* 7 he discusses the matter on purely Christian grounds again with reference to Dives and Lazarus: *corporalitas animae in ipso evangelio relucebit: dolet apud inferos anima cuiusdam et punitur in flamma et cruciatur in lingua, et de digito animae felicioris implorat solatium roris*: and this cannot be taken for a mere parable, since the name of Lazarus shows it to be real: and even if it were a parable it still testifies to the sentient, and therefore corporal, nature of the soul. At *De Anima* 55, 56, there is a somewhat confused discussion of what happens to souls immediately after death, but with the general conviction that, except for certain privileges of the martyrs, and special cases dependent on the will of God, there is no entrance to Paradise until the judgement: John, in the spirit (Apoc. 6. 9), saw beneath the altar, which represents Paradise, only the souls of the martyrs, and *Perpetua fortissima martyr sub die passionis in revelatione paradisi solos illic commartyres suos vidit.* So also *Scorp.* 12, in an exhortation to martyrdom. The judgement referred to is apparently that which precedes the first resurrection: cf. *De Monogamia* 10, where the wife is assumed to pray for her deceased husband—*pro anima eius orat et refrigerium interim postulat ei et in prima resurrectione consortium, et offert annuis diebus dormitionis eius.*

2 repraesentandam, with *carnis repraesentatio* (below, line 11), means, as frequently in Tertullian, 'be brought into court'—a use for which there seems to be no classical parallel, though *pecuniam repraesentare,* 'to pay up a debt', is Ciceronian. *Exhibere* is used in the same sense: so *exhibitione carnis* below (line 31).

4 nos autem, etc. The volume referred to is perhaps the treatise *De Anima.* This however is possibly of somewhat later date, and in that case the reference here will be to the earlier work *De Censu Animae,* which has not survived. *Proprium genus substantiae soliditatis* (all the MSS.) will construe, and may be correct: or Engelbrecht's insertion of *ac* may be the solution: *substantivae soliditatis* would be unusual, though who could say that Tertullian did not write it? *Quid* might here have been nominative, except that *sentire quid* (line 11) shows it to be accusative.

8 probabit (*MP*) seems more natural than *probavit* (*TX*): if Tertullian had meant that the proof was already made, he would have said *probat.* The reference is no doubt to Luke 16. 20, for which see also *De Idol.* 13: the other Lazarus is mentioned *De Carne Christi* 12 and below, § 52. Apparently *T* once read *Eleazari,* perhaps by confusion with 2 Macc. 6. 18: also at *De Anima* 7 this form appears in cod. Agobardinus: but I see no reason to restore it to the text on all occasions, in defiance of the MSS. both of St Luke and of Tertullian.

21 requirerentur, 'brought under review', as at Ovid, *Her.* VI. 31, *tua facta requirere coepi,* 'I began to rehearse in my mind'—but apparently this line and the seven following are not by Ovid.

25 etsi habet membra: see the sentence from *De Anima* 7 quoted above. Tertullian apparently thought his doctrine of the corporeity of the soul so important that he eventually felt bound to leave both the Church and the Montanists and to found a sect of his own. G. Säflund (*De Pallio und die stilistische Entwicklung Tertullians*, Lund, 1955) suggests that the outward mark of this secession was the assumption of the *pallium*, and that *De Pallio* is one of the later works.

CHAPTER XVIII

Thus far we have done preparatory work with a view to the protection of the meaning of the Scriptures which promise the resurrection of the flesh. We have insisted on the dignity of the flesh, the power of God to raise it, and on the need for it to be brought to judgement: so that even without the Scriptures the resurrection of the flesh might well be assumed. The Scriptures therefore must be understood in conformity with this assumption.

Before we come to the Scriptures themselves we must examine the terms in which the promise is expressed. 'Resurrection' implies the reconstruction of that which has fallen: and as it is the body, not the soul, which falls in death (as it does in sleep) it must be the flesh that is to rise again. Likewise 'of the dead' refers to the body, not to the soul, as is evident from Abraham's words in requesting a burying-place for his dead.

Chapters 5–17 have at the same time removed objections to the idea of resurrection and shown its intrinsic reasonableness, without particular reference to the Scriptures. Chapters 18–25 are transitional, intended to clear up one further point before the actual scriptural evidence is discussed. The expression 'resurrection of the dead' is to be understood in its literal sense, and may not be allegorized away in the manner of those who claim that it refers to the Christian life, in which we are already risen again in Christ. For the prophets, though they sometimes spoke in figures, did not do so when they were concerned with the essentials of the faith: and it is evident that this hope is fixed at the second coming of Christ, the signs of which, as noted by the apostles, are not yet in view.

2 cui cum tot, etc. *Patrocinium* is the defence of the weaker by the stronger: cf. §38, *ut tota hominis salus dimidiae patrocinaretur*. So

Cicero, *De Off.* II. 8. 27, says that formerly Roman magistrates still sought the benefit of their provincials, *itaque illud patrocinium orbis terrae verius quam imperium poterat nominari*: hence also the defence of a client in court, by a *patronus* or *advocatus* (neither of whom was permitted to receive payment). *Iusta patrocinia* will then be legal support afforded by those who, through close association with the client, have the right to give it. If *rationes iudicii* are the principles in God's mind when instituting it, *necessitates ipsius* will be the implications which follow as a necessary corollary from the fact of its institution.

7   **quia incredibile, etc.** These two clauses, with *quia* and *non quia*, are at first sight contradictory. The key is in the previous *de sola incredulitate*. The people in question refuse to believe, not because (*non quia*) they can give any articulate reason for disbelief, but simply because (*quia*) they regard it as incredible that a substance once destroyed can be restored.

10   **plane incredibile...nisi quod, etc.** Here again there is an apparent contradiction, deliberately over-emphasized so as to enforce what is really a self-correction.

13   **personat** (*TMPX*) must stand: *cum* regularly construes with the present indicative, and *personet* (*Rig. Brf.*) is not needed.

15   **quonam titulo, etc.** Tertullian imagines the divine doctrine posted up in public view, like the praetor's edict, with the short heading over it, *resurrectio mortuorum*. This perhaps precludes us from identifying the *edictum dei* with the Creed, where these words come not at the head but at the foot: and moreover it is by no means certain that the Creed known to Tertullian contained these words. (So, by implication, Kelly, *Early Christian Creeds*, p. 84.) In his *regula fidei* we have *De Virg. Vel.* 1, *venturum iudicare vivos et mortuos per carnis etiam resurrectionem*, and *De Praesc. Haer.* 13, *facta utriusque partis* [sc. the holy and the profane] *resuscitatione cum carnis restitutione*: both of which assume the answer to the question here to be discussed. The same is the case *De Praesc. Haer.* 36, where the agreement of the Roman Church with the African is thus summarized: *unum deum dominum novit creatorem universitatis et*

Christum Iesum ex virgine Maria filium dei creatoris, et carnis resurrectionem, where the unusual order *Christum Iesum* suggests that this is a credal form. We must therefore probably go back to the New Testament for the edict in question. There we have, Matt. 22. 31, περὶ δὲ τῆς ἀναστάσεως τῶν νεκρῶν, and Luke 20. 35, οἱ καταξιωθέντες...τῆς ἀναστάσεως τῆς ἐκ νεκρῶν, where St Luke's form of words might have given Tertullian's adversaries a small opportunity, which however they do not seem to have taken. In the apostolic preaching also we have: Acts 4. 2, καταγγέλλειν ἐν τῷ Ἰησοῦ τὴν ἀνάστασιν τὴν ἐκ νεκρῶν: but at Acts 23. 6, 24. 21, περὶ ἀναστάσεως νεκρῶν, and at 1 Cor. 15. 12 *sqq.* ἀνάστασις νεκρῶν, ἡ ἀνάστασις τῶν νεκρῶν: as also at Heb. 6. 2, ἀναστάσεώς τε νεκρῶν καὶ κρίματος αἰωνίου. This then, in the New Testament itself, seems to be the divine edict which Tertullian is to expound.

25 ipsa substantia indutus is the MS. reading, and must stand: Engelbrecht (followed by Borleffs) reads *ipse*. But 'himself clothed with substance' would have no meaning for Tertullian, since *substantia* means real existence, or a really existent entity: and that our Lord was already, before the Incarnation. So 'that very substance' is required, if we are to mean the Body which he assumed and to which he referred as 'this temple'.

33 sicut ipsa est, etc. The reference here, as in the following sentence, is not to the resurrection which is to be, but (as *inflata* shows) to the entry of the soul into the body at the creation: Gen. 2. 7. (If the resurrection had been meant, Tertullian would have written *inflata fuerit.*) Therefore read *suscitavit* (TR³).

37 agitatur in somnis: no one appears to have suggested *somniis*.

39 sequens nunc vocabulum, etc. In these sentences make a period after *insideat*, and place a comma after *communicaturae*, so as to end the second sentence at *suae sorti*. The heretics who ascribed mortality to soul will be the Valentinians who regarded soul as a semi-material thing, a substantification of the passion of Achamoth. The only part of human nature which these regarded as capable of salvation was 'spirit', a kind of divine substance which Achamoth unwittingly inherited from her mother the errant Wisdom and equally unwittingly imparted to her son Craftsman who again unwittingly at the creation imparted it to the elect: cf. *Adv. Val.* 25 and *De Carne Christi* 19, *semen illud arcanum electorum et spiritalium,* and my note on the latter. Tertullian will not at present allow himself to be sidetracked by this question.

47 divinae familiaritatis virum: perhaps a reference to Isa. 41. 8, 'the seed of Abraham my friend' and James 2. 23 'was called the friend of God': but Lat. vg. in both places has *amicus,* not *familiaris.*

50 mortuum meum (*T Gel.*) is evidently masculine, not neuter: so *mortuus* (twice) below. *MPX* have here the feminine, which is due to an editor: below they have (correctly) *mortuus corpus est,* where *T* and Mesnart wrongly have the neuter. At Gen. 23. 3, 4, LXX has τὸν νεκρὸν αὐτοῦ, τὸν νεκρόν μου, which might be supposed to avoid the question of gender, for νεκρός as an adjective is sufficiently uncommon: Lat. vg. has *mortuum meum.* Spurrell, in a note on the Hebrew text, says that מֵתִי is common gender, and adds further references to Lev. 21. 11, Num. 6. 6, quoting Delitsch to the effect that the distinction of gender in the case of a dead person is less regarded than in that of a living person —which is begging the question, supposing there is one.

CHAPTER XIX

Our insistence that these words mean what they say will serve to stultify a further device of our adversaries. Observing that the prophets frequently speak in parables, they claim that 'death' stands for ignorance of God, that 'resurrection' means acknowledgement of the truth, and that they are 'with the Lord' when they have put him on in baptism. By 'resurrection' however they privately among themselves understand knowledge of secret heretical doctrines. Some of our people are misled by these: while others think that 'death' means this present world, or this material body, and that the resurrection is the soul's departure from it as from a tomb.

In this chapter and in those which follow Tertullian seems to have in view three classes of persons in error. The first (from *nacti enim quidam* to *in baptismate induerint*) are those who, mistakenly but apparently in good faith, think that by death the prophets mean ignorance of God, and by resurrection acceptance of the Christian faith. The second (from *hoc denique ingenio* to *apud illos resurrectio*) are deceivers who use Christian terms so as to attract the ignorant, reserving to themselves *tacite secundum conscientiam suam* their own interpretation of these terms for later use after they have won their hearers' confidence. From *sed et plerique* we have a third group, of sincerely mistaken people, who for two allied reasons regard death as itself a resurrection. Such, at the present day, is probably the view of a large number of Christians who would be very surprised, and somewhat pained, to be told that this idea is without any support in Scripture or in authentic Christian teaching.

1 **dispectio tituli, etc.** *Titulus* still seems to mean no more than the heading of the decree: for that is all that has been examined so far. *Praeconium* originally meant the office of public crier, as at Cicero, *Ad Fam.* VI. 18. 1, *eos qui facerent praeconium vetari esse in decurionibus*, 'those who held the office of public crier could not be town-councillors', but its meaning was extended to mean *laudatio*, in which sense it has already occurred in § 11, with which compare Ovid, *Amor.* III. 12. 9, *quid enim formae praeconia feci?* Here there seems to be a further extension, to mean the contents of the decree, or (more accurately) the implications of its title.

3 **manifestiora quaeque, etc.** For a similar commonsense rule cf. *Adv. Prax.* 20, *regula autem omni rei semper ab initio constituta in prioribus et in posteriora praescribit, utique et in paucioribus* (where my note tries to explain the last four words as an impatient summary of another expression of the rule). This rule is again referred to in § 21, *supra demandavimus incerta de certis et obscura de manifestis praeiudicari*. Whether or not Tertullian wrote *de incertis* (*T* omits *de*), that is what he meant: the dative would naturally refer not to uncertain *data* but to uncertain interpreters of them.

NOTES AND COMMENTARY

5 sollemnissimam eloquii prophetici formam: cf. *Adv. Marc.* III. 5, where Tertullian, discussing *ipsarum scripturarum formam et ut ita dixerim naturam*, indicates two prophetic practices: (1) *qua futura interdum pro iam transactis enuntiantur*, e.g. *per Esaiam, Dorsum meum posui in flagella*, which whether (as Christians maintain) it refers to Christ, or (as the Jews allege) it refers to the prophet himself, is manifestly a future event expressed as past: and (2) *qua pleraque figurate portenduntur per aenigmata et allegorias et parabolas, aliter intellegenda quam scripta sunt*, a practice recognized by the apostle himself, 1 Cor. 9. 9, 10. 4; Gal. 4. 22; Eph. 5. 32. In the present chapter and those which follow Tertullian claims, first that there are many places where the prophets state plain facts in plain language: and again that even when they speak in parables there have to be plain facts in the background, or the parables will have no meaning: and thirdly, that the allegories and parables support his view and not his adversaries'. *Imaginarius* frequently means 'unreal': but cf. § 20, *omnia prophetas per imagines contionatos*, which suggests that the meaning here is 'metaphorical', though still with the sense of 'unreal': cf. *De Carne Christi* 5, *nativitatis et infantiae imaginariae vacua ludibria*.

12 itaque et resurrectionem, etc. So Irenaeus, *Haer.* II. 18. 2, *esse autem resurrectionem a mortuis agnitionem eius quae ab eis dicitur veritatis*: for *adita veritate* cf. § 1.

17 quem in baptismate induerint (*T*) is justified by Gal. 3. 27, ὅσοι γὰρ εἰς Χριστὸν ἐβαπτίσθητε Χριστὸν ἐνεδύσασθε (but not Rom. 13. 14, ἐνδύσασθε τὸν κύριον Ἰησοῦν Χριστόν), and is perhaps what Tertullian wrote: *MPX* have *cum baptisma induerint*, which he may quite well have written, to mean the same thing.

21 secundum conscientiam suam: for this sense of *conscientia* cf. *Adv. Prax.* 13, *ceterum si ex conscientia* ('that private Christian knowledge') *qua scimus dei nomen et domini et patri et filio et spiritui sancto convenire deos et dominos nominaremus*, etc. Cf. also a similar use above, § 3, *utar et conscientia populi contestantis deum deorum*.

CHAPTER XX

It cannot be true that the prophets spoke all things in parables, for if there were no realities to base them on, how could there be parables of anything? Also it is evident from the facts themselves that the prophets did say many things which have been literally fulfilled. It is true that we ourselves interpret spiritually, as referring to the soul, the diseases which our Lord healed: but we can only do that because there was actual healing of diseases of the flesh. Thus the prophets are seen to have spoken both literally and figuratively, but for the most part literally of things literally fulfilled: so that the prophetic writings and the facts of history are in correspondence with each other.

1 primam praestructionem. Souter, followed by Borleffs, at first sight plausibly, reads *primum*, which would be balanced by §22 *post haec*, as if Tertullian were outlining the course of his own argument: and cf. §33, *hic quoque occursurus prius*. But (1) in that case we should have expected to read here *eam primum praestructionem* so as to balance the relative pronoun which follows: and (2) we have a reference to the present expression at §26, *unum adhuc respondebo ad propositionem priorem allegoricarum scripturarum*: so that the MS. reading had better stand.

2 ff. imagines, figurae, umbrae, aenigmata seem to have much the same meaning, of unsubstantial images in a mirror: so *quomodo speculum obtendes? Aenigma* is connected with a mirror at 1 Cor. 13. 12. Below, *figurate* seems equivalent to *oblique*, both being the opposite of *manifeste*.

9 nam et virgo concepit, etc. Isa. 7. 14 is discussed *Adv. Marc.* III. 12, 13, where Marcion is reported as saying that the Christ prophesied by Isaiah ought to have been named Emmanuel, and to have taken the strength of Damascus and the spoil of Samaria, etc., none of which has in fact happened. Tertullian replies that the whole context must be considered, *ut cohaerentia quoque utriusque capituli recognoscas.* He points out that Emmanuel means *Nobiscum deus,* a reference to Matt. 1. 23 which Marcion would have refused, and says that Marcion does not deny that in Christ God is with us, adding that there are Hebrew Christians, and even Marcionites, who use the Hebrew word: *atque ita constat venisse iam illum qui praedicabatur Emmanuel, quia quod significat Emmanuel venit, id est Nobiscum deus.* Similarly Marcion is following the sound rather than the sense of the words when he says that the prophecy indicates that Christ will be a warrior. Here also he must look at the context, which says that this will be when Emmanuel is still a child, and as it is impossible (except perhaps in Pontus) that a child should be a warrior, *sequitur ut figurata pronuntiatio videatur.* Also the context speaks of a sign: *signum autem a deo nisi novitas aliqua monstruosa iam signum non fuisset,* which is why the Jews, objecting to the sign, read *iuvencula* for *virgo.* Some of what follows is a sign, some is not. For an infant to eat butter and honey, that is, *malitiae non assentari,* is no sign, for all infants are like that; but to receive the strength of Damascus is a sign, and needs to be interpreted. The reference is to the Magi, who came from the East, which is the home of gold and incense, and the spoils of Samaria are their conversion from idolatry: *nec hoc enim novum est creatori, figurate uti translatione nominum ex comparatione criminum.* The same argument is repeated *Adv. Iud.* 9, in much the same language, but with some additions and stylistic improvements: *adversus regem Assyriorum* means *adversus diabolum.* There are, he adds, other places where Christ is prophesied as a warrior, notably Psalm 45, where again there is an evident need for interpretation, which is given at some length: e.g. the sword upon his thigh is *sermo divinus, bis acutus duobus testamentis legis antiquae et legis novae, acutus sapientiae suae aequitate, reddens unicuique secundum actum suum.* See also *De Carne Christi* 17, 21, 23, for a discussion of the positive implications of *virgo concipiet.*

12 **venturum in iudicium**, etc. Isa. 3. 14 is quoted again *Adv. Marc.* IV. 42, also in connection with Ps. 2. 1, 2 and Isa. 53. 7 *sq.*

13 **tumultuatae sunt gentes**, etc. At *Adv. Marc.* IV. 42 (in a comment on Luke 23. 1, 2) the verses are quoted in full, with *nationes* instead of *gentes*, and the explanation, *nationes, Romani qui cum Pilato fuerant: populi, tribus Israelis: reges, in Herode: archontes,*

in summis sacerdotibus. Cf. *Adv. Marc.* I. 21, where we read *magistratus* for *archontes*: and *Adv. Prax.* 28, *et si adstiterunt reges terrae et archontes congregati sunt in unum adversus ⟨dominum et adversus⟩ Christum ipsius, alius erit dominus contra cuius Christum congregati sunt reges et archontes,* i.e. if, as the monarchians allege, Christ is identical with the Father, there will have to be some other lord besides, who is the lord of this Christ-Father.

17 tanquam ovis, etc. Isa. 53. 7 is quoted *Adv. Marc.* III. 17, with the comment that the whole passage is a good description of *meus Christus,* but not of the idealized Christ of Marcion: at *Adv. Marc.* IV. 40 (in reference to Luke 22. 7) with the comment that the reason why our Lord kept the passover is because he himself is the paschal lamb: ibid. IV. 42, *non aperuit os suum quia dominus dederat ei linguam disciplinae*: *Adv. Jud.* 13, with the comment, *hunc enim oportebat pro omnibus gentibus fieri sacrificium.* There are also references, of no special interest, *De Fug.* 12, *De Pat.* 3, *Adv. Jud.* 9. The rest of the sentence, from *dorsum suum ponens,* is a cento of quotations from Isa. 50. 6; 53. 12; Ps. 22. 16, 18; 69. 21; 22. 7; Zech. 11. 12 = Matt. 27. 9. Similar sequences of texts occur *Adv. Marc.* IV. 40 and elsewhere: especially *Adv. Jud.* 10, where there is the comment: *quae quidem omnia ipsa perpessus non pro actu suo aliquo malo passus est sed ut scripturae implerentur de ore prophetarum: et utique sacramentum passionis ipsius figurari in praedicationibus oportuerat, quantoque incredibile tanto magis scandalum futurum si nude praedicaretur, quantoque magnificum tanto magis obumbrandum ut difficultas intellectus gratiam dei quaereret.*

29 animalium vitiorum, diseases of the soul. For various uses of *animalis* cf. §22, *animales istos, ne dixerim spiritales,* an ironical reference to allegorizers: §33, *corporalitas animalis,* the fact (as Tertullian supposes) that soul, like everything real, is body of some sort: §53, *corpus animale,* a soul-informed body (σῶμα ψυχικόν).

CHAPTER XXI

Despite our admission, 'sometimes and in some cases', we insist that the prophecies of the resurrection have to be taken literally: first, because the whole tenor of Scripture demands in this instance a literal interpretation: and again, because the stringent demands of Christian discipline call for an unambiguous declaration of rewards and punishments. God's temporal decrees are clearly stated: his eternal decrees, being of greater moment, require to be no less clearly pronounced: and God does not suffer from that weakness of character which at times restrains us from plain speaking.

6 supra demandavimus, § 19.

10 ea species sacramenti in effect means 'that sentence of the creed'.

20 lucem sui fugerint. If *sui* is correct, perhaps the explanation is that it is an appositional genitive, 'the light that is themselves': so also § 30, *imago ipsa in veritate est sui*. The reading of *T* is *lucem suffuerint*, which a corrector has altered to *suffugerint*: this gives a good sense, but is too easy a way out of what is not a real difficulty, since both Hoppe and Bulhart agree that Tertullian frequently uses the genitive of the pronoun instead of the possessive adjective.

24 cavillatur here seems to be passive, and to mean 'is expressed with reserve'. The verb is given by Lewis and Short only as deponent, with the meaning 'jeer' or 'scoff', and (in a secondary sense) 'quibble'. At Appuleius, *Metam.* IX. 28 *cavillatum* is passive, meaning 'teased'.

CHAPTER XXII

Scripture itself excludes the idea that resurrection either consists of present apprehension of the truth or ensues immediately after death. The hope of it is fixed at the coming of Christ, at the end of the world, of which there will be warning by manifest signs. So our Lord himself taught, when he spoke first of the fall of Jerusalem and then of the end of the age, specifying the signs which would indicate that it was coming, not that it had already come. No one yet has seen either that Christ has come or even that the signs have occurred: heretics themselves, though they profess to have risen again, are still subject to this life's disabilities.

2 animales istos. Because they admitted a resurrection of the soul alone, Tertullian claims to identify them with the 'natural men', the ψυχικοί, of 1 Cor. 2. 14. They called themselves *spiritales*, πνευματικοί, in St Paul's language a complimentary term, which Tertullian will not allow. A few years later he apparently, as a Montanist, called himself πνευματικός, as he called non-Montanists ψυχικοί: cf. *Adv. Prax.* 1.

5 aeque non licebit...ante constitui. By supplying this clause, missing in the other authorities, *T* has clarified the sentence and made unnecessary the slight verbal rearrangements of the early editors.

7 in adventum, etc. This sentence is built up of phrases from various places of Scripture: *in transitum mundi*, the general sense of Isa. 13. 13, ὁ γὰρ οὐρανὸς θυμωθήσεται καὶ ἡ γῆ σεισθήσεται ἐκ τῶν θεμελίων αὐτῆς: *diem irae*, Zeph. 2. 2, ἡμέραν θυμοῦ Κυρίου: *retributionis*, Hos. 9. 7, ἥκασιν αἱ ἡμέραι τῆς ἐκδικήσεως: *nec ulli...notum*, Acts 1. 7: *et tamen signis*, etc., Luke 21. 9 *sqq*.

13 interrogatus, etc. This and the following sentences summarize the apocalyptic passage of Luke 21. 9 *sqq*., of which verses 9–24 treat of the fall of Jerusalem, and verses 25–8 of the end of the world. At *Adv. Marc.* IV. 39 there is a discussion of this passage, illustrated by many texts from the prophets, designed to show that Christ's words are in harmony with the Creator's: *cuius dispositiones confirmat impleri oportere, quas ut optimus tam tristes quam atroces abstulisset potius quam constituisset, si non ipsius fuissent*: and again, *praemiserat oportere haec fieri tam atrocia tam dira, deus optimus, certe a prophetis et a lege praedicata: adeo legem et prophetas non destruebat, cum quae praedicaverant confirmat perfici oportere. Eruperat* as a transitive verb occurs e.g. Lucretius I. 723, *faucibus eruptos iterum vis ut vomat ignes*: so that *eruperant* (Gelenius) is not necessary. *Conclu-*

sionem nationum is a literal translation of συνοχή ἐθνῶν (Luke 21. 25): Lat. vg. *pressura gentium*.

27 emergetis...elevabitis...adpropinquaverit. The Greek has ἀνακύψατε...ἐπάρατε...ἐγγίζει with a variant ἤγγικεν: *Adv. Marc.* IV. 39, Tertullian has *erigetis vos et levabitis capita... appropinquabit* (so apparently the MS. and Rhenanus: Pamelius substituted *appropinquavit*). In the following sentence Tertullian has the present, *appropinquare*: *Adv. Marc.* IV. 39, *appropinquasse*. Souter's *app. crit.* to Luke 21. 28 needs correction: ἐγγίζει Tert. ¼ ἤγγικεν ²⁄₄ ἐγγίσει ¼

38 in agnitione sacramenti means either 'at acceptance of the faith' or 'at reception of baptism'—which for practical purposes would in Tertullian's day have meant the same thing.

39 quis ergo, etc. A further cento of scriptural phrases: *ad confringendam terram*, Isa. 2. 19, θραῦσαι τὴν γῆν: *subiecit pedibus eius*, Ps. 110. 1: *talem conspexit*, etc., Acts 1. 11: *tribus ad tribum*, etc., Zech. 12. 12, καὶ κόψεται ἡ γῆ κατὰ φυλὰς φυλάς: *quem pupugerunt*, John 19. 37, from the Hebrew of Zech. 12. 10, where LXX has καὶ ἐπιβλέψονται πρός με ἀνθ᾽ ὧν κατωρχήσαντο: *fugit antichristum*, Rev. 12. 6: *Babylonis exitum flevit*, a summary of Rev. 18. 9 *sqq.*

CHAPTER XXIII

The apostle certainly speaks of baptism as a spiritual dying and rising again, but not in such a sense as (even in the same context) to exclude a corporal resurrection in the future. In fact his words throughout this passage demand a future resurrection, as do those of St John, of St Paul himself elsewhere, and of St Peter in the Acts.

The two indirect quotations from Col. 1. 21; 2. 12, in the opening sentence, which justify the idea of a present spiritual resurrection, are balanced by four further quotations from the same context which show that a corporal resurrection is still to be expected. Further citations from other apostles and from St Paul elsewhere support this contention.

2 alienatos et inimicos sensus domini hardly gives the sense of the Greek (Col. 1. 21), ἀπηλλοτριωμένους καὶ ἐχθροὺς τῇ διανοίᾳ, which evidently means the converts' own minds: Lat. vg. *alienati et inimici sensu*.

5 et vos, cum mortui essetis, etc. Col. 2. 13. The Greek is καὶ ὑμᾶς νεκροὺς ὄντας τοῖς παραπτώμασι, κτέ: Lat. vg. has *in delictis* (so also *T Gelenius*). *Donatis* stands for χαρισάμενος: Lat. vg. *donans*: so also Tertullian, *Adv. Marc.* v. 19. *Donare* meaning 'forgive' is classical, cf. Ovid, *Ex Ponto* II. 7. 51, *culpa gravis precibus donatur saepe suorum*: and Horace, *Carm.* III. 3. 33, *Marti redonabo* seems to mean 'I will forgive for Mars' sake'.

7 si cum Christo, etc. Col. 2. 20: *mortui essetis*, the MS. reading, hardly represents ἀπεθάνετε: Rhenanus and subsequent editors have *mortui estis* (so Lat. vg.). *Quomodo quidam* is in all the MSS., but there is no τινες in the Greek: perhaps it was a false recollection by Tertullian of 1 Cor. 15. 12, πῶς λέγουσιν ἐν ὑμῖν τινες ὅτι ἀνάστασις νεκρῶν οὐκ ἔστιν; in which case it must be retained (so all editors except Borleffs). *Sententiam fertis*, δογματίζεσθε, Lat. vg. *decernitis*: St Paul's meaning seems to be 'pass laws for other people to keep', or even 'invent sins for other people not to commit'.

12 si conresurrexistis, etc. Col. 3. 1: so Borleffs writes, on the authority of *TX*, *cū resurrexistis*: Lat. vg. *consurrexistis*, Gk. συνηγέρθητε. *Quae deorsum*, τὰ ἐπὶ γῆς, *quae super terram*.

18 et nondum, etc. 1 John 3. 2: *similes eius* (*MX*) is perhaps what Tertullian wrote: Gk. ὅμοιοι αὐτῷ: Lat. vg. *similes ei*.

26 si qua...concurram, etc. Phil. 3. 11 *sqq.*: *concurram in* (Lat. vg. *occurram ad*) is for καταντήσω εἰς: *ad palmam incriminationis* is for εἰς τὸ βραβεῖον τῆς ἄνω κλήσεως, the last word (as Borleffs observes) being misread as ἀνεγκλησίας—a word which occurs once, Eusebius, *Praep. Evang.* page 274 D in a quotation from Bardesanes: but the adjective ἀνέγκλητος is classical and not uncommon. Lat. vg. *supernae vocationis*. The words that follow are not part of St Paul's text, but are either Tertullian's explanation or are due to a slip of his memory.

36 det illi dominus, etc. 2 Tim. 1. 18: the Greek has εὑρεῖν ἔλεος παρὰ κυρίου.

38 custodire mandatum, etc. An indirect quotation of 1 Tim. 6. 14, 15: *in adparentiam* (Lat. vg. *usque in adventum*) is for μέχρι τῆς ἐπιφανείας. *Et dominus dominantium* was added by Gelenius, apparently without authority.

41 paeniteat itaque, etc. Acts 3. 19 *sqq.*: for *respicite* Erasmus suggested *resipiscite*, which is even further from the Greek, ἐπιστρέψατε (Lat. vg. *convertimini*): *ex persona dei*, ἀπὸ προσώπου τοῦ κυρίου (vg. *a conspectu domini*): *praedesignatum*, τὸν προκεχειρισμένον (which, if classical usage is any guide, would mean 'was prepared beforehand')—Lat. vg. *qui praedicatus est* seems not to go quite deep enough into the matter: *ad usque tempora exhibitionis*, ἄχρι χρόνων ἀποκαταστάσεως, which according to classical usage ought to mean 'restitution' (so Lat. vg. *in tempora restitutionis*) though it appears that *exhibitionis*, by which Tertullian means 'delivery', or 'fulfilment', is more in keeping with the clause that follows: *de ore*, διὰ στόματος: Tertullian omits ἀπ' αἰῶνος αὐτοῦ before *prophetarum* as do some New Testament manuscripts (Souter plausibly suggests that the words have slipped into the text of Acts from Luke 1. 70).

CHAPTER XXIV

Concerning the time of the resurrection St Paul writes to the Thessalonians, expounding the manner of our Lord's coming and of our being brought into his presence. None of this has yet happened, and those persons are seriously in error who, by setting their hope in this life only, lose the promise of the life to come. The day of the Lord, the apostle says, will come suddenly and unexpectedly, but not until Antichrist has come first: and this cannot be, so long as the Roman empire continues to act as a restraint upon that mystery of iniquity which is already at work.

The selections from the Thessalonian epistles in this chapter follow St Paul's order. They are designed to show (1) that our Lord's coming is expected: and (2) what are the accompanying circumstances of his coming and of our meeting with him. Tertullian then observes that none of these things have yet occurred, and remarks upon the error of those who place all their hope in this present life. Returning to St Paul he quotes (3) to the effect that our Lord's coming will be sudden and unexpected, and (4) that men must be on their guard against false and premature announcements of it: for (5) this will not occur until the disruption of the Empire permits the appearance of Antichrist, whom our Lord at his coming will destroy.

2 qualiter conversi sitis, etc. 1 Thess. 1. 9, 10.

4 quae enim spes, etc. 1 Thess. 2. 19: *quam ut et vos* is a mistranslation of ἢ οὐχὶ καὶ ὑμεῖς, which is the beginning of a new sentence, the answer (in the form of a question) to the question preceding.

6 coram deo et patre nostro, etc. 1 Thess. 3. 13: 'before our God and Father' (so English R.V., correctly).

These first three quotations serve to show that our Lord's coming is a well-authenticated Christian expectation: the one that follows outlines the manner of it and its accompaniments.

9 si enim credimus, etc. 1 Thess. 4. 14–17. In this passage *T* seems to show evidence of editing into conformity with the Greek:
   resurrexit TB, for ἀνέστη: Lat. vg. *mortuus est et resurrexit*: *MPX resurrexerit*.
   in adventum domini nostri: *T* and the Greek omit *nostri* (so Lat. vg.).
   et in voce: *T* and the Greek (not Lat. vg.) omit *et*.
   qui simul: *T* omits *qui*: the Greek has οἱ περιλειπόμενοι, Lat. vg. *qui relinquimur*, which should perhaps be restored.
   obviam Christo, MPX: *obviam domino Christo, T*, perhaps again bringing into partial conformity with the Greek εἰς ἀπάντησιν τοῦ κυρίου.
All the MSS. have *in sermone dei*, where Pamelius wrote *domini*: *primi resurgent* is for ἀναστήσονται πρῶτον, Lat. vg. *resurgent primi*.

22 miserrimi revera, etc., a paraphrase of 1 Cor. 15. 19. Phygellus and Hermogenes are mentioned at 2 Tim. 1. 15 as having

NOTES AND COMMENTARY 253

deserted St Paul in Asia: I suspect that Tertullian has confused them with Hymenaeus and Alexander (1 Tim. 1. 19) who, having cast off faith and a good conscience, made shipwreck concerning the faith.

27 de temporibus, etc. 1 Thess. 5. 1–3: *tuta sunt omnia* represents the single word ἀσφάλεια, Lat. vg. *securitas*.

31 obsecro autem vos, etc., 2 Thess. 2. 1–7: *per adventum*, ὑπὲρ τῆς παρουσίας, 'in respect of the coming': *insistat*, ἐνέστηκεν, 'has arrived': *in omne quod dicitur*, εἰς πάντα λεγόμενον, where Tertullian apparently misread πάντα as πᾶν τὸ: *adfirmans*, ἀποδεικνύντα, 'displaying': *tantum qui nunc tenet, TMP* add *teneat*, which is a misguided attempt to correct St Paul, who deliberately, so as not to be too precise, left the sentence incomplete. It is not impossible that Tertullian attempted the correction: Lat. vg. has *tantum ut qui tenet nunc teneat donec de medio fiat*. For various interpretations of ὁ κατέχων, τὸ κατέχον, it must suffice to refer to the commentaries.

44 in decem reges dispersa, Rev. 17. 12–14.

45 et tunc revelabitur, etc., 2 Thess. 2. 8–10: the antecedent of *cuius* is of course *iniquus*.

CHAPTER XXV

The Apocalypse of John also sets out the order of the last times, and (like the rest of the Scriptures) places the harvest of Christian hope at the end of the world. Consequently, the heretical pretension of a present resurrection through baptism is either false, or at all events is without prejudice to that which is expected at the end of the age. Also, for the very reason that the supposed present resurrection is spiritual, the other must be admitted to be corporal, seeing there is no indication that it is spiritual, and no prophecy to that effect. Thus the suggestion of a spiritual resurrection upon entrance into the faith is rather in our favour than our adversaries'.

The first sentence of this chapter is a closely knit series of references to the Apocalypse, as follows:

martyrum animae	6. 9, 10
de pateris angelorum	15. 7; 16. 1 *sqq.*
prostituta civitas	17. 1 *sqq.*
a decem regibus	17. 12
dignos exitus	17. 16
certamen ecclesiae	19. 19, 20
in abyssum religato	20. 2, 3
interim (1000 years)	20. 2
primae resurrectionis praerogativa	20. 4, 5
a soliis	20. 4
diabolo igni dato	20. 9, 10
universalis resurrectionis censura de libris	20. 12

The sentences that follow leave aside the specific reference to the Apocalypse and repeat the tenor of all the Scriptures: though if justification were sought for *corporalis agnoscitur* it could be found in the reference (Rev. 20. 13) to the sea giving up the dead.

In two places the MS. text has been needlessly altered by editors: *religato* (line 7) is evidently correct, being based upon Rev. 20. 2, 3, καὶ ἔδησεν αὐτὸν χίλια ἔτη καὶ ἔβαλεν αὐτὸν εἰς τὴν ἄβυσσον: *vindicetur* (line 16) is the reading of three MSS. and could well stand. On line 18, the additions made by Gelenius are evidently necessary. At line 7, *de soliis ordinetur*, I wonder if Tertullian wrote *ordiatur*: or possibly *ordinetur* should be understood in that sense.

CHAPTER XXVI

We also can find support for our view from figurative Scriptures. For example, mankind is referred to as 'earth', because man was taken from the earth, and it was earth ⟨as yet without the animating soul⟩ which first received the designation 'man': so that blessings and curses pronounced against 'earth' really apply to man. So in David, 'the earth shall rejoice', and in Isaiah, 'ye shall eat the good things of earth'. For it is inconceivable that God should have proposed to attract obedience by the promise of such things as he has already given to all alike, including the ungodly. The Jews, by hoping only for earthly goods, lose those that are heavenly, even as they misinterpret 'holy land' to mean the soil of Palestine, when it really means our Lord's flesh, by virtue of which the flesh also of those who have put on Christ becomes holy land, and even that Jerusalem which Isaiah commands to arise ⟨from the dead⟩. Such words as these can never apply to that Jerusalem which slew the prophets and its own Lord, or even to any earth at all, for the whole earth is to pass away. Even if 'holy land' means Paradise, it is the Paradise of the Fathers that is intended, and restitution to Paradise is a promise made to the flesh, so that man may return thither in that state ⟨of completeness of flesh and soul⟩ in which he was when cast out.

It will hardly be possible to accept Tertullian's interpretations of the passages quoted. Their 'spiritual' sense may be worth seeking; but their primary meaning is precisely that of which he denies the possibility. *Terra es et in terram ibis* is one of his favourite texts: he has cited it already in §§6 and 18, and it will recur in §52: see also *Adv. Marc.* v. 9 and *De Anima* 52. Psalm 97 will probably be best understood as a poetical personification of the earth rejoicing at God's kingship: and the hills melting like wax as the poetically imagined consequence of the lightning which declares God's power. Isa. 1. 19, *Bona terrae edetis* means precisely what Tertullian denies, that if the men of Judah and Jerusalem are willing and obedient they will have good harvests which will not be destroyed by foreign invaders. Isa. 51. 9, *Exsurge exsurge Hierusalem* follows LXX: the Hebrew has 'O arm of the Lord', and the words are a prayer for deliverance, with an assurance that deliverance is near at hand. In the Hebrew, at verse 17, 'Awake, awake, stand up O Jerusalem' is the beginning of a prophecy, continued in chapter 52, of the restoration of the nation after the captivity of Babylon. Certainly the 'good things of the land' can be interpreted as things which the eye hath not seen nor the ear heard: and undoubtedly Jerusalem stands for the eternal city of God: but the primary historical sense need not be denied so as to establish the prophetic and secondary meaning: and Tertullian's suggestion that 'land' means 'flesh' is too far-fetched to be credible. The same remarks will no doubt apply to the larders of the following chapter: the unstained garments are a different matter, for the context from which they are taken is itself a 'spiritual' one.

1 unum adhuc respondebo. This theme, that our case no less than the heretics' can be supported by allegory, is continued in §§ 27 and 28. It is assumed that we have the better right to this method because we use it in conformity with the other Scriptures, and not so as to explain them away. *Proinde* here stands for *perinde*, as often: 'we no less than they'.

8 quia nec proprie, etc. *Proprie* either 'in a strict sense' or 'on its own account'. *In figuram*, etc.: Tertullian seems by a slip of memory to have confused Gen. 3. 17, ἐπικατάρατος ἡ γῆ ἐν τοῖς ἔργοις σου, addressed to Adam, with 4. 11, καὶ νῦν ἐπικατάρατος σὺ ἐπὶ τῆς γῆς, addressed to Cain: but he still suggests that 'earth' here means figuratively the flesh of Cain the homicide.

11 nam et si, etc., makes a slight admission, that it is just possible that the curse was addressed to the earth itself; but, even so, it is man, and not the earth, who suffers from it.

17 exultabit terra: at Ps. 97. 1 LXX has ἀγαλλιάσεται: the Hebrew seems to have the jussive meaning, *exultet*. It is just possible that in this, as in other places, the editor of *T* corrected his text into conformity with the Scripture, Tertullian having originally written *exultavit*. Below, *quo supra regnante exultavit* (*MPX*) has the appearance of being correct, 'has just been said to rejoice'.

20 et videbunt enim eum qui, etc. This reading (of *T*) seems best to explain the other variants. John 19. 37, ὄψονται εἰς ὃν ἐξεκέντησαν is referred to again § 51, *agnoscendus scilicet et eis qui illum convulneraverunt* and *De Carne Christi* 24, *agnoscent qui eum confixerunt*. In the gospel this seems to be a quotation from the Hebrew (not LXX) of Zech. 12. 10.

21 adeo, as often, is for *ideo*: *simpliciter*, the opposite of allegorically.

25 reformatam, 'brought again into shape', i.e. out of dissolution: for *angelificatam* see a note on § 36, *similes enim erunt angelis*.

29 **homini addicta conditione**, Gen. 1. 28, 'have dominion'.

36 **de caelesti**, as the more difficult reading, must probably stand: it refers to Exod. 16. 4 (not, as far as the Jews were concerned, to John 6. 51), ἰδοὺ ἐγὼ ὕω ὑμῖν ἄρτους ἐκ τοῦ οὐρανοῦ, but it is not easy to explain the adjective, unless perhaps Tertullian read οὐρανίου. *Vigorare* occurs as a transitive verb, *De Pud.* 2, *effeminantia magis quam vigorantia disciplinam*, and Appuleius, *Met.* IX. 21, *vigorati iuvenis* ('who had recovered his courage'): there seems no parallel to the present intransitive sense, 'obtaining strength'. *Ex vite Christo* (*T*) is no doubt correct: cf. John 15. 1.

39 **quae exinde**, etc. *Quae* has for its antecedent not *carnem domini* but flesh in general, which when it has put on Christ becomes 'holy land'. *Vere lacte ac melle*, the common reading, may be what Tertullian wrote: the Greek of Exod. 3. 17 has accusatives, as Borleffs observes—εἰς γῆν ῥέουσαν γάλα καὶ μέλι: but it is always possible that the editor of *T* corrected the text into conformity with the Greek. So also below, *in primordio diei*, ὡς ἐν ἀρχῇ ἡμέρας, though here probably *T* is correct.

42 **vere Iudaea**, etc. There seems here to be a reference to a supposed Hebrew meaning of the name Judah. At Gen. 29. 35 and 49. 8 it is connected with ידה, 'praise', which gives us no help here. I suspect that Tertullian has confused Judah with Israel, which was thought to mean *vir videns deum*, Gen. 32. 30, 'I have seen God face to face'. So I read here *per dei familiaritatem*, with *MPX*.

Tertullian had written, or afterwards wrote, a treatise *De Paradiso*, which has not survived: *De Anima* 55, *habes etiam de paradiso a nobis libellum quo constituimus omnem animam apud inferos sequestrari in diem domini*. See the whole chapter, which begins with a description of *in fossa terrae et in alto vastitas et in ipsis visceribus eius abstrusa profunditas*, where Christ was for three days in the heart of the earth. This itself (in Tertullian's view) is not Paradise, for from it the patriarchs and prophets came into Paradise at the time of our Lord's resurrection. But it is not to be expected that all, even all Christians, will go to Paradise immediately after death: the realm of Paradise was revealed to John (Apoc. 6. 9), who saw there only the souls of the martyrs beneath the altar: and Perpetua, *fortissima martyr*, on the day of her martyrdom saw in a vision of Paradise only the souls of her fellow-martyrs: therefore *tota paradisi clavis tuus sanguis est*. At *Apol.* 47 in a (hardly serious) comparison of Christian concepts with heathen fables, he says, *et si paradisum nominemus, locum divinae amoenitatis recipiendis sanctorum spiritibus destinatum, maceria quadam igneae illius zonae a notitia orbis communis segregatum, Elysii campi fidem occupaverunt*. At *Adv. Iud.* 2 he says, *primordialis enim lex data Adae et Evae in paradiso quasi matrix omnium praeceptorum dei*: if they had kept this law there would have been no need for any other, concerning either circumcision or sabbath. So *De Patientia* 5, *innocens erat et deo de proximo amicus et paradisi colonus*: *Adv. Marc.* II. 2, because man had not faith, *etiam quod videbatur habere ademptum est illi, paradisi gratia et familiaritas dei per quam omnia dei cognovisset si oboediisset*. Apparently Tertullian does not distinguish between this 'Paradise of the Fathers' and that of the martyrs: *Adv. Marc.* II. 10, space (i.e. time) was left for a contest, so that man might overthrow the adversary with the same freedom of will with which he had fallen before him, *probans suam non dei culpam...et deus tanto magis bonus inveniretur sustinens hominem gloriosiorem in paradisum ad licentiam decerpendae arboris vitae iam de vita regressurum*. This is part of what he means in our present text, in which he admits for the sake of argument a suggestion made by others, not necessarily his adversaries: but he adds that if man has the promise of restoration to Paradise, that promise is given to his flesh, so that he may return there in flesh, even as in flesh he was driven out. From this it appears that he has not yet adopted the view that Paradise is where the martyrs only await the day of the Lord, but still thinks that none go there before the resurrection.

CHAPTER XXVII

The mention of garments in the Apocalypse and by Isaiah is also an allegory of the resurrection of the flesh, and Isaiah's injunction to enter into secret chambers is a reference to those graves and sepulchres from which the flesh will be withdrawn after the indignation is overpast.

2 hi sunt, ait, etc. is a conflation, probably by a slip of memory, of Apoc. 14. 4, οὗτοί εἰσιν οἱ μετὰ γυναικῶν οὐκ ἐμολύνθησαν, παρθένοι γάρ εἰσιν, and ibid. 3. 4, ἃ οὐκ ἐμόλυναν τὰ ἱμάτια αὐτῶν. *Castraverunt*, cf. Matt. 19. 12: *in albis vestibus*, Apoc. 3. 5, ὁ νικῶν οὕτως περιβαλεῖται ἐν ἱματίοις λευκοῖς, and ibid. 7. 13: *indumentum nuptiale*, Matt. 22. 11, where Tertullian is wrong if he thinks this implies no more than *sanctitas carnis*.

7 itaque Esaias, etc. This sentence as printed by Dr Borleffs is not in syntax: the easiest remedy would be to omit *inquit*, which, though apparently in all MSS., merely repeats *subicit*. Isa. 58. 8, τότε ῥαγήσεται πρόϊμον τὸ φῶς σου καὶ τὰ ἰάματά σου ταχὺ ἀνατελεῖ, where Tertullian misread ἰάματα as ἱμάτια. *Subsericam*, introduced into the text by Gelenius, is a brilliant emendation of *MPX subscribam*, which is meaningless: but both the word and the garment are very uncommon. On Trebellius Pollio, *Divus Claudius*, Isaac Casaubon has a learned note beginning 'Familiare est in re vestium ut solis adiectivis sine substantivis nominentur' (*Hist. Aug. Script.*, Paris, 1603, vol. II, pp. 495, 499). *Subucula* (Mesnart) would mean much the same thing but without the suggestion of effeminacy.

12 allegorice is in all MSS. Kroymann says it is a Greek substantive, in which case *defensio* is complementary to it: Borleffs thinks it is an adverb, in which case *defensio* is the subject of the sentence.

13 populus meus, etc. Isa. 26. 20, βάδιζε λαός μου, εἴσελθε εἰς τὰ ταμεῖά σου, ἀπόκλεισον τὴν θύραν σου, ἀποκρύβηθι μικρὸν ὅσον ὅσον ἕως ἂν παρέλθῃ ἡ ὀργὴ Κυρίου. *Promus* is usually a substantive, meaning the steward's deputy who distributes provisions, and so forth: Tertullian alone, and only here as it appears, makes it an adjective: Lat. vg. *cubicula*, English R.V. 'chambers'. *Quae extinguet antichristum*, cf. Apoc. 20. 10, where however the actual word 'wrath' does not occur, though the whole context abundantly suggests it.

After *ortum carnis* (line 11) *T* fails until §28, line 20, *occidens per*.

CHAPTER XXVIII

There are allegories of fact as well as of words. The reviving of Moses' hand is a forecast of the resurrection of the whole man. In fact the three signs given to Moses (Exod. 4. 2–9), of the serpent overcome, of the hand brought back to life, and of the water to be turned into blood, are a parable of the triple power of God in vanquishing Satan, in raising the dead, and in exacting vengeance for bloodshed. Moreover blood cannot be avenged in its absence: and as there can be no blood without flesh, this also signifies the resurrection. There are also some statements of resurrection which, though not figurative, need to have their meaning made plainer by a short explanation: such is 'I will kill, and make alive'.

8 apud eundem propheten, i.e. Moses, Gen. 9. 5.

19 apud Esaiam is in error: Deut. 32. 39 (the song of Moses), and cf. 1 Sam. 2. 6 (the song of Hannah).

CHAPTERS XXIX–XXXI

Ezekiel's vision of the Valley of Bones first describes and then promises the resurrection of the actual substances of human flesh.

Some attempt to treat this as an allegory of the restoration of the Jewish nation from its dispersion. But what when they die again? Is there another resurrection? Other prophecies say so: consequently this must refer to it. Moreover there could be no allegory based on resurrection if there were no actual resurrection: you cannot make a parable out of that which does not exist. If the reference here had been to the re-establishment of the Jewish state, the explanation 'These bones are the whole house of Israel' would have come at the beginning. Actually what happens here is that God first tries and then confirms the prophet's faith in a real resurrection (which the Jews were denying) and afterwards applies the parable.

There was as yet no dispersion for the people to mourn over: but they had often enough given up hope of the resurrection, and it was of this that they needed to be assured. Moreover, even if there had been present distresses, it was more to be expected that they should be turned away from consideration of them towards the hope of eternal salvation through the resurrection: for it is of this that Malachi and Isaiah (in several places) speak in similar terms to Ezekiel's.

The interpretation of this chapter of Ezekiel is generalized and concluded in §32.

Complete agreement with Tertullian's interpretation of this vision will not be easy. He may be right in his supposition that if there had been no physical resurrection there could have been no parable based upon it: but there can be little doubt that what Ezekiel chiefly had in mind was to comfort the people during the captivity in Babylon by the promise of the restoration of their nation—not of the Jews only who had been taken captive in 597 and 586, nor of those slain in the massacres in Jerusalem, but of the whole house of Israel, including the dispersed of the northern kingdom. Tertullian, saying that the dispersion had not yet taken place, was thinking only of the events of A.D. 70 and 130, and preferred to forget the previous history recorded in the Book of Kings. His observation that if the vision had had Jewish history in view the explanation to that effect would have come earlier, shows a strange lack of the sense of literary climax. His further suggestion that if there had been national distresses, the remedy would have been not the promise of temporal restitution but the promise of eternal salvation, is couched in Christian rather than Jewish terms: for the prophets said many things which meant present comfort to their contemporaries, but which Christians interpret as parables of a better hope.

The text of Ezekiel quoted here is not translated from the Septuagint but appears to be an independent version of a faulty Hebrew text. In the analysis of variants which follows the English Revised Version is intended to represent the Hebrew (of which it is a translation): the Latin vulgate also is (as was to be expected) closer to the *Hebraica veritas* than is the Greek.

Ezek. 37. 1-14

	Tertullian	LXX	English R.V.	Lat. vg.
1	ossibus refertus	μεστὸν ὀστέων ἀνθρωπίνων	full of bones	plenus ossibus
2	multa	πολλὰ σφόδρα	very many	multa valde
3	Adonai domine tu scis	Κύριε σὺ ἐπίστῃ ταῦτα	O Lord God thou knowest	Domine Deus tu nosti
5	dominus Adonai... spiritum, et vivetis	Κύριος... πνεῦμα ζωῆς	the Lord God... breath...and ye shall live	Dominus Deus... spiritum, et vivetis
6	spiritum (*leg.* nervos) ...dabo in vobis spiritum	νεῦρα...δώσω πνεῦμά μου ἐφ' ὑμᾶς	sinews...put breath in you	nervos...dabo vobis spiritum
7	ecce vox...accedebant ossa ad ossa	[*caret*] προσήγαγε τὰ ὀστᾶ ἑκάτερον πρὸς τὴν ἁρμονίαν αὐτοῦ	there was a noise... the bones came together, bone to his bone	facta est autem sonitus ...accesserunt ossa ad ossa unumquodque ad iuncturam suam
8	circompositae sunt eis carnes	ἀνέβαινεν ἐπ' αὐτὰ δέρματα ἐπάνω	flesh came up, and skin covered them	carnes ascenderunt et extenta est in eis cutis desuper
8 *sqq.*	spiritus } ventus }	πνεῦμα	breath, wind, spirit רוּחַ	spiritus, ventus
9	dominus Adonai	Κύριος	the Lord God	Dominus Deus
9	veni, spiritus	ἐλθὲ	come...O breath	veni, spiritus
10	ad spiritum...in ea ...valentia	[*caret*] εἰς αὐτούς... συναγωγή	[*caret*] ...into them...army	[*caret*] ...in ea...exercitus
11	avulsi sumus in eis	διαπεφωνήκαμεν	we are clean cut off [i.e. spadones facti sumus]	abscissi sumus
12	propheta ad eos	προφήτευσον καὶ εἰπόν Τάδε λέγει Κύριος	prophesy and say unto them, Thus saith the Lord God	vaticinare, et dices ad eos, Haec dicit Dominus Deus
2 *sqq.*	sepulchra	{ τάφοι { μνήματα	graves קְבָרוֹת	sepulchra, tumuli
13	ego dominus aperuerim...et eduxerim vos de sepulchris vestris, populus meus	ἐγώ εἰμι Κύριος ἐν τῷ ἀνοῖξαί με...τοῦ ἀναγαγεῖν με ἐκ τῶν τάφων τὸν λαόν μου	...I am the Lord, when I have opened ...and caused you to come up out of your graves, O my people	...ego Dominus cum aperuero...et eduxero vos de tumulis vestris, popule meus
14	spiritum...requiescetis...fecerim	τὸ πνεῦμά μου... θήσομαι ὑμᾶς... ποιήσω	my spirit...I will place you...and performed it	spiritum meum... requiescere vos faciam...et feci

CHAPTER XXIX

4 speciali seems here to mean 'specific' rather than 'special'.

13 nervos is Kroymann's necessary correction into conformity with the Hebrew: *MPX* have *spiritum*: *T* omits from *dabo* to *vivetis et*.

22 valentia no doubt stands for δύναμις, 'army': Hebrew חיל: LXX συναγωγή.

30 locutus sum et fecerim: *TMX* have *sum*: *P* has *sim*: at the repetition of this sentence at the end of §30 *T* again has *sum*, the others *sim*. As the more difficult reading, *sum* in both places appears to be right: but if so *fecerim* must stand for *fecero*. The use of future perfect for simple future is not uncommon (though there is nothing to this effect in Rönsch, *Itala und Vulgata*), and Tertullian in the last clause of §30 seems to take the speaking as already past, but the doing as still future, *si aliter facturus quam locutus*. LXX has καὶ ποιήσω: Lat. vg. *et feci* (so also English R.V.): the Hebrew וְעָשִׂיתִי can apparently mean either. The Bishop of Bradford kindly informs me that the future is probably correct. For the future perfect in *-erim*, see §16, *satisfecerim*, and probably §56, *si non meminerim me esse qui merui, quomodo gloriam deo dicam?*

CHAPTER XXX

11 respirari, 'be made to breathe again', seems to be Tertullian's coinage, used only here: below is its verbal noun, *reviscerationem et respirationem*. Oehler quotes Franciscus Junius who surmises that the verb is equivalent to ἀναψυχοῦσθαι: otherwise *respirare* means 'breathe' or 'recover' (from surprise, etc.), and is always intransitive.

18 denique hoc ipso, etc. This and the next few sentences make a good debating point, which is very competently put: but it is to be feared that it will only persuade those who are already persuaded. An argument in support of it, which Tertullian does not in fact introduce (though similar arguments on other texts had occurred to Justin) is that the restoration of the Jewish polity, as Ezekiel envisaged it, did not in fact take place, and consequently, since prophecy must be fulfilled, it has to be fulfilled either in the moral or in the transcendental sphere: i.e. the vision signifies either the moral restoration of those dead in sin, or the corporal resurrection of those who are, or will be, physically dead—or perhaps both of these together. This in fact is the sense in which Christian interpreters have usually interpreted the vision.

21 **figmentum,** a post-classical word, means an image: Lewis and Short give examples from Aulus Gellius and Ammianus Marcellinus, e.g. *aerea figmenta*, 'images made of bronze': the meaning 'fiction' or 'falsehood' also occurs, e.g. Appuleius, *Met.* IV. 27, *nec vanis somniorum figmentis terreare*. The meaning here is 'model': so below, *qualis adfingitur*, 'such as is modelled upon it'. Cf. also §40, *figmento iam homini appellato*, of the clay which God had brought into human shape.

22 **in veritate est sui.** I take *sui* here to be a genitive of apposition, 'the truth which it is itself': so Appuleius, *De Mundo* 24, *neque ulla res est tam praestantibus viribus quae viduata [dei] auxilio sui natura contenta sit*. But see above, §21, *lucem sui fugerint*: the explanation there given may well serve here also.

36 **sed quoniam praedicabatur, etc.** It is hardly true to say that the resurrection of the dead was so clearly preached that Israel could be expected to have apprehended it. There are indeed places like Ps. 16. 10, 11 (Thou wilt not leave my soul in hell, etc.) which envisage it: but all of them are obscure enough to have, for a time at least, and until they received fuller inspiration, escaped the notice of the Apostles (cf. John 20. 9). Tertullian is throwing back into the past the fuller knowledge of an age enlightened through Christ.

38 **habitum senescentis sepulturae.** *Habitus* means 'state' or 'condition'. *Sepultura*, by metonymy, seems to mean the corpse:

and *senescens*, 'getting old', is another way of saying 'now a long time dead'. There is perhaps a hidden reference to John 11. 39, ἤδη ὄζει, τεταρταῖος γάρ ἐστι.

CHAPTER XXXI

2 exitum is the direct object of the verb *queri*, involved in the adjective *querulus*.

12 ad hoc enim, etc. By a slip of memory Tertullian regards this text as belonging to Ezekiel: Mal. 4. 2, καὶ ἐξελεύσεσθε καὶ σκιρτήσετε ὡς μοσχάρια ἐκ δεσμῶν ἀνειμένα, καὶ καταπατήσετε ἀνόμους. *Gaudebit*, etc. Isa. 66. 14: the comment on it has a hidden reference to John 12. 24, I Cor. 15. 36, οὐ ζωοποιεῖται ἐὰν μὴ ἀποθάνῃ.

20 de omnibus enim, etc. Isa. 26. 19: LXX, ἀναστήσονται οἱ νεκροὶ καὶ ἐγερθήσονται οἱ ἐν τοῖς μνημείοις...ἡ γὰρ δρόσος ἡ παρά σου ἴαμα αὐτοῖς ἐστι. Tertullian follows neither LXX nor Hebrew: *medulla* for *medela* is a natural enough alteration for *T* to have made, with *ossibus* in his text: or Tertullian himself, having changed αὐτοῖς to ὀστέοις, might equally well have written it if he had been acquainted with the Hebrew (not LXX) of Prov. 3. 8, 'health to thy navel and marrow to thy bones'. This text seems to have no bearing on Tertullian's postulate of a universal resurrection: that which follows (Isa. 66. 23) is no doubt universalist, but has no bearing on the resurrection, for it signifies the gathering of all nations to worship at Jerusalem. *Supra enim*, i.e. in the previous verse, Isa. 66. 22, which again has only in a secondary sense a bearing on the resurrection: the concluding verse, Isa. 66. 24 (*et videbunt*, etc.), also needs interpretation, which Tertullian gives. *Et erit satis conspectui*, LXX καὶ ἔσονται εἰς ὅρασιν: the Hebrew apparently means 'and they shall be an abhorring'.

CHAPTER XXXII

To make it abundantly clear that it was a corporal resurrection the prophets had in view, it is said that even the fishes will give up the dead they have devoured, and according to Moses men's blood will be required of every beast. Of the fishes giving up the dead Jonah is a sufficient example: though there is no need to suppose that beasts and fishes will have part in the resurrection, for the beasts signify the men, and the angels of wickedness, who have shed Christian blood. In the face of such evident testimonies it is sheer perversity to interpret bones and flesh and skin and sinews as anything but what they are. Moreover if prophecies about the body are to be interpreted as parables, prophecies about the soul will also have to be explained away: for it is inconceivable that the one sort should be figurative and the other not.

As the continued reference to bones and flesh, etc. indicates, this chapter is the conclusion and summary of Tertullian's interpretation of Ezekiel's vision. His protest against the inconsistency of allegorizing prophecies relating to the body, while abstaining from allegorizing those which refer to the soul, is no doubt sound: but that some discretion is required as to what is allegory and what is fact appears from his own allegorizing of the references to fishes and beasts, which have no part in the resurrection though included in the prophecies. In what follows Tertullian will base his argument on the Gospel and the Apostles, where there are clearer indications such as neither need nor admit of allegorizing.

2 **et mandabo, etc.** This might be supposed to be derived from Rev. 20. 13, καὶ ἔδωκεν ἡ θάλασσα τοὺς νεκροὺς τοὺς ἐν αὐτῇ, though the sentence itself is quoted from the Book of Enoch. This book is cited several times by Tertullian, who regarded it as canonical Scripture and as the actual words of the patriarch, communicated to his descendants, preserved in Noah's memory, and thus escaping destruction by the Deluge, so as to be written down later: cf. *De Cultu Feminarum* I. 2, 3, where he repeats its story that cosmetics, along with philtres, astrology, and other black arts, were communicated to their wives by the fallen angels (Gen. 6. 2), and remarks that this book is not received by some because it is not in the Jewish canon (*armarium*), and because they think it could not have been preserved during the Flood—a supposition he argues against as above indicated, adducing as a parallel the recon-

struction from memory of the whole Hebrew canon by Ezra after the captivity in Babylon, and adding that the probable reason why the Jews refuse this book is that it prophesies of our Lord: and finally, the apostle Jude acknowledges it. Cf. ibid. II. 10: also *De Idololatria* 15, *haec igitur* [heathen tutelary deities of doorways] *ab initio praevidens spiritus sanctus etiam ostia in superstitionem ventura praececinit per antiquissimum propheten Enoch.* But it is to be feared that Tertullian's eagerness to have the book accepted as canonical stemmed from the opportunity it gave him of using the story of the fallen angels both as a warning to women and as a reproach to such of them as disregarded his strictures on their apparel.

10 puto autem, etc. I have punctuated both these sentences about Jonah as a parenthesis in the main argument, which now concerns beasts in general rather than fishes in particular, and is taken up again at *salvo eo*. Kroymann thinks *conditae* is from *condire* ('embalm'): I thought so myself when I first met with this passage (in a college exercise in 1907), and still think so, while regretting that I have to disagree with Dr Borleffs, who reads *condĭtae*, and translates 'tidy'.[1]

17 iniquitatis angelos, etc. These will be those whose existence and activity in instigating persecution is hinted at, *Apol.* 2, *suspecta sit vobis ista perversitas, ne qua vis lateat in occulto quae vos adversus formam adversus naturam iudicandi, contra ipsas quoque leges ministret*: and, less allusively, ibid. 27, *vice rebellantium ergastulorum sive carcerum vel metallorum vel hoc genus poenalis servitutis erumpunt adversus nos*, etc.

30 in aliquam speciem corporalem. *Species* here apparently means 'aspect', as below *altera species*, body and soul being two aspects of one and the same humanity, *tam enim corpus homo quam et anima*: cf. *infra*, § 40, *nec anima per semetipsam homo quae figmento iam homini appellato postea inserta est, nec caro sine anima homo quae post exilium animae cadaver inscribitur*.

[1] If (as I suspect) 'tidy' is an English word, I should remark (1) that it is not a natural translation of *condĭtus*, and (2) that 'tidy burial' is not a natural English expression.

CHAPTER XXXIII

When we refer to the Gospels, there are those who allege that as our Lord spoke all things in parables his references to the resurrection can be explained away. Certainly he always spoke in parables to the Jews, and sometimes also to the disciples. It follows that there were times when he did not speak in parables: and when he did do so, he either supplied an interpretation, or the evangelist indicates the way for one, or else the meaning can easily be surmised. Moreover there are plain statements which are not parables. Such are those made concerning judgement, the kingdom of God, and the resurrection: and as these three terms mean what they say, and are not parables, we must consider that the further implications of the terms refer to objective corporal fact. We have already remarked that soul is corporal, but this must not be allowed to exclude the flesh, which is no less corporal: for both soul and flesh must share in the judgement and the kingdom and consequently in the resurrection.

It seems likely that the texts Tertullian discusses in the chapters that follow are for the most part those which his adversaries had already misinterpreted.

1 **instrumento,** documentary authority: cf. *Apol.* 18, *instrumentum litteraturae,* 'literary evidence': *De Carne Christi* 2, *originalia instrumenta Christi,* 'documents bearing on Christ's origin', i.e. the nativity stories of Matthew and Luke.

3 **proinde,** if it stands for itself, means 'consequently': if for *perinde,* 'likewise', i.e. no less than the prophets.

16 **commentatore,** cf. *De Carne Christi* 22, *Matthaeus fidelissimus evangelii commentator.*

25 **nomina absoluta,** 'complete nouns', are, according to the grammarians, nouns which have their meaning in themselves, without further definition or qualification: see Lewis and Short, s.v. *absolvo,* who also refer to Cicero, *De Inventione* II. 57. 170,

where it is observed that we sometimes say 'necesse est' with an expressed or unexpressed condition, sometimes without: *esse quasdam cum adiunctione necessitudines, quasdam simplices et absolutas.*

28 quae ad dispositionem, etc. The meaning of this sentence seems to be that, seeing that the terms themselves have their meaning evident, it being perfectly clear what is to be understood by 'judgement', 'kingdom', and 'resurrection', it will follow that not only the three 'things' but also their circumstances and accompaniments, as well as all that is essential to them or results from them, must be understood in a literal sense. *Dispositio* and *transactio* will be, from God's side, the establishment and the conduct of the kingdom, the judgement, the resurrection, while *passio* will be, from man's side, the experience of them. The older editions, following *MPX*, had *passionem regni iudicii et resurrectionis*, which is difficult (as the editors seem not to have noticed) because of the omission of *et* after *regni*. For *iudicii* T has *Iudaici*, and then *resurrectionem*, which Borleffs accepts: but there has been no mention of, or even remote reference to, the Jewish kingdom, and (as appears from §22) Tertullian thought (quite rightly) that other Scriptures, in particular Luke 29. 9 *sqq*., referred to the fall of it, but would have denied that any prophecy gives reason to expect a future re-establishment of it: any Old Testament prophecies which seem to have that meaning he would have interpreted 'spiritually'. Therefore *Iudaici* should probably be rejected, and along with it any reason for *resurrectionem* also disappears. It might be desirable to regularize the syntax by inserting *et* before *iudicii* (or removing the *et* that follows), in which case the three verbal nouns would naturally distribute among themselves the three genitives, 'establishment of the kingdom, conduct of the judgement, experience of resurrection'.

31 On **corpus animae** see a note on §17: Tertullian here admits that few accept this doctrine, and indeed it appears that he subsequently left both the Church and the Montanist sect to found a sect of his own of which this was the peculiar tenet: G. Säflund, *De Pallio und die stilistische Entwicklung Tertullians* (Lund, 1955), pp. 27–52.

CHAPTER XXXIV

Christ came to save that which was lost (Luke 19. 10). It was the whole man that was lost, not a part only—the soul through desire of the forbidden fruit, the flesh through tasting of it. Consequently the whole man will be saved, as in the parable the whole of the lost sheep was. God is not less generous than secular princes, so as to grant less than plenary indulgence: and man cannot truly be said to be saved, if part of him perishes. The soul may perhaps be regarded as saved (i.e. exempt from total destruction) because of its natural immortality: so that that which is lost will be the flesh, and it too will be saved. Alternatively, if the soul is destructible, the flesh, also destructible, will also be saved. Whatever part of man is not destructible, does not perish, and whatever part is destructible will be saved: and thus you have the restitution of the whole man. Moreover our Lord said that of all that the Father had given him he would lose nothing: so that, as the Father had given him, at the Incarnation, complete manhood, it is complete manhood that he will save. Also he says that those who see him, and believe in him, will have eternal life: and since it is the flesh which sees and the soul which believes, both of them merit, and will obtain, eternal life. And if anyone objects that this pronouncement only applies to those who then saw and believed, we answer that those who have not seen and yet have believed are pronounced more blessed: and such they cannot be if one part of them is to be lost.

3 siquidem transgressio, etc. The transgression of Gen. 3, as the original of all transgressions and of universal condemnation, is referred to *Adv. Marc.* I. 22, *homo damnatur in mortem ob unius arbusculae delibationem, et exinde proficiunt* (= *proficiscuntur*) *delicta cum poenis, et pereunt iam omnes qui paradisi nullum caespitem norunt.* See also *De Cultu Feminarum* I. 1, where the responsibility is put upon Eve, and in rhetoric which loses both its head and its manners is transferred to women in general. So also, in less offensive terms, *De Carne Christi* 17. *Instinctu*, usually in the ablative, commonly refers to divine (or demonic) inspiration of pagan prophecy: but at Tacitus, *Hist.* I. 70 we have *instinctu decurionum*, where it seems that the cavalry officers' mind was formed more by happy guesswork than by accurate knowledge of the facts: Tertullian, *Adv. Marc.* I. 2, *passus infelix huius praesumptionis instinctum*, 'the suggestion of this piece of guesswork': ibid. II. 10, *diabolum...instinctorem delicti*: and (if the MS. is correct) ibid. v. 16, *erit eis instinctum fallaciae* (= 2 Thess. 2. 11, ἐνέργεια πλάνης), a nominative form which Lewis and Short do not recognize.

12 After **minus facere** there is something missing: I suggest *quam faciat homo*, Kroymann's *quam censuram humanam* being syntactically impossible, and therefore not very clear in its meaning.

18 carne scilicet, etc. I suspect that these six words should be marked as a supposed reply to the preceding question, and that *nisi quod iam*, etc. is Tertullian's comment on that reply. Throughout this passage there persists an equivocation on the meaning of *perire*, which sometimes stands for *interire*, perish altogether and (at least until the resurrection) cease to exist, and sometimes (as the author remarks) for *supplicio adfici*. An attempt is made, somewhat half-heartedly, to disentangle the two senses, the result being merely to complicate the argument.

29 eum salus destinet either means 'salvation points out his way', or else stands for *salus ei destinetur*, 'salvation is his destiny'.

39 ut omne quod dedit, etc. It will not be supposed that Tertullian is correct in his suggestion that 'what the Father hath given' is the actual humanity assumed by the Son at the Incarnation: John 6. 39 seems most naturally to have reference to all those who are predestined to eternal life: in which case it would have been a legitimate deduction if Tertullian had claimed that 'all this' must mean not only all the persons but also both their human constituents, body as well as soul. Throughout this passage, and elsewhere, the MSS. seem not to agree, even with themselves, on the gender of *dies*.

47 hoc est patris voluntas, etc. John 6. 40. In this sentence T, reading *haec* for *hoc*, and *videt* for *aspicit*, has manifestly been assimilated to Lat. vg.

55 feliciores enim, etc. John 20. 29 has μακάριοι, though it might be arguable that 'more blessed' (i.e. than Thomas) is a justifiable deduction from the context.

CHAPTER XXXV

The possibility of both soul and body being slain in hell (Matt. 10. 28–31) is further evidence in our favour. The soul cannot be slain by man: the body can. But the flesh cannot be slain in hell unless it has first been raised up again. By 'body' we mean the flesh with all its material constituents, not some alleged 'occult' body—of the existence of which there is no evidence at all. Nor shall we be misled by reference to the 'body' of the soul, for in this text both soul and body are mentioned as distinct from each other. Slaying in hell must be understood to be for punishment, not for destruction: for as the fire of hell is eternal, so must be the substances of flesh and soul on which they feed: and moreover it would be absurd that the body should be restored to existence merely so that it might for a second time cease to exist. If one sparrow out of two does not fall except by God's will, neither will the flesh, more valuable than many sparrows, be outside God's care. And for what purpose are our hairs all numbered, except that they may be raised up again? Those who are in hell will need eyes to weep with and teeth to gnash, and those cast out of the marriage-feast will need hands and feet that may be bound. Also those who recline at the feast or sit on thrones or eat of the tree of life will not be able to do so without bodies.

1 eum potius timendum, etc. Tertullian is no doubt right in his interpretation *id est dominum solum*: for (1) there is a significant change of construction from μὴ φοβήθητε ἀπὸ τῶν ἀποκτεινόντων τὸ σῶμα (with the preposition) to φοβήθητε δὲ μᾶλλον τὸν δυνάμενον, κτέ (with the direct accusative), the former meaning the fear of shrinking, the latter the fear of reverence;

NOTES AND COMMENTARY 273

for it appears that neither LXX nor New Testament ever use such an expression as φοβεῖσθαι ἀπὸ τοῦ θεοῦ: and (2), as A. H. M'Neile observes (*ad loc.*), it would not be true to say that the devil has either δύναμις or ἐξουσία in this respect. Tertullian has throughout this chapter the accusative *in gehennam*: the Greek has ἐν γεέννῃ.

4 anima immortalis natura. *Natura* is here equivalent to the Aristotelian φύσει, which is somewhat unusual: it is just possible that we ought to read *animae*. *Recognoscitur* serves a double purpose, first with *anima* as subject, and again as an impersonal passive with the accusative *resurrectionem* and its infinitive.

9 ego corpus humanum, etc. Oehler's Index (s.v. *corpus*) confuses this passage with *De Carne Christi* 9, which compares the several parts of the human body with the elements of the earth from which it was taken and which (the allegation is) it still resembles. If *arcanum aliquod corpus* means anything definite, it may refer to those supposed 'animal' or 'spiritual' or 'choic' bodies, of gnostic origin, which are discussed *De Carne Christi* 10–16. *Arcana* at *Apol.* 21 means 'archives', *eum mundi casum* (the darkening of the sun at midday, Matt. 27. 45, etc.) *relatum in arcanis vestris habetis*: below, §63, *arcana apocryphorum blasphemiae fabulae* are gnostic additions to the Scriptures: and so here the word seems to mean 'occult', a theosophical euphemism for 'fanciful'.

40 nisi quia hoc est, etc., an addition to the interpretation of this text which was given in §34.

45 Kroymann changed **operibus** to *opertibus*, of which Souter and Borleffs approve. It is difficult to disagree with such great authorities, but I am not convinced. The word *opertus* occurs at Appuleius, *De Magia* 56 (where Lewis and Short have a wrong reference) in the dative singular along with two other verbal nouns of similar form, all of which are more verbs than nouns: *lini seges...non modo indutui et amictui sanctissimis Aegyptiorum sacerdotibus sed opertui quoque rebus sacris usurpatur*. I know of no evidence that it can be a concrete noun or be used in the plural, and I suspect that *operibus* must be retained, as Tertullian's quite legitimate interpretation of ἔνδυμα γάμου, the literal meaning of these words being already fully represented by *in nuptiis...indutus*. The 'good works' will be such as are recounted at Matt. 25. 31 *sqq.*, from which comes the reference to *fletus et dentium frendor*, above.

CHAPTER XXXVI

Matt. 22. 25-33; Mark 12. 18-27; Luke 20. 27-40

Our Lord's reply to the Sadducees' question about the woman with seven husbands bears directly on our subject. The Sadducees raised objections to the resurrection on precisely those grounds where objection is easiest, namely the flesh: for it was the flesh which they thought of as involved in marriage. Thus our Lord's answer refutes them on the same grounds. He does not say that men will not rise again, but that they will not marry, being made like the angels. They could have raised no question regarding either marriage or resurrection except by throwing doubt upon the flesh, which is specifically involved in death, as in marriage. Thus our Lord is found to affirm what the Sadducees denied, a whole and entire resurrection.

Luke 20. 27-40 is discussed *Adv. Marc.* IV. 38. The subject of the Sadducees' question was the resurrection, and we must take it that this also was the subject of our Lord's answer: *neminem timuit, ut quaestiones aut declinasse videatur aut per occasionem earum quod alias palam non docebat subostendisse*, i.e. he did not, as Marcion alleged, give secret hints of a hidden doctrine of Marcionite pattern. Our Lord's answer begins with the statement that the sons of this age marry, i.e. that marriage belongs to this age, to which death also belongs. In that age there will be no marriage, for they will be like the angels. The answer is still framed in terms of the question, and is an answer to it and to it alone. It affirms the resurrection, of which the Sadducees were raising doubts: it has no reference at all to a Marcionite 'other god', nor does it question the Jewish law of marriage. If you make Christ answer a question he was not asked, you suggest that he could not answer the question he was asked, and that the Sadducees had the better of him. The Marcionites, in quoting the text, join together words that are not meant to join. It appears that οἱ δὲ καταξιωθέντες τοῦ αἰῶνος ἐκείνου τυχεῖν καὶ τῆς ἀναστάσεως τῆς ἐκ νεκρῶν had been mistranslated *quos vero dignatus sit deus illius aevi possessione et resurrectione a mortuis*: Tertullian does not question the translation, but denies the Marcionite grouping *deus illius aevi* by which they claim to prove both the existence of their supposed superior god, and that even already he has prohibited from marriage these Marcionites, whom he has deemed worthy of the possession and of resurrection from the dead: they also allege that *filii huius aevi* are the Creator's men. He adds that as the Sadducees' question was concerned with the marriages not of this world but of the other, it was the latter which the answer denied. It was in this sense that the bystanders understood the answer, for the scribes comment, 'Master, thou hast well said', being pleased that he had confirmed their own belief in the resurrection, as against the Sadducees' denial: and finally, our Lord did not refuse the approval of those who understood him in this way, for he went on to quote the scribal teaching that Christ is the Son of David, and to supplement (not deny or supersede) it with David's testimony that Christ is David's lord.

1 Concerning the **Sadducees** cf. *De Praesc. Haer.* 33, *Paulus in prima ad Corinthios notat negatores et dubitatores resurrectionis. haec opinio propria Sadducaeorum: partem eius usurpat Marcion et Apelles et Valentinus, et si qui alii resurrectionem carnis infringunt.* He says *partem eius* because the heretics mentioned did not deny the survival or the resurrection of the soul, as the Sadducees apparently did: so *De Carne Christi* 1, *fidem resurrectionis ante istos Sadducaeorum propinquos sine controversia moratam. An* here stands for *annon*, as frequently, e.g. *De Carne Christi* 3, *an ergo voluerit nasci consideremus*, where see my note. *Elidens, erexerit*, involve a metaphor from the overthrowing and setting up of defence-works or of buildings: cf. *Adv. Prax.* 16, *turrem superbissimam elidens*: so below, *destructio, labefactatur*.

4 **ex qua...specie.** *Species* can mean the particular application of some *forma*, or rule of law: so perhaps here 'under which heading'. Or it can mean some part or aspect of a thing, or a

particular instance of some species or genus (for which see my note on *De Carne Christi* 13, towards the end): so that the meaning here would be 'in respect of which part or aspect of human nature'. The latter seems more in point.

11 scripturarum ignaros, μὴ εἰδότες τὰς γραφάς, i.e. that when God says 'I am the God of Abraham, of Isaac, and of Jacob', since he is not God of the dead but of the living (*apud deum vivorum*), it is evident that at the time of Moses the three patriarchs, though deceased, were still alive, and that therefore the conditions existed which ensured their resurrection.

12 virtutis dei incredulos, μηδὲ τὴν δύναμιν τοῦ θεοῦ, possibly (as Tertullian says) *idoneae mortuis resuscitandis*, but also (certainly) competent so to transmute human nature that with it questions of physical marriage will not arise.

20 sed resuscitati seems to hang in the air, and the MSS. and editors have attempted various amendments, none of which are very convincing, though the best of them, by Engelbrecht, might stand: *sed resuscitati similes [enim] erunt angelis*. Thornell defends the MS. text, but in spite of his great authority I am not quite convinced, and suggest (as I wrote in the margin of Oehler forty years ago) that *virgines manebunt* has fallen out after *resuscitati*.

20 similes enim erunt angelis, an indirect reference to Luke 20. 36, ἰσάγγελοι γάρ εἰσι (where Matthew and Mark have ὡς ἄγγελοι). On this text see *Adv. Marc.* III. 9, *si deus tuus veram quandoque substantiam angelorum hominibus pollicetur*: and especially ibid. IV. 38, where the whole episode is fully discussed: and below, §62. Tertullian never entirely adopts the erroneous view that at the resurrection redeemed men will be transmuted into angels, though he often comes perilously close to it, as at *De Orat.* 3, *angelorum si meruerimus candidati*: and here that would have been the case if *per substantiae demutationem* had meant 'exchange' and not just 'change' of substance, such a change as in fact St Paul indicates at 1 Cor. 15. 52, καὶ οἱ νεκροὶ ἐγερθήσονται ἄφθαρτοι καὶ ἡμεῖς ἀλλαγησόμεθα (on which cf. §51).

28 solidam resurrectionem, a complete and entire resurrection, i.e. of both the human substances, body and soul: from the testamentary use of *solidus* = *ex asse*, 100%, for which see my note on *De Carne Christi* 6, and notes above on §§2 and 4.

CHAPTER XXXVII

The statement that the flesh profiteth nothing (John 6. 63) must be read in its context, where there precedes 'It is the Spirit that quickeneth', and there follows, 'The words that I speak are spirit and are life'. That means that it is the word or discourse which makes alive, and our Lord naturally identifies his flesh with this word, because the Word was made flesh: so also he gives us his flesh to eat as a cause of life, having already said that it is bread from heaven. Thus the text in question has no bearing on the resurrection: and yet it has, because the flesh is one of those things, themselves unprofitable, which can receive profit from elsewhere—in this case, from the Spirit. In this way the text confirms the resurrection, because there is the Spirit which quickens the flesh. On a previous occasion (John 5. 25) our Lord had said that the dead would hear his voice and would live: that is, it is he, the Voice, Word, Spirit, who will raise the dead. At that point he adds (John 5. 28) that all that are in the tombs will hear his voice and will rise again: and evidently it is bodies, flesh, which are laid in tombs. The suggestion that 'tombs' here means sinners is untenable: for the text says that both the good and the evil are to rise again: and how can tombs rise out of tombs?

The text *Spiritus vivificat ⟨in regnum dei⟩, caro nihil prodest* is quoted again in §56 in a comment on 1 Cor. 15. 50.

1 **sic et si** (Gelenius, for the MS. *licet si*: *T, licet sic*) is probably correct: the reading of *T* would almost make sense, though it would be difficult to explain *sic*. In the text as printed, *sic et* refers back to the previous chapter, where also we have had a suggestion by the opponents that our Lord's words support their view. So here they quote *caro nihil prodest*, and again Tertullian replies that when taken in its context it is in conformity with his view. With

materia dicti cf. *Adv. Marc.* IV. 38, *haec fuit materia quaestionis, haec substantia consultationis* (of the Sadducees at Luke 20. 27).

2 durum et intolerabilem...sermonem, σκληρός ἐστιν οὗτος ὁ λόγος, τίς δύναται αὐτοῦ ἀκούειν; Perhaps *intolerabilem* has crept in by a slip of memory from John 16. 12, οὐ δύνασθε βαστάζειν ἄρτι. *Sermo* throughout this passage, and usually in Tertullian, stands for λόγος: *verba*, below, is for ῥήματα, and *vox* is for φωνή. As a rule ῥῆμα is the jussive word (so also ἐρρέθη at Matt. 5. 21, etc.), and at John 6. 63 it refers to the series of commands implied in the preceding discourse, beginning with the direct imperative ἐργάʒεσθε (verse 27). Λόγος is the discursive word, of which *sermo* is the best Latin equivalent: it appears from *Adv. Prax.* 5 that the African church at least was already accustomed, by what Tertullian calls the artlessness of the translation, to say that *sermo* was in the beginning with God (John 1. 1). Tertullian thinks *ratio* would have been better, as meaning the thought in the mind of God; though even so, he adds, it makes no difference, for thought itself is a kind of unspoken speech, a conversation which the thinker holds with himself. Φωνή (John 5. 28, quoted below) is the recognizable sound of a voice already known, involving an invitation, or perhaps a summons, as at Gen. 3. 8, etc., τὴν φωνὴν Κυρίου τοῦ θεοῦ, and Isa. 40. 3, φωνὴ βοῶντος. *Quasi vere carnem suam* refers back to John 6. 52, πῶς δύναται οὗτος ἡμῖν δοῦναι τὴν σάρκα φαγεῖν;

4 ut in spiritum disponeret, etc. is not easy to explain. *Status salutis* may possibly mean 'state of salvation' in the Augustinian (medieval and modern) sense of that phrase: for *status* in Tertullian commonly (in such a connection as this) indicates that assemblage of attributes which constitute the *natura* of an object or person, and the meaning here seems to be those attributes of personal character and divine relationship which salvation assures and of which it consists: so that *salutis* is an appositional genitive. The difficulty is to find a consistent interpretation of *spiritus*, which neither here nor in the rest of this chapter means the human spirit, nor apparently is that its meaning in John 6. 63: far less is 'spirit' to be taken in its illegitimate and highly misleading modern sense of a certain attitude of mind or an upthrust of human emotion. Tertullian here (as elsewhere, e.g. *Adv. Prax.* 26, *De Carne Christi* 18, 19) identifies the Word with the Spirit. This does not mean that he identifies the second and third Persons of the divine Trinity, but that beginning from John 4. 24, πνεῦμα ὁ Θεός, he thinks that 'spirit' is a description of the divine Substance, the kind of substance God is. Thus in whatever context he finds the term 'spirit' he can apply it to that One of the three Persons whom the text before him seems to require: as for example he equates 'the Spirit of God' at Luke 1. 35 (for so he read the text) with the Word who was made flesh (*Adv. Prax.* 26); and here in John 6. 63 he finds support for a similar identification, it being easy enough tacitly to change over from *verba* to *sermo*, so as to identify the words which were spoken with the Word who was made flesh— *spiritus et vita sermo*—so that the Word incarnate is the Spirit that giveth life. That this is not too far removed from the meaning of the gospel text should perhaps be admitted: though probably the meaning originally intended was (1) that the Holy Spirit is capable, and alone is capable, of giving understanding of the 'hard saying', and (2) that the same Holy Spirit, by the consecration of the bread of the Eucharist, makes it the flesh of Christ, of which a man will eat and not die. A point which Tertullian misses is that this effect (in both senses) is contingent on our Lord's ascension (John 6. 62, ἐὰν οὖν θεωρῆτε τὸν υἱὸν τοῦ ἀνθρώπου ἀναβαίνοντα ὅπου ἦν τὸ πρότερον;).

8 qui audit, etc. John 5. 24 (after the healing of the cripple at Bethesda): *veniet* is for ἔρχεται (so also below, *veniet hora* for ἔρχεται ὥρα, John 5. 28): possibly Tertullian wrote the future so as to avoid confusion between *vĕnit* and *vēnit*. *Transiet,* for μεταβέβηκεν, is in all the MSS.; Gelenius wrote *transibit*: *transiit* would stultify Tertullian's argument. The better MSS. of Tibullus 1. iv. 27 have *transiet aetas*.

12 in causam vitae is again difficult, since Tertullian as a rule uses *causa* not for the efficient but for the final cause (cf. e.g. *De Carne Christi* 6 and 14, where the word is repeatedly used in this sense): so perhaps here 'for the purpose of obtaining life'.

Evidently *adpetendus* stands somewhat apart from the three other gerundives which follow it.

14 paulo ante, i.e. at 6. 51, of which Tertullian's indirect quotation is a summary.

25 veniet enim inquit hora. John 5. 25 (the preceding verse having already been quoted): *enim* is not part of the quotation, but is Tertullian's connecting word: the Spirit, he says, is of profit to the flesh, because (as our Lord says) those who hear the voice of the Son of God will live, and he has already identified the Son (the Word) with the Spirit that quickeneth.

30 ne miremini. John 5. 28, 29: *filii dei vocem* is for τῆς φωνῆς αὐτοῦ, i.e. the Son, to whom the Father has given authority to execute judgement, because he is Son of man: *qui mala*, abbreviated from οἱ δὲ τὰ φαῦλα πράξαντες.

CHAPTER XXXVIII

Our Lord's actions have the same purport as his words. His raising of people from the dead was not merely a present display of power, but a token of the resurrection to be, which must therefore be as complete a resurrection as these tokens of it were. It is not true that these examples were corporal only because the souls, being invisible, could not have been seen to be rising again: souls can be made visible, as witness the souls of the martyrs beneath the altar. We prefer to think that God cannot be deceptive, as that he should give examples of complete resurrection in token of a partial one: for the fact represented by an example must be not less, but greater, than the example. Such is the case here: the resurrection to be is of both flesh and soul, as those examples were: but this is greater, in that those persons had to die again, whereas we shall not.

The reference here is to Jairus' daughter, Matthew 9. 18–26, Mark 5. 22–43, Luke 8. 41–56: to the widow's son, Luke 7. 12–16; and to Lazarus, John 11. 1–46. Luke 8. 41 *sqq.* is discussed *Adv. Marc.* IV. 20, with reference only to the woman from among the

NOTES AND COMMENTARY 281

multitude: Luke 7. 12 *sqq.* is referred to briefly *Adv. Marc.* IV. 18: for Lazarus see below, §53.

5 ad fidem...sequestrandam. *Sequestrare* is a late formation for *sequestro dare,* 'put into the hands of a trustee': Tertullian is apparently the first user of it: cf. §27, *corpora sepulchris sequestrantur: Adv. Val.* 25, *peculium quoddam seminis spiritalis, sicut et ipsa Achamoth in filio Demiurgo sequestraverat, ne hoc quidem gnaro.* Prudentius could have got the word from Tertullian, *Cathemerinon* 10. 125 *sqq., nunc suscipe terra ferendum | gremioque hunc suscipe molli: | hominis tibi membra sequestro, | generosa et fragmina credo.* At 1 Macc. 11. 34 (Lat. vg., the Greek having nothing to correspond) *sequestrari* seems to refer to the setting aside ('ear-marking') of the revenues of certain territories for the service of the sanctuary.

8 in carne quoque decucurrisse, the reading of *T,* is perhaps correct: *praecucurrisse (MP)* is attractive, being certainly what Tertullian meant, even if he did not write it: *in carnem (MPX)* may also be what he wrote, for the distinction between ablative and accusative with *in* was becoming blurred, and in any case the accusative here (in its full sense) would be defensible. There is nothing to be said for Kroymann's *procucurrisse* or Souter's *percucurrisse.*

11 quod non putant. We must here supply in thought a second *eum posse*: Tertullian deliberately writes a foolish sentence to stigmatize a foolish suggestion.

11 instrumentum Iohannis: Rev. 6. 9, εἶδον ὑποκάτω τοῦ θυσιαστηρίου τὰς ψυχὰς τῶν ἐσφαγμένων. Tertullian insists on the full sense of εἶδον. On *instrumentum* cf. *Apol.* 18, *instrumentum litteraturae* (i.e. the Old Testament), where Oehler notes that Tertullian regularly says *instrumentum* for *apparatus*, and gives a number of examples: so also §33, *de prophetico instrumento*, and §39, *apostolica instrumenta.*

16 immo ne si, etc. *T* here has *immo si nec,* which will only make sense if it begins a new sentence, and if the *non* before *valuit* is omitted (so Borleffs). This is rather rough treatment of the authorities, and it seems preferable to punctuate with a comma after *videatur*, read *immo ne si* with *MPX*, and retain *non* (all the MSS.), with *possit* (*MPX*) at the end of the sentence. A superficial objection to this might be that the part of the sentence following *immo* is on a different theme from what precedes: but this is to miss the force of *immo*, which indicates the author's own correction of, or supplement to, his previous words. Our opponents' suggestion, he says, would lead to the idea that God can be deceptive (or disappointing) in offering proofs which promise more than he is going to fulfil: we cannot accept that idea—nay rather (*immo*), if he could not accomplish a temporal resurrection without including the flesh, much more, we claim, he could not accomplish the final, more difficult, resurrection without it (reading *sine eadem substantia*, with *T*, and *possit* with *MPX*).

20 resuscitabuntur, 'are going to be raised up again', a future of impatience with an intolerable idea, 'if we once allow the possibility of souls along with bodies being raised up for a proof of their rising without bodies': Ursinus' *resuscitarentur* is therefore unnecessary. *Corpore* (*MPX*, both times) is perhaps right, there being no particular thought of either singular or plural, but merely adjectival phrases, 'embodied', 'bodiless'.

24 secundum nostram veritatem (*T*), 'according to the truth as we see it', is probably what Tertullian wrote, and what he meant: *veri aestimationem* (Leopold's correction of *MPX*) amounts to the same thing, and looks like an attempt to interpret the more unusual expression.

CHAPTER XXXIX

The apostolic writings also indicate what manner of resurrection Christ affirmed. In their dealings with Israel the apostles based themselves on the Old Testament, saying nothing new about the resurrection except its connection with the triumph of Christ. Thus St Paul in the Acts assumes without further ado that the resurrection was what Moses and the prophets had taught, namely a corporal one: and the Athenians would have found nothing to mock at if he had spoken only of the restitution of the soul. It is only when gentile believers begin to be troubled with doubts that St Paul discusses the matter in detail, maintaining that there is a resurrection, that it has not yet taken place, that it is a corporal one, and that it is not corporal in any abstruse sense of that word.

This chapter summarizes the evidence of the Acts, in which the only controversy that appears is with the Sadducees, who deny the resurrection altogether: for the rest, the Old Testament evidence is sufficient both for the apostles and for the Pharisees who agree with them, and this evidence is of a corporal resurrection. But the apostles still had to relate the resurrection to the triumph of Christ: that is, that though they found agreement concerning the fact and the nature of the general resurrection, they still had to persuade their hearers that Jesus himself had risen again: and this it was that others, who were not Sadducees, were capable of denying.

3 veteris testamenti resignandi. *Resignare* can mean (*a*) open or explain, (*b*) cancel or delete, (*c*) carry forward (as a term of accountancy, equivalent to *rescribere*). (*a*) For 'open' cf. *Apol.* 6, *ob resignatos cellae vinariae loculos*: *De Carne Christi* 23, *idem illud sexus resignavit*, 'the same sex performed that opening' (*illud* being a cognate accusative, and not as I wrote in my note on that sentence): and perhaps *De Virg. Vel.* 5, *sed ingeniose quidam de futuro volunt dictum, Vocabitur mulier, quasi quae hoc futura esset cum virginitatem resignasset*, but more probably here 'cancelled'. (*b*) For 'cancel', *De Poenit.* 5, *poenitentiam...semel cognitam atque susceptam nunquam posthac iteratione delicti resignari oportere*: *Adv. Marc.* IV. 20, *Ionathan...resignati ieiunii culpam deprecatione delesse*: *Adv. Nat.* I. 5, *caelum ipsum nulla serenitas tam colata purgat ut non alicuius nubeculae flocculo resignetur* (= *maculetur*). (*c*) For 'carry over', *De Orat.* 22, adolescent girls *et membris et officiis mulieribus resignantur*: and perhaps *Adv. Marc.* I. 28, *signat igitur hominem nunquam apud se resignatum, lavat hominem nunquam apud se coinquinatum*, where the reference is to baptism, and (with an obvious play upon words) the meaning apparently is that Marcion's god must be supposed to mark as his own a person who has never stood to his account. In the present passage, as the sequence shows, 'cancel' would be out of place, and the meaning must be 'open' or 'unseal' or 'expound': so that *consignare* will mean 'seal' or 'confirm', as *Adv. Prax.* 25, the subscription at John 20. 31, *consignat haec scripta*.

4 For **potius iam** *T* reads *potentiam*, which is attractive; but as the word is written by another hand in an erasure, it must unfortunately be taken as a conjecture by some reader of that MS. *In Christo* is to be construed with *contionandi*, not as attributive to *dei*: the modern equivocation 'God in Christ' (which is constructively Photinian and was perhaps so intended by some of those who made it fashionable forty years ago) is due to a misreading of 2 Cor. 5. 19, where ἦν should be construed with καταλλάσσων as a periphrastic imperfect.

10 sub tribuno, Claudius Lysias, the χιλίαρχος of Acts 21 *sqq.*: cf. esp. 23. 6. The reference below, to Agrippa, is to Acts 26. 22, 23, and 27. The resurrection is *praecipuus fidei articulus*, first, because in the apostolic preaching (as the speeches in the Acts clearly show) it was on the attested fact of the resurrection of Jesus of Nazareth that the proof of his messiahship was based; and secondly, because the hope and expectation of the resurrection of the dead and eternal judgement was (and still is) a potent motive towards conversion.

27 frequentiorem praesumptionem. *Praesumptio* here, as elsewhere, seems to mean an assumption, based on no tangible evidence: see my note on *De Carne Christi* 10 (page 129). Plato at least regarded soul as fundamentally indestructible, and so did the Pythagoreans: the Stoics thought it for some time survived death, but eventually dispersed: Aristotle, treating it as an entelechy of the body, was bound to think it disappeared when the body dissolved: the Epicureans, regarding it as material in constitution, held a similar view of its dissolution. It is somewhat doubtful whether any theory of the restitution of soul was *frequentior*; though Tertullian is right in remarking that if that had been what St Paul was saying, the Athenians would have understood what he meant, and would not have been moved to derision.

32 esse eam (*MPX*) must be correct: *esse iam* (*T*) would imply the opposite of *nondum transactam*, namely, that the resurrection is past already, which St Paul denies (2 Tim. 2. 18). At the end of the sentence *dubitatur* (*T*) is perhaps correct: there were questions in apostolic times whether there was a corporal resurrection (*quaerebatur*): but the suggestion 'corporal in a different sense' was more modern (*insuper dubitatur*), contemporary with Tertullian himself.

CHAPTER XL

2 Cor. 4. 16–18, compared with Eph. 3. 16, 17; Rom. 8. 17, 18; and 2 Cor. 7. 5

The heresies have seized upon the apostle's distinction between the outer and the inner man, as though the former were the flesh that is to perish, the latter the soul that is to be saved. But neither soul nor flesh by itself is man, and the apostle means by 'the inner man' not the substance of the soul, but its content, as becomes clear when he writes to the Ephesians that Christ should dwell in our hearts by faith—and the heart, in fact, is part of the flesh. So also here, the decaying of the outer man is that which the flesh suffers by persecutions and distresses, as appears from the sentences that follow: and likewise the inner man is here and now, not after the resurrection, renewed from day to day by the supply of the Spirit. To the future belongs neither daily suffering nor daily renewal, but the eternal reward, as the apostle writes to the Romans of jointly suffering so that we may be jointly glorified—of which he himself had been an example in Macedonia.

Chapter 40 begins a new section of the work. Tertullian has insisted that plain statements of Scripture concerning the resurrection of the dead are not to be allegorized away, but must be understood in their natural and literal sense. His next concern is to answer quibbles based on three of the apostle's statements which, it was suggested, justified, or even made necessary, the allegorizing of the rest. These statements are, first, that our outward man is perishing (2 Cor. 4. 16), expounded in §§ 40–4: secondly, that the old man is perishing according to the lusts of deceit (Eph. 4. 22), explained in §§ 45–7: and thirdly, that flesh and blood cannot inherit the kingdom of God (1 Cor. 15. 50), expounded in §§ 48–

56. The method in each case is to examine the apostle's words in the light of their own context and of similar expressions elsewhere. There can be little doubt that (except perhaps in one or two small details) Tertullian has given the true interpretation of the apostle's words, making it impossible for them to be used to support unbelief: and in fact, if there are any who wish to deny the resurrection they can only do so by repudiating St Paul, not by explaining him away.

9 figmento iam homini appellato, cf. *supra*, § 5: God's handiwork, even before the inbreathing of the soul, was already called 'man'.

13 porro apostolus, etc. The relation expressed here between *anima* and *animus* is that common in Latin—*anima est qua vivimus, animus est quo sapimus*: so Juvenal, *Sat.* xv. 140 *sqq.* of the difference between men and animals: *mundi | principio indulsit communis conditor illis | tantum animas, nobis animum quoque, mutuus ut nos | adfectus petere auxilium et praestare iuberet*, etc. Tertullian however assigns the foremost rank to *anima*: cf. *De Anima* 13, which concludes, *habes animae principalitatem, habes in illa et substantiae unionem, cuius intellegas instrumentum esse animum, non patrocinium*. On the relation between the bodily organs, the soul, and the perceptions, cf. *De Corona* 5, *puto autem naturae deus noster est, qui figuravit* [forsan leg. *figulavit*] *hominem et fructibus rerum appetendis iudicandis consequendis certos in eo sensus ordinavit per propria membrorum quodammodo organa*... *per haec exterioris hominis ministeria interiori homini administrantia fructus munerum divinorum ad animam deducuntur a sensibus*.

19 non substantiva...sed conceptiva. *Substantivus*, as Oehler remarks (Index, *s.v.*), stands for οὐσιώδης, and in that case means, not pertaining to, or possessing, but being the *substantia*, which is the thing itself: so *Adv. Prax.* 7, *non vis enim eum* [sc. *sermonem dei*] *substantivum habere in re per substantiae proprietatem ut res et persona quaedam videri possit*, etc., and ibid. 26, *quodsi spiritus dei tanquam substantiva res non erit ipse deus*...*virtus altissimi*... *sapientia*...*providentia*...*substantiae non sunt sed accidentia unius-*

cuiusque substantiae: on which see my notes, and the Introduction, pages 39–45. Also *Adv. Hermog.* 19, *nam et ipsum principium in quo deus fecit et caelum et terram aliquid volunt fuisse quasi substantivum et corpulentum quod in materiam interpretari possit*: ibid. 26, *quis enim tibi concedit motum in secundam partem substantiae deputare, cum substantiva res non sit...sed accidens si forte substantiae et corpori? Conceptivus* is not quoted from elsewhere in Oehler's Index; but as *conceptus* (participle) means 'conceived in the womb' and *conceptus* (substantive) means 'conception', *conceptivus* can be taken to mean 'belonging to (or consisting of) the contents' of such and such a *substantia*: so here, faith and love are not substances, constituent parts, of soul, but are part of its content: hearts, however, are *substantiae*, parts of that composite substance which is flesh. This leads to the conclusion that the apostle, by associating 'inner man' with the heart, has reckoned it (or him) as belonging to the flesh—a good enough debating point against people as literal-minded as Tertullian himself, who were capable of forgetting that 'heart' in scriptural language has no anatomical significance, but is used, both in the Old Testament and the New, to indicate the determinative understanding, the intelligence which proceeds to resolution and consequent action.

27 per suggestum spiritus, cf. Phil. 1. 19, διὰ τῆς ὑμῶν δεήσεως καὶ ἐπιχορηγίας τοῦ πνεύματος Ἰησοῦ Χριστοῦ. Lewis and Short (*s.v.* B) observe that this use of *suggestus* (= supply, provision) is post-classical and very rare, quoting only Tertullian, *De Spect.* 7, *circensium paulo pompatior suggestus*, and ibid. 12, *in ipsorum honorum suggestu*, in both which cases the meaning really seems to be 'proud trappings': so also *De Cor.* 13, *ab ipso incolatu Babylonis illius in Apocalypsi Iohannis submovemur, nedum a suggestu*, where Oehler notes that the word means *ornatus, apparatus* (giving three further examples) and refers to a note by Salmasius on *De Pallio*, page 362 [§ 4, *superque omnes apices et titulos sacer suggestus deducit oculos*, where, with many examples, the conclusion is, '*suggestus itaque pro quovis eximio ornatu*']. Salmasius however has missed this other meaning (= *suppeditatio*), of which there are several examples, e.g. *Adv. Hermog.* 16, *per substantiae suggestum*:

De Anima 1, *ex materiae potius suggestu quam ex dei flatu ⟨animam⟩ constitisse*: and *De Res. Carn*. 46, *ne ita quis existimet ex aliorum vel cohaerentium sensuum suggestu procurantem*. A further meaning is 'suggestion', e.g. *Apol*. 18, the Hebrew Scriptures were translated *ex suggestu Demetrii Phalerii*.

30 quod enim ad praesens, etc. 2 Cor. 4. 17, 18 and Rom. 8. 17, 18 (in reverse order) are quoted at *Scorp*. 13 with some slight verbal variations such as could be due either to quotation from memory or to extemporized translation from the Greek, and with comments similar to the present.

41 siquidem compatimur, etc. Rom. 8. 17, κληρονόμοι μὲν θεοῦ, συγκληρονόμοι δὲ Χριστοῦ, εἴπερ συμπάσχομεν, ἵνα καὶ συνδοξασθῶμεν, where evidently the prepositions stand for σὺν Χριστῷ. Tertullian here (somewhat perversely) pretends that the joint-suffering and the joint-glory are of the body with the soul, which suffer, and are to be glorified, together: at *Scorp*. 13 he shows that he knows better, *siquidem compatiamur, uti et cum illo glorificemur*.

CHAPTER XLI

2 Cor. 5. 1, 2; 1 Thess. 4. 15–17

The apostle continues to the same effect, that the rewards are greater than the distresses. By the earthly house of our tabernacle being dissolved, he may mean: (1) that because the flesh is dissolved through sufferings we shall obtain the kingdom of heaven, not thereby denying the restitution of the flesh (for to it the reward is due) but remembering that our Lord has promised to those who suffer persecution a heavenly abode: or more probably he means (2) that our earthly house is this present world, and that when this is dissolved there is promised us an eternal dwelling-place in heaven. The words that follow do refer to the flesh, for the apostle says that we desire to be clothed upon with the heavenly grace of immortality without being divested of the flesh: and this refers to those of us who are still alive in the flesh at our Lord's coming, and are to have the privilege of immortality without having died, as the apostle explains to the Thessalonians.

NOTES AND COMMENTARY 289

There can be little doubt that Tertullian's first interpretation of 2 Cor. 5. 1 is the correct one, and that he is wrong in suggesting a change of subject at *Nam et in hoc gemimus*. He is also correct, as the apostle's words show (verse 4, οὐ θέλομεν ἐκδύσασθαι ἀλλ' ἐπενδύσασθαι), in his insistence that the flesh cannot be supposed to be excluded from the future reward: and it is at least possible that he is justified in interpreting the apostle's allusive language here in the light of the more precise terms of 1 Thess. 4. 15–17.

1 eandem adhuc sententiam, etc. This sentence is easier to paraphrase than to translate, greater weight resting on the participle than on the indicative verb: 'To the same effect in what follows, he continues to speak of the rewards as greater than the vexations.'

2 scimus enim, etc. Tertullian has *etsi* for ἐάν (Lat. vg. *si*) and, if we take the reading of *MPX*, attaches ἡμῶν to τοῦ σκήνους instead of to οἰκία: *T* reads *nostra*, which may be an accommodation to Lat. vg. He omits altogether οἰκοδομὴν ἐκ θεοῦ.

6 beati, etc. Matt. 5. 10: Lat. vg. has *patiuntur* (and so here *MPX*) for the Greek οἱ δεδιωγμένοι, and *quoniam ipsorum*. The same text as quoted at *Scorp.* 9 agrees with Lat. vg., but with *ob* for *propter*.

11 ipsi domui...meliorem domum, etc. A captious critic, remembering from §27 *quomodo de monumentis monumenta procedent?*, might here ask *quomodo domum domus habitabit?* The objection could hardly be sustained, for it appears that throughout this passage St Paul is thinking both of the body as a dwelling-place of the soul, and of the eternal dwelling which is one of the mansions in the Father's house, without being concerned to notice that strictly speaking these are two different types of dwelling.

17 divisionem enim facit, etc. The meaning here seems to be that the apostle introduces a change of subject, yet within the same sphere of discourse: in both sentences he is speaking of houses, but of different houses in the one case and the other. *Divisio* according to the rhetoricians was the arrangement of the subject-matter under its several heads. Lewis and Short (*s.v.* II) give references to Cicero and Quintilian, none of which is precisely applicable to our present context, the nearest being Quintilian, *Inst. Orat.* v. 10. 63, where it is said that Cicero *divisione adiuvari finitionem docet, eamque differre a partitione quod haec sit totius in partes, illa generis in formas*. It is probably not true that the apostle changes the subject, even slightly: he seems throughout the paragraph (5. 1–10) to be speaking of the two houses as though they were of the same type.

18 nam et in hoc, etc. Oehler's punctuation (followed by Borleffs) with a comma after *nostrum* and not after *gemimus* seems intended to mean 'We groan with desire for this our dwelling-place (sc. the dwelling eternal in the heavens), desiring to be clothed upon with that thing which is from heaven'. It is possible that Tertullian intended this, though the Greek shows that *hoc* is ablative: καὶ γὰρ ἐν τούτῳ [sc. τῷ σκήνει] στενάζομεν, τὸ οἰκητήριον ἡμῶν τὸ ἐξ οὐρανοῦ ἐπενδύσασθαι ἐπιποθοῦντες. Lat. vg. *nam et in hoc ingemiscimus, habitationem nostram quae de caelo est superindui cupientes,* agrees that *hoc* is ablative, though since all the preceding substantives are feminine it can only mean *in hoc tempore*, which is a possible meaning of ἐν τούτῳ, 'meanwhile'. Tertullian apparently read ἐκδυσάμενοι, which he explains in the sentence following: the apostolic text ἐνδυσάμενοι, *vestiti*, strangely enough is capable of the same explanation.

25 hoc enim dicimus, etc. 1 Thess. 4. 15–17 has already been quoted in §24, with variants which suggest either quotation from memory or *ad hoc* translation from the Greek. There are further references, *Adv. Marc.* III. 24; v. 15.

CHAPTER XLII

1 Cor. 15. 51–3, still commenting on 2 Cor. 5. 3, 4

The change which will then take place is elsewhere described by the apostle as the corruptible thing putting on incorruption and the mortal thing putting on immortality: and this incorruption and immortality will be the same thing as the dwelling-place which is from heaven. Obviously those are at an advantage who undergo the change without passing through death, and without experience of hell. But since all have to be changed, both those who are found alive and those who have died, it follows that the flesh of those who have died must rise again so that there may be something which can be changed, something mortal which may be swallowed up of life. It is not true to say that in the case of those who have died the swallowing up will have already taken place. Apart from the fact that there will be some so recently dead that their corpses will be still fresh (and indeed we know of cases where buried corpses have remained fresh for centuries), yet even if decay has taken place this will not have been a swallowing up by life, but by death: and we are taught to expect a swallowing up by divine power, not by natural processes. So then there will have to be present that which may be swallowed up, and this can only be the flesh raised again: which is what the apostle meant when he said that even after being unclothed we shall not be found naked—namely, that we shall first be reclothed with the flesh, so that we may be further clothed upon with immortality.

The text of Tertullian's quotation from 1 Cor. 15. 51 must be regarded as at least doubtful. *Omnes quidem resurgemus non autem omnes demutabimur* is in all the MSS. (except that T omits the first three words), and is practically equivalent to Lat. vg., *Omnes quidem resurgemus sed non omnes immutabimur*. But this is almost the opposite of what Tertullian proceeds to say, namely that we shall not all rise again (for some of us will by-pass death by being alive at the last day), but we shall all be changed, either by passing into a state of incorruptibility without dying, or by being reclothed with our resuscitated flesh so that we may receive the additional garment of immortality. Thus there is much to be said for Kroymann's reading, *Non omnes quidem resurgemus, omnes autem demutabimur*. Against it we must admit that there is no authority for it in the MSS. either of Tertullian or of the New Testament: though the first hand of Cod. Graeco-Latinus Parisiensis (D) reads πάντες ἀναστησόμεθα, οὐ πάντες δὲ ἀλλαγησόμεθα (from which Lat. vg. is derived), which by an almost impossible change of punctuation could be read as πάντες ἀναστησόμεθα οὔ, πάντες δὲ ἀλλαγησόμεθα, thus giving Kroymann's text. It is just possible that Tertullian read the Greek that way, because it suited his argument: as also, in the following verse, *Et mortui resurgent*, he has omitted to translate ἄφθαρτοι which would have caused him difficulty (quoting the same text at *Adv. Marc.* v. 10 he has *resurgent enim mortui incorrupti*).

Doubts about his biblical text will not be supposed to destroy the value of Tertullian's argument. He could have got the same result from the common Greek text, πάντες οὐ κοιμηθησόμεθα πάντες δὲ ἀλλαγησόμεθα (so Cod. Vat. (B) and the great number of MSS.), unless perchance this should be taken to mean, 'We shall none of us sleep', etc., which is manifestly not what St Paul meant. Cod. Sin.(ℵ) and other authorities have πάντες κοιμηθησόμεθα οὐ πάντες δὲ ἀλλαγησόμεθα, which again is manifestly untrue and not what St Paul meant, unless again we invert the sense by an almost impossible punctuation and accentuation of οὔ.

The text is summarily discussed *Adv. Marc.* v. 10: *resurgent enim mortui incorrupti, illi scilicet qui fuerant corrupti dilapsis corporibus in interitum: et nos mutabimur in atomo in oculi momentaneo motu. oportet enim corruptivum hoc* (tenens utique carnem suam dicebat apostolus) *induere incorruptelam, et mortale hoc immortalitatem, ut scilicet habilis substantia efficiatur regno dei: erimus enim sicut angeli. haec erit demutatio carnis, sed resuscitatae: aut si nulla erit* [if it has ceased to exist], *quomodo induet incorruptelam et immortalitatem? aliud igitur facta per demutationem tunc consequetur dei regnum, iam non caro nec sanguis sed quod illi corpus deus dederit*. With some superficial differences this is in agreement with what is repeated here. So also *Adv. Marc.* v. 12 (again commenting on 2 Cor. 5. 2–4): *hic enim expressit quod in prima epistula strinxit: Et mortui resurgent incorrupti, qui iam obierunt, et nos mutabimur, qui in carne fuerimus deprehensi a deo. et illi enim resurgent incorrupti, recepto scilicet corpore, et quidem integro, ut ex hoc sint incorrupti, et hi propter temporis ultimum iam momentum et propter merita vexationum antichristi compendium mortis* [a by-passing of death] *sed mutati consequentur, superinduti magis quod de caelo est quam exuti corpus*: which is in complete agreement with what is said here, and with the apostle's argument. It will be observed also that Tertullian avoids the difficulty which ἄφθαρτοι

NOTES AND COMMENTARY 293

might have caused him, by making it proleptic. At §§ 50, 51 there is further discussion of this sentence, in its own context of 1 Cor. 15.

5 hac ergo prius, etc. *Dispositio* occurs *Adv. Prax.* 3 with reference to the divine Trinity: *numerum et dispositionem trinitatis*: and again ibid. 4, *dispositionem et dispensationem eius* [sc. *monarchiae*], i.e. διάθεσίν τε καὶ οἰκονομίαν: so that it indicates something neither fortuitous nor contingent, but as it were essential to the divine being, or here, to the divine purpose: 'this predetermined order of events'. There seems no sufficient reason for Kroymann's alteration of *prospecta* to *perspecta*.

10 gravari nos ait, etc. 2 Cor. 5. 4, καὶ γὰρ οἱ ὄντες ἐν τῷ σκήνει στενάζομεν βαρούμενοι, ἐφ' ᾧ οὐ θέλομεν ἐκδύσασθαι ἀλλ' ἐπενδύσασθαι, of which the last clause may possibly mean, 'in that we wish not to be unclothed but to be clothed upon', i.e. we wish to escape being divested of the body by death, and yet to obtain the additional garment of immortality. So Tertullian understands it, and so apparently Lat. vg., *eo quod nolumus expoliari sed supervestiri*.

17 abhinc enim, etc. 'At this point I make the dogmatic statement which I shall henceforth insist on.' *Habitus* in the sense of 'clothing' appears frequently from Suetonius onwards: and so probably here 'angelic attire'. *Illam* (*T*), the superficially more difficult reading, is apparently correct: 'the flesh it is that will by means of change take upon it angelic attire'.

28 devoratum non aliud existimas, etc. 'You are mistaken in the idea you have of "swallowed up": you think it means "entirely and utterly destroyed", whereas my contention is that when a thing is swallowed up it is not destroyed but remains itself.' But the Greek is not 'eaten up', but 'drunk up', καταποθῇ.

30 nec gigantum autem, etc. The source of this information is apparently Pliny, *H.N.* VII. 16: there are further references by Aulus Gellius, *N.A.* III. 10 and by Augustine, *De Civ. Dei*, XV. 9 (with a reference to Pliny). At *De Anima* 51, Tertullian mentions a number of instances of arrested decay, for which he suggests there may have been natural causes.

32 in ista civitate: certainly (as Oehler says) Carthage: Rome was not *civitas* but *urbs*. *Odei* is Gelenius' correction of the MS. reading *hodie*: nothing else seems to be known of it. *Sacrilega* may well stand (as against Engelbrecht's suggestions *sacrilegio* or *apertura sacrilega*), meaning 'the foundations which caused desecration to a large number of ancient graves': Tertullian (or any other writer of a living language) would be quite capable of giving the word this extended sense.

37 fructificaturi, the MS. reading, is probably correct: the editors, following Junius, read *fruticaturi*. Likewise in § 52 Borleffs has substituted *fruticaturam* for *fructificaturam*. But it is the seeds which sprout: the body, when risen again, may be regarded as a ripened fruit. At §22 Pamelius read (probably correctly) *in agnitione sacramenti fruticat, sed in domini repraesentatione florescit atque frugescit*: which justifies the MS. reading in the other two places.

38 For **invenietur** perhaps we should read *inveniatur*, since this is a mere supposition which Tertullian allows for the sake of argument, but not (as appears from his own words) one which he will accept as a probability.

40 porro qui, etc., as the indicative verbs show, refers specifically to St Paul, who by the fact that he says the swallowing up will be by life, excludes any thought of swallowing up by natural causes.

47 siquidem exuti, etc. The explanation which follows shows that Tertullian took this to mean, 'if so be that we shall not be found unclothed and naked', which (as already remarked) gives the same sense as the Greek εἴ γε καὶ ἐνδυσάμενοι, κτέ.

CHAPTER XLIII

2 Cor. 5. 6–10

So again 'at home in the body, on pilgrimage from the Lord', and 'we walk by faith, not by sight', is not directed to the belittling of the body but to the enhancing of the glory of martyrdom, that being the only way of passing out of this life directly into the Lord's presence. Also 'on pilgrimage' refers to such as will sometime return home. In the verse following, when it says that we must all stand before the judgement-seat of Christ, by 'all' it means also 'the whole', body no less than soul: and the recompense referred to, in whatever way we disentangle the syntax of this clause, is either directly promised to the body or else is owed to it for the deeds it has done. The whole passage must be interpreted in conformity with its ending.

4 offuscatio, *offuscare*, are only used by late writers and only in a figurative sense: so *Adv. Nat.* I. 10, the new custom of swearing by Caesar, *et ipsum ad offuscationem pertinet deorum vestrorum*: *Adv. Marc.* II. 12, *ne...iustitiam de causa mali offusces*, 'vilify justice as being the outcome of evil'.

8 boni ducentes (*T*), a genitive of price or value, εὐδοκοῦμεν: the other MSS. have *bonum ducentes*.

12 nemo enim peregrinatus, etc. Cf. *De Anima* 55 where Tertullian controverts the opinion that the souls of the faithful enter Paradise immediately after death, without visiting hell: in that case, he asks, how is it that John in the Apocalypse had shown to him the region of Paradise, which is beneath the altar, and saw there no other souls except those of the martyrs? *quomodo Perpetua fortissima martyr sub die passionis in revelatione paradisi solos illic commartyres suos vidit, nisi quia nullis romphaea paradisi ianitrix cedit nisi qui in Christo decesserint, non in Adam? nova mors pro deo et extraordinaria pro Christo alio et privato excipitur hospitio...tota paradisi clavis tuus sanguis est.* The argument however is somewhat confused: Tertullian thinks he is making a distinction between the death of a Christian and the death of a heathen; but he speaks as if the only possible Christian death were martyrdom, and does not envisage, in the immediate future, any amelioration of the estate of a Christian who dies a natural death, *in mollibus febribus et in lectulis*.

The suggestion that **peregrinari**, ἐκδημῆσαι, indicates that the traveller will sometime return home will no doubt stand: it would suit Tertullian's argument (though he does not enforce this point, as it would raise complicated questions) that as the soul after death is absent from the body that is the home which will be reconstituted for it at the resurrection. *Revertetur* (so all the MSS.) must be restored: it is not true that at any particular point any and every traveller is actually on his way home.

20 si omnes, et totos is not a logical argument, but a mere assumption. The fourth *omnes*, changed by Gelenius to *totos*, is defensible and should perhaps be restored: the argument (such as it is) is not necessarily *per soritem*.

23 quasi turbate, etc. The Greek is quite clear: ἵνα κομίσηται ἕκαστος τὰ διὰ τοῦ σώματος πρὸς ἃ ἔπραξεν, εἴτε ἀγαθὸν εἴτε φαῦλον: so is Lat. vg., *ut referat unusquisque propria corporis prout gessit, sive bonum sive malum*. The equivocation Tertullian refers to appears only in the reading of MP, *ut unusquisque reportet per corpus*, etc.: TX, inserting *quae*, make the Latin as clear as the Greek. Hyperbaton, according to Quintilian, *Inst. Orat.* IX. 3. 91, is *verborum concinna transgressio*: cf. ibid. VIII. 6. 62, where its correct management is discussed, with examples: ibid. IX. 1. 6, *in hyperbato commutatio est ordinis*: from which it appears doubtful if Tertullian is using the term correctly.

CHAPTER XLIV

2 Cor. 4. 6–14

The words of the apostle which precede the mention of the outer and the inner man are also to the honour of the flesh. He says that the light of God shines in our hearts: and when he adds that we have the divine treasure in earthen vessels he surely indicates that the vessels will have to be conserved: otherwise the treasure would be lost. Also the intention is that the life of Christ should be made manifest in our mortal body—mortal by sin, but vital by grace: and it cannot be that the eternal life of Christ should be made manifest in a thing alien to salvation. For observe that the life of Christ the apostle refers to is not that which he lived before his passion—that is already manifest in all the world—but that which will break the bars of death: and that life will thenceforth be ours. Thus the resurrection is involved: for the apostle's words preclude the restriction of this manifestation to present morals and conduct, seeing that he makes the express statement, in the future, 'will raise us up along with him'.

This concludes Tertullian's discussion of the outer and the inner man: there will follow an explanation of what the apostle means by the old and the new man.

3 quod illuxerit, etc. *Quod* may be the relative pronoun, a cognate accusative: otherwise *illucescere* appears to be always intransitive, except in Plautus where it (twice at least) means 'shine upon'. But the Greek ὃς ἔλαμψεν is intransitive, 'God hath shined', so Lat. vg. *ipse illuxit*. Tertullian has already remarked (§15) that the heart is part of the flesh, and so has no need here further to insist upon it. *Persona Christi* was apparently taken by Tertullian to mean 'person': St Paul (ἐν προσώπῳ) probably meant 'face': Lat. vg. *in facie*.

7 conditorium, according to Lewis and Short, is used by Pliny and Suetonius for a coffin or a sepulchre; by Ammianus for a storehouse or armoury: there seems no parallel to the present use 'receptacle'.

10 plane, si periturus: so the MSS., which Rhenanus altered to *plane sic*: but the point is that we can only suppose the receptacle to perish if the treasure also perishes—which latter is inconceivable. *Plane* expresses an ironical assent to the preceding question.

16 ut et vita manifestetur, etc. In what follows Tertullian legitimately enough takes this subjunctive of purpose to have a future reference; so (three times) he represents it by *manifestabitur*.

21 iam et dei vita. *Iam* stands for *iampridem*, 'already', i.e. from all eternity the life of Christ is the life of God.

31 intentio, 'statement of the case', a legal term signifying the praetor's instruction to the court, indicating in what direction the petitioner's interests lie: so almost §31, *non idcirco in parabola accipienda esset revelationis intentio*, and *Adv. Marc.* II. 29, *aufer titulum Marcionis et intentionem atque propositum operis ipsius*.

31 **si enim nos:** 2 Cor. 4. 11, ἀεὶ γὰρ ἡμεῖς: Tertullian misread ἀεί as εἰ. At the end of the sentence the Greek has ἐν τῇ θνητῇ σαρκὶ ἡμῶν, which would have suited the argument even better than *in corpore nostro mortali* (Lat. vg. *in carne*).

CHAPTER XLV

Eph. 4. 22–4, 25–32

Our adversaries unintelligently misinterpret the apostle's reference to the old man and the new, alleging that the former, which is being corrupted according to deceitful lusts, is the flesh, while the latter is the soul. But the soul is in fact no newer than the flesh. At the creation very little time elapsed between the formation of the one and the inbreathing of the other: and even if the time had been longer, since the flesh had to wait for the soul, the soul has a logical priority. Adam himself was wholly new: and at each human conception and birth the procreation and nativity of soul and body are contemporaneous. Certainly they are two substances, but they together make one man. We may conceivably be old or new: we cannot be both at once. But the apostle's meaning is plain: he says 'corrupt according to deceitful lusts' and 'put off according to former conversation', distinguishing not between two substances but between two sets of moral acts, as the following verses make clear. If the old man, which is to be put off, is the flesh, these people ought to bring death upon themselves. We however are convinced that, since even the life of faith has to be lived in and by means of the flesh, the difference between old and new is not a physical but a moral one: and so we understand that the putting off of oldness and corruption is a stripping off not of corporeity but of bad conduct.

The discussion is continued in §§ 46 (on Rom. 8) and 47 (on Rom. 6).

2 **deponere nos,** etc. This is evidently a free quotation, changed throughout from the second to the first person plural. The omission of κατὰ τὴν προτέραν ἀναστροφήν (restored by Tertullian later, line 23) may be due to tendentious alteration by the oppo-

nents. For the rest the translation fairly represents the Greek, and agrees with Lat. vg. except for *desideria erroris...spiritu mentis vestrae...creatus est...sanctitate veritatis*. The expression ἐνδύσασθαι τὸν καινὸν ἄνθρωπον might have given Tertullian further support, for καινός represents newness of character rather than later emergence. The plural *concupiscentias* (*T*, here and below, line 47) may be an editorial correction into conformity with the Greek.

7 defendant (*T Gel.*) seems to be what Tertullian wrote: the singular verb (*MPX*) is the mistake of a copyist who thought *hic* was a nominative pronoun.

9 quantulum enim temporis, etc. According to Gen. 2. 7 the formation of Adam's body and the inbreathing of the soul were practically contemporaneous. In the following sentence *prior anima caro* must be correct. The reading of *TB* (followed by Borleffs), *prior anima quam caro*, stultifies the argument both of Tertullian and of his adversaries. They claimed that the flesh is older than the soul, or was brought into existence before it: he replies (*a*) that the difference in time was so short as to be negligible, and (*b*) that, even if the lapse of time had been greater, the soul has a logical priority.

12 omnis enim consummatio, etc. This difficult sentence universalizes the theme exemplified in the case of body and animating soul, namely, that the factor which by supervening perfects the composite product, has itself a logical priority. The difficulty lies in the phrase *effectu anticipat*, apparently the reading of most manuscripts, which would naturally mean 'is previous in effect'—which is not true, unless (as Tertullian would hardly do) we use 'in effect' in the loose sense it has acquired in spoken English. *T* reads *positum, adecfectum*: evidently the copyist did not understand his text: but perhaps it might be permissible to extract from this *postumat, effectum anticipat*, with the meaning 'exists before its completed activity'. Something of this kind is apparently what Tertullian intended to say.

15 nam et exinde, etc., i.e. since Gen. 1. 28, 'be fruitful and multiply'. Tertullian's theory of the origin of the individual soul was traducianist—a view also held in a less crude form by Gregory of Nyssa, but in later times generally considered heretical. Cf. *De Anima* 27, where the question is proposed, *Quomodo igitur animal* [the living being] *conceptum? simulne conflata utriusque substantia corporis animaeque, an altera earum praecedente? immo simul ambas et concipi et confici et perfici dicimus, sicut et promi, nec ullum intervenire momentum in conceptu quo locus* [space of time] *ordinetur*. The argument follows: (1) That the end is proof of the beginning: since death is the disjunction of body and soul, life is the conjunction of them: *si disiunctio simul utrique substantiae accidit per mortem, hoc debet coniunctionis forma* [quaero an legendum *formam*] *mandasse pariter obvenientis per vitam utrique substantiae*: this conjunction, we affirm, takes place at conception. (2) If we grant priority to either of them, time must elapse between their pro-creation: but this would involve a separation of the two species, the body and the soul, which we insist are *indiscretae* and therefore *contemporales eiusdemque momenti*. (3) After a sort of apology for speaking of such matters, *in concubitu...scimus et animam et carnem simul fungi, animam concupiscentia, carnem opera, animam instinctu, carnem actu* (where the emphasis, as here, is on *simul*): and, after more detail, *hoc erit semen animale protinus ex animae distillatione, sicut et virus illud corporale semen ex carnis defaecatione*. (4) This corresponds to the original creation: the *corporale semen* is represented by *limus* (*quid aliud limus quam liquor opimus?*): the *semen animale* by *afflatus dei*. It will be admitted that Tertullian makes out a strong case for his traducianist theory, which would have the further advantage (not referred to by him) of making easier for him the doctrine of original sin. But there are manifest objections to it, the most serious being that it would make it difficult to account for the genesis of the soul of Christ.

18 contemporare, *contemporalis* (*Adv. Hermog.* 6), as well as *coaetare*, *coaetaneus*, seem to occur only here: *coaetaneant* appears to have been invented by Gelenius, and *coaetaneo* should be removed from Lewis and Short as a *vox nihili*. Kroymann's reading *duo isti homines...eduntur* misses the point: the subject of the sentence is *caro atque anima*: it is these which produce the 'two men', certainly of double substance, yet really one man, seeing that neither has the priority, and therefore the distinction of 'old' and 'new' cannot apply on this ground.

20 citius est is unusual, but not sufficiently so to justify Oehler's alteration to *rectius*: it is a natural enough development from the Ciceronian *citius dixerim* (*Phil.* II. 11. 25 and elsewhere). Kroymann's *unum et alterum* is attractive and may be correct: *unum* could have dropped out by confusion with *enim*. If Tertullian wrote *possumus* (*T*), this was to avoid rhyming with *nescimus*.

22 expone, of putting off a garment, is here (except for its mood and number) the correct translation of ἀποθέσθαι: but below, for ἀποθέμενοι Tertullian reverts to *deponentes*.

25 et alibi, Gal. 5. 19, φανερὰ δέ ἐστιν τὰ ἔργα τῆς σαρκός, κτέ.

26 deponentes, etc. Eph. 4. 25-32. Tertullian's Latin fairly represents the Greek, except for

ad proximum suum, μετὰ τοῦ πλησίον αὐτοῦ.
qui furabatur (so Lat. vg.), ὁ κλέπτων (*MPR*[1], qui furatur).
operando manibus, ἐργαζόμενος τὸ ἀγαθὸν ταῖς χερσίν (where the Greek MSS. vary).
ad aedificationem fidei, πρὸς οἰκοδομὴν τῆς χρείας (*v.l.* πίστεως).
ira [animi], θυμὸς καὶ ὀργή (Lat. vg. ira et indignatio).

Membra alterutrum, for μέλη ἀλλήλων, seems to be in all the MSS., and must apparently be tolerated: below, *in alterutrum* stands (correctly) for εἰς ἀλλήλους: *ira animi* (*T* only) may be what Tertullian wrote, for if not it is difficult to imagine where it came from: *donantes*, here and Lat. vg., is for χαριζόμενοι, which the English versions translate 'forgiving', and perhaps *donare* had acquired that sense (cf. Ovid, *Ex Ponto* II. 7. 51, *culpa gravis precibus donatur saepe suorum*, which is hardly parallel, but tends in that direction).

45 atque ita pariter, etc. A badly balanced sentence, which reads better by the omission of the commas after *hominem* and after *non secundum carnem*: *corrumpi ita dictum* is balanced by *quemadmodum et veterem,* 'he is said to be under corruption according to deceitful lusts in the same sense as he is called old according to former conversation': and *corrumpi secundum concupiscentias* is again balanced (this time in the negative) by *non secundum carnem per interitum perpetuum,* the corruption referred to being a moral corruption according to deceitful lusts, not physical corruption by perpetual destruction: and finally, this last clause is expanded and explained in a positive form by *ceterum salva carne,* etc., i.e. as far as the flesh is concerned he is conserved (or saved) either in the physical or the moral sense (*salvus* being the opposite of *corruptus*), and is the same man as he always was, having stripped off his bad character but not his bodily characteristics. Whether or not we accept *salva* (Borleffs' correction of *salve,* in *T* only) the meaning is the same, though this reading emphasizes again the fact that the flesh as such *non corrumpitur. Corpulentia* occurs in Pliny, meaning 'corpulence': apparently only Tertullian makes it mean 'corporeity'.

CHAPTER XLVI

Rom. 8. 8–13

The apostle regularly condemns the works of the flesh, yet always shows by the context that it is not the flesh itself which is being condemned. When he says that those who are in the flesh cannot please God, he makes it clear by what follows that to be in the flesh signifies carnal living; and when he adds that the body is dead because of sin but the spirit is life because of righteousness, he shows that his condemnation is directed against moral delinquency and not against physical constitution. Moreover his condemnation would have been pointless unless it had been possible for life to expel death from the body. But there is no need for argument: the apostle in the same context says that God will quicken our mortal bodies, from which it is clear that even if (as some assume) the soul is a mortal body, the flesh certainly is one, and therefore will be raised up again. So again, in the sentence that follows, he speaks of mortifying the actions of the flesh: and generally, it is not the flesh itself, but the work of the flesh, which is opposed to salvation, and as we have been set free from the law of sin and death which was in our members, evidently our members are free from it. The Son of God has condemned sin in the flesh, not the flesh in sin: the mind of the flesh, not the flesh itself, is enmity against God, and this must mean the soul when it acts in accordance with the flesh. If sin dwells in the flesh, that is because it is already in the soul. So in another place, when he says, Why, as though living in the world, etc., the apostle is addressing not dead men, but men who ought to have ceased to live in worldly fashion.

The texts here quoted nearly enough represent the Greek, except for these variants:

at Rom. 8. 11 Tertullian omits to translate ἐκ νεκρῶν on its first appearance, and translates ἐγείρας and ζωοποιήσει by the same verb *suscitare*: his Greek text had διὰ τὸ ἐνοικοῦν πνεῦμα (so BDG and the cursives):

at Rom. 8. 12 he omits κατὰ σάρκα (which Kroymann restores):

at 8. 13 he translates the present verbs ζῆτε and θανατοῦτε by the future perfects *vixeritis, mortificaveritis*:

at 8. 2 he has *manumisit te* (so ℵBG and others) for ἠλευθέρωσέ με:

at 8. 3 he translates ἐν ᾧ by *in quo*, apparently (and perhaps correctly) dependent on τὸ ἀδύνατον, 'that in which it was weak'; περὶ ἁμαρτίας (presumably meaning 'as a sacrifice for sin') is mistranslated *per delinquentiam*:

at Col. 2. 20 *sententiam fertis* misses the point (made clear by the context) of δογματίζεσθε.

Here and throughout this work Tertullian translates ἁμαρτία by *delinquentia*: *peccatum* (Lat. vg.) can often be a self-excusing word: *delictum* is a tort, a wrong done to a person.

14 ceterum frustra, etc. The repeated *illic...ubi* from the previous sentence makes probable *illuc...ubi* (Latinius) in the sentence following, where all MSS. have *illud*.

17 et quid ego, etc. The adjective *nodosus*, meaning 'intricate', is found in classical writers, and in Horace in the secondary sense of 'well versed in intricacies': *Serm.* II. 3. 69, *nodosi Cicutae*, of a tricky moneylender. The adverb apparently is found only here, and seems to mean 'in this involved manner', with a suggestion that a result obtained by argument is more hesitant, or less convincing, than the 'unreserved' pronouncement of the apostle.

21 ut et si animam, etc. It does not appear that any definite persons had suggested that by 'mortal body' the apostle meant the soul: it seems to be a mere supposition or passing suggestion of Tertullian that someone might think so. He himself insists (*De Anima* 6 and elsewhere) that soul is itself a body, neither *animale* nor *inanimale*. But this is no more than a Stoic way of saying that it is a real thing: its bearing on the present suggestion is only that it supplies the argument that if soul, being body, can rise again, there is no *a priori* reason why flesh, which is also body, should not do the same, *secundum eiusdem status communionem*, because they both have the same natural characteristics, at least as far as corporeity is concerned.

25 secundum carnem (the first time), added by Kroymann, is certainly required: Pamelius and Rigaltius took *ut secundum carnem vivamus* from the vulgate.

28 ut ad singula quaeque, etc. The key to the meaning here is that throughout this section of his treatise Tertullian is not producing his own arguments for the resurrection of the flesh, but is replying to his adversaries' objections to it. In the present chapter he has established the general principle that the apostle (1) habitually condemns the works of the flesh in such terms as to seem (but only to seem) to condemn the flesh, and (2) distinctly says that God will raise up our mortal bodies. He now replies to a series of objections (*singula quaeque*) apparently based on the apostle's remarks in Rom. 8—that the flesh is hostile to salvation, that the law of sin and of death dwells in our members, that God has condemned sin in the flesh, and that the mind of the flesh is death—all of which, briefly referred to, are briefly explained.

43 cui ergo dices, etc. *Substantia* here apparently means 'the thing itself', in the Aristotelian sense of οὐσία, but with a further Stoic suggestion that it is the ὑποκείμενον to which the attributes pertain: cf. *De Anima* 38, *omnia naturalia animae ipsi substantiae inesse*. *Plane* admits, with the intention of immediate exception, the positive implication of the adversaries' supposed question—

NOTES AND COMMENTARY 305

sensus carnis ipsa substantia [*ipsa caro*] *est*. But this cannot be true, for the flesh in itself has no sensations and no mind: cf. *De Anima* 17, *unde sensus si non ab anima? denique carens anima corpus carebit et sensu*—the whole chapter being a notable argument for the general trustworthiness of the senses.

48 et ideo habitare, etc.: cf. *De Anima* 38, *certe enim domus animae caro est, et inquilinus carnis animus: desiderabit itaque inquilinus ex causa et necessitate huius nominis profutura domui toto inquilinatus sui tempore*, etc.

CHAPTER XLVII

Rom. 6. 6–13; 19–23

That the difference between the old and the new man is a matter of morality and not of corporeity appears also from the apostle's previous words, when he says that the old man has been crucified together with Christ—which is not true in a physical but only in a moral sense. And so throughout that chapter the apostle speaks of moral revival during this present life, though of course with the intention that the flesh, which now shares in the revival, should share in the future reward. If it were not so intended, the flesh would have no right to baptism, in which, as the apostle has just previously said (Rom. 6. 3, 4), there is a figure of Christ's death and a pledge of the reality of life eternal: for where the death was, namely in the flesh, there the life must surely be, for what death destroys, that must the life restore. To the same effect are other texts, which speak of the mortal being swallowed up by immortality, and of our citizenship being in heaven from whence our Lord Jesus Christ will come to transfigure our body into conformity with his own. Therefore it is that, as the apostle says again (Rom. 12. 1), our bodies must be presented to God as a holy and acceptable sacrifice: and this they could not be, except that our whole body and soul and spirit are to be preserved without reproach at the Lord's appearing (1 Thess. 5. 23).

In these texts Tertullian seems to be quoting the Greek from memory, and translating as he goes: typical of his own style is *uti hactenus delinquentiae serviamus*, where Lat. vg. has (more literally) *ut ultra non serviamus peccato*. His memory, and his translation, are accurate enough, except as follows:

Rom. 6: 8, *commortui in Christo* ἀπεθάνομεν σὺν Χριστῷ.
6: 12, *ad obaudiendum illi* εἰς τὸ ὑπακούειν ταῖς ἐπιθυμίαις αὐτοῦ.
6: 13, *et ad exhibendum* μηδὲ παριστάνετε.
arma iustitiae omits τῷ θεῷ.
6: 19, *immunditiae et iniquitatis* (genitive dependent on *famula*) τῇ ἀκαθαρσίᾳ καὶ τῇ ἀνομίᾳ (dependent on παρεστήσατε: Lat. vg. interprets δοῦλα by *servire*). So probably also *famula iustitiae* δοῦλα τῇ δικαιοσύνῃ, and 6: 20, *liberi eratis iustitiae* ἐλεύθεροι ἦτε τῇ δικαιοσύνῃ.
6: 21, *fructum habebatis* omits τότε.
6: 3, *in Iesum* εἰς Χριστὸν Ἰησοῦν.
6: 4, *surrexit*, active (as also vg.) for ἠγέρθη, omitting διὰ τῆς δόξης τοῦ πατρός (as also Irenaeus, *Haer*. III. 17. 9).
6: 5, *consati sumus simulacro* (apparently instrumental ablative) σύμφυτοι γεγόναμεν τῷ ὁμοιώματι (Lat. vg. *complantati facti sumus similitudini*).

The remaining quotations, Rom. 5. 21 and 1 Thess. 5. 23, are close to the Greek.

1 **haec enim erit, etc.** *Enim* is not in *T*, and should perhaps be removed, unless it can be shown to mean *itaque*: *esse* (deleted by Kroymann) must be retained. *Corporalitas* elsewhere means the fact of possessing bodily substance: so *Adv. Herm.* 36: Movement is not, as Hermogenes professes, 'an incorporal substance of matter': all things are movable, either of themselves or by impulse from without, *tamen nec hominem nec lapidem et corporalem et incorporalem dicemus quia et corpus habeat et motum, sed unam omnibus formam solius corporalitatis, quae substantiae res est*: i.e. corporeity is in the category of οὐσία, motion in the category of ποιεῖν or πάσχειν: *De Anima* 7, *corporalitas animae in ipso evangelio relucebit*: ibid. 9, *sed nos corporales quoque illi* [sc. *animae*] *inscribimus lineas, non tantum ex fiducia corporalitatis per aestimationem, verum et ex constantia gratiae per revelationem*. In the present place *corporalitas* seems to mean not the fact of possessing bodily substance, but the bodily substance itself. *Moralitas* is not in Oehler's Index: it signifies moral characteristics, in the category of ποῖον.

NOTES AND COMMENTARY 307

3 ceterum si...convivemus illi. This sentence (printed by Borleffs as one, by Oehler with a period after *serviamus*) seems in either case to be out of syntax. The remedy might be to point with a colon after *perpessa est*, and to change *sicut* to *sic* (so as to balance *quemadmodum*), reading *et ut* as equivalent to *ut et* (a transposition which is not infrequent: examples are given by V. Buchart, *Tertullian-Studien*, page 19). Otherwise we must understand a positive *perpessa est* after *sed*: 'yet in fact it has suffered with him, in the sense in which the apostle has added, That the body of sin should be destroyed'. The former seems easier: which is perhaps an argument in favour of the latter.

31 nec ipsum baptisma. At *De Baptismo* 4 Tertullian says there are no marks of sin on the flesh, but only on the spirit: *tamen utrumque inter se communicant reatum, spiritus ob imperium caro ob ministerium: igitur...et spiritus in aquis corporaliter diluitur et caro in eisdem spiritaliter mundatur*: cf. also above, § 8, *caro abluitur ut anima emaculetur*, etc.

36 ac ne de ista, etc. The grouping of this and the following sentences seems to be that the quotation *Si enim consati*, etc. illustrates *ne de ista tantum vita*, and *per simulacrum*, etc. expounds the quotation. Then comes a new quotation, *Ut sicut regnavit*, on which *quomodo ita*, etc. is a comment. But what is the connection between *Ut sicut regnavit* (Rom. 5. 21) and what has gone before? It seems possible that Tertullian, quoting from memory, thought it followed on from Rom. 6. 3–5, and with it summarized and clinched this series of quotations.

47 devoraverat mors invalescendo: a quotation (repeated in § 54 *ad fin.*) of Isa. 25. 8 LXX, κατέπιεν ὁ θάνατος ἰσχύσας, where the Hebrew means, He hath swallowed up death for ever: Irenaeus, *Haer.* v. 12. 1, quotes from LXX in a discussion of the resurrection, which was certainly known to Tertullian. On *contentio* see a note on § 51, line 26.

49 sic enim et gratia, etc. This sentence is a series of reminiscences, of Rom. 5. 20, 2 Cor. 12. 9, and Ezek. 34. 16, where LXX has τὸ ἀπολωλὸς ζητήσω καὶ τὸ πλανώμενον ἐπιστρέψω καὶ τὸ

20-2

συντετριμμένον καταδήσω καὶ τὸ ἐκλιπὸν ἐνισχύσω καὶ τὸ ἰσχυρὸν φυλάξω καὶ βοσκήσω αὐτὰ μετὰ κρίματος, Tertullian adding a few clauses of similar nature, and translating the rest loosely from memory. *Municipatum*, πολίτευμα, Phil. 3. 20: cf. *Adv. Marc.* III. 24, *in civitate divini operis Hierusalem caelo delata quam et apostolus matrem nostram sursum designat et politeuma nostrum, id est municipatum*. *Salutificator* also occurs *Adv. Marc.* II. 19 = Ps. 24 (23). 4: *De Ieiunio* 6 = Deut. 32. 15: *De Pud.* 2 = 1 Tim. 4. 10: in every case for σωτήρ: there seems no good reason for the editorial variant *salvificatorem*.

61 placibilem deo: Rom. 12. 1, εὐάρεστον τῷ θεῷ, Lat. vg. *deo placentem*. The variant *placabilem* would mean 'able to propitiate', but would require the genitive *dei*.

69 qui clavis est resurrectionis may refer to Apoc. 1. 18, ἔχω τὰς κλεῖς τοῦ θανάτου καὶ τοῦ ᾅδου, though that text has no immediate bearing on the second Advent.

CHAPTERS XLVIII–LVI

Chapters 48–56 answer a cavil based on the apostle's statement that flesh and blood cannot inherit the kingdom of God. This the adversaries regard as the key to their position. Tertullian omits to remark that the introductory words τοῦτο δέ φημι mean 'This I admit', rather than 'This I affirm', and indicate that as the cavil had already been raised at Corinth the apostle is himself engaged in answering it. But he rightly claims that the apostle's words must be interpreted in the light of their context, and proceeds to examine sentence by sentence the whole of 1 Cor. 15.

In chapter 48, after a brief reference to St Paul's recapitulation of the evidence for the resurrection of Christ, Tertullian quotes almost in full the argument (verses 12–18) that an outright denial of the resurrection of the dead would involve a denial of Christ's resurrection and thereby stultify both the apostolic preaching and the Christian faith. Evidently, Tertullian continues, any fact must be in accord with the precedent adduced to prove it: and consequently our resurrection must be a copy of that of Christ. So again, as the mention of Adam shows (verse 22), the same thing is to live again in Christ which in Adam has died, namely, the flesh. 'Every man in his own order' (verse 23) means order of merits and of rewards, and introduces the moral factor. The practice of baptism for the dead, and the dangers and conflicts the apostle undergoes, being the concern of the flesh, in mere justice demand that it shall rise again. The question, 'With what kind of body' (verse 35) is deferred for later consideration (in § 52).

In chapter 49 Tertullian passes on to 1 Cor. 15. 50, which contains the text under discussion, and asks in what sense flesh and blood are disinherited. Looking back to verse 47 he observes that the contrasted χοϊκός and ἐπουράνιος imply no difference of substance (for both these are epithets attached to 'man') but a difference of discipline (or conduct) and dignity 'in (or 'within') the same substance.' Hence the exhortation (verse 49), 'Let us bear the image of the heavenly', which is only intelligible in a moral sense, of the adoption of Christian discipline and conduct. Here Tertullian (following Irenaeus) inserts the particle 'for', which is not in the apostolic text, and by reading 'For this I say' brings the statement that flesh and blood cannot inherit, into causal connection with the contrast of earthly and heavenly, once more obtaining for these terms an ethical meaning. He also remarks, with examples from elsewhere, that it is not unusual for the apostle to specify a substance when he means the works of that substance: so that 'flesh and blood' here means the works of flesh and blood, some of which have already been condemned in verse 32 in the strictures on those who say 'Let us eat and drink for tomorrow we die'.

Chapter 50 opens a new line of argument by bringing under consideration the remaining words of the apostolic text. A distinction is drawn between the kingdom of God, which flesh and blood cannot inherit, and the resurrection of the dead in which they have to be involved. Flesh and blood, of themselves, are incompetent to inherit: it is the Spirit which gives life and makes them competent. Therefore it is that by the act of God they are to be clothed upon with incorruptibility and immortality, in the case of those only who are to inherit the kingdom of God. A suggestion had been made that by 'flesh and blood' the apostle meant Judaism: Tertullian mentions this, but apparently does not think it of much account.

In chapter 51 we leave for a moment the consideration of particular texts and state a principle which covers them all: namely, that the apostle cannot be thought to have summarily excluded all flesh from the kingdom of God, when the fact is that Jesus himself, in the flesh and blood which he has made his own, is already seated at the right hand of God, having taken up to heaven that human nature which he has received from us, as a token and pledge that the whole will sometime be accepted there. After this noble piece of writing, one of the most eloquent in all his works, Tertullian observes that flesh and blood, though not themselves corruption, are capable of the corruption which is death: the corruption which, as the apostle says, cannot inherit incorruption, is death itself; so that flesh and blood, when freed from death, can and will inherit incorruption and immortality.

In chapter 52 Tertullian returns to verse 35, to the question, 'In what body do they come?' The apostle's parable of the seed is examined and expanded. Bare grain is sown: grain in the ear, with all its accoutrement, is raised again. So also the flesh, when raised again, will have from God something which it had not before, by addition and not by abolition. There follows a somewhat fanciful explanation of what the apostle means by the various kinds of flesh (verses 39, 40), with the comment that once more the difference will be not of substance but of glory.

Chapter 53 controverts the suggestion that 'natural body' (σῶμα ψυχικόν, *corpus animale*, verse 44) means the soul. The soul is not 'sown' after death: and the example of Lazarus is evidence that it is the body which is buried and which rises again. When the apostle says 'this corruptible thing', 'this mortal thing', he as it were touches or points to his own body as he says it. When the body is buried it is *corpus animale*: when raised again it will be *corpus spiritale*. Soul, though it is itself a body (of its own kind), is not *corpus animale* or *animatum* but *corpus animans*. As we so understand the matter we are in agreement with the apostle when he says that the first man is from the earth, earthy, and the second

Man is the Lord from heaven; the first Adam a living soul, the last Adam a quickening spirit.

The next two chapters continue the subject, with a discussion in chapter 54 of 'swallowed up' at verse 54 and at 2 Cor. 3. 4: and in chapter 55 of the meaning of 'change' (verse 52). Swallowing up does not of necessity involve destruction: and change is concerned with attributes and not with substance. Chapter 56 repeats a previous observation, that it would be inconsistent with divine righteousness for one body to have done the work and another to enjoy the reward.

CHAPTER XLVIII

1 Cor. 15. 1–34

The apostolic statement that flesh and blood cannot inherit the kingdom of God must be considered in terms of its context. The apostle has placed the sum total of his gospel in the preaching of the death and resurrection of Christ, and maintains that denial of the resurrection of the dead, by involving a denial of Christ's resurrection, stultifies the Christian faith and hope. Evidently he is here equating our resurrection with Christ's: so that, as Christ's flesh died and was buried and rose again, so also will ours. Hence also the contrast between Adam in whom all die, and Christ in whom all will be made alive: in the flesh they die because of Adam, and in the flesh they will be made alive because of Christ. 'In his own order' implies 'in his own body': for the order is an order of merits, and seeing that merits are attributed to the body, the body must rise again so as to enjoy them. Baptism for the dead also has reference to the body: for the soul is assured of salvation not by the washing but by the act of faith. Likewise the perils and afflictions of the apostolic office, being corporal sufferings, require the resurrection of the flesh so that its sufferings may be rewarded. The question in what body we shall rise again, we defer until later.

1 **hereditate possidere,** κληρονομῆσαι. *Possidere* has its proper sense, 'obtain' or 'take possession of'. Throughout these chapters the MSS. vary between *hereditati* and *hereditate*. *Hereditas* can mean either the act or fact of inheriting, or the property inherited. If the

former is the intention here, the ablative is correct: and this is perhaps to be preferred, as nearer the sense of the Greek. The dative could be explained, but hardly justified, as a kind of predicative dative attached to *regnum dei*, 'obtain for an inheritance the kingdom of God'. The printed text of Irenaeus has the ablative.

5 disiectis. *TFR*^mg·: *deiectis PM*. *Deicere* is the more obvious word for throwing down a road block, which is good enough reason for thinking that Tertullian (who often avoids the obvious word) used the more violent term *disiectis*.

5 expetent is only in *P*, but seems to give the best sense: *expectent* of the usually better MSS. is in the wrong mood: *expediet* (Kellner's conjecture) is in the right tense, but seems somewhat weak. The second hand of *T* inserts *non* before *praeiudicet*, which is due to misunderstanding of Tertullian's use of this verb: cf. § 5, *nec idcirco restitutio mundi praeiudicabitur*, 'cannot be taken for a proof that the world will be reconstituted'—i.e. 'prejudice' in a positive, not a negative, sense.

9 demandatione is a reminiscence of St Paul's παρέδωκα γὰρ ὑμῖν (1 Cor. 15. 3) as *unde constaret* is of ἐν ᾧ καὶ ἑστήκατε.

14 inanis est et fides vestra is not in *MPX*: the others vary between *inanis* and *vacua*. Possibly Tertullian, who in any case is abbreviating slightly, omitted the clause, and the copyists afterwards added it. *Inanis* here stands for κενόν, κενή, void of content: *vacua* (below) for ματαία, destitute of purpose.

41 si autem et baptizantur, etc. There are said to be more than two hundred explanations of St Paul's reference to baptism for the dead, most of them concerned to explain away the apparent superstition of the practice or to excuse the apostle's failure to rebuke it. Tertullian takes the passage to mean what it says, but by adding *hoc eos instituisse* hints that the Corinthians were doing this without apostolic authority. *Portendit* need not be altered: no copyist is likely to have introduced this uncommon word, in this unusual sense of 'suggest': its regular meaning seems to be 'presage'. *Non nisi alias* can hardly be right: Engelbrecht would omit *nisi*.

NOTES AND COMMENTARY 313

45 qui et ipsos, etc. There is no pressing need to alter *qui* to *quid*: it could mean 'how' or 'in what sense': though *quid* would better represent St Paul's τί καί. *Id est* is difficult: Dr Borleffs reads *id est lavari*; but it seems unlikely that there could have been any need for Tertullian to inform a Christian audience that *baptizare* is the Greek word for 'wash'. I suspect that after *baptizari ait* some words have dropped out, e.g. *si omnino mortui non resurgunt*, answering to St Paul's εἰ ὅλως νεκροὶ οὐκ ἐγείρονται, and that *id est si non*, etc. is Tertullian's comment on this.

46 anima enim, etc. This is a careless remark, made for the purpose of present effect, and inconsistent with what has been said above, §8, *caro abluitur ut anima emaculetur*, etc. But if *PMX* are right, reading *animae*, the meaning is that for the soul the sacramental act is completed not by the washing but by the *responsio fidei*: which is perhaps less objectionable.

52 super quam supra (*MPX*) represents St Paul's καθ' ὑπερβολὴν better than *super quam* (*T*) which omits the second member of comparison demanded by *quam*. *Citra vires* is for ὑπὲρ δύναμιν, a not unparalleled use of *citra* for *ultra*: cf. *De Ieiunio* 13, *citra illos dies quibus ablatus est sponsus*, where *citra* is equivalent to *praeter*: and *supra*, §39, *citra* (= ἐκτός) *quam prophetae adnuntiassent*.

59 ex hoc quoque genere: an uncommon use of *genus*: the meaning seems to be 'from this class of argument'.

CHAPTER XLIX

1 Cor. 15. 50

We now ask on what conditions the apostle excludes flesh and blood from the kingdom of God. Once more we refer to the context. The apostle has said that the first man is from the earth, earthy, and the second Man is Christ from heaven, and that there are earthy and heavenly persons, after the likeness of the one or the other of them. We ask, after what sort of likeness: and we must answer that the contrast between them cannot be in respect of substance (for both are designated 'man') and so must be in respect of character. As Christ, who alone is truly heavenly, is in his earthly nature no different from others of earthly origin, we have to conclude that those who after his likeness are heavenly are so not because of their present substance but because of the glory that is to be: for there is a difference of dignity, even as star differs from star, in glory but not in substance. Only in view of this moral sense can we understand the injunction, Let us bear the image of the heavenly: for this does not mean that we are to divest ourselves of the flesh, but that we ought to imitate Christ's character: the injunction is in the present tense, and so of necessity is concerned with moral conduct. As it is in this connection that the apostle says that flesh and blood cannot inherit the kingdom, evidently by flesh and blood he means this image of the earthy, which we have already seen is a matter of discipline, not of substance. The apostle not infrequently mentions a substance when he means the works of that substance, and he has elsewhere (Gal. 5. 21), while enumerating the works of the flesh, indicated that those who do them will not inherit the kingdom of God: and this again gives us the moral sense here required.

1 Evidently a word has dropped out before *revera*: Kroymann's suggestion of *cardinem* seems to meet the case. The same play upon words has already occurred in §8, *adeo caro salutis est cardo*.

4 **choicus**, χοϊκός, is apparently found only in this passage of St Paul and places dependent on it. Lat. vg. translates by *terrenus*: Tertullian keeps the Greek word, possibly with the intention of rescuing it from fanciful gnostic misinterpretations, for which cf. *Adv. Val.* 24 (copied from Irenaeus, *Haer.* I. I. 10). The demiurge, in creating the semi-celestial prototype of man, *substantiam ei capit non ex ista, inquiunt, arida quam nos unicam novimus terra...sed ex invisibili corpore materiae illius scilicet philosophicae*, which was a condensation of the tears of Achamoth: *figulat ita hominem Demiurgus et de afflatu suo animat: sic erit et choicus et animalis*. There is in truth nothing abstruse about the word: it is naturally enough derived from χοῦς, which means earth heaped up by digging. Cf. *Adv. Marc.* V. 10, where Tertullian has *primus homo de humo terrenus*:

apparently he was making his own translation from the Greek, as each case required.

8 nec Adam ex semine caro, etc. So *De Carne Christi* 16, *recordentur Adam ipsum in hanc carnem non ex semine viri factum: sicut terra conversa est in hanc carnem sine viri semine, ita et dei verbum potuit sine coagulo in eiusdem carnis transire materiam.* So also Irenaeus, *Haer.* III. 19. 6, ὥσπερ γὰρ διὰ τῆς παρακοῆς τοῦ ἑνὸς ἀνθρώπου τοῦ πρώτως ἐκ γῆς ἀνεργάστου πεπλασμένου ἁμαρτωλοὶ κατεστάθησαν οἱ πολλοὶ καὶ ἀπέβαλον τὴν ζωήν, οὕτως ἔδει καὶ δι' ὑπακοῆς ἑνὸς ἀνθρώπου, τοῦ πρώτως ἐκ παρθένου γεγενημένου, δικαιωθῆναι πολλοὺς καὶ ἀπολαβεῖν τὴν σωτηρίαν.

14 supercaelestis (and again below) and *superterrenorum* are needlessly precise translations of ἐπουράνιος, ἐπίγειος, for which Lat. vg. is rightly satisfied with *caelestis, terrestris*.

25 portemus: so Lat. vg.: the Greek MSS. seem about equally balanced between φορέσομεν and φορέσωμεν (which when the MSS. were copied were probably almost identical in sound). A little later Tertullian uses this (to him, present) imperative to support his argument that 'image of the heavenly' has a moral, not a physical, sense.

30 non iam dei: with a reference to Ps. 82. 6 and John 10. 34.

40 hoc enim dico, etc. The MSS. and editors have made heavy weather of this sentence, though in Oehler's text it is almost intelligible. I suspect that the text as I have printed it is correct, with the meaning given in my translation. *Propterea* is a dittography from *propter ea*: the second *est* (P only) must be rejected. But it is to be observed that *enim* is Tertullian's addition to St Paul's words: there is nothing in the Greek to justify it, though Irenaeus, *Haer.* v. 11. 2, has *hoc enim dico fratres*.

CHAPTER L

The apostle's exact words must be noted. He does not say that flesh and blood will not rise again, but that they cannot inherit the kingdom of God. The general resurrection is not excluded by the fact that some will rise only to judgement and not to the kingdom. So on this ground also it must appear that flesh and blood are to be taken in a moral and not a physical sense. Also it is true that flesh and blood, of themselves, cannot inherit the kingdom, but (since it is the Spirit that quickeneth, while the flesh profiteth nothing) only as they are empowered by the Spirit to do the works of the Spirit. At the resurrection all flesh and blood will rise again in its own quality, and thereafter those who are to come to the kingdom will be clothed upon with incorruption and immortality: and thus flesh and blood, being 'changed' and 'swallowed up', will inherit the kingdom—and that not without having been raised again. There are some who think that in this text, as at Gal. 1. 16, St Paul, in speaking of flesh and blood, means Judaism.

14 spiritus enim est, etc. John 6. 63. The original intention of this text seems to have been to mitigate the 'hardness' (i.e. almost 'offensiveness') of the σκληρὸς λόγος about eating the flesh and drinking the blood of the Son of Man. This will be possible, our Lord explains, because of his ascension into heaven, and because of the working of the Holy Spirit upon certain earthly bread and upon the recipients of it. The words which follow, τὰ ῥήματα ἃ ἐγὼ λελάληκα, κτἑ, seem to indicate that the flesh which is in nothing profitable means the natural uninspired understanding of the words lately spoken. Tertullian's extension of the words to natural human flesh and to the Spirit which quickens it would be justified by the whole tenor of the discourse in John 6, and (if he had known that epistle) by 2 Pet. 1. 4, θείας κοινωνοὶ φύσεως. So also Irenaeus, *Haer.* v. 12. 4 (commenting on Phil. 1. 22): *fructus autem operis spiritus est carnis salus: quis enim alius apparens fructus eius est qui non apparet spiritus quam maturam efficere carnem et capacem incorruptelae?*

16 spiritus, et per spiritum, etc.: i.e. the flesh receives profit, first from the spirit itself (or the Holy Spirit himself—though Tertullian's Montanism made him blind to this possibility, of which Irenaeus was well aware), and consequently from the moral 'works of the Spirit' (Gal. 5. 22).

16 resurgunt itaque, etc.: i.e. all the dead will rise again in their natural condition, and only thereafter will those who are to come to the kingdom of God be clothed upon with immortality. Tertullian is not in disagreement with the doctrine expressed by Irenaeus, *Haer.* v. 2. 2, ὁπότε οὖν καὶ τὸ κεκραμένον ποτήριον καὶ ὁ γεγονὼς ἄρτος ἐπιδέχεται τὸν λόγον τοῦ θεοῦ καὶ γίγνεται ἡ εὐχαριστία σῶμα Χριστοῦ, ἐκ τούτων δὲ αὔξει καὶ συνίσταται ἡ τῆς σαρκὸς ἡμῶν ὑπόστασις, κτὲ. This appears to mean that even in this life the natural body may become endowed with a certain divine quality—a possibility for which Tertullian has allowed in the preceding sentence, *prodesse tamen*, etc. But the body retains its natural quality, however much it be prepared for the life to come by assimilation to the perfect humanity of Christ through the operation of the Spirit: it is still *in qualitate sua*, and *in qualitate sua* it will rise again. Probably Tertullian would add that it will remain *eiusdem qualitatis*, as true human flesh (though not *eiusdem condicionis*) even when it has been clothed upon with, or swallowed up by, immortality.

21 cum devorari habeat, etc.: *devorari* here (instead of *induere*) is an anticipation of κατεπόθη εἰς νῖκος at the end of the sentence: it may have been suggested by the close association of ἐνδύσασθαι and ἵνα καταποθῇ at 2 Cor. 5. 4: *ex demutatione* carries a reference back to ἀλλαγησόμεθα, 1 Cor. 15. 51.

CHAPTER LI

The apostle cannot be supposed by these words to exclude unconditionally all flesh and blood from the kingdom of God, when the fact is that Jesus, the eternal Word of God, is, in the flesh and blood which he has made his own, seated at the right hand of the Father, and is to return again in like manner as he ascended, still recognizable as himself. As he has given to us an earnest of his Spirit, so has he received from us an earnest of our flesh, which he has taken up into heaven in pledge that the whole amount will in due time be transferred thither. If flesh and blood are in Christ, and Christ is in heaven, it cannot be denied that they too will be taken there.

'Corruption', the apostle says, 'cannot inherit incorruption.' Flesh is not itself corruption, but rather is subject to the corruption which is death. So the apostle goes on to say that death itself is swallowed up in striving. The sting and the power of death is sin, and the strength of sin is that other law in the members which fights against the law of the mind. But he has already said that death is the last enemy to be destroyed: and this will be, he now indicates, when the dead rise again incorruptible and the mortal flesh and the corruptible blood put on immortality and incorruption. Also when he says 'this mortal thing, this corruptible thing', he as it were points to his own body as he says it. A corruptible thing is one thing, corruption is another: and it follows from our text that the same thing which now suffers corruption and mortality will eventually enjoy incorruption and immortality.

3 clausis quod aiunt oculis: so *Apol.* 3, *quid quod plerique clausis oculis in odium eius impingunt?* and *De Pall.* 2, *quod clausis vel in totum Homericis oculis liquet.* The other examples cited by Salmasius on the latter passage have a literal and not a proverbial sense.

4 sine distinctione, without distinguishing between one man and another: *sine condicione,* without considering the conditions under which flesh and blood can be competent to inherit the kingdom. *Passim,* meaning 'generally', is unusual, its proper sense being 'at random': but Tertullian frequently says *passivus* for 'general', e.g. *Ad Uxor.* 1. 2, *per licentiam tunc passivam materiae subsequentium emendationum praeministrabantur,* 'general permission' to the patriarchs to have more than one wife: a natural enough deduction from the root *pandere*: cf. also *Apol.* 9, *suppeditante materias passivitate luxuriae,* 'the general prevalence of debauchery'.

8 puriora seems the better attested reading and makes a better rhythm, though *purior* would be more in sequence with *Adam novissimus, sermo primarius* and the other singular nominatives. There was no need for Kroymann to alter *qua* to *quam*.

10 sequester dei et hominum: 1 Tim. 2. 5, μεσίτης θεοῦ καὶ ἀνθρώπων, referred to again in §63. In post-Augustan Latin *sequester* can mean 'mediator', e.g. Lucan, *Phars.* x. 472, *orator* *regis pacisque sequester*, where Haskins quotes Seneca, *Dial.* xii. 5, *qui inter patres ac plebem publicae gratiae sequester fuit*. But Tertullian having perhaps found the word in his Latin version, or more probably having himself made a tendentious translation, prefers to understand *sequester* in its original sense of trustee or depositary: so *Adv. Prax.* 27, *sic et apostolus dei et hominum appellans sequestrem utriusque substantiae confirmavit*. At *De Carne Christi* 15, where the emphasis is on the manhood of Christ, Tertullian has *mediator dei et hominum homo Christus Iesus*. Lat. vg. has *mediator* both here and at Gal. 3. 19, 20.

12 depositum, money or goods entrusted to another for safe-keeping, as in Juvenal, *Sat.* 13. 60, *nunc si depositum non infitietur amicus...* | *prodigiosa fides et Tuscis digna libellis*. In Christ the *depositum* of his human flesh becomes an earnest or token of the whole of humanity, a suggestion taken up from 2 Cor. 5. 5, θεὸς ὁ δοὺς ἡμῖν τὸν ἀρραβῶνα τοῦ πνεύματος: i.e. as God has given us certain spiritual gifts, or the gift of the Holy Spirit, as an earnest or token of what he will do for us hereafter, so (Tertullian says) Christ has taken of us a deposit, as a token that he will afterwards lay claim to the whole sum of humanity. *Arrabo, arra,* ἀρραβών, is a Hebrew word which appears in Greek as early as Isaeus, and in Latin as early as Plautus, apparently by borrowing from Phoenician traders: *pignus* is here used in much the same sense, though its correct meaning is a pledge left in security for money borrowed: but at Juvenal, *Sat.* 6. 27, *tu digito pignus fortasse dedisti*, possibly the meaning is of a token of something promised.

16 usurpastis, 'have taken seizin of': so Cicero, *De Orat.* iii. 28. 110, *amissam possessionem ex iure civili surculo defringendo usurpare*.

16 aut si negent, etc. At first sight it is tempting to read *aut negent vos in Christo aut negent in caelo Christum*, etc. But the present text is intelligible: Tertullian's adversaries did in fact deny that flesh and blood were in Christ, and did deny heaven to flesh and blood: he advises them, not in logical consequence but as a further piece of impiety, to go on and deny that Christ is in heaven. But this sequence of thought is difficult, and perhaps some emendation is required.

26 **in contentione,** 1 Cor. 15. 54, εἰς νῖκος (= εἰς νίκην) misread as εἰς νεῖκος, as frequently: e.g. Augustine, *Enchir.* 121, *quando contentio mortis nulla erit.* In the next sentence Tertullian follows the order of textus receptus, and reads *potentia* for νῖκος: cf. §47, where he has the same order, but *contentio* for νῖκος. At §54 he reads *in contentionem...contentio tua*.

28 **virtus autem delinquentiae lex.** This sentence has little to do with St Paul's actual argument at 1 Cor. 15, and it seems possible that he wrote it because at that time he was engaged on the composition of the Epistle to the Romans. In that case his meaning here will be that expressed more fully at Rom. 7. 7–25. Tertullian perhaps unduly restricts it to one single theme, at verse 23, βλέπω δὲ ἕτερον νόμον ἐν τοῖς μέλεσί μου ἀντιστρατευόμενον τῷ νόμῳ τοῦ νοός μου, κτἑ.

34 **cum in atomo, etc.** Here the quotation from St Paul is interlaced with Tertullian's explanations. As the text is quoted the *et* before *mortui* must be read as 'both', balanced by the *et* before *nos demutabimur*. There is no further insistence by Tertullian on the somewhat artificial distinction between the flesh as mortal and the blood as corruptible: the two things and the two qualities are at this point indistinguishable: but cf. §57 where he distinguishes between immortality and incorruption, the former envisaging the resurrection, the latter redintegration.

40 **ac ne putes, etc.** I once thought that something like *aspice illum* had fallen out from before *providentem sibi*: so, I now learn, does Kroymann. The text will however construe, though somewhat unnaturally, 'And lest you should suppose the apostle has anything else in mind while he takes precautions and is anxious for you to understand that his words refer to the flesh, when he says "this corruptible thing", and "this mortal thing" he touches his own skin as he says it.' But possibly, with Kroymann, read *aspice ipsum.*

CHAPTER LII

In answer to the question 'With what body do they come', the apostle by the illustration of the seed that is sown shows that the flesh which will be brought to life again will be that which has

NOTES AND COMMENTARY 321

died. 'Thou sowest not that body that shall be', should cause us no difficulty: for, if we stand by our example, whatever kind of grain is sown, the same kind rises again: the corruption of the seed is still the seed. 'Bare grain' gives us the clue: the seed sown is bare grain: the seed when it comes to life, when God gives it a body as it pleases him, is fuller and richer, clothed and protected with husk and halm. Into this body the seed is changed not by destruction but by enlargement. So likewise our flesh when it rises again will be the same that was sown, but fuller and richer: not another flesh, but the same in another form. With this in mind the apostle distinguishes various kinds of flesh, of differing degrees of glory, each of which suggests a figure of different sorts of men: and when he continues, 'So also is the resurrection of the dead', he indicates that the only difference will be of degrees of glory. The same thing, he says, which is sown in corruption, rises again in incorruption, is sown a natural body and is raised a spiritual body. It was the divine sentence, 'Into the earth shalt thou return', which suggested to the apostle the thought of the sowing of seed, which is placed in the earth for the express purpose of being brought out of it again: which is why he adds, 'And so it is written'.

4 hoc ergo iam, etc. The older authorities here have *constet*, which must be allowed to stand, for this is the deduction which Tertullian wishes to draw concerning the flesh. *Constat* (below, line 20) is also correct, for this is not a matter of a deduction to be drawn, but of a fact to be observed, concerning the seed.

16 ergo salvum est, etc. The argument is that if God gives 'it' a body, there must still be existent something, the original seed or what remains of it, to which the body is given. Tertullian follows St Paul almost verbally: *cui dare habet deus corpus* is a paraphrase of ὁ δὲ θεὸς δίδωσιν αὐτῷ σῶμα.

22 additicium erit corpus still refers to the seed as it is brought again to life: but Tertullian no doubt has in mind 2 Cor. 5. 1–4, especially ἐφ' ᾧ οὐ θέλομεν ἐκδύσασθαι ἀλλ' ἐπενδύσασθαι, which refers to the body either at the resurrection or (in that particular context) to the heavenly clothing which St Paul conceives that some will receive when found alive by our Lord at his coming. So Tertullian says (still referring to the seed) *non abolitione sed ampliatione*. The application to the human body is made a few sentences later: *suggestum et ornatum qualem deus voluerit superducere*.

32 fructificaturam is the reading of all the MSS., and must stand: the point here is not merely that the body will show evidence of life, but that it will be amplified, and in that sense will bear fruit. See a note on §42, line 37.

39 figurata subicit exempla. In spite of Tertullian's remonstrance below, *ceterum si non figurate*, etc., we may suppose that he has drawn from St Paul's words more than they were intended to imply. The apostle's intention was apparently to indicate that there are various kinds of bodies, of different texture and of differing degrees of glory, but all of them real bodies: Tertullian's comments will appear to have homiletic rather than doctrinal value. After *stella enim a stella differt in gloria* it seems as if a few words have been lost: the usual comment is missing at this point, and the words which follow are not in grammatical sequence: nor is the difficulty overcome by Rhenanus' alteration of *Iudaeos scilicet et Christianos* to the nominative singular. What seems to be missing is some comment on 'one star differeth from another star in glory' and then some words like *sicut iam dixerat* before *et corpora terrena*. On the idea that the stars, though of varying brightness, are all of the same quality, cf. Irenaeus, *Haer.* II. 22. 1, where the subject under discussion is the Valentinian aeons to which apparently this text had been referred: *etenim si stella a stella in claritate differt, sed non secundum qualitatem nec secundum substantiam secundum quam passibile aliquid vel impassibile est: sed aut universos* (sc. *aeones*), *ex lumine cum sint paterno, naturaliter impassibiles et immutabiles esse oportet, aut universi cum paterno lumine et passibiles et commutationum corruptionis capaces sunt*.

55 seminatur, inquit, etc. It is grammatically possible that the repeated σπείρεται, ἐγείρεται, in these sentences may be impersonal verbs, 'there is a sowing in corruption and a rising again in incorruption', etc. This would, it appears, ease (if it did not quite

NOTES AND COMMENTARY

remove) a difficulty which some have found in envisaging a physical resurrection. But Tertullian will have none of it, as he comments, *certe non aliud resurgit quam quod seminatur*: and apparently St Paul was of the same mind, for *corpus spiritale*, σῶμα πνευματικόν, cannot mean a body composed of spirit, any more than *corpus animale*, σῶμα ψυχικόν, can mean a body composed of soul. The difference between them, Tertullian would say, is not of *substantia*, or of *qualitas*, but of *condicio*: and as now the σῶμα ψυχικόν is informed and directed by soul, so hereafter the same body, become πνευματικόν, will be so informed and directed by spirit that the *condiciones* of its mortality will be swallowed up by life.

65 sic enim scriptum est. Tertullian refers these words to the implied scripture, *terra es et in terram ibis*: by inserting *enim*, which is not in the Greek, he connects this with what precedes. There is no doubt that St Paul meant the phrase to introduce ἐγένετο ὁ πρῶτος ἄνθρωπος εἰς ψυχὴν ζῶσαν (a paraphrase of Gen. 2. 7), on which he adds his own comment ὁ ἔσχατος 'Αδὰμ εἰς πνεῦμα ζωοποιοῦν. On this Tertullian comments indirectly in the following chapter.

CHAPTER LIII

The suggestion that 'natural body' means the soul, cannot stand: soul does not die, nor is it buried. The example of Lazarus shows that it is the flesh, not the soul, which is buried and is raised again. St Paul, in the passage before us, refers again to the Scripture that Adam was made into a living soul: and this can only mean that his flesh (which was there before the soul was) was by the accession of soul made into a soul-informed body. At death the body ceases to be soul-informed: at the resurrection it will again become soul-informed so that it may also become spirit-informed. Soul certainly (like all real things) is a body; but it is not a soul-informed body: rather does it by accession to some other body cause that to be soul-informed. So likewise when the flesh receives the spirit it will become spirit-informed. By the comparison which he draws between the first and the last Adam the apostle shows clearly that the distinction between 'natural body' and 'spiritual body' lies within the same flesh: for Christ is Adam because he is man, and man because he is flesh, forasmuch as flesh was man before soul was. The terms 'first' and 'last' imply identity of substance: totally unlike things cannot be set in that kind of sequence. Moreover the second Man is from heaven according to the Spirit: for all that, he is man according to the flesh. As then this distinction applies to the flesh, so does that other, 'That was not first which is spiritual, but that which is natural', and we are brought again to see the identity of that which is sown with that which rises again. It may be thought that the flesh even now, having received the spirit, has become a spiritual body: but not so, for we have as yet only an earnest of the spirit, but of the soul not an earnest but the fullness, so that the body is 'natural' because there is present in it more soul than spirit.

3 ad ipsius rei exhibitionem. *Exhibere* is a legal term meaning 'produce in court'. Lewis and Short quote from the Digest, *Exhibere est in publicum producere et videndi tangendique hominis facultatem praebere*, referring to a person illegally detained: so too of an article in dispute, Petronius, *Sat.* 15, *indignatus rusticus quod nos centonem exhibendum postularemus.* So also below, *stilus apostoli comparet*, 'is present to give evidence'.

14 quadriduo, 'four days earlier' is unusual: Cicero has the opposite sense, *Pro Rosc. Amer.* 7. 20, *quadriduo quo haec gesta sunt, res ad Chrysogonum defertur,* 'four days after', or perhaps 'within four days of this being done'.

20 caro autem homo ante animam: either 'the flesh was man before the soul was' or 'the flesh was man before the soul was breathed into it': cf. *supra,* §§ 7, 45, and notes. Here apparently the former is meant: but either would suit the argument.

29 anima vero etsi corpus. On the Stoic idea of the corporeity of all real things cf. *Adv. Prax.* 7, *quis enim negabit deum corpus esse?* and my note, which refers to *De Anima* 6, *bene autem quod et artes Stoici corporales affirmant: adeo sic quoque anima corporalis si et artibus ali creditur*: ibid. 7, ⟨*anima sub terris*⟩ *nihil si non corpus*: *De Carne*

Christi 11, *omne quod est corpus est sui generis: nihil est incorporale nisi quod non est.*

31 f. accedens (twice: *T* only) is evidently correct: Lewis and Short, *s.v.* II. B. 2 give a number of examples with 'the accessory idea of increase': they also remark that this verb often so closely approaches the sense of *accidere* that it has been suggested that the latter word should be substituted for it (so here *MPX*, *accidens*).

35 in Adam quoque et in Christo: i.e. the distinction the apostle draws is not between Adam and Christ, but between 'flesh' and 'living soul' in Adam, and between 'flesh' and 'quickening Spirit' in Christ.

38–45 si enim et primus homo...in utroque homine praestruxit. These eight lines form a single sentence: the protasis, *si enim...non quia anima* is answered by the apodosis *ecquid... praestruxit*, the intervening clause *atque ita subiungit...utrumque Adam* (with the citation of 1 Cor. 15. 46) being parenthetical. In that case there is no need for Kroymann's insertion of *si* before *subiungit*. *Ecquid* (a correction by Gelenius of the MS. readings) stands for *nonne*: Tertullian uses the interrogative particles in ways peculiar to himself.

45 ex qua enim substantia...deputarentur. Here again the punctuation in the text is mine. Previous editors have made a query at *Christus et Adam*, with a period or a colon after *carne*, after *sunt*, and after *homo*, beginning a new sentence with *ex illa*. I have suggested that *ex qua substantia* is not interrogative but relative, and is balanced by *ex illa*: *scilicet ex carne* defines *substantia* (*scilicet* does not commonly introduce the answer to a question: that as a rule would be *plane*): *licet et...caro homo* is parenthetical, summarily disposing of a possible objection which is at this stage of the argument not likely to be pressed, having often enough been dealt with already.

50 de substantia apparently qualifies *diversa* (not *disponi*).

54 de caelo secundum spiritum. Tertullian, always with a reference, tacit or overt, to John 4. 24, *deus spiritus est*, habitually uses or interprets 'spirit' as indicating Christ's divine nature: and so here. For his own justification of this practice see *Adv. Prax.* 26, with my notes (pp. 313, 314) and my Introduction (pp. 63-70).

63 totum de homine, etc. The punctuation here follows Oehler. These three clauses have no grammatical connection with what precedes, and must be treated as a brief recapitulation of its content.

64 habet caro spiritum ex fide. The primary reference here is to Gal. 5. 5, ἡμεῖς γὰρ πνεύματι ἐκ πίστεως ἐλπίδα δικαιοσύνης ἀπεκδεχόμεθα, which explains Tertullian's *ex fide*: but Rom. 8. 23 is also in his mind, καὶ αὐτοὶ τὴν ἀπαρχὴν τοῦ πνεύματος ἔχοντες ἡμεῖς: and so is 2 Cor. 5. 5, τὸν ἀρραβῶνα τοῦ πνεύματος (already referred to in §51) which suggests the argument of the following sentence.

67 itaque etiam, etc. The manuscripts here twice read *in qua*, which Ursinus in both cases altered to *in quo*: but *in qua* could well stand, referring first to *maioris substantiae* (i.e. the soul, 'in which', being *corpus animale*, it is buried), and afterwards to *plenitudinem spiritus* (i.e. not the *arrabo* but fullness, in which as *corpus spiritale* it is to rise again). As it rises again it will at first be *animale* and then (after an unmeasurably short interval) *insuper spiritale*, as it was stated earlier in this chapter that *animale corpus efficitur, ut fiat spiritale*.

At the end of the chapter there is an assonance between *conferta* and *respersa* which my translation has not very successfully tried to reproduce.

CHAPTER LIV

Equivocal terms, here as elsewhere, have caused trouble. 'Swallowed up of life' has been taken to imply the destruction of the mortal thing that is to be swallowed up. But 'swallow' can mean 'hide' or 'clothe' or 'contain', as it does in this text. Here it may be objected that in that case death, when swallowed up unto contention, will also survive. Not so: for death is not capable of immortality, its own opposite. In reference to the 'mortal thing',

NOTES AND COMMENTARY 327

'swallowed up of life' means the same as to be clothed upon with immortality. Death will be swallowed up into destruction, because that is what itself 'strives' to do: life will have the opposite effect, and will swallow up not to destruction but to salvation.

2 de verborum communionibus: cf. *Adv. Marc.* IV. 10 where, referring to nouns rather than verbs, Tertullian remarks that *nominum communio simplex si forte videri potest*, 'may be supposed perhaps to have no special significance', adding however that he has maintained elsewhere (ibid. III. 15, 16) that this will not justify the Marcionite suggestion that there could be two Christs both named Jesus: even less could it justify an equivocation over 'Son of man', for this is not a name but an appellation, and when used by our Lord of himself must be supposed to identify him with the prophetic character in Daniel to whom it was first applied.

3 uti devoretur, etc. 2 Cor. 5. 4, already discussed in passing in §42.

6 continere, and below, *continetur,* 'enclose' or 'confine'—something stronger than the modern English meaning of 'contain': the same idea is represented below by *includitur in ipsam*, an expression justified by St Paul's use of *induere*, as of putting on clothing.

18 devoravit, inquit, mors invalescendo, Isa. 25. 8 (LXX), κατέπιεν ὁ θάνατος ἰσχύσας, where English R.V. has, 'He hath swallowed up death for ever': Lat. vg. *praecipitabit mortem in sempiternum*. The text has already been referred to in §47. Cf. also Irenaeus, *Haer.* v. 12. 1, *si enim mors mortificavit, quare vita adveniens non vivificabit hominem, quemadmodum Esaias propheta ait, Devoravit mors potens, et rursus, Deus abstulit omnem lachrimam ab omni facie?* The quotation of 1 Cor. 15. 55 is repeated from §51. *Per contentionem tuam* (at the end of the sentence) makes no evident sense, and the presence of *tuam* is difficult to account for, unless perhaps as a dittography from three lines above: *T* omits the word, as did Gelenius: Junius read *suam*, which is possibly correct. *Devoraverat* (the MS. reading) is certainly correct, and Kroymann's future *devoraverit* uncalled for: the text of Isaiah, in LXX as in the

Hebrew, refers to some past event, which Tertullian does not trouble exactly to define, though perhaps he thought the LXX text referred to the primal sin and its effect, Gen. 3. 3.

CHAPTER LV

'And we shall be changed' does not imply the destruction of that which is changed, but rather its conservation, though in another form. If the change that takes place after the resurrection were to involve destruction, the resurrection might as well not occur. Change and destruction are in fact mutually exclusive. Moreover a man changes in many respects and many times over during his lifetime, yet remains the same man. Examples of such change, with continuance of identity, are recorded in Scripture: Moses' hand was the same hand both before and after it was touched with leprosy, and he himself remained the same when his face was so bright that the people could not bear to look upon it: Stephen was the same when his face shone like an angel's: our Lord himself, as well as Moses and Elijah, remained the same, recognizable as such, during the Transfiguration. And so St Paul says that our Lord will transfigure the body of our humility. If transfiguration had involved a change of substance, Saul when changed into another man would not have been the same Saul, and Satan when transfigured into an angel of light would cease to be Satan: which evidently is not the case.

4 licet aliunde iam caesae, as for instance the text *et nos immutabimur* has already been discussed in §42 and referred to in §51.

15 ne esset is Dr Borleffs' excellent emendation. The MSS. (except *T*, which omits the clause) have *necesse est*, which is meaningless: from this Rhenanus derived *nec esse*, which would make sense.

15 non miscebuntur: a good example of Tertullian's practice of using the future to express a necessary or self-evident assumption or conclusion: 'cannot be confused'.

NOTES AND COMMENTARY

20 habet enim esse: *esse* here is a substantive, the object of *habet*, an imitation of the Greek, ἔχει γὰρ τὸ εἶναι, ὅπερ οὐ πάντως διαφθείρεται: and *non omnino* possibly means *omnino non*, but I am not sufficiently sure of this to have put it into my translation.

23 substantiā quidem ipse sit: cf. below, *quodsi et transfigurationem et conversionem in transitu substantiae cuiusque defendis*: and *cum salute substantiae*. In my introduction to *Adversus Praxean* I have shown (apparently to the satisfaction of a number of good scholars) that one of the meanings of *substantia* is 'the thing itself' (or the person himself), in the Aristotelian sense of πρώτη οὐσία. That seems to be the case here: 'in his essential being he is the same person as he was'. In my translation, 'in substance remains himself' must be understood in this sense, and not in the modern English misusage by which some say that a thing is substantially (or essentially) the same when they mean that it is really quite different. Later in this sentence, when Tertullian says that during his lifetime a man changes *ipsa corpulentia* he comes near to the modern discovery that the physical constituents of the human body all change and are replaced in the course of seven years; but he can hardly have been aware of that, and *corpulentia* probably means much the same as *habitus*.

28 nec alius...sed aliud seems to be written with less than Tertullian's usual accuracy. It ought to mean, 'not another person but another thing', i.e. substantially different: but the argument above shows that this is not the meaning, but rather 'the same in person (i.e. substantially the same) but with different attributes'.

29 Moses' hand, which died and came to life again, has been referred to in § 28 as a prophecy of resurrection.

35 The Transfiguration is discussed *Adv. Marc.* IV. 22. Marcion, in retaining this episode in his gospel, was inconsistent with himself: the presence of Moses and Elijah showed that Christ had not come to destroy the law and the prophecy which these represented, but to confirm it.

CHAPTER LVI

It would be unjust, and altogether unworthy of God, that one flesh should have lived this life and another be rewarded or punished in the life to come. Better that there should be no resurrection at all. It is not conceivable that the memory of this life should be abolished hereafter, for in such a case the resurrection would be otiose and pointless: without memory and consciousness of continuity we shall know no reason to give glory to God. Such a theory as this should involve the resurrection not only of other flesh, but of another soul: which is patently ridiculous.

This is a continuation of the argument of the preceding chapter. A similar theme has been treated in § 15, of the injustice of the soul alone being rewarded or punished for the conduct in which the flesh has been its partner. The last sentence of the present chapter is evidently heavily ironical.

7 Marcionem pro Valentino resuscitari is the only instance in this work of those conversational asides which belong more properly to a speech than to a treatise: the clause could be removed without doing any damage either to the argument or to the syntax. Grammatically the four words will either go with what precedes, under the same mark of interrogation: or they can be treated as an exclamation, feigning shocked amazement. There had in truth been no suggestion that one man would be substituted for another, but that in place of the body that had decayed another would be substituted, composed of supposedly better materials. Of this Tertullian was well aware.

7 quando neque mentem, etc. *Quando* marks this as a dependent clause. It can hardly be dependent on what precedes, or on the two sentences *si non meminerim* and *cur autem solius* which immediately follow, the connection of thought in either case being too remote. It seems then that from *si non meminerim* to *praefuit carni* must be treated as a double parenthesis, commenting on and expanding the *quando* clause, and that the apodosis to that clause begins at *quale est ut eadem anima*. *Mutatorium*, as a substantive, occurs at Lat. vg. Isa. 3. 22 (where English R.V. has 'festival robes') and at Zech. 3. 4 (R.V. 'rich apparel'): and this is perhaps the meaning here, but also with a reference to the text *et nos immutabimur*. *Scilicet* marks this ablative clause as a consequence of the affirmation of what is denied in the previous clause: 'since in that case', etc.

11 **meminerim** seems to be a future perfect, for *meminero*: for which cf. §16, *et huic quoque argumentationi satisfecerim*, and §29 *ad fin.* (where see note). *Excipitur*: Lewis and Short, s.v. *excipere* I. B. 2. b give two examples, both post-Augustan, of the meaning 'expressly mention': this I have taken to be the meaning here.

CHAPTER LVII

The fear that if the same flesh is raised again it will again be subject to its old diseases and mutilations, is quite groundless. We must assume that God will restore the body in its integrity, to its true nature, not to its accidental defects. He is competent to do this, and in Christ has both promised and performed it: the apostle also means this when he says the dead will be raised incorruptible. There will therefore be no recurrence hereafter of old disabilities, for the grace of God is stronger than natural law. A slave manumitted has no further fear of servile treatment from his former owner: even so will our condition, though not our nature, be so changed by God's act that there can be no fear of its relapsing.

This theme has already had a passing mention in §4, in connection with the heretical supposition that the flesh as such is unworthy of redintegration: *rursus ulcera et vulnera et febris et podagra et mors redoptanda?* There the heretics are said to begin their attack at a point at which they have some common opinion on their side, *de communione favorabili sensuum*: here *vulgaris incredulitas* is the lack of faith, not of heretics but of the general more or less Christian public. The difficulty continued to be felt, as is shown by the care St Augustine takes (*Enchiridion* 84–90) to answer questions of this nature: it has not yet ceased to cause trouble.

This chapter begins the last section of the work, in which Tertullian resolves a few additional difficulties.

1 argutia in the singular is very uncommon: it probably ought to mean 'stridency', though evidently here it does not.

3 itaque et caeci, etc. There is an anacoluthon after *paralytici, erunt* being understood: the rest of the sentence generalizes what has begun as an enumeration of particular cases.

16 naturae non iniuriae reddimur. *Iniuria* in later Latin can apparently mean damage or injury, in which no question of injustice arises: so probably Suetonius, *D. Aug.* 14, *qui desiderabatur repente comparuit incolumis et sine iniuria*. *Natura*, here, and again in this chapter, means (as usual) the totality of those attributes which are essential, and without any one of which the object would not be itself: see my note on *De Carne Christi*, pp. xxxv *sqq*. It follows that *vitiatio accidens res est*. In spite of the mention of *gratia* twice in this chapter, it would be a mistake to suppose a distinction, in the Pauline or Augustinian sense, between nature and grace: *gratia* perhaps means a free gift of divine bounty, and by this gift, it appears, nature is not superseded but brought back into being. God has indeed, if he should so wish, the power even to change nature: actually what he will do is to restore the nature of human flesh, while changing its *condicio*, those secondary attributes which now leave it open to disease and injury. Tertullian does however make an opposition between law and grace, again taking his terminology from St Paul, but not in a strictly Pauline sense: *legem adversus gratiam impie adseris*: where 'law' means neither the Law of Moses nor quite what are now called the laws of nature, but 'what you regard as the law regarding nature and its possibilities', to the exclusion of what God can do with it by an act of his own beneficence, his *potestas* and his *liberalitas*: so also § 58, *ut et deum potentiorem credamus omni corporum lege*.

25 in Christo spopondit, apparently by the apostolic saying, 'Even so in Christ shall all be made alive': *et ostendit*, by Christ's own resurrection and in those whom he raised from the dead. In the following clause probably we should continue to read (with

NOTES AND COMMENTARY 333

the MSS.) *resuscitatorem* and *redintegratorem* (removing the comma after *ostendit*): the former with reference to people raised from the dead, the latter to persons healed of leprosy, palsy, and other diseases.

35 omnis substantiae integritatem: 1 Thess. 5. 23, spirit, soul, and body, quoted above, §47.

37 admittere should be retained: the occurrence of *amiserat* later in the sentence was no reason for reading *amittere* here (Rigaltius first made the change). If we can say *facinus admittere* for committing a crime, no doubt we could have said *vitium admittere* for contracting a fault or injury, and *nihil admittere* for 'contract no fault' or 'receive no injury'.

44 stulta mundi, etc. 1 Cor. 1. 27 is often quoted by Tertullian (e.g. *De Bapt.* 2: *De Carne Christi* 4): apparently he wrote *sapientia* for the Greek τοὺς σοφούς: the MSS. vary between *sapientia* and *sapientiam* and (very rarely) *sapientes*.

52 eatenus passibilis, etc. The flesh in Tertullian's view will need to remain passible (as the soul also is) to the extent of being (in the case of some) capable of chastisement, and yet impassible in the sense of no longer being subject to natural corruption: moreover, in the case of all, it must remain passible in the sense of being capable of sensation, for this is part of that *natura* without which it could have no experience of the joys of the life to come, of which it is to partake along with the soul.

CHAPTER LVIII

The everlasting joy, with the removal of sorrow and the wiping away of tears, which is promised after the resurrection, postulates the absence of all corruption, as well as immunity against injury and temptation. The conservation of even the garments of the Israelites in the wilderness, and of the barbarian clothing of the three holy children in the Babylonian furnace: the preservation of Jonah in the sea-monster's belly, and the present integrity of Enoch and Elijah who did not die: all these are, to use the apostle's words, examples to prove to us that God is more powerful than natural law, and will be able to conserve what he will have restored.

1 iocunditas, etc. Isa. 35. 10 LXX: *aufugit*, ἀπέδρα, where the Hebrew requires *aufugiet*: *et maeror*, καὶ λύπη, is not in the Hebrew, and is queried in one of Swete's MSS. of LXX.

7 et mors hactenus: Apoc. 21. 4, καὶ ὁ θάνατος οὐκ ἔσται ἔτι. *Hactenus*, equivalent to *haud diutius*, is a favourite expression of Tertullian: its presence here suggests that he is making his own translation from the Greek. Cf. above, §6, *hactenus terra ex quo aurum*, 'it ceases to be earth as soon as it becomes gold': *De Praesc. Haer.* 11, *vidua a iudice...ubi audita est hactenus institit*, 'ceased to press him': *De Pall.* 2, *hactenus Sodoma*: *Adv. Marc.* 1. 24, *carens denique anima caro hactenus peccat*. See also §§47 and 60.

14 ubi necessitas, etc. The Index to Ritter and Preller, s.vv. ἀνάγκη, τύχη, εἱμαρμένη, directs to a number of extracts which illustrate the development of this theme by the philosophers, the most interesting being these: 463 a. Epicurus rejected the physicists' theory of fate or necessity, κρεῖττον ἦν τῷ περὶ θεῶν μύθῳ κατακολουθεῖν ἢ τῇ τῶν φυσικῶν εἱμαρμένῃ δουλεύειν· ὁ μὲν γὰρ ἐλπίδα παραιτήσεως ὑπογράφει θεῶν διὰ τιμῆς, ἡ δὲ ἀπαραίτητον ἔχει τὴν ἀνάγκην: 512, Cicero, *De Fato* 41, describes the attempt of Chrysippus, by distinguishing different kinds of causes, to reconcile necessity and liberty: 544 a, Cicero, *De Fato* 31, Carneades repudiates the idea of fate, because it suppresses human liberty and responsibility. On this subject as it affected the common mind at about this period there is an interesting discussion in Dr Gilbert Murray's *Five Stages of Greek Religion*, ch. IV, *The Failure of Nerve*: to which could be added the lyric fragment beginning τύχα μερόπων ἀρχὰ καὶ τέλος (Bergk–Hiller, *Anthol. Lyr., melica adesp.* 79).

19 unguium et capillorum, etc. *Crementa* is apparently correct: cf. *De Anima* 51, *Democritus crementa unguium et comarum in sepulchris aliquanti temporis denotat*: so read with *MXP*, but omit *et* with *T*: unless perhaps Tertullian wrote *excrementa*.

22 quanquam Iudaeis aliena: a similar contempt for these garments is expressed *De Pall.* 4, Alexander the Great *triumphalem cataphractam amolitus in captiva sarabara decessit* (where Salmasius rightly observes that *sarabara* is neuter plural, and that *decessit* does not mean 'died'). The clothing of the three children is again referred to at *De Orat.* 15. See also Novatian, *De Trin.* 8, *cuius etiam cura et providentia Iraelitarum non sivit nec vestes consumi nec vilissima in pedibus calciamenta deteri, sed nec ipsorum postremum adulescentium captiva sarabara comburi.*

28 immunitatem carnis ediscunt: the verb could mean 'are acquiring', but more probably means 'now experience'. But cf. *Adv. Prax.* 16, *ita semper ediscebat et deus in terris cum hominibus conversari,* referring to the theophanies, as also *De Carne Christi* 6, *qui iam tunc et adloqui et liberare et iudicare humanum genus ediscebat in carnis habitu non natae adhuc quia non moriturae,* and *Adv. Marc.* III. 9, *carnis...discentis iam inter homines conversari:* so perhaps here 'are becoming accustomed to'.

32 The **et** before **conservatorem** (omitted by *T*) perhaps indicates that we ought to read *redintegratorem et conservatorem.*

CHAPTER LIX

It is no good argument against us to say that the world to come is of a different, an eternal, dispensation: for that dispensation too was made for man, as the apostle says, 'All things are yours'. And though Isaiah says that all flesh is grass, he also says that all flesh will see the salvation of God: for the judgement of God will condemn some and save others, though the flesh of both is the same. So again Isaiah says in one place that the nations are dust and spittle, and in another that they will trust in the name of the Lord: but the nations to which Christ has appeared are all within our ocean and under our sky, and there is no difference of nature between those which believe and those which do not. Likewise any distinction between one flesh and another is not of substance or material, but of reward.

5 sive mundus, etc. I Cor. 3. 22, where the Greek has εἴτε ἐνεστῶτα εἴτε μέλλοντα. Tertullian is quoting from memory, as in the following references to Isaiah. *Omnis caro foenum,* Isa. 40. 6:

et alibi, by a slip of memory, for *videbit omnis caro* is from Isa. 40. 5, *salutare dei* being an inexact recollection of the beginning of that verse, 'The glory of the Lord shall be revealed', and of Isa. 52. 10, 'All the ends of the earth shall see the salvation of our God'. Probably here read *salutare dei*, with *MPX*, and below (line 11) *salutare domini* and again (line 15) *domini salutare*, also with *MPX*: for it seems that Tertullian first quotes what he thinks is the scriptural text, and on further reference twice interprets it as referring to our Lord. So there was no need for Pamelius to read *dei* all three times: 'cave ne corrigas ipsum scriptorem'. The references below (line 17) to the Name and the arm of the Lord are an inexact recollection of Isa. 51. 5 and 52. 10.

20 intra oceanum, etc. Perhaps Tertullian had in mind the suggestion made in Plato's *Timaeus* that there are on the earth's widespread surface numerous other low-lying places like our world within the Ocean, inhabited perhaps by nations unlike ours, and with which, by virtue of the high country between, we can never have contact. Tertullian would probably deny this, but would add that in any case these nations have no bearing on the question before us.

CHAPTER LX

Another quibble arises from the question of what use the several parts of the body will be in a life in which there is to be no eating and drinking, no procreation, and so forth. We answer that though not needed for these purposes, they are required so that the whole man may stand before the judgement of God. We have seen a ship restored in all its parts, though not again intended for use: and there is nothing to prevent God from reconstituting the whole human body, even if not for use. For all that, in God's presence it will be for use, as we shall proceed to show.

16 praestruximus, i.e. §§ 55 *sqq*.

24 detinentur is Löfstedt's correction, which it now appears was in the first hand of *M*: *retinentur* means the same thing, and is in more common use.

NOTES AND COMMENTARY 337

26 etenim is my conjecture: it is difficult to account for the presence of *enim* unless it has some right to be there, and *et* could have been lost after *licet*: *etenim* for *siquidem* is not impossible, and some such word is required to mark the importance of the relative clause.

37 an deus, followed later by *an eandem*, must be retained: Tertullian is, for the sake of argument, still treating two of three questions as open: it is agreed that God has designed man for salvation: we are still discussing, secondly, whether he has included the flesh in that design, and thirdly, whether it is his will that it should be the same flesh.

CHAPTER LXI

The mouth was made for speaking and for praising God, as well as for eating and drinking: the teeth are for an ornament of the mouth and a help to speech, as well as for chewing. So also of other parts of the body. In the life to come the lower functions will cease, even as now they are by some people sparingly used or totally unused. If this is possible during this present life, it will be the more easily possible in the life to come, especially if we have during this life trained ourselves for that other.

Heretical disparagement of the physical functions of the flesh has already been mentioned at §4, which recapitulates what has been said at *De Carne Christi* 4.

4 Adam gave names to all cattle, Gen. 2. 19: Tertullian regards this as a form of prophecy, not in the sense of foretelling the future, but of speaking words of which God expressed approval: 'for that was the name thereof'.

11 potuum defluxus is my own suggestion: *MPX* have *defluxura*, which (if it is meant for a neuter plural substantive) is impossible, and Kroymann's amendment to *defluxurae* would have to be accepted: *T* has had trouble at this point. *Potuum defruta*, the usual reading, is from Gelenius, and is perhaps possible, though very improbable, for *defrutum* is wort or must boiled down to the required consistency. *Defluxus* (in the singular) occurs at Appuleius, *De Deo Socratis* 11, of the clouds flowing back to earth as rain: perhaps it is in place here, in the plural.

14 quatenus is for *quandoquidem*, as always in Horace, e.g. *Serm.* I. I. 64 *iubeas miserum esse, libenter | quatenus id facit*, 'since he is willingly doing that already'.

CHAPTER LXII

The word of our Lord shall conclude the matter. He says redeemed men will be as the angels. Angels have on occasion appeared in the outward form of men, yet without ceasing to be angels: it is equally possible for men to acquire the likeness of angels without ceasing to be men, retaining their human substance yet relieved of some of the concomitants of that substance. But observe that our Lord said not 'They shall be angels' but 'They shall be as the angels', being careful not to deny the continuance of manhood.

On the text Matt. 22. 30 see on § 36, where there are references to *De Anima* 26 and *De Monogamia* 7. The angelic visitation of Gen. 18 and 19 is fully discussed *Adv. Marc.* III. 9 and *De Carne Christi* 3, but with nothing that specially bears on the present passage.

CHAPTER LXIII

The flesh, we conclude, will rise again in its integrity. Meanwhile it lies on deposit with Jesus Christ, the intermediary of God and men, who has made in himself an alliance of flesh and Spirit, as of bride with bridegroom. Even if the soul were the bride, the flesh would go with it as its dowry. But in truth it is the flesh which is the bride, while the Spirit is the bridegroom, a bridegroom of blood. The flesh, with the soul, is for a while in retirement: it will in due course be brought out of retirement, this time to be called truly Adam, as knowing the evil it has escaped and the good it has entered into. The soul ought not to hate the flesh, but to desire its resurrection, as it would do if it were not led astray by heretical fables.

Since there are in Scripture certain ambiguities which minister to heretical perversity, God has in these latter days sent forth the Paraclete to resolve all doubts and expound all parables. Any who drink of this fountain will suffer no thirst.

2 in deposito est, etc. For this, and Tertullian's use of 1 Tim. 2. 5, see above on §51. *Spiritus* is regularly used by Tertullian for Christ's divine substance: for this see *Adv. Prax.* 26 and my Introduction, pp. 63 *sqq*.

9 ut collactanea: presumably the serving-maid, who went with the Roman bride as part of her dowry, was often enough of the bride's own age and herself the daughter of the bride's own wet-nurse: this would create an almost natural bond of affection between them.

11 sponsum per sanguinem: a reminiscence of Exod. 4. 25, *Tulit illico Sephora acutissimam petram et circumcidit praeputium filii sui: tetigitque pedes eius* [sc. *Moysis*] *et ait, Sponsus sanguinum tu mihi es*: but of course with reference to the Blood of redemption. By *secessum scias esse* possibly a reference is intended to the bride's few days' seclusion before marriage.

20 in deo nascitur, that is, in baptism: cf. §8.

24 ipsum sermonem dei, αὐτὸν τὸν λόγον τοῦ θεοῦ: *sermo* was in regular use by African Latin Christians as a translation of λόγος in John 1. 1–14: Tertullian would for some purposes have preferred *ratio*: see *Adv. Prax.* 5 *sqq*.

26 atenim deus omnipotens, etc. This paragraph, and one sentence concerning Prisca in §11, are the only explicit references to Montanism in this work. Both of them could have been added after the work was complete: and neither makes any notable addition to the argument. Tertullian often claims that the Montanist revelations give help in the interpretation of the Scriptures: but neither here nor elsewhere does it seem that they have contributed anything that could not either have been derived from previous non-Montanist Christian teachers, or thought out for himself by any instructed Christian of good intelligence and reverent mind.

The Montanist claim in fact was seriously overdrawn, and it is surprising that so great a man as Tertullian was taken in by it.

32 haereses esse oportuerat: 1 Cor. 11. 19 is first quoted *De Praesc. Haer.* 4 and 30, and several times in later works, usually with some such comment as, *non tamen ideo bonum haereses quia esse eas oportebat,* with examples of other things which 'had to be', and yet are evil, but which brought the good to light.

44 refrigeraberis: Leopold's correction of the MS. reading *refrigerabis* must probably be accepted, there being no evidence elsewhere of the intransitive use of this verb.

INDEX OF SCRIPTURAL REFERENCES

According to chapter and sentence of the Latin text. The upright figures indicate direct quotations, the italic figures bare references or allusions

Genesis		1 Kings	
1. 26	5. 6; 6. 4	19. 8	*61. 5*
1. 27	5. 6; 6. 4		
1. 28	*45. 4*	2 Kings	
2. 7	5. 8; 7. 3; *40. 3*	2. 11	*58. 9*
2. 8	5. 8		
2. 23	7. 2	Psalms	
3. 19	6. 7; 18. 6; 26. 2; *52. 17*	2. 1, 2	20. 4
		22. 7	*20. 5*
3. 21	*7. 2*	22. 16, 18	*20. 5*
3. 22	63. 4	49. 20	*52. 12*
4. 11	*26. 2*	69. 21	20. 5
5. 24	*58. 9*	92. 12	*13. 3*
6. 3	10. 2	96. 1	*56. 4*
9. 5	28. 3; *32. 2; 39. 5*	97. 1	26. 4
18. 4–8	62. 2	97. 4, 5	26. 5
23. 4	18. 12	107. 16	*44. 7*
31. 3	*26. 14*	110. 1	*22. 9*
48. 21	*26. 14*		
		Isaiah	
Exodus		1. 19	26. 7
3. 5	*26. 11*	2. 19	*22. 9*
3. 17	*26. 11*	3. 14	*20. 3*
4. 2–9	28. 1	6. 9	*33. 2*
4. 6, 7	28. 1; *55. 8*	7. 14	*20. 3*
4. 25	63. 3	8. 4	*20. 3*
24. 18	*61. 5*	13. 13	22. 2
		23. 1	*20. 8*
		25. 8	*47. 13; 54. 5*
Deuteronomy		26. 19	31. 6
8. 3	26. 9; *61. 5*	26. 20	*27. 4, 6*
8. 4	*58. 6*	29. 5	*59. 5*
29. 5	*58. 6*	35. 5, 6	*20. 6*
32. 39	9. 4; *28. 5*	35. 10	58. 1
		40. 5, 6	10. 2; *59. 2*
1 Samuel		40. 15, 17	*59. 5*
2. 6	*28. 5*	44. 20	*3. 3*
10. 6	*55. 11*		

Isaiah (cont.)

51. 5	59. 5	5. 28	15. 4
51. 9	26. 12	5. 45	26. 8
52. 10	59. 5	8. 12	35. 12
53. 6, 7	20. 5	9. 4	15. 4
53. 12	20. 5	9. 17	44. 3
58. 8	27. 3	10. 7	33. 7
66. 14	31. 4	10. 28	35. 1
66. 22	*31. 7; 31. 8*	10. 29–31	35. 9, 10
66. 23	31. 7	10. 31	*13. 4*
66. 24	31. 9	11. 24	33. 7
		12. 13	33. 2
		13. 10	33. 2
Ezekiel		13. 13	*33. 3*
18. 23	9. 4	13. 18–23	33. 5
34. 16	47. 14	13. 34	33. 1
37. 1–14	29; 30; 31	17. 2–8	55. 10
		19. 12	27. 1
Daniel		19. 17	9. 3
3. 27	*58. 7*	19. 26	57. 11
7. 13	*22. 5*	22. 13	*27. 2; 35. 12*
		22. 23–33	*2. 1; 36. 1*
Hosea		22. 30	62. 1
9. 7	*22. 2*	22. 32	*36. 4*
		22. 37	*9. 3*
Joel		23. 27	19. 4
2. 28	*10. 2; 63. 7*	23. 37	*26. 13*
		25. 30	*35. 12*
Jonah		25. 46	35. 6
2. 1	*32. 14; 58. 8*	26. 38	*18. 7*
2. 11	*32. 14*	27. 9	20. 5
Zephaniah		Mark	
2. 1	*22. 2*	2. 22	44. 3
		12. 18–23	*36. 1*
Zechariah		16. 19	*51. 1*
11. 12	*20. 5*		
12. 10	*22. 10; 26. 5; 51. 1*	Luke	
12. 12	*22. 10*	4. 4	26. 9; 61. 5
		5. 31	9. 4
Malachi		5. 37	44. 3
4. 2	31. 4	12. 59	42. 3
4. 5	*22. 10*	13. 6–9	*33. 5*
		13. 34	26. 13
Matthew		14. 14	33. 7
1. 23	*20. 3*	15. 4–6	*34. 2*
4. 4	*26. 9; 61. 5*	18. 1–5	*33. 5*
5. 10	41. 2	18. 9	33. 4
5. 26	*42. 3*	18. 19	*9. 3*

INDEX OF SCRIPTURAL REFERENCES

Luke (cont.)
19. 10   9. 4; *34. 1*
19. 37   *26. 5*
20. 27–38   *36. 1*
20. 36   *36. 4, 5*
20. 37   *36. 3*
21. 9–24   *22. 3*
21. 25–8   *22. 4–6*
21. 29–31   *22. 7*
21. 36   *22. 8*
24. 26   *39. 2*

John
1. 3   *5. 6*
2. 19   *18. 6*
2. 21   *18. 7*
5. 24   *37. 2, 5*
5. 25   *37. 6*
5. 28, 29   *37. 8*
6. 38, 39   *34. 9*
6. 39   *35. 11*
6. 40   *34. 11*
6. 51   *26. 10; 37. 4*
6. 53   *37. 1*
6. 63   *37. 1, 2, 5; 50. 4*
11. 1–18   *53. 3, 4*
14. 2   *41. 3*
15. 1   *26. 10*
19. 37   *26. 5; 51. 1*
20. 29   *34. 12*

Acts
1. 7   *22. 2*
1. 11   *22. 9; 51. 1*
3. 19–21   *23. 12*
7. 59, 60   *55. 9*
9. 15   *23. 8*
17. 32   *39. 7*
23. 1–9   *39. 3*
23. 6   *39. 3*
26. 22   *39. 4, 5*

Romans
1. 25
2. 28, 29   *26. 9*
5. 20   *26. 11*
5. 21   *34. 3; 47. 14*
6. 3, 4   *47. 12*
    47. 10

6. 5   *47. 11*
6. 6   *47. 1* (ter)
6. 8   *47. 1*
6. 11   *47. 2*
6. 12, 13   *47. 3*
6. 19–23   *47. 4–7*
7. 17   *46. 11, 14*
7. 18   *10. 3*
7. 23   *46. 10; 51. 6*
8. 2   *46. 10*
8. 3   *16. 13; 46. 11*
8. 6, 7   *46. 12*
8. 8   *10. 3; 46. 2*
8. 9   *46. 2*
8. 10   *46. 4*
8. 11   *46. 6*
8. 12, 13   *46. 8*
8. 17, 18   *40. 11*
9. 20   *7. 5*
12. 1   *47. 16*
13. 14   *3. 4*

1 Corinthians
1. 20   *3. 3*
1. 27   *57. 11*
2. 9   *26. 7*
3. 16   *44. 4*
3. 16, 17   *10. 4*
3. 19   *3. 3*
3. 22   *59. 2*
6. 15   *10. 4*
6. 20   *10. 4; 16. 14*
7. 31   *5. 5; 26. 13*
10. 11   *58. 10*
11. 19   *40. 1; 63. 8*
12. 23   *9. 4*
15. 1–9   *48. 2*
15. 3, 4   *48. 7*
15. 12–18   *48. 3–5*
15. 19   *24. 7*
15. 21   *48. 8*
15. 22   *48. 9*
15. 23   *48. 10*
15. 26   *51. 7*
15. 29   *48. 11*
15. 30–2   *48. 12*
15. 32   *49. 13*
15. 35   *48. 14*

1 Corinthians (cont.)

		Galatians	
15. 35, 36	52. 1	1. 16	50. 7
15. 37	52. 3	3. 27	3. 4
15. 37, 38	52. 5; 52. 9	5. 5	23. 6; 53. 18
15. 39	52. 11	5. 19	45. 6
15. 40, 41	49. 5; 52. 12, 13	5. 21	49. 12
15. 42–4	52. 16	6. 9	23. 10
15. 44	53. 17	6. 17	10. 4
15. 45	49. 2; 51. 1; 52. 18; 53. 5; 53. 12	Ephesians	
		3. 16, 17	40. 4, 5
15. 46	53. 13, 16	4. 22	19. 3; 37. 9; 45. 6; 49. 7
15. 47	49. 2		
15. 48	49. 4	4. 22–4	45. 1
15. 49	49. 6	4. 24	49. 7
15. 50	48. 1; 49. 9; 50. 4; 51. 4, 7	4. 25–32	45. 7–13
		6. 12	22. 11
15. 51, 52	42. 1; 51. 8	6. 13–17	3. 4
15. 52	57. 8		
15. 53	42. 2; 50. 5, 6; 51. 8; 54. 2, 4; 57. 9	Philippians	
		2. 6	6. 4
15. 54–6	51. 6	3. 11, 12	23. 8
15. 55	47. 13; 54. 5	3. 12–14	23. 8, 9
		3. 20, 21	47. 15
2 Corinthians		3. 21	55. 11
1. 8	48. 12		
3. 7	55. 8	Colossians	
4. 6	44. 2	1. 21	23. 1
4. 7	7. 5; 44. 2	2. 11	7. 6
4. 10	44. 4	2. 12	23. 1
4. 11	44. 4, 9	2. 13	23. 2
4. 14	44. 10	2. 20	23. 2; 46. 15
4. 16	40. 2; 44. 1	3. 1, 2	23. 4
4. 17, 18	40. 6	3. 3	23. 5
5. 1	41. 1	3. 9	19. 3; 37. 9
5. 2, 3	41. 5		
5. 3	42. 12	1 Thessalonians	
5. 4	42. 2, 5, 9; 54. 1	1. 9, 10	24. 1
5. 5	51. 2; 53. 18	2. 19	24. 2
5. 6, 7	43. 1	3. 13	24. 2
5. 8	43. 3	4. 4	16. 11
5. 9, 10	43. 6	4. 8	16. 11
5. 10	59. 7	4. 13–18	57. 9
7. 5	40. 12	4. 14–17	24. 4–6
10. 3	49. 11	4. 15–17	41. 7
11. 14	55. 12	5. 1–3	24. 9, 10
12. 9	9. 4; 47. 14	5. 23	47. 17, 18; 57. 9

2 Thessalonians
2. 1–7	24. 12–18
2. 8–10	24. 19, 20

1 Timothy
1. 19	24. 8
2. 5	51. 2; 63. 1
2. 7	23. 8
6. 14, 15	23. 11

2 Timothy
1. 15	24. 8
1. 18	23. 10

1 John
2. 8	59. 6
3. 2	23. 6

Revelation
1. 18	47. 18
2. 7	35. 13
3. 4	27. 1
3. 5	27. 2
5. 9	56. 4
6. 9–11	25. 1
6. 9	38. 4
7. 17	58. 2
12. 6	22. 10
14. 4	27. 1
15. 7	25. 1
16. 1	25. 1
17. 12–14	24. 18; 25. 1
18. 9	22. 10
19. 19, 20	25. 1
20. 2–4	25. 2
20. 9	25. 2
20. 10	58. 5
20. 12	25. 2
21. 4	58. 3

INDEX VERBORUM LATINORUM

Siquae vel ipsa inusitatiora sunt vel paullo inusitatiore sensu usurpantur

abhinc iam 42. 4
abrupte 51. 1
absentiae 12. 3
absolute 46. 6
absolutus 33. 8
absolvere 46. 12
accidens res 57. 4
acerbe 22. 9
actus (*subst.*) 10. 3
adaequare 5. 6; 19. 4
addiscere 9. 3
additicius 52. 6
adfectio 6. 3
adfectus 60. 8
adfingere 30. 6
adflatus 7. 4
adhuc 5. 8
adhuc proxime 1. 5
adlegere 22. 4
adparere 7. 9; 16. 3
adplaudere 11. 9
adulari 8. 4
adversari 46. 9
aemulus 3. 6
aenigma 19. 1; 32. 8
aestuare 4. 5
agitare 27. 6
agnitio 22. 8; 25. 3
aliqui 2. 12; 3. 2
aliter 2. 3; 39. 2, 8; 52. 10
allegoria 28. 5; 37. 4
allegorice 27. 4; 31. 1
allegoricus 19. 2; 20. 9; 26. 1 *et al.*
allegorizare 27. 1; 30. 2
alligare 8. 2 (*v.l.*)
alterutrum 45. 6, 13
ambiguitas 63. 7
angeli 5. 2; 32. 4 *et al.*
angelicus 36. 5; 42. 4
angelificare 26. 7

animalis 20. 7; 22. 1; 33. 10; 53. 7 *et al.*
animare 53. 8
ante (= antea) 12. 8 (*v.l.*); 47. 13
antecursor 22. 8
anticipare 45. 3
antistare 13. 4; 35. 9; 61. 1
apostolicus 39. 1 *et al.*
apponere 52. 14
apud deum 2. 1
arbitrium 60. 7
arcanum 19. 6; 24. 18; 35. 4; 63. 6
archigallus 16. 6
argilla 7. 4 *sq.*
argumentari 37. 9; 44. 8; 60. 1
argumentatio 16. 1, 9; 30. 1
argumentum 3. 5; 29. 1; 32. 7
argutia 57. 1
arrabo 51. 2; 53. 18
artifex 6. 5
artius dicam 18. 9
auctor 14. 6; 48. 8
auctoritas 18. 2
aura 7. 8

Babylonius 58. 7
baptisma 47. 9 *sqq.*; 48. 11
bene quod 5. 4
boni ducere 43. 3 (*v.l.*)
brachium domini 59. 5

caedere 55. 1
calculus 45. 4
capacitas 16. 12
caput (= origo) 53. 11
cardo 8. 2; 49. 1 (*v.l.*)
carere 2. 12; 28. 5
carnaliter 11. 1; 46. 3
carnes (*pl.*) 11. 2
castigatio 9. 1

INDEX VERBORUM LATINORUM 347

causa 2. 8; 13. 3; 14. 3 sqq.; 15. 2; 36. 1; 46. 9
cavillare (act.) 21. 6
cellae promae 27. 4, 5
cellarium 27. 6
censura 15. 8; 25. 2
census (subst.) 6. 8
cessare (= desinere) 58. 3
choicus 49. 2 sqq.
circumcisio 7. 6
circumferre 7. 9
circumstantiae 30. 9
citius est 45. 5
citra 39. 4; 48. 12
claritas 27. 2
clausula 25. 5; 30. 10; 43. 9
clavis 47. 18
coaetare 45. 5
cogitatorium 15. 5
collactaneus 63. 2
collegium 15. 3; 40. 14; 49. 6
collocare 37. 6
commentari 32. 5
commentarius 45. 4
commentator 33. 5
committere 60. 4
communes sensus 3. 1, 2, 6; 5. 1
communicare 15. 8; 16. 2, 9; 18. 10
communio 16. 12; 46. 7; 52. 11; 54. 1, 3
communio sensuum 4. 1
comparare 63. 1
comparari 5. 6
comparere 42. 7
compassio 3. 6; 40. 12, 13
compati 40. 12
compendium 41. 6
compensare 17. 8
compensatio 41. 2; 47. 8
competere 6. 5; 30. 5; 47. 9
compungere 10. 3
conari (= niti) 52. 12
concilium prophetarum 22. 5
concipere 52. 18
conclusio 22. 5
concretio 7. 9
concupiscentia 45. 1, 16
concurrere 41. 6
concussio 2. 9; 22. 2

concutere 2. 11; 30. 1; 39. 8
condicio 2. 5; 5. 1, 7; 8. 1; 25. 5; 38. 6; 62. 1 et al.
condimentum 27. 5
condire 32. 3
conditio 11. 5; 13. 1; 26. 8, 9
conditorium 44. 2
confercire 53. 19
configurare 30. 5
conflictatio 8. 4; 22. 2; 31. 3; 48. 13
conformalis 47. 15
congregatio 14. 11
congressio 61. 6
congressus (subst.) 4. 7; 55. 1
congruenter 2. 6
congruentia 7. 8
congruentissimus 14. 8
coniectare 33. 5
coniectura 20. 1
coniunctio 49. 9
conmortuus 47. 1
conresuscitare 23. 1
conscientia 3. 2; 19. 6; 56. 3
consecratio 16. 8
consecutio 52. 14
consepelire 23. 1
consequentiae 4. 5
conserere 47. 11
consignare 22. 3; 39. 1
consistorium 26. 3
consors 2. 4
consortium 5. 9; 40. 14; 49. 6
constabilire 2. 11
constantia 30. 9
constare 5. 6; 6. 2
constitutum 22. 9
contemplatio 23. 7
contemporare 45. 5
contendere 31. 5
contentio 47. 13; 54. 5
contentioso fune deducere 34. 7
contextus (subst.) 15. 1
continuare 42. 3
e contrario 1. 5
convenire 18. 4
conversatio 45. 6; 49. 9
convulnerare 51. 1
coronare 61. 2

corporalitas 33. 9, 10
corporaliter 23. 3
corpulentia 17. 3; 45. 16; 55. 7; 60. 1
corpus 2. 14
corpusculum 5. 2
corruptela 51. 5 sqq.
crates (pl.) 42. 7
credens (subst.) 1. 1
cremare 1. 3
crementum 58. 6
criminosus 4. 2
cuneus 2. 11
cura 9. 2

daemonicus 58. 5
decisus 18. 4
declinari (pass.) 2. 10
decoquere 12. 5
decurrere 38. 3 (v.l.); 56. 5
defectio 2. 13
defendere 45. 1, 15; 57. 11
definitio 33. 6; 41. 2
defluxura 61. 3
deformare 30. 1
defruta 61. 3 (v.l.)
defunctus 1. 2
dehaustus (ptc.) 11. 9
delibatio 7. 2
deliniare 20. 1
delinquentia 15. 7; 46. 4, 10; 47. 1 sqq.; 51. 6
delinquere 34. 2
demandatio 48. 2
demutatio 2. 9; 6. 8; 36. 5; 41. 6; 42. 1; 55. 2 sqq.
demutator 32. 7
depositum 51. 2; 63. 1
depretiare 2. 9
deputare 16. 5
desperatio 31. 1
despoliatio 7. 6
destinare 32. 5 sq.; 47. 18; 60. 4
destinatio 14. 8
destructio 36. 1
determinare 29. 1; 37. 1; 46. 4
detersus 18. 4
detexere 43. 9
detinere 60. 5 (v.l.)

devorare 7. 3; 54. 1 sqq.
devoratio 54. 1
dictare 6. 3
differentia 5. 7; 25. 5; 45. 15
digerere 2. 11
dignitas 49. 5 sq.
diicere 48. 1
dilutior 7. 1
directo 50. 2
dirigere 28. 4
disceptatio 2. 7; 62. 1
disciplina 26. 2; 44. 8; 45. 16; 48 2
dispectio 19. 1
dispersio 31. 2
disponere 2. 7
dispositio 3. 1; 35. 13; 59. 1; 62. 2 et al.
dispungere 14. 11; 56. 1
disputare 52. 1
distantia 5. 6
distinctio 12. 3; 48. 2; 53. 16
distinguere 59. 2
diversa pars 19. 1
diversitas 2. 10
diversus 53. 15; 55. 5
divertere (intrans.) 7. 12
divinitas
  altera 2. 2, 8, 9
  secunda 5. 2
  una 2. 8
divisio 41. 5
domicilium 41. 1, 4
dominicus 48. 6; 62. 1
donare 23. 2; 45. 13
boni ducere 43. 3
dure 2. 8
duriores doctrinae 5. 4
durus 37. 1

ecclesiasticus 48. 2
edictum 18. 4; 21. 1
ediscere 48. 9
edissertare 33. 5 (v.l.)
eleganter 41. 3
elidere 2. 10; 34. 3; 36. 1; 47. 14; 52. 17
eligere 6. 5; 8. 2 (v.l.); 27. 3
eliminare 49. 13
eliquare 6. 8

INDEX VERBORUM LATINORUM

elogium 4. 2
eloquium 19. 2
emolumentum 61. 7
enim 49. 9
Epicurei 2. 1
eradere 60. 1
eradicatio 27. 6
eructuare 32. 1
erumpere 22. 3; 49. 13; 52. 1, 4
esculenta 1. 2
ethnicus 3. 3, 6; 4. 7 et al.
evacuare 47. 1; 51. 7 et al.
eventus 55. 12
evocare 11. 9
exaggerare 51. 5; 60. 1
excīdere 52. 3
excludere 46. 5, 9
excudere 6. 5
excusare 6. 8
exheredare 49. 1
exhibere 14. 11; 38. 4; 42. 11; 47. 16
exhibitio 17. 9; 53. 1
exilium 8. 5; 40. 3
exitus 4. 2; 59. 2
exodium 25. 3
expeditus 18. 4
expellere 40. 10
exponere 45. 6; 49. 7
expungere 14. 8; 25. 5; 41. 6
exsequi 28. 2; 37. 2
exstruere 34. 11; 48. 6
exsuscitare 31. 5
exterminare 52. 7
extrudere 51. 1

facultas 17. 3; 30. 2
familiaritas 3. 6; 18. 12; 26. 11
famosus 13. 2
famulus (*adi.*) 5. 7
fastigium 6. 5; 55. 9
fatum 58. 5
favorabilis 4. 1
fenerare 52. 8
ferrugo 7. 8
fibula 40. 3
fidelior 3. 6
fiducia 1. 1
figmentum 5. 9; 6. 2; 30. 5; 40. 3

figulatio 5. 4
figura 19. 1; 20. 2; 58. 10
figurare 13. 1; 19. 2; 21. 1 et al.
figurate 20. 3
fingere 6. 6
florescere 7. 2; 22. 8
folliculus 52. 8
forma 5. 6; 8. 1; 19. 2; 49. 11; 50. 3; 51. 1; 59. 6 et al.
fortuna 58. 5
frictrix 16. 6
fructificare 22. 8; 42. 8 (*v.l.*); 82. 10
fructuosus 34. 12
fructus (= fruitio) 26. 4
frugescere 22. 8
frustrari 24. 8
fruticare 22. 8 (*v.l.*); 42. 8 (*v.l.*); 52. 10 (*v.l.*)
fulcimentum 61. 4
fundamentum 52. 8
funestari 12. 1
fungi (*forsan pass.*) 14. 11

gehenna 34. 5; 35. 1
generalis 50. 2
genitura 45. 4
genus 48. 14; 57. 4
gestire 43. 6
gloria 38. 7; 39. 2
gloriosus 7. 7
gradus 2. 10
grana candentia 7. 8
gratia 38. 1; 41. 6; 57. 2; 63. 7
gratiosus 56. 5
gravitas 56. 2
gustus 38. 6

habilitas 58. 6
habitaculum 19. 7
habitudo 51. 8; 55. 10
habitus 18. 8; 31. 7
hactenus 6. 8; 47. 1; 58. 3; 60. 8
haereses 2. 11
haereticus 3. 3, 6; 4. 7 et al.
ἡγεμονικόν 15. 5
hereditas 48. 1 et saepius
hodiernus 86. 3
hyperbaton 43. 7

igneus angelus 5. 2
illucescere (*trans.*) 44. 2
imaginarius 19. 2
imago 18. 9; 20. 1; 30. 5
immortalitas 50. 5 *sq.*
impingere 45. 1
implere 34. 1
imprimere 52. 18
inclarescere 20. 6
incolumitas 60. 6
inconsiderantia 51. 1
incontemplabilis 55. 8
incorruptela 51. 5
incorruptibilitas 38. 7; 50. 5 *sq.*
incriminatio 23. 9
incursio 2. 13
inducere 10. 5; 17. 8; 38. 5
infirmare 46. 11
infulcire 42. 12; 49. 13
infuscare 6. 5; 10. 1
ingenium 8. 5
ingerere 47. 3
ingestus (*subst.*) 42. 9
inhabilis 18. 1
iniuria 31. 2
inmiscere 7. 9
inquilinus 46. 14
inscribere 2. 5
inserere 7. 9
insidēre 18. 10
insignia (*subst. pl.*) 57. 1
insignis 57. 1
insinuare 2. 10
insinuatio 2. 8
ad instar 33. 5
instare 33. 5
instigare (*v.l.*) 2. 10
instinctus (*subst.*) 34. 1
instrui 3. 3, 4; 55. 11
instrumentum 33. 1; 38. 4; 39. 1, 8 *et al.*
instrumentum sensuum 7. 11
intempestive 22. 9
intentio 31. 3; 44. 8
intercedere 60. 4
interibilis 34. 5, 6
interstruere 4. 1
invadere 63. 4

invalescere 47. 13; 54. 5
invehi 7. 10
invidia 16. 7
irreformabilis 5. 5
istud 51. 9
iterum 12. 6
ius dei 60. 7
iustitia 58. 6
iustitium 12. 1

laborare 63. 7
lactes (*pl.*) 4. 3
lancinare 8. 5
laniare 8. 5
lătus 2. 11
liberalitas 9. 2; 32. 6; 57. 7
licentia 11. 3
liniamenta (*pl.*) 6. 3; 61. 5

macellum 61. 2
macerare 8. 5
machinatio 8. 5
maiestas spiritus sancti 24. 9
manifestatior 2. 8
manifestus est (*c. ptc.*) 31. 2
manūs dei 6. 1, 2
martyrium 43. 4
materia 4. 2; 6. 2, 5, 6; 7. 4; 11. 6; 14. 1; 16. 10; 37. 1; 42. 5 *et al.*
matrimonii dissimulatio 8. 4
matrix 6. 8; 63. 4
cum maxime 2. 13; 14. 1
medicare 27. 5
menstruus numerus 12. 3
ministra 7. 13
modulari 11. 9
moliri 6. 6; 11. 9
molitio 9. 2
monstruosus 13. 2
monumentum 37. 8 *sq.*
moralis 45. 15
moralitas 47. 1
mortalitas 18. 10
mortificatio 44. 4
mundialiter 46. 15
mundus (*i.e.* ornatus) 8. 5
municipatus 47. 15
munitio 57. 13

libertate mutare 57. 12
mutatorius 56. 3

natare 4. 5
nationes 59. 5
natura 14. 4; 18. 6; 57. 11
naturaliter 2. 8; 3. 1
necessarior 31. 3
necessitas 58. 5
nodose 46. 6
nomen 2. 14; 4. 2; 8. 1; 16. 5
notare 10. 2
novitas 45. 1, 15
nubilus 20. 7
nudus 20. 7

obaudire 47. 3
obducere 2. 6
obfulgere 59. 6
oblaqueare 7. 8
oblatrare 61. 4
oblique 20. 3
obliterare 7. 3
obliteratio 57. 9
obloqui 30. 8
obsoletus (*adi.*) 6. 8
obstringere 46. 12
obstruere 48. 1
obtentus 2. 8; 36. 1
obvenire 50. 2
occupare 5. 8
occurrere 45. 14
offendere 1. 3
offuscatio 43. 1
omnino 39. 7
onerare 2. 9; 10. 3 (*v.l.*)
minus digna opera 35. 12
orbis 58. 9
ordinarie 2. 8
ordinarius 2. 13
ordo 2. 7; 53. 11
organum 7. 11
origo 4. 2

parabola 31. 3; 32. 8; 33. 1 *sq.*; 63. 9
paracletus 11. 2; 63. 9
paradisus patrum 26. 14
parentare 1. 2

parēre 8. 6; 14. 11
pariare 53. 14
pariari 6. 4 (*v.l.*)
parilitas 48. 6
pariter 7. 7
partiarius 2. 2
patrocinari 38. 6
patrocinium 18. 1
pelliciae tunicae 7. 2, 6
pendēre 23. 8
penes 2. 11; 3. 1
pensare 43. 8
peraequare 34. 7
peraequatio 52. 11
percutere 19. 6
in perdito constitui 34. 4
peregrinari 43. 5
perennare 42. 8
perpetuus 44. 6
perseverantia 60. 1
persona 20. 4; 23. 12; 44. 2
perversitas 63. 7
petras (*vox nihili*) 5. 1
phantasma 2. 5
philosophari 5. 1
philosophi 11. 5
phoenix 13. 2, 3
pignus 6. 5
placibilis 43. 6
portae adamantinae 44. 7
portendere 28. 1; 39. 7; 48. 11
portio 5. 5; 16. 12
portionalis 57. 3
possessio 23. 7
posteritas 13. 2
postumare 45. 3
mundi potentes 22. 11
humanae potestates 35. 1
praeceptivus modus 49. 8
praeconium 11. 1; 19. 1
praefatio 6. 4
praeiudicare 5. 5; 18. 2; 21. 2; 25. 4; 48. 2
praeiudicium 2. 4; 18. 1, 10
praelatio 5. 6
praelibare 2. 14
praeluminare 33. 5
praeparare 2. 2

praerogativa 8. 1; 25. 2; 43. 4; 52. 11
praescribere 2. 6; 12. 7; 19. 1; 57. 3, 11
praesidere 16. 4
praestantia 43. 4
praestringere 2. 13
praestructio 18. 1; 20. 1; 49. 13
praestruere 2. 11; 4. 1; 53. 13; 60. 4
praesumere 1. 2; 18. 2; 32. 5; 34. 7
praesumptio 39. 7; 48. 11
praeterire 26. 13
praetimere 35. 6
praevertere 37. 4
pressura 40. 6; 48. 12
pridianus 42. 6
primarius 51. 1
principalis 2. 7
principalitas 15. 5
privilegium 5. 9; 41. 6
probabilis 63. 8
problema 36. 1
professor 39. 3
proinde (= perinde) 26. 1
promereri 1. 3
pronuntiatio 62. 1
prophetia nova 63. 9
prophetis 11. 2
propositio 26. 1; 30. 7; 37. 6
proprietas 2. 5; 14. 4; 18. 11; 40. 12
proscribere 18. 4
prosternere 48. 1
provocare 5. 6; 53. 1
pseudopropheta 25. 1
publicum naturae 11. 4
publicus 8. 1
non pudendum 4. 5
pusillitas 6. 1

quadriduo 53. 3
quaestio 2. 8, 11; 3. 6; 39. 2, 8
qualitas 1. 6; 2. 3, 5; 7. 3; 39. 2; 50. 5
qualiter 16. 4
quandoque 4. 3
quatenus 61. 4
querulus (c. acc.) 31. 1

ratio 3. 6; 5. 7; 12. 5; 14. 3; 21. 1; 35. 11; 43. 5; 48. 11 et al.

reaedificare 11. 3
recenseri 1. 5; 6. 7
receptorius 27. 5
recidivatus 1. 6; 18. 1; 30. 4; 53. 1
recidivus 12. 6
recogitatus 37. 5
reconsignare 52. 18
recorporare 31. 5
recorporatio 30. 4
redanimare 13. 1; 19. 4; 31. 5
redanimatio 30. 4; 38. 1
redemptor 2. 6
redhibitio 32. 2
redintegratio 47. 13
redintegrator 57. 7
redoptare 4. 6
refectio 2. 13
reformare 13. 1; 26. 7
reformatio 7. 2; 11. 7
refrigerare 63. 10
regula 52. 3
religare 25. 2
religio 9. 2; 45. 1
religiosus 30. 7; 32. 5
reliquiae 31. 5
relucere 52. 2
remeabilis 1. 5
remissio 40. 12
reportare 43. 6
repraesentare 17. 1; 63. 4
repraesentatio 14. 10; 17. 3; 23. 7
reputare 16. 5
requirere 17. 6
rescindere 12. 2; 39. 3
rescissio 57. 9
resignare 39. 1
resorbere 63. 4
respicere 23. 12
respiratio 30. 6
responsio 48. 11
restitutio 5. 5; 39. 7
restitutor 12. 8
restruere 11. 3; 31. 2
resuscitatio 46. 7
resuscitator 12. 8; 57. 7
retexere 9. 1; 53. 5
retinere 60. 5

INDEX VERBORUM LATINORUM 353

retractatu (vb. sup.) 2. 12
retro (= antea) passim
revalescere 20. 6
revincere 2. 6; 51. 1
revincibilis 63. 8
revisceratio 30. 6
revivificare 19. 4
revocare 6. 7
rhetoricari 5. 1
robustus 7. 4
ructuare 16. 6 (v.l.)
rudis 2. 11; 5. 1
rumae 4. 3

sacramentum 2. 8; 21. 3; 25. 3
sacrosanctus 22. 2
saecularis 19. 7; 34. 3
saeculum 1. 6; 3. 3
salutificator 47. 15
sancire 48. 11
sanctificium 47. 4 sqq.
sanctimonia 47. 8
sanctitas 27. 2
sapere 44. 10
sapor 40. 4
sarabara 58. 7
satis erit 31. 9
scandalizare 30. 9
schola 1. 4
scrupulus 2. 9
secessus 55. 10; 63. 3
secta 2. 1
securitas 34. 9
seductio 45. 1
semel ad summam 40. 7
senium 45. 6; 57. 8
sensus 2. 9; 3. 1, 3; 4. 1; 23. 1; 34. 9;
   42. 2, 6; 47. 8 et al.
sententia 3. 2; 17. 5; 26. 2; 33. 6; 46.
   15; 52. 17 et al.
sepultura 12. 2; 30. 9
sequester 51. 2; 63. 1
sequestrare 38. 2
sequestratorium 52. 18
serae escae 8. 4
sermo dei 5. 6; 6. 4; 37. 3; 49. 2; 51. 1;
   63. 6
servire 52. 10

signatior (adi. comp.) 13. 3
significantia 21. 1
simplex 20. 7
simplices 2. 11; 5. 1
simplicior quisque 17. 1
simplicitas 3. 6; 28. 5
simpliciter 26. 6
simulacrum 46. 11; 47. 11
singularitas 13. 2
sitire 11. 4; 28. 5
soliditas 17. 2
solidus (adi.) 2. 5; 4. 3; 36. 7
sollemnis 19. 2; 62. 3
soror 9. 2
sors 18. 11
sortiri 18. 5
spatium 23. 7; 40. 6
specialis 29. 1; 50. 2
species 11. 7; 15. 4; 20. 7; 32. 8; 36. 1;
   43. 3 et al.
speculum 52. 10
spiritalis 22. 1; 25. 4; 53. 7 et al.
spiritaliter 19. 2; 20. 7; 23. 3 et al.
spiritus 37. 3 sqq. et passim
spolium 7. 6
spurciloquium 4. 7
stabulum 37. 8; 60. 3
status 12. 6; 30. 1, 3, 4; 36. 5; 37. 1;
   46. 7; 56. 3 et al.
stigma 57. 12
stigmata Christi 10. 4
stilus 2. 13; 4. 7; 10. 3; 22. 2; 53. 4;
   63. 6
strues 35. 3
subicere 2. 12
subiectus 51. 9
subministrare 63. 8
subserica 27. 3 (v.l.)
subspargere 63. 9
substantia 2. 2, 4, 12; 6. 7; 7. 2; 8. 1;
   10. 3; 11. 7; 13. 3; 16. 10; 18. 1, 6;
   36. 3; 40. 4; 42. 12; 47. 18; 49. 3
   sqq.; 51. 1; 55. 7; 59. 1, 2 et al.
substantialis 45. 15
substantivus 40. 5
subtexere 22. 8
succensio 12. 3 (v.l.)
suffragium 8. 1

suffundere 61. 4
suggestio 12. 3 (*v.l.*)
suggestus 12. 2; 40. 7; 46. 1; 52. 10
suggillare 49. 13
suggillatio 10. 3; 15. 4
sui (= suus) 21. 5; 30. 5
summa 51. 2
superabundare 47. 15
supercaelestis 49. 5; 52. 13
superducere 7. 6; 52. 10
superficies 62. 1
superinduere 41. 5; 42. 2 *sqq.*
superindumentum 42. 5, 9
superinundare 63. 9
superstruere 7. 6; 60. 4
supparatura 61. 4
supplementum 49. 9
suspirare 22. 2
sustinere 17. 9; 25. 1; 40. 14

taxare 50. 1
temperare 2. 9; 5. 1; 57. 9
temporalitas 60. 4
temporaneus 27. 3
tenerescere 22. 8
testaceus 7. 5
testatio 12. 7
textura 34. 10
tiara 58. 7
tinguere 47. 10
titulus 2. 11; 18. 4; 19. 1; 50. 7
torquere 39. 8
tractatio 62. 2
tractatus 2. 9
tradux 7. 2
transfingere 32. 7
transgressio 26. 12; 34. 1

transitus 22. 2
turbate 43. 7

ultro 2. 10; 33. 5
unio divinitatis 2. 11
universitas 5. 5; 11. 6; 13. 1
urgentior 2. 8
usurpare 51. 3

vacare 9. 5; 16. 10, 15; 60. 3 *et al.*
vacuus 30. 5
vagina 9. 2
vanitas 2. 5
vapor 7. 5
vaporeus 7. 3
vasculum 16. 3, 9
veritas 1. 1, 6; 18. 9; 19. 4
vernaculus 39. 7
versutia 63. 9
vetus homo 19. 4; 45. 1 *sqq.*
vetustas 45. 1, 15; 49. 10
vice (= instar) 16. 3; 19. 7
viderit 2. 12
vigorare 26. 10
vilitas 6. 6
virtus 41. 5
vis 50. 5
  vis dei benefica 9. 5
  vires divinae 14. 1; 18. 1
vitiatio 57. 4
vivacitas 9. 1
vivere 42. 7
vividus 28. 1
vivificare 47. 14
vivificatio 28. 6
vocabulum 4. 2; 5. 8; 18. 8
voluntarius 61. 6
votum 4. 6; 22. 2

INDEX NOMINUM PROPRIORUM

Ab ipso scriptore commemorata

Abraham 18. 12; 52. 13
Adam 7. 2; 45. 4; 49. 2, 3; 53. 5 *sqq.*;
    61. 1; 63. 4
Adam et Eva 7. 2; 26. 14
Adam novissimus 49. 2; 51. 1; 52. 12
    sqq.
Aegyptius 36. 4
Aegyptus 20. 8
Agrippa 39. 4
Annas 20. 5
Apelles 2. 3; 5. 2
Arabia 13. 4
Aristoteles 2. 12
Asiaticus 38. 12
Athenienses 39. 7

Babylon 20. 8; 22. 10
Babylonius 58. 7
Basilides 2. 3

Caesar 22. 11
Caiaphas 20. 5
Carthaginienses 20. 8

Damascus 20. 3
Daniel 22. 4
David 20. 6; 22. 9

Emmanuel 20. 3
Empedocles 1. 5
Enoch 58. 9
Ephesus 48. 12
Epicurei 2. 1
Epicurus 1. 4
Esaias 20. 6; 22. 9; *falso citatur* 28. 5
Euphorbus 1. 5

Helias 22. 10; 55. 10; 58. 9; 61. 5
Herodes 20. 4, 5
Heth 18. 12
Hieremias 20. 6
Hierusalem 22. 3, 4; 26. 12, 13
Homerus 1. 5

Idumaea 20. 8
Ioel 22. 4
Ionas 32. 3
Israel 20. 4; 30. 1, 8; 31. 3, 5;
    58. 6
Iudaea 26. 11; 30. 2
Iudaeus 26. 10; 30. 1; 33. 3; 52. 13
Iudaicus 22. 3; 26. 11; 30. 3, 6, 7;
    33. 8
Iupiter Olympius 6. 6

Lazarus (*in parabola*) 17. 2
Lazarus (*Bethaniensis*) 53. 3, 4
Lucanus 2. 12

Macedonia 40. 12
Marcion 2. 3, 11; 14. 6; 56. 2
Marcus 5. 2
Menander 5. 2
Moyses 55. 8, 10; 61. 5

Paulus 10. 4
Petrus 55. 10
Pharisaei 19. 4; 39. 3, 6
Phidias 6. 6
Pilatus 20. 4
Plato 3. 2
Platonici 1. 5
Prisca 11. 2
Pythagoras 1. 5

Romanus status 24. 18

Sadducaei 2. 1, 2; 36. 1, 2; 39. 3, 6
Samaria 20. 3
Sarra 18. 12
Seneca 1. 4
Stephanus 55. 9

Tyrus 20. 8

Valentiniani 59. 6
Valentinus 2. 3; 56. 2

INDEX LOCORUM
[Secundum paginas huius libri]

Tertullianus [secundum ordinem librorum ab Oehlero dispositorum]

De Spectaculis

7	287
12	287
26	222

De Idololatria

13	237
15	267

Apologeticus

2	267
3	318
6	283
9	318
11	222
17	202, 217, 233
18	268, 288
21	273
27	267
39	189
47	202, 205, 236, 258
48	xii, 191, 236

Ad Nationes

i. 5	283
i. 10	295
i. 12	207
i. 15	210

De Testimonio Animae

	202
1	190
4	xii, 192, 236

De Corona

4	204
5	286
13	287

De Fuga

9	224

Scorpiace

1	203
12	237
13	288

De Oratione

3	276
5	233
13	204
15	235
22	283

De Patientia

5	258

De Baptismo

4–8	219
4	307

De Paenitentia

5	283

Ad Uxorem

	220
i. 2	318

De Cultu Feminarum

i. 1	270
i. 2, 3	266
i. 10	267

De Exhortatione Castitatis

5	223
10	224

INDEX LOCORUM

De Monogamia

	220
7	338
10	237

De Pudicitia

2	257
17	234
21	224

De Ieiunio

13	313

De Virginibus Velandis

1	239
5	283

De Pallio

2	318, 334
4	287, 334

De Praescriptione Haereticorum

4	340
11	214, 334
13	189, 239
30	340
33	208, 275
36	239

Adversus Marcionem

i. 2	271
i. 3	197
i. 10	271
i. 21	245
i. 22	222, 270
i. 23	204
i. 24	195, 334
i. 28	283
i. 29	204
ii. 2	258
ii. 10	258
ii. 12	295
ii. 21	203
ii. 29	297
iii.	197
iii. 5	243
iii. 9	276, 335, 338
iii. 12, 13	244
iii. 16	195
iii. 24	308
iv. 10	205
iv. 11	222
iv. 18	281
iv. 19	198, 204
iv. 20	280, 283
iv. 24	203, 290
iv. 27	222
iv. 37	217
iv. 38	274, 278
iv. 39	205, 248, 249
iv. 40	246
iv. 42	245, 246
v. 4	223
v. 9	255
v. 10	292, 314
v. 12	292
v. 14	235
v. 15	235, 290
v. 16	271
v. 17	192
v. 19	250
v. 20	212
v. 34	236

Adversus Hermogenem

3	189, 197
6	300
7	209
16	287
19	198, 287
26	287
36	306
45	211

Adversus Valentinianos

3	198
19, 20	209
24	215, 314
25	241, 281

De Carne Christi

	196
1	205, 208, 218, 275

De Carne Christi (cont.)

2	268
3	189, 198, 275, 338
4	337
5	242
6	229, 277, 279, 335
9	273
10–16	273
10	229, 284
11	229, 235
12	202, 203, 237
13	203, 216, 276
14	203, 204, 279
15	319
16	234, 315
17	215, 245, 270
18, 19	279
19	241
20	223
21, 23	245
22	268
23	283
24	231, 256

De Resurrectione Carnis

3	205, 243
6	221
7	217
11	xxiv
17	xiii
21	242
22	199 (bis), 201, 246
25	199
26	244
27	289
30	247
31	297
32	246
39	313
40	267
46	205, 288
52	205
53	246
56	263

De Anima

1	288
5 sqq.	235
6	324
7	236, 237, 306, 324
9	210
11	223
13	286
17	202
23	208
24	214
27	217, 300
28	191
31	191
32	192
33	191
35	224
38	304, 305
42	190 (bis)
51	293, 334
52	255
53	214
54	191
55	xxv, 257, 295
55, 56	236

Adversus Praxean

1	248
3	196, 207, 293
5	204, 218, 339
7	213, 235, 286, 324
8	200
9	234
13	198, 243
16	275, 335
20	198, 242
26	279, 286, 339
27	319
28	246

Adversus Iudaeos

2	258
9	245
10	246
13	246

INDEX LOCORUM

Appuleius
  Metamorphoses
    iv. 27   264
    v. 156   195
    ix. 21   257
    ix. 28   247
  De Mundo
    24   264
  De Magia
    56   273
  De Deo Socratis
    11   338

Aristoteles
  De Anima
    ii. 1   201 (*bis*)

Athenagoras
  Supplicatio
    10   209
    36   xxviii
  [*De Resurrectione Mortuorum*]
               xxviii *sqq.*

M. Aurelius Antoninus
  Meditationes
    xii. 14   231

S. Aurelius Angustinus
  De Civitate Dei
    xv. 9   293
  Enchiridion
    84–90   331
    121   320

S. Iohannes Chrysostomus
  Ad I Corinth.
    i. 18   234

Cicero
  Pro Roscio Amerino
    7. 20   324
  Ad Familiares
    vi. 18. 1   242
  De Oratore
    iii. 28. 110   319
  De Inventione
    ii. 57. 170   268

  Disp. Tusculanae
    i   190
    i. 10. 20   231
    i. 25. 61   233
  De Natura Deorum
    ii. 11. 29   231
  De Officiis
    ii. 8. 27   239
  De Fato
    41   334

S. Clemens Romanus
  Epistula
    i. 24   226
    i. 25   227

Diogenes Laertius
  Vitae Philosophorum
    vii. 159   231

Dionysius Periegetes
  Orbis Descriptio
    1103   217

Empedocles
               191
Epicurus
               190, 334
S. Epiphanius
  Haereses
    43   201

Eusebius Caesariensis
  Praeparatio Evangelica
    p. 274 D   250

Aulus Gellius
  Noctes Atticae
    iii. 10   293

Heliodorus
  Aethiopica
    vii. 20   213

Herodotus
    ii. 73   227

Hesiodus
  Frag. 171   227

INDEX LOCORUM

Hippolytus
  Philosophumena
    vii. 37   200
    vii. 38   208
    viii. 27   208

S. Irenaeus
  Adv. Omnes Haereses
    i. 1. 10   215, 314
    i. 5   196
    i. 7   208
    i. 15   206
    i. 17   207
    i. 19. 2   195
    ii. 18. 2   243
    ii. 21. 1   322
    iii. 19. 6   315
    iv. *praef.*   211
    iv. 31. 1   211
    iv. 51. 2   196
    v. 1–15   xxxii
    v. 1. 3   211
    v. 2. 2   317
    v. 11. 2   315
    v. 12. 1   327
    v. 12. 4   316
    v. 28. 3   211

S. Iustinus Martyr
  Apologia
    i. 6   209
    i. 8   xxv
    i. 18, 19   xxv
    i. 52, 53   xxvi
    i. 61   220
    ii. 9   xxvi
  Dialogus
    69   xxvi
    80, 81   xxvii
  [*De Resurrectione*]
         xxvii

Iuvenalis
  Satira
    vi. 27   319
    xiii. 60   319
    xv. 140 *sqq.*   286

Lucanus
  Pharsalia
    v. 69   197
    x. 472   318

Lucretius
         216
  De Rerum Natura
    i. 723   248

Martialis
    v. 29. 3   213

Minucius Felix
  Octavius
    34   226

Novatianus
  De Trinitate
         234
    8   335

Origenes
  De Principiis
    iii. 6. 1   212
    iv. 4. 10   212
  Contra Celsum
    ii. 27   201
    iv. 98. 1   228

Ovidius
  Heroidum Epistulae
    vi. 31   237
  Metamorphoses
    xv. 60–478   191
  Amores
    iii. 12. 9   242
  Ex Ponto
    ii. 7. 51   250

Petronius
  Saturae
    15   324

Plato
  Phaedrus
    p. 245 E *sqq.*   203

INDEX LOCORUM

Plinius
  Historia Naturalis
    vii. 16   293
    x. 2   227
    xxxvii. 2, 6   217
    xxxvii. 9   219
    xxxviii. 5   217

Prudentius
  Cathemerinon
    10. 125   281

Quintilianus
  Institutio Oratoria
    v. 10. 63   290
    vi. 4. 21   210
    viii. 6. 62   296
    ix. 1. 6   296
    ix. 3. 92   296
    xi. 3. 1   221

Seneca
  Troades
    397 *sqq.*   190
  Dialogus
    xii. 5   319

Suetonius
  D. Julius
         190
  D. Augustus
         332

Tacitus
  Annales
    i. 3   196
    iv. 11   221
    vi. 28   227
    xiii. 26   213
  Historiae
    i. 70   271

S. Theophilus Antiochenus
  Ad Autolycum
    i. 7   xxxii
    i. 8   xxxi
    i. 13   xxxi, 226
    i. 14   xxxi
    ii. 3   213

Trebellius Pollio
  D. Claudius
         259

Varro
  De Lingua Latina
    iv.   201
  De Re Rustica
    ii. 11. 10   225

Virgilius
  Aeneis
    i. 455   213
    ii. 182   200
    v. 77 *sqq.*   189

www.ingramcontent.com/pod-product-compliance
Lightning Source LLC
Chambersburg PA
CBHW071231290426
44108CB00013B/1369